Christopher Berry-Dee

Talking
with
Psychopaths
and Savages

**LETTERS FROM
SERIAL KILLERS**

A chilling study of murderers' minds

First published in the UK by John Blake Publishing
an imprint of Bonnier Books UK
4th Floor, Victoria House
Bloomsbury Square
London WC1B 4DA
England

Owned by Bonnier Books
Sveavägen 56, Stockholm, Sweden

www.facebook.com/johnblakebooks
twitter.com/jblakebooks

First published in paperback in 2023

Paperback ISBN: 978-1-78946-658-4
Trade paperback: 978-1-78946-657-7
Ebook ISBN: 978-1-78946-659-1
Audiobook ISBN: 978-1-78946-660-7

British Library Cataloguing-in-Publication Data:

A catalogue record for this book is available from the British Library.

Design by www.envydesign.co.uk

Printed and bound in Great Britain by Clays Ltd, Elcograf S.p.A

1 3 5 7 9 10 8 6 4 2

John Blake Publishing is an imprint of Bonnier Books UK
www.bonnierbooks.co.uk

Health warning

This book contains extremely disturbing material written by highly dangerous, psychopathic criminals. It is not for the faint of heart, or intended as a snug-as-a-bug bedtime read.

Envelope addressed to the author by Arthur Shawcross, 'the Genesee River Killer',

sent from Sullivan Correctional Facility, New York State.

Contents

Prologue

*There are road trips and then there are road trips. Christopher
and I travelled to the four corners of the USA, covering twenty-
two states by car, truck, boat and plane filming* The Serial
Killers, *the ratings-topping thirteen-part TV series.
Etched on my mind are many unforgettable experiences from
the streets of New York to the 'one-horse' prairie towns of
Texas and from the depths of death rows to the boulevards of
Hollywood. Deadly serious in parts but also great fun in others.
An experience I would undertake again tomorrow if there was
a chance. After all, who could resist being one of two English
guys driving along the unbelievable long straight mid-western
roads singing country music songs out loud. 'Look out — the
boys were back in town.'*

THE LATE FRAZER ASHFORD, ARPS (1951–2022)

Way back in the 1970s, television producer Frazer took a brave step into the unknown when he enabled me to interview many of the most notorious serial killers in the United States of America. I say 'a brave step' because although there are countless documentaries broadcast in the same genre today, back then we broke all the rules because this had never been achieved before.

The genesis for this idea came about because I had been corresponding with these criminal psychopaths for a long time; learning their stories, gaining their trust. I had a wealth of unique material to hand. The plan was for Frazer and me to go on some road trips across 'The Land of the Free' doing recces: talking to cops, attorneys, judges and the grieving next of kin of some of the victims; visiting crime scenes or newspaper offices to hoover up articles and documents; eating junk food; bickering; getting on each other's nerves; trying to avoid any mass-murder event (an almost weekly ritual in the US – see my book *Talking with Psychopaths and Savages: Mass Murderers and Spree Killers)*. And generally do all the things needs must before hauling in a film crew with all their kit to repeat what we had done in reverse order.

Before we went on our road trip into murder most foul, I'd never met a serial killer in the flesh. But throughout the years of corresponding with them, I now felt comfortable about getting up close and personal with this hellish evil. The TV series would allow the killers to talk on camera about their lives and terrible crimes. It was screened as *The Serial Killers*. One can still buy the DVDs of these programmes online, but it also occurred to me that I should write a book about my experiences. John Blake bravely stepped in as publisher, to spawn the best-selling brand: *Talking with Serial Killers*. Today, its many sequels have been translated into quite a few languages, including Polish, German, Russian and even Japanese. It may strike the reader as rather strange that true-crime fans from across the world are so fascinated with monsters thousands of miles away who have committed abominable crimes. Actually, there is a very good reason for it. Allow me to explain.

It matters not from which country one hails, nor which language one speaks, because heinous acts of serial homicide, mass-murder, rape and spree or rampage killing are committed by offenders with very similar mindsets – mindsets being universal too. A sadosexual serial killer at large in Poland or the sovereign state of the Czech Republic will have very similar motivational drivers as one from North America, the United Kingdom or the Russian Federation.

To clarify: the crimes committed by sadosexual serial murderer Ted Bundy are mirrored by killers in other countries and vice versa. The motives can be almost identical. The methods such killers use to hunt their human prey are often strikingly similar. This is not to suggest that these are 'copycat killings'. It is because when it comes down to committing mass murder (as distinct from serial homicide), the motives are usually religious, political or grudge-driven, and not usually sexual gratification, which is mostly a serial killer's motive. Mass murder and serial homicide are a universal phenomenon, are they not? For that reason, I believe this book may prove an enlightening read, for the letters featured here could have been penned by any offender without conscience from any country at any time past, present, or into the future.

Initially, there was some mild criticism about Frazer and me allowing these disgusting monsters to spew out what they needed to say on camera. However, we consulted some of the victims' next of kin, who often had tears streaming down their cheeks as they talked about their departed loved ones, and they agreed that we should go ahead. They felt that despite the tragedies these wanton beasts had heaped upon their lives, if we allowed these murderers to tell it how it was, then society might learn a few lessons from them.

As my loyal readers will know, I always treat the relatives, close friends and work colleagues of the deceased – not forgetting the police who have to clear up the sickening mess in the aftermath of a murder – with the deepest respect, for they are victims too. I always imagine how I'd feel if it were one of my children or a loved one who had been used, abused, raped, tortured, murdered, then dumped like so much garbage. As you read through this book, you might think about that, too.

This book goes way back to some of the letters these killers wrote to me years ago, alongside some more recent missives. We will analyse them in a way never previously attempted in the history of criminology – something that once again, I would argue, breaks new ground. I write from my heart and, as always in my books, I say it exactly as it should be, with no leftie PC BS thrown in to appease anyone, whatever side of the moral aisle they sit on.

On a lighter note, and in relation to Frazer's observations at the start of this chapter, our road trips took us through big cities, little cities, small towns and one-horse towns, with the rich tapestry of American history seamlessly woven throughout. Our research demanded we visit strip-joints, aka clip-joints, only to leave hastily. We called in at pool rooms, where the cigarette smoke drifted like grey smog two feet below the ceilings and where almost every patron, including the women, seemed to be genetically cloned from everyone from miles around. We did visit some nice locations and several quite nice motels, and some mean old penitentiaries too.

So, as I've done in my previous books, I invite you to come along and join me for the ride. I hope you enjoy it.

And now to the letters, please.

CHRISTOPHER BERRY-DEE

SOUTHSEA, UK, AND EL NIDO, PALAWAN, PHILIPPINES

christopherberrydee.com

Introduction

There is nothing to writing. All you do is sit down
at a typewriter and bleed.
Ernest Miller Hemingway (possibly ...)

Now that I've typed this book's first flush of enthusiasm onto my keyboard, the reader will have cottoned on to me having some literary 'fun' with our American cousins. However, allow me to acknowledge that their republic is awash with some of the finest true-crime writers in the world, past and present across the world, and I truly applaud them. That said, I rather doubt that if perchance any of these talented people read the book you have in your hands they will reciprocate. I say this because at the time of writing, the USA is a politically divided place to be. Fifty per cent of the population, including most probably the majority of its writers and TV broadcasters, support the somewhat wishy-washy Democrats, while the rest believe that the storming of the Washington Capitol on 6 January 2021 was simply about a lot of innocent sightseers anxious to visit the place where Americans allege democracy was born, as opposed to a semi-illiterate Trump-incited armed mob of insurrectionists determined to kill police officers then lynch some politicians; to rip up and shit-can one of the greatest documents ever penned in the history of mankind: the Constitution of the United States. I wonder what the Founding Fathers would have made of 'the Donald'?

Still, as this book is all about correspondence, as is par for the literary course I shall start by explaining that the quote at the head of this chapter is not, as many − including me − had previously thought, from Ernest Hemingway. Nope, it is generally attributed to the distinguished American sportswriter Walter 'Red' Smith, of whom Hemingway was an admirer. Paul William Gallico, an American author and sportswriter is in the mix here too, I am told. 'Pedantic maybe, yet I rather think that the quote applies to everyone who wishes to see their work published,' says my editor-in-chief, putting me straight on that point. Well, we learn something new every day!

For several reasons, I very much like Ernest Hemingway: to wit, he sported a beard similar to mine; he had steely blue eyes that twinkled (mine do not). Moreover, he wrote in longhand while standing up, on account of him having damaged his feet while serving as a volunteer in the Great War. That's a strange thing, is it not? One might have thought that having dodgy feet, one would want to sit down as often as possible. Although my feet are in perfectly good order, I type sitting down using a PC, employing a word-processing system that most often seems to have a mind and vocabulary of its own. And, my computer has the damned impertinence of frequently insisting that I am American because my car has 'tires'; the noun crudely misapplied because the 'tyres' on my car are not 'tire[d]' – only when they are flat.

Occasionally, Dutch pops up, my PC reminding me that I am talking 'double Dutch', with even French *un peu* or Swahili *kidogo* thrown in. Then, just about when I think I have things about right, up pops a local undertaker's ad followed in short order by a will-writing service implying that my community and family would be better off without me and who might be lucky enough to cash in when my sell-by date expires. Ernest Hemingway, who honed his signature sparse style as a reporter and often covered crimes, never had any of these problems, even less so after he shot himself in the head. And I almost forgot to add that he was a literary alchemist who turned ink into gold – mucho dollars, to be precise – so on this score, I like him: his writing, bad feet and all.

I can hear you muttering, 'Hey, Christopher, let's get with the programme, shall we? *Letters from Serial Killers* is what we need; it's advertised on the tin.' But as my tens of thousands of loyal readers around the world already know, I do venture into trivia from time to time. Occasionally it's my wont to use it to lighten the load, because we are soon heading off to a dark, terrible place, a foul homicidal literary landscape. I want this book to have some 'fun' in it, simply because real-life murder is a wretched business.

Handwriting is an electrical impulse originating in the brain. The hand and the pen are its tools, and inky traces.
Margaret Gullan-Whur, *Discover Graphology:*
A Straightforward and Practical Guide to
*Handwriting Analysi*s (1991)

You are now embarking on a homicidal literary road trip with me and we will find signposts to direct us along our way. The above quote from Margaret Gullan-Whur will be a fundamental guide in helping us to try to understand the mindsets of the monsters we will meet on our journey. As part of the process, we will also be looking at Locard's 'Exchange Principle' in a completely different light. According to that well-established criminological principle 'every contact leaves a trace', and I will apply this not only to what is written on the page, but to what the offender is hiding between the lines, or intentionally neglects to say.

To assist us further: we all know that an offender's modus operandi (MO) – his or her method of operation – can vary over time. Indeed, even you and I have our own particular way of doing different things; we get set in our ways, then we change those ways as we develop better practical and social skills. During the course of this book, I will also develop in detail the theme of a criminal's modus vivendi (MV), in other words the manner in which he or she lives their life. But how can we more accurately define handwriting as 'an electrical impulse originating in the brain'?

Without becoming entangled in the complex psycho-analytical studies of Carl Gustav Jung and Sigmund Freud, and with great impertinence on my part, I think that I have rediscovered the congruent way of thinking or 'modus cogitandi' (MC). Initially, this idea took a bit of tweaking as all of my brain's 120 billion neurons sent chemical and electrical signals whizzing along my neural extensions, sometimes bumping into each other in a confused way, before hooking up with other neurons across tiny junctions called synapses, to form my own thoughts about the phrase 'modus cogitandi' and how to apply this and then permit to travel in fits and starts down to my fingers and onto the typed page. I suggest this is because MO and MV have to originate from our MC.

Phew! That was a bit heavy was it not? Gosh, no doubt I'll soon be receiving thousands of grumpy emails and text messages from psychologists and psychiatrists across the world, all of them using their own cogitandi to inform me that it was Heraclitus 'The Obscure' (or 'The Dark One') of Ephesus, and the later Greek philosopher Parmenides, who came up with this jolly good idea – and a long time before a Mr Morris invented the Morris Minor. Nevertheless, as far as I can tell, neither Jung, Freud nor the ancient thinkers such Heraclitus and Parmenides, nor any forensic shrink since, have studied in depth such reams and reams of letters by fully emerged sexual psychopaths as I have.

We will also examine a killer's behavioural 'trophy-taking' from his victims (and all the killers bar one are male in this book) from a different perspective. These 'trophies' need not just be physical items, such as a lock of hair, jewellery, items of underclothing or crime-scene photographs, they can also be sickening memories that the perpetrator relives, and often masturbates to, long after he has been incarcerated. In *Letters from Serial Killers*, we will witness these mental trophies being transmitted from an evil mind onto paper. And this may not make for nice reading at all.

Grim stuff, you will agree, but as mentioned earlier, I do periodically digress into trivia by way of relief. I prefer to go off the wall rather than up the fucking wall, because getting into the minds of these monsters can be a debilitating process, so trivia is my form of escapism, like it or not.

Finally, for your edification and at no further cost to you, the reader, we will be visiting some fascinating locations en route – at least, I find them so. And I can reassure you that although I will be having a pop at our American cousins across the pond from time to time, I ~~truly love~~, ~~deeply admire~~, okay, okay – I mean I quite like them, if you can read between those lines.

Hershey bar, anyone?

Pens and Ink Can
Cause a Stink

How wonderful it is to be able to write someone a letter!
To feel like conveying your thoughts to a person, to sit at your
desk and pick up a pen, to put your thoughts into words like
this is truly marvellous.

HARUKI MURAKAMI, *NORWEGIAN WOOD* (1987)

Long gone are those times when bleary-eyed writers gazed into glasses of dark porter, candles nearby spluttering to cast eerie shadows on a wall of a Fleet Street pub, and dipped their well-trimmed goose quills into pots filled with iron gall ink to scribble-scratch away. Back then, parchment and ink were more than a trifle expensive. Back then, geese were so scared they suffered incontinence on an hourly basis. Back then, one had to actually 'think' before a single scratch of ink touched the page. No Tipp-Ex, back-spacing key, or spell-checker to make good your mistakes. Allegedly, William Shakespeare said that when starting with a blank sheet of vellum, it 'was God's will what

1

happened next' and confessed 'to be heartily relieved' when he reached the end of a work.

Back then – before, I think, America was properly invented then patented as a republic – most of the British population were illiterate, so writing really was a craft. As Haruki Murakami notes above, it represents an extension of one's creative thinking processes (the modus cogitandi, or 'way of thinking') as transmitted to others in what one sets down. This is what the great wordsmiths, writers, historians, soothsayers, novelists, romanticists, poets, mystery-makers were all about – an extension of one's thoughts, emanating from the wondrous machine that is our mind, travelling down to our fingers via electrical impulses, to dip quill into ink. And most often in the spirit of 'Let the Devil take the hindmost', to quote a popular proverb probably dating back to the sixteenth century, those people had time on their hands because it took a good while to trim a quill – even longer when 'Gerry the Goose' was having none of it. None of this nipping across the street to pick up a biro from a 7-Eleven store malarkey, that's for sure.

So, as this book is all about writing, let us consider this not insignificant fact. Every letter – including the correspondence from serial killers and their ilk discussed here – book, news article, menu, potboiler, magnum opus, magazine piece, script, poem, document, dissertation, indeed every single piece of reading material that has ever been written or chiselled into stone for the benefit of those to follow has involved grey-matter-thinking. The same is true today, of course, when typed or twittered into one's PC, laptop, notebook, or the gadgets we call mobile phones – some of which even try to translate our spoken words into the written word, as in when you tell someone to 'Go and duck off!'

Take the British Library, which holds some 14 million printed books and e-books, as well as millions of periodicals and thousands of rare manuscripts. Within its King's Library alone (works collected by George III), you can, if you have nonillions of hours to play with, read through some 65,000 volumes of printed books. The British Library has a major collection of manuscripts, along with around 19,000 pamphlets, music scores and historical items, some dating back to 2000 BC. This collection is calculated at approximately 150 million bits and pieces in more than 400 languages. As to the latter, I think that they need to pull their socks up because there are roughly 7,000 languages in the world today, so the bibliothecaries are falling a tad short, if you ask me!

Take away from Genesis the belief that Moses was the author, on which only the strange belief that it is the word of God has stood, and there remains nothing of Genesis but an anonymous book of stories, fables, and traditionary or invented absurdities, or of downright lies.

Thomas Paine, *The Age of Reason*
(three parts, 1794, 1795, 1807)

Thomas Paine was an English-born philosopher and writer who supported revolutionary causes in America and Europe. In later life, he had to contend both with poverty and ill health (worsened by being continually chemically unbalanced with the drink), but indubitably Thomas was a man of remarkable insight and his cogitandi was very much up to scratch – when it wasn't floating around in ale, that is. Thomas was born in the British market town of Thetford. His father, a corsetier and farmer, had high ambitions for his son, but by the age of twelve the lad had fallen out of school due to his shortcomings, then went on to become such a respected and influential writer. There is a gilded bronze statue of him standing on a stone plinth outside King's House on King Street in Thetford. There is also one of him in New Rochelle, New York, dedicated to the perpetuating legacy of this Founding Father. I would ask the reader to read up on this guy. Okay, he was sozzled for much of his waking time, but what would one expect when there are many breweries close by!

If you can't make it to the British Library in London, amble into any bookstore, wander around any Sunday car-boot sale ('swap meet' in the US) or your local public library, and marvel at how many different pieces of literature there are, all researched and written by someone anxious to see their words passed down for the benefit of generations to come. And according to Exodus, the Ten Commandments were inscribed by the finger of God on two stone tablets. Well I don't like being 'commanded' to do anything, do you? There is far too much of this damned impertinence these days, so had God been a bit more diplomatic he might have titled them the 'Ten Polite Requests', since people would then have been less likely to break them.

Moving on, it should be noted that Fran Lebowitz wrote in *Metropolitan Life* (1978), 'Contrary to what many of you might imagine, a career in letters is not without its drawbacks – chief among them the unpleasant fact that one is frequently called upon to actually sit down and write.' However, as all people of letters know – be they long gone deep in graves with the sides falling in, those at it today, or those to come – the craft can become addictive. It has been said that if one takes away a professional writer's pen, he or she could become so depressed they might kill themselves!

Still, it's hard work, this writing business, I can tell you that much. Between you and me, previously I have become so distraught over it that I started looking for a way out – planting my head inside a gas oven seeming the best option open to me. Then I realised that I only have an electric hob, so I gave up on that idea altogether, a microwave oven being completely out of the question.

It is also to be noted that many writers are prone to sensitivities, are subject to fragile mental states, and there is some substance to this because writing can be a lonely profession; one where occasionally fantastic flights of fantasy reign supreme. So let's get down to some nitty-gritty, some claret and brains splattered over some walls, for in 1961, aged sixty-one, the aforementioned Ernest Hemingway, he with the bad feet, shot himself in the head. The narrative of this remarkable man's life is fascinating, ranging from the highs of his literary success and fame to the lows of the mental anguish that eventually led him to his death.

In 2005, aged sixty-seven, Hunter S. Thompson also shot himself. Aged fifty-nine, Virginia Woolf, who suffered from various mental illnesses for years, committed suicide by drowning in 1941, leaving a note to her husband, Leonard, that read in part: 'Dearest, I feel certain that I am going mad again. I feel we can't go through another of those terrible times. And I shan't recover this time. I begin to hear voices, and I can't concentrate. So I am doing what seems the best thing to do.' It also included this somewhat small compensatory flourish for him: 'You have given me the greatest possible happiness.'

So, a risky occupation, this writing business can be. A few more examples: Author Louis Adamic shot himself in 1951, aged fifty-three. In 1963, thirty-year-old poet Sylvia Plath placed her head in a gas oven to dispatch herself, having sealed off the kitchen with wet towels to stop the fumes drifting into the room where her children were sleeping. Off-kilter humourist Richard Brautigan popped his clogs using a pistol in 1984, aged forty-nine. In 1989, social activist and wordsmith Abbie Hoffman overdosed on barbiturates aged fifty-two. In 2004, forty-four-year-old Drake Sather fired a live round into his literary head, he being best known for his contributions to TV comedy shows such as *Saturday Night Live* and *The Larry Sanders Show*. Troubled, like so many of the above, by years of depression, forty-six-year-old David Foster Wallace – a novelist, essayist and short story writer – hanged himself in 2008. And five years later, twenty-six-year-old tech wizard, Reddit co-founder and writer Aaron Swartz signed himself off in the same way. And one would be remiss if one missed out Oscar Fingal O'Flaherty Wills Wilde (1854–1900): an Irish poet and playwright best known for his epigrams and plays, his criminal conviction for gross indecency for consensual homosexual acts in one of the first celebrity trials – almost monthly events these days – his imprisonment, and early death from meningitis at the age of forty-six.

Coleridge was a drug addict. Poe was an alcoholic. Marlowe was killed by a man whom he was treacherously attempting to stab. Pope took money to keep a woman's name out of a satire, then wrote the piece so she could

6

be recognised anyhow. Chatterton killed himself. Byron was accused of incest. *Do you still want to be a writer – and if so, why?*

Bennett Cerf, *Shake Well before Using* (1948)

So if you are still inclined to take up the idea of writing, you might wish to consider this: the mean terminal age of the wordsmiths above is about fifty years, which is considerably less than blind-as-bat lumberjacks, one-armed steeplejacks and perhaps even all-weather lightning-rod installers. After I wrote my first book, *Dad, Help Me Please*, decades ago, I swore in God's name I'd never go through the same pen-pushing trauma again, but I did. I am still above ground, and not under it with a wooden stake driven through my heart – so far.

I had considered writing my memoirs old chap, but as you know I made a mess of things and in a bit of a fix right now. They are going to hang me in a few days. Damned inconsiderate it is too.

Neville George Clevely Heath,
undated letter from the condemned
cell to an acquaintance, 1946

The killers whose correspondence features in this book had, or have, time on their hands: pitiless chains of days, months and years. And it's not always what they say, or the competency of their handwriting, their literacy skills or their previous education – if they had any schooling worth mentioning – that matters. It is their thinking processes, concealed like invisible ink between the lines they write, that should concern us most.

To Speak or Not to Speak? That is the question.
Billy Fallon, Professor of Communication,
San Diego State University (2007)

I recall interviewing killers who have consciously attempted to present themselves as socially acceptable people. As I have discussed extensively in other books, this presenting of normality is the mask they wear to hide the beast breathing deeply within, and in almost every instance this is *precisely* what we see when reading their writings, for this generally conceals what is 'hidden between the lines'. And, often, what the killers do *not* say in their correspondence (because they do not want to say it, or they conveniently forget to say it) matters much more to us in terms of our understanding their psychopathologies, for they have a cunning knack of knowing when to speak or not to speak.

To add a little literary seasoning here, when examining the killers' letters published in this book, perhaps we might think of them as three-dimensional exercises, combining 'the written word against the true facts' versus 'what is hidden between the lines' versus 'the offenders' modus cogitandi, or actual thinking process'. If we can bring the three together, we might be able to learn more about their mindsets, because we cannot see the whole picture until all three of these components are in place.

When I've interviewed serial killers behind bars, they sometimes come across as conciliatory, remorseful, wearing a hangdog expression, perhaps with watery eyes or rounded shoulders; they present, in short, as lost souls. All of which is designed to elicit a compassionate response. I referred earlier to letter writing as merely the extension of one's thought-processing system transferred via pen to paper. These criminals' letters are more or less echoes of what we would physically see when interviewing one of these beasts in the flesh.

> Look Chris. Letters, letters everywhere. Piles of letters from adoring women. Ya know, I am even learning to write Braille in efforts to help the blind. I've got so many books, to store them they've given me the empty cell next to mine.
>
> Michael Bruce Ross: from his condemned
> cell to the author, 26 September 1994

I have interviewed serial killers who rant and rave. The highly intelligent, articulate Connecticut-born, Connecticut-executed Michael Bruce Ross came across as a bookish, bespectacled fresh-faced all-American guy. Previously a door-to-door Prudential Insurance salesman, on death row he gloated and boasted to me during a TV interview about his terrible killing of young women and two little schoolgirls, one of whom he anally raped post-mortem. He revelled in it all, often breaking into hysterical fits of giggles. He wrote extensively to me about his crimes too and if one looked carefully enough, one could see Michael's twisted psychopathology writ large across every page. Because he was Cornell University-educated, he had a way with words. He once said to me: 'Chris, I'm not afraid of dying. I just don't want to be around when it happens.' On that score, I am inclined to feel the same way. The reader can find a photo of me chatting to Michael through the bars of his death row cell at christopherberrydee.com.

With my Polish readers in mind, we will meet Phillip Jablonski soon enough. His letters reveal the thought processing of a highly dangerous schizophrenic (and 'highly dangerous' in this case is one of the biggest understatements in criminal history), while the beguiling correspondence from petite former nurse Melanie Lyn McGuire proves just what a cunning and manipulative 'Black Widow' she truly is.

Gentlemen, you must not mistake me. I admit that the French Emperor is a tyrant. I admit he is a monster. I admit that he is the sworn foe of our nation, and, if you will, of the whole human race. But, gentlemen, we must be just to our great enemy. We must not forget that he once shot a publisher.

Poet Thomas Campbell (1777–1844):

an apocryphal toast to Napoleon

Regarding penmanship: my publisher's editor-in-chief writes exquisitely, as does my colleague Frank Pearce, and the once upscale 'hot-to-trot' prisoner #584496, Melanie McGuire, whose letters are written behind the walls of the Edna Mahan Correctional Facility (EMCF) in Clinton, New Jersey. Their correspondence is a delight, yet such examples of handwriting perfection are as rare as hens' teeth these days. So as we are talking about correspondence, let's consider the implements involved for a moment. I would be remiss in not doing so, because pens have been used to kill people – prisoners make them into 'shanks' to stab each other – proving that, to paraphrase the well-known saying: 'Sometimes the pen truly is mightier than the sword.' And so on to pens.

While praying that the following trivia doesn't damage what credibility I do possess and while Lewis Waterman (founder of Waterman pens) is said to have invented the fountain pen, he was merely improving on an idea patented by a Romanian inventor called Petrache Poenaru.

Genius is one percent inspiration and ninety-nine per cent perspiration.

> Thomas Edison, American inventor
> (1847–1931), circa 1900

Edison was a bright spark, but so was Petrache Poenaru (1799–1875) who, when aged twenty-one, came up with an idea that had popped into his cogitandi while studying geodesy and surveying at the École Polytechnique in Paris. Poenaru was so occupied with note-taking and writing that he devised a new kind of pen that utilised a swan's quill, which served as a reservoir of ink. Alas, history fails to inform us from where he got the quill. On 25 May 1827, the Manufacture Department of the French Ministry of the Interior registered Poenaru's invention with the code number '3208' and the somewhat over-hyped description: *'plume sans fin portative . . . qui s'alimente d'encre d'elle-même'* ('never-ending portable pen, which recharges itself with ink'). This was a seminal landmark in the history of writing; a eureka moment, so much so that in 2010 Posta Română issued a 5 lei stamp portraying Poenaru alongside some working drawings for his famous creation. Sadly, this belated recognition all rather passed over Poenaru's grave, for the last time his pen touched paper was when he signed his will with him expiring probably before the ink had dried on the paper.

My invention consists of an improved reservoir or fountain pen, especially useful, among other purposes, for marking on rough surfaces – such as wood, coarse wrapping-paper, and other articles where an ordinary pen could not be used.

John Jacob Loud 1888

Although the first 'true' ballpoint pen was invented by inventor John Jacob Loud, and patented in 1888, it was not a commercial success for reasons unknown to us even today, and indeed to Mr Loud himself, it seems to me. There were certainly plenty of murders to write about circa this time. One contemporary killer who knew how to read and write perfectly well was Theodore 'Ted' Durrant, aka 'The Demon of the Belfry'. He was a San Francisco Sunday school teacher who raped and strangled two women who rebuffed his advances, then dumped their bodies in the church's library and bell chamber. Somewhat ironically, Theo was to find himself, in 1898, suspended, like a church bell, but at the other end of a rope.

George Chapman, who turned himself into an Englishman when he took the surname of his mistress Annie Chapman (he was born Seweryn Antonowicz Kłosowski in Poland in 1865, moved to London in his early twenties, went to live in the US then returned to London), poisoned *three* of his mistresses with tartar emetic. He was suspected at the time of his hanging in 1903 to be the real Jack the Ripper and it's alleged that he declared 'I am Jack the Rip—' before being cut terminally short as he plunged to his doom. Well, he would have said that to get a stay of the inevitable – wouldn't you? But I hasten to add if one were to ingest tartar emetic, one would certainly experience vomiting, severe chest pains, cardiac abnormalities, renal and hepatic toxicity and some stress (as in: mega stress) – all very similar symptoms to someone who has overdosed on American TV soaps. If you end up in intensive care you will still wish you'd never been born, as you'll find yourself as bald as a goose egg, as white as a mortician's sheet and forced to wear incontinence panties for the remainder of your days.

Not to be outdone by Loud, in 1938 Hungarian-Argentine inventor and journalist László József Bíró invented a 'miraculous pen' – a ballpoint that actually worked. Bíró had noticed that the type of ink used for printing newspapers dried quickly and did not smudge the paper. Making a complete mess of his kitchen and truly upsetting spouse Elsa, he decided to make a pen using the same type of ink. However, printers' ink could not flow through a normal pen, so he tried something else. I could say that 'Bíró had a lot of balls', but my publisher will scold me. Nevertheless, that is how the ballpoint, as we know it today, works: 'the ink inside the pen covers one side of the tiny ball at the pen's nib; this rotates as the writer moves the pen on paper and the ink is transferred to the page' – in case you are not sure.

Initially, ballpoints were very exciting writing implements, at least for our cousins across the pond; nonetheless, it took some time for them to figure out exactly what was the point of a point with a ball on it? Not surprisingly, initial sales were extremely low. They finally did cotton on, however, and throughout 1946 hundreds of people were queuing up to buy them, despite the fact that just one biro cost around $150 in today's dollars. Can you imagine buying a pack of twelve at $1,800 – I can't! As a matter of fact, I get lots and *lots* of letters from criminals using biros. These days they can only use the inner ink reservoir; the plastic outer casing is taken away from the cons because of its usefulness, referred to earlier, as a weapon (shank) with which to stab other inmates or the prison guards – something our László never intended it to be used for. I get Christmas cards from killers too; mostly handwritten, or occasionally a typed letter, as was Peter Sutcliffe's wont. Some crayon cartoons on the envelopes. 'Charles Bronson' (Charles Arthur Salvador), does it. Phillip Carl Jablonski once did, for he died some time ago.

Some of the homicidal scribes featured within these pages vehemently profess their innocence. Others glorify in their heinous crimes. The now deceased Harvey 'The Hammer' Louis Carignan would send me reams of stuff about his rapes and murders. At one time he used a typewriter called 'Clyde', but that broke. When I asked him why he called it 'Clyde', he stoutly replied: 'That's one of my pearls of wisdom. The answer is amongst [*sic*] secrets I hold that I'll never reveal to anyone.' I firmly responded with: 'Okay, Harvey, so you will call your next typewriting machine 'Bonnie', correct? So fuck you, too!' Indeed, as one of his prison guards – correctional officers who can never correct any of their charges – at the Minnesota Correctional Facility (MCF) in Stillwater, Minnesota, told me: 'Sir, I had never seen a typewriter fly before. It went straight outta the window. Mr Carignan was truly pissed because we didn't have the funds to repair it.' Nonetheless, not to be deterred from producing further pages of what amounted to drivel, Harvey resorted to using a pen.

As an aside, your author enjoys etymology. 'Pen' derives from *penna* (Latin for 'feather') through to *penne* (Old French) and thence to *pen* (Middle English). How the Italians turned a writing instrument into a penne pasta dish only the 'Saint of Writing', aka Catherine of Bologna OSC, might know. But wait a moment: maybe it was a bolognese?

Putting his serial killing aside for a moment, you would have probably liked Harvey. He spoke in a very soft, grandfatherly voice, yet – resembling a character from *The Planet of the Apes* – he was an immensely strong guy. Some fifteen years ago he could do one-arm pull-ups for ten minutes without breaking sweat. I went to a zoo once and saw some apes doing the same thing. It was well worth the quarter of a banana I tossed them. And this is another strange thing: the chimpanzee and bonobo are said to be genetically our closest living relatives – certainly with my late mother-in-law – because we share as much as 98.8 per cent of their DNA (but then we share about 90 per cent with cats). In the context of this 'Tree of Life' stuff, quite obviously the missing 1.2 per cent covers an ability to read, write, vote and use the internet, which must have taken the wrong branch at some time.

You may be shocked by the contents of Harvey's letters, but those from female killers can be just as horrific, or even more so. On that note, we will very briefly consider Joanne Dennehy. Dennehy, a manipulative British serial killer who despatched three men, also attempted to stab to death two male dog walkers in broad daylight, after which she licked their warm blood from her blade. Step aside Rose West, there's another psycho-bitch on the block and she is most certainly the most dangerous female inmate held within the 'British Correctional Estate', as the Home Office describes its prisons. Of some inconsequential note, these institutions are most often farmed out to private companies who treat their inmates as 'clients'. And get this: these firms get paid bonuses for the amount of time cons are allowed *out* of their cells (or 'peters') than in. Later, we'll examine letters from the upscale Melanie McGuire, aka 'The Ice Queen' – articulate, cogent and a million miles away from the horrific crime she committed, but she's in a US prison and that place is a hellhole.

> That's not a red lipstick kiss, Chris. That's menstrual blood.
>> Keith Hunter Jesperson: to the author, referring to a letter from one of his countless murder groupies

Dubbed by the media 'The Happy Face Killer', interstate 'mother trucker' Keith sent taunting correspondence to police adding a 'smiley' ☺. This Canadian-born American monster wrote hundreds of letters to me, as he will to you if you should show even the *slightest interest* in his life from foetus stage until the day you contact him. He will expansively expound on backhoes, and how mean and cruel his pa was in insisting that as a fresh-faced kid he spend much time out in the wild enjoying healthy pursuits: fishing, shooting small game, making a log cabin and learning how to use a bow and arrow. You will not even have to mention his murders, because he will boastfully go on and on about them – especially if you include a photograph of some busty blonde Russian model and hint that it's you. Of course, as his hundreds of supportive pen friends will rail that I really should not suggest such a thing, but why not? Think about this for a moment. If every reader of this book sent Keith a letter along with an alleged selfie of a 'Miss Rock Your Socks Off Tatiana Hotski', while complimenting him on his rugged looks, detailing their own avid interest in backhoes, Big Mack trucks and whether his pecker really is the size of a Californian redwood, they *will* get a response. Whether the American paper industry will be able to supply his stationery needs is another matter entirely.

On a more serious note, Keith once reviewed one of my books, *Talking with Serial Killers*. No other multiple murderer has done this before with any true-crime author. He sent the book back to me, annotating page by page where I'd got things wrong and giving me his own professional psychological analysis [quotation marks removed] on the killers featured throughout my book. I mean, one could not make this up if one tried!

So, with all of that done and dusted, in this book we will focus not so much on what these killers say – their penmanship; the way they structure a page, or even whether they choose to write with a pen or to type; it is what's missing that counts. Then, when you compare these written offerings with what we know as fact about each offender's criminal antecedents, I hope that you might come to understand a little more about the murderous instincts that lie deep within their modus cogitandi.

Psychopaths Using Pens

You really should learn to use your own English grammer
[sic] effectively. I'm sick and tired of correcting yours [sic]
errors. You dont [sic] learn do you [missing a ? mark]. My
lives [sic] story is very important and your readers should
appreciate what I have done.

KEITH HUNTER JESPERSON, RANT IN THE FORM
OF A LETTER TO THE AUTHOR CORRECTING YOURS
TRULY ON MY GRAMMAR

Quite why we should 'appreciate' what Jesperson has done remains a tad unclear. However, what one *can* appreciate when researching, writing about, then visiting heinous killers of any ilk, are the road trips involved. Gig Harbor, where we filmed the once dishy VerLyn (Veronica Lynn Compton) at the Washington Corrections Center for Women (WCCW), is set among the pine-clad San Juan Islands in north-west Washington State. Taken in the round, this area is breathtaking. It is as if America imported lots of Norway's fjord water and around this planted many trees. And they do the best clam chowder at the local Tides Tavern, where Frazer and I spent two lazy evenings eating buckets of blue crab, drinking ice-cold beers, pledging to be friends till the end of time (until the following morning, when sobriety called for serious business) in the course of getting femme fatale VerLyn to spill the beans about her sordid and almost murderous relationship with the psycho-twisted serial killer Kenneth Alessio Bianchi, and her previous penpally plans to open a mortuary with the serial killer Douglas Daniel Clark aka 'The Sunset Slayer', and have sex with the dead.

Nevertheless, if you *are* keen to visit serial killers in the US you'll need to pack a liking for travel – lots and *lots* of travel. It's nothing like buying a day-return rail ticket and visiting hubby having a comfy time in HMP Woodhill, Milton Keynes. In the states, most always you are entering 'The Twilight Zone'; places where, like anywhere else in 'The Land of the Free', you stand a very good chance of being caught up in one of the country's daily, de rigueur mass-murder events or perhaps far worse: having to attend one of Donald Trump's fascinating and eloquently choreographed mass-produced redneck 'Make America Great Again' (MAGA) stuffed rallies.

During some tumbleweed-strewn road trips to interview killers, we interviewed greet-and-meet cops and visited crime-scene locations. Small-town cops wearing Stetsons and packing heavy heat are very proud of their crime scenes, you know. They insist on being filmed precisely where some mother-in-law was chopped up, in a case probably dubbed 'The Granny Axe Murder', or pointing to a row of Tommy-gun bullet holes in a bank's ceiling. At one place near Wichita

Falls, we filmed a local sheriff proudly holding his Remington twelve-gauge, but we signally failed to tell him that he was standing atop a fire ant hill. Of some minor interest, Wichita is quite famous: it boasts the 'world's littlest skyscraper' – the narrow, four-storey Newby–McMahon Building. Make of that what you will.

Yes, dear reader, we had to drive dusty, arrow-straight, meltingly hot long-haul roads, such as in Texas to meet death-row inmates Henry Lee Lucas and Kenneth Allen McDuff. To come a-calling in places dubbed 'cities' yet where the population numbers just a few hundred. Rosebud, for example, where Texas Longhorns have the right of way, and guess what – most of them have a 'Boot Hill', a misnomer if ever there was one. The deceased back in them thar good ole Wild West days were never buried boots-on because, and you'll doubtless have already guessed this, the boots were removed by the undertaker to help pay for his undertakings. Any lead he found in the corpses he recycled, selling it to other gunslingers to make more bullets, which inevitably brought in more clientele – an eminently sound, environmentally almost green business practice, it seems to me.

I certainly digressed there so please forgive me as I momentarily went off-piste, so let's get back with the programme. The following (complete with original spelling mistakes) is a letter sent by Clyde Barrow to motor mogul Henry Ford. After it was published in the national press, sales of Ford V8s rocketed, in the best marketing wheeze in automotive history.

Tulsa Okla

10th April

Mr. Henry Ford

Detroit, Mich.

Dear Sir:—

While I still have got breath in my lungs I will tell you what a dandy car you make. I have drove Fords exclusivly when I could get away with one. For sustained speed and freedom from trouble the Ford has got every other car skinned and even if my business hasen't been strickly legal it don't hurt enything to tell you what a fine car you got in the V8 –

Yours truly

Clyde Champion Barrow

Dubbed by the media 'The Death Car' – more formally, a 1934 Ford Fordor Deluxe sedan – the automobile in which Bonnie and Clyde died is now parked up on a plush red carpet next to the main cashier's cage at Whiskey Pete's Casino, 100 W Primm Boulevard, Primm, Nevada. Come to think of it, this V8 must have been the first automobile in auto history to have through-and-through air conditioning: 167 air vents in total – not including the shot couple who were well ventilated with bullet holes too.

That is a very American thing to do, is it not? I cannot think of any British, European, or any-place-else country on planet Earth where one goes into a casino for a flutter, complete with gratis free snacks, to be confronted by a 'death car', and right up close and personal to a cashier's desk where one throws one's hard-earned money into a trash can. And all the while, the clerk gives one a wry smile and says: 'Thank y'all. You have a nice day, y'all, and ya come back soon, y'all hear,', while she's really thinking: 'Thanks for being a losing dummy and paying my wages.'

Now back to whether it is the desire for the thrill of the fear these killers induce, or in trying to understand how their evil minds work, or where their bullet-peppered cars are presently parked, we find ourselves inextricably, weirdly fascinated by the stories of the killers who wreak havoc in our communities. We are fixated by the likes of the bank-robbing, shoot-'em-up gang led by Bonnie and Clyde outrunning the law, a motley mob with a sexy young tartlet posing over the hood of a souped-up Ford V8 with a Thompson submachine gun. They wrote many love letters to each other, too. Frazer and I visited the site of one of the banks they robbed when making a TV documentary about Henry Lee Lucas. It's now a café, but one of its outside walls still has the bullet holes from their raid – a memento of the day when Bonnie and Clyde made a cash withdrawal in a 'not strickly [sic] legal' sort of way!

If you ask me, I think that the couple's letters to each other are *very* romantic. You can find a few of them online. Oodles of *real* love; evangelical, deep-seated tenderness dished out in spades. One can almost feel Bonnie's heart thumping as her adoration for Clyde flows unabated onto each page. None of this E.L. James *Fifty Shades of Grey* love malarkey here. Nothing erotic, seedy or explicit. Clyde Barrow and Bonnie Parker were no Christian Grey and Anastasia Steele. These days such written appreciations of a loved one come by way of a text, Messenger or WhatsApp as in: 'Hey hun. Fancie a curry tonite and a quick fuck under the pier. Luv U', which to my mind leaves something to be desired, and is most certainly not designed to knock anyone off their feet, unless their IQ is about six.

If you do decide to read Bonnie and Clyde's correspondence, you will find it is very much like the quilled letters exchanged between high-society Lord Nelson and Emma, Lady Hamilton; the latter having climbed the social ladder using her 'charms'. Her sequin-embroidered curriculum vitae included roles as a model, maid, actress and dancer. She began her career moving in the less salubrious circles of eighteenth-century London, opening her legs to a series of wealthy men and culminating within Lord Nelson's britches – when he wasn't sinking just about every French and Spanish man-o'-war ever built with cannon fire, that is. Yes, Bonnie and Clyde's letters prove that they enjoyed a low-key sexual enterprise based solely upon gunslinging, pumping red-hot lead into lots of innocent folk with discreet hints of some shagging thrown in between these very naughty events. My authority on this is – as might be expected – the 1967 biographical crime film starring Warren Beatty and Faye Dunaway.

Perhaps the first issue we should get our heads around is that the letters featured throughout this book are written by people bereft of morals. They are penned by homicidal psychopaths, some sadosexual psychopaths with a few one-off killers and a wild card being an oddball thrown in for good measure. They are devoid of conscience. Their character profiles prove that where any sense of right and wrong should exist, there is a black hole. They have no concern for others; are so reprehensible that they abduct, torture, rape and commit serial homicide just for the fun of it. Then, when finally behind bars, many of them miraculously find Jesus Christ and/or entice some halfwit women to fall in love with them; sometimes it even ends in marriage. It works vice versa, with men being just as foolish too.

> Christopher, I promised the authorities that if they let Art out of prison I will make sure that he keeps taking the pills then you can be the Best Man at our wedding.
>
> Clara Neal, serial killer Arthur Shawcross's
fiancée: during a filmed interview with the author,
September 1998

Once a criminal psychopath always a criminal psychopath. Psychopathy can be defined as a neuropsychiatric disorder marked by deficient emotional responses, lack of empathy, and poor behaviour, all of which, unfortunately, often result in persistent antisocial deviance and criminal behaviour, and in their letter writing as well. These people have been found to have weak connections among the components of the emotional systems in their brains. It is also claimed by professionals much brighter than me that psychopaths are not good at detecting fear in the faces of other people. I strongly disagree with that. Many of the serial killers I have interviewed gained a great sexual kick out of terrifying their victims to death. Serial killer Michael Ross could only fulfil his sex needs if the victim fought for her life. He told me that he felt cheated if they just went limp, thus, the more passive the victim, the less excitement the killer receives as a sexual reward. Psychopaths, specifically sado-psychopaths, get pleasure from hurting or humiliating others. We will see this in Phillip Jablonski as he relives his murders in ink.

While there are those who will differ with me, I state that sexual psychopathy *cannot* be cured with pills or any form of medication because more often than not this disorder is ingrained into these killers' formative years by bad parenting, poor diets, disruptive schooling, familial abuse and a whole raft of other issues related to the nature and nurture debate. All of which the child begins to accept as being the norm. We will see how this can happen when we examine some of these killers-holding-pens later.

> I hated all my life. I hated everybody. When I first grew up and can remember, I was dressed as a girl by my mother. And I stayed that way for two or three years. After that I was treated like what I call the dog of the family. I was beaten. I was made to do things that no human bein' would want to do.
>
> Henry Lee Lucas (1936–2001)

There is no empirical evidence to prove that criminal psychopaths are more intelligent or less intelligent than most of us. With their absence of empathy and the blunting of other affective states, they exist across cultures and ethnic groups. It's been estimated that approximately 1 per cent of males and 0.3–0.7 per cent of females could be classified as psychopathic. Rose West, Cathy May Wood, Joanne Dennehy and Melanie McGuire are among this 'deadlier than the male of the species' breed. When you read McGuire's correspondence, this lack of empathy leaps from the pages. An innate ability to manipulate and control others stands out with most of them. One can go online and find out just how many psychopathic killers have been released from mental institutions after receiving years of medication and psychiatric counselling, after the shrinks, who should have known better, and some half-wit parole board have rubber-stamped the release papers, signing off: 'In our professional opinion, the patient is now cured and fit to return to society.' Then, what happens? Yes, you've guessed correctly – the freed man goes homicidally ape. Take just two examples: Arthur John Shawcross (US) and arch-poisoner Graham Young (UK). Both of them were freed from mainline prisons or mental institutions to kill again and again. In Henry Lee Lucas's case, he didn't want to be freed and he reiterated this when I interviewed him while he was still on death row at Ellis Unit, Texas. I can understand that when a one-time murderer's tariff expires, then release might be the right thing to do – if, and only *if*, he or she has shown solid signs of rehabilitation. However, once a sexual psychopath *always* a sexual psychopath. So I would urge a major rethink by governments: never mind the thirty-year tariff – life should mean natural life with no quibbling about it.

Some among us may be inclined to think that psychopaths – most especially serial killers – have a superficial charm. Ted Bundy, Michael Ross, John Cannan and John 'J.R.' Edward Robinson are regarded as good-looking men, in some quarters. That said, any high intelligence that such individuals may have is deeply undermined by a litany of crippling character flaws: poor judgement and failure to learn from experience, pathological egocentricity and incapacity for love, impulsivity, grandiose narcissistic sense of self-worth, pathological lying and manipulative behaviour. And in any case, many serial murderers have extremely low IQs and are ugly specimens of manhood – witness Henry Lee Lucas, although I must admit that his handwriting was quite neat, that's if someone didn't put pen to paper at 'Enry's behest.

When they put me out on parole [from the Ionia State Mental Hospital], I said I'm not ready to go. I told them all, the warden, the psychologist, everybody that I was going to kill.

Henry Lee Lucas: to the author at interview,

death row, Ellis Unit, Huntsville, Texas,

February 1996.

Lucas was literally dragged protesting and screaming out of the gates and thrown into the road. The next day, the body of a young girl who had been raped and beaten to death was discovered just under a mile away.

If we look at psychopathy through the other end of the behavioural telescope, we can identify 'recidivism': a tendency to relapse into a previous condition or mode of behaviour, especially into criminal behaviour. It describes criminals of all sorts who despite spending periods behind bars cannot refrain from committing crime once they have been released only to be arrested, over and over, ad infinitum. These characters know what they are doing is wrong, yet they simply don't care about the consequences to their victims, their own kith and kin – and themselves, come to that. Simply put, they never learn from the errors of their ways. Low-level recidivists include impulsive shoplifters and drivers who continually break the speed limits; moving up the scale, we get to burglars, sex offenders, rapists and serial killers. We will see much of this warped psychopathology in the letters that follow, so bear with me please.

A more recent example closer to the British home was the release from a life-licence tariff of British double child-murderer and rapist Colin Pitchfork. He was the first killer in criminal history to be convicted using DNA profiling after he murdered two schoolgirls in 1983 and 1986. He was given a thirty-year minimum term and despite massive public protests he was granted parole in June 2021. On 19 November 2021, he was arrested and returned to prison after being seen by police stalking young girls in Portsmouth – and he'd only been out of jail since the start of September, for God's sake! The Parole Board wrote to me stating that they *had* to release Pitchfork, which is patently untrue. He had being conning the prison's psychiatrists, falsifying regular polygraph tests and boasting about his murders to his fellow cons, all of which the Parole Board were very much aware of, and this being so, I would certainly dock their wages, do you agree?

What I am now about to propose will deeply offend everyone who leans so far to the left they might be inclined to topple over. But let's get real, now. Imagine that you were the parents of Pitchfork's victims – Lynda Mann and Dawn Ashworth, both aged fifteen – and thirty-some years after you'd lost your precious daughter to a craven sex monster, you see press photos of him out on day release, parading himself around the city of Bristol wearing expensive trainers, a smug smile from ear to ear. Then follows a national outcry because he is due for release on licence, wearing a tag of course. Out of the prison gates, he is provided with an all-singing, all-dancing multi-geared cycle courtesy of HM Government, fancy clothes, given *free* accommodation at the taxpayers' expense with more benefits than most, and then starts following young girls in your town or city. If one of those murdered girls had been my daughter, I would have wanted him executed from the get-go. Sadly the Parole Board doesn't see it that way. But then, none of those pen-pushers have lost a loved one that way. Period!

Graham Frederick Young

To give the reader some initial insight as to what to start looking for in an offender's correspondence (and an insight into a total botch-up by psychiatrists and the Home Office), we need look no further than a small sample penned by serial killer Graham Young, aka 'The Teacup Poisoner' (1947–90). Young had been confined in the Broadmoor mental asylum since the age of twenty for poisoning his parents and a sister. However, despite the concerns of many of the nurses, just eight years later – during which time he is widely believed to have killed another patient and *is* known to have attempted to poison hospital staff with bleach in their tea urn – on 4 February 1971, the blinkered authorities set Graham free on the recommendation of the hospital's shrinks.

Almost immediately, Young sought employment, applying for a job at John Hadland Ltd, a company in Bovingdon, Hertfordshire that specialised in high-speed photographic and optical equipment. The firm's stocks of extremely toxic substances were more than substantial. In his initial application letter, Young wrote: 'I previously studied chemistry, organic and inorganic, pharmacology and toxicology.' All fake hyperbole with huge red flags. By way of a reference, the hospital psychiatrist, Dr Udwin, provided Hadland's with the following letter:

This man [Graham Young] has suffered a deep-going personality disorder which necessitated his hospitalisation throughout the whole of his adolescence. He has, however, *made an extremely full recovery* and *is now entirely fit for discharge*, his sole disability now being the need to catch up on his lost time. [Author's italics]

One could cynically suggest that Dr Udwin meant 'lost time in killing people' but I won't suggest anything of the sort; nonetheless he wrote his letter to John Hadland not on Broadmoor stationery but his own, so the company was not aware that this 'hospital' was a nuthouse containing some of the most dangerous individuals in the UK. With Mr Hadland reassured, Young was given the job as an assistant storekeeper with access to enough lethal substances to kill most of the country's population, and he wrote the following letter to thank the firm for accepting him. I quote verbatim:

Dear Mr John Hadland
I am pleased to accept your offer, and the conditions attached, thereto, and shall, therefore, report for work on Monday, May 10th at 8.30 a.m.
    May I take this opportunity to express my gratitude to you for offering me this position, notwithstanding my previous infirmity as communicated to you by the Placing Officer [Dr Udwin]. I shall endeavour to justify your faith in me by performing my duties in an efficient and competent manner.
    Until Monday week, I am, Yours faithfully, Graham Young

Young repaid his gratitude to Mr Hadland by killing two of his employees and attempting to fatally poison others. But what does the tone of that brief letter smack of? It's obsequious, ass-licking, over-flowery – especially when the first paragraph would have been more than sufficient, with something like: 'Cheers, mate, I will start on Monday.' Hidden between the lines however we find a man who likes to hear himself talk, perhaps expansively, probably a 'Mr Know-All', like Donald Trump even, so taking what's on the page and what's hidden between the lines, in Young's letters we should instantly sniff an arrogant, jerry-built, boastful individual Donald Trump again). I can confirm this, because once settled in at Hadland's, Young held forth on all matters concerning toxicology: what he didn't know about ratsbane, hemlock, deadly nightshade, datura, henbane, monkshood and vomica one could write on the back of a postage stamp. As for expounding on the unpleasant effects following ingestion of corrosive drain cleaner, battery acid, prussic acid and every other lethal substance known to mankind, or an 'A to Z' of the periodic table of elements, he knew it all. And it was this that *finally* – after a very long time – led to suspicion falling upon him and his arrest.

Young got a perverse kick out of people falling ill; watching and gloating as they writhed around in agony, and leaving the staff at Hadland's – and previously the doctors and nurses at Broadmoor – completely in the dark as to the cause of these terrible symptoms. Being a homicidal voyeur, Young then had the gall to advise the attending medics and a canny police officer on what that problem might be. It's mind-bending, isn't it? Here we have a fully emerged psychopath more or less pointing a finger at himself with the shrinks bickering among themselves as to whether or not the problem lies in their county's contaminated water supply, radiation from some unknown source or some red berries, or even laurel leaves from a bush.

> We have a cure for sexual psychopathy and serial killers. We strap them down on that gurney there and inject the goodnight juice. Hurt? Of course it hurts. It's like having acid pumped through your veins.
>
> > Death row warden, Neil Hodges: execution
> > suite, 'The Walls Prison', Huntsville, Texas,
> > to the author at interview

In the UK we have something like a polite note being passed to a sexual psychopathic murderer saying: 'Hi, there, the Parole Board are delighted to inform you that your prison tariff has now expired and all of us at the Home Office apologise for having detained you so long.'

Way to go, bro! These stone-cold American killers know all too well what the ultimate penalty could be if they get arrested for committing first-degree aggravated homicide: a fry-up in an electric chair, a good dose of toxic drugs given as a bolus injection or 'The Long Drop'. Therefore, quite effectively they are committing judicial suicide, with the state merely providing the terminal means to dispatch them.

Selecting which of the homicidal ink-slingers out of my vast collection of letters to include in this book has been a momentously difficult task. There will be critics who will say that I have not included a 'Mr So-and-So', even a 'Mrs So-and-So & Sons'. On that score, I can only reply that I will include in a sequel those individuals I've left out this time around.

One thing the reader will quickly notice is the complete lack of contrition among these killers. In my face-to-face, up-close-and-personal interviews, and/or correspondence with around thirty serial killers and mass murderers, I can say that never ever once has *any of them* exhibited a flyspeck of remorse.

> I was born with the devil in me. I could not help the fact that I was a murderer, no more than the poet can help the inspiration to sing [...] I was born with the evil one standing as my sponsor beside the bed where I was ushered into the world, and he has been with me since.
>
> Herman Webster Mudgett, aka H.H. Holmes or
> 'The American Ripper' (1861–96)

On the rare occasions that a monster has expressed any form of remorse, it's accompanied by a crocodile tear or two with some sackcloth and smoke-blown ashes into my yard to gain my sympathy. This charade is phoney. If they appear to be upset, it is because of the unfortunate fix they now find themselves in – some often having just been moved to the death-house suite a few short steps from the electric chair or lethal injection gurney. You will see this writ large in some of their letters to me.

A fine example of this 'hollowness' is the two-faced shifty, sly Ted Bundy's filmed interview with author and evangelical Christian, Dr James Dobson. The reader can find it on YouTube. Look at Bundy's face: his expression as fake as a hooker's smile, the occasional flickering glance up into Dr Dobson's eyes to see if his bullshit is being believed, that Dr Dobson is being taken in. Many of my colleagues and guests who attend the annual CrimeCon event in London will spot this false-presenting in a heartbeat. So, please watch this interview with Dr Dobson then can you see Bundy's fake mask of suggested normality, the phoney contriteness, the blame-shifting onto his early exposure to pornography? Ted's psychopathological mind working flat out in pathetic mitigation as his end draws nigh, when his head will be shaved prior to being strapped down hard into the electric chair after a tampon has been stuffed into his rectum and an elastic band pinged around his penis to prevent his urine from shorting out the electrode strapped to his leg.

When we watch a live criminal trial on Court TV or YouTube, we often see a defendant apologising to the judge, with his attorney laying on mitigating bullshit faster than a cook ladles soup into a bowl. These killers do not mean that they're sorry at all. One wonders if they even understand what that adjective means; besides, as with Bundy, you can see pretence written across their stony faces, and throughout the following letters, you will spot the pretence too, with no mention of 'I'm sorry' too.

Judges have long since cottoned on to this, as is clear from the collected accounts of the first trials at the Old Bailey, which were published in 1674. During one later murder case, the defendant, pleading to be spared, begged: 'M'lud, please don't top me. I'd like a prison sentence best.' The judge, Sir Horace Edmund Avory, was 'thin-lipped, utterly unemotional, silent, humourless, and relentless towards lying witnesses and brutal criminals' according to *Brewer's Dictionary of Phrase and Fable*. Among the legal fraternity he was dubbed 'The Acid Drop', Wrapped up in ermine and as cold as a wintry day, he glared at the prisoner in the dock and replied: 'I don't give you what *you* like I give you what *I* like.' He donned the black cap, read the dread words, after which he did what all murder trial judges did in those days – he snapped off the nib of his pen (a symbolic act signifying that he'd never use the same pen again) and ordered the guards to 'Take him down.'

I like Judge Avory, don't you too? He's my kind of guy. Pity there are none like him on the benches today, hanging the illiterate little asswipes who beat old ladies to death to steal their pension money just collected from the post office. Oh, my gosh. I sound a bit like grumpy Victor Meldrew from the British sitcom *One Foot in the Grave*, do I not?

Moving swiftly on. Many years ago at the Federal Correctional Institution in Tallahassee, Florida, I interviewed the grossly obese Cathy May Wood on camera for our *The Serial Killers* TV series. Along with Gwendolyn Gail Graham, Wood was the other half of the killing tag team dubbed the 'Lethal Lovers' by the media, because during the ice-cold winter of 1987, they burked (i.e. suffocated by kneeling on their victims' chests, pinching their noses and forcing their hands over dry mouths and pursed lips) five elderly residents of the Alpine Manor nursing home in the homely Walker suburb of Grand Rapids, Michigan. I also interviewed the scrawny, self-harming Graham at the Women's Huron Valley Prison in Michigan.

Cathy Wood was released from prison on 16 January 2020. Graham will only be freed wearing a cardboard coffin. Meanwhile, Wood – the prime instigator – whistled a plea-bargain deal to get herself a lighter sentence, oozing regret, to the point of tears with phoney facial expressions that she'd hoped would melt anyone's heart, but as soon as she left the interview room, my crew and I overheard her snigger and say: 'I bet I fooled those fuck-suckers in there!' And what a fine example that is: the crew and me had no idea what was going through her mind during the interview, yet now we see Wood presenting as someone she patently was not, with pretence writ large over her podgy face.

So there is a parallel example of what I mean when I talk about reading between the lines of a letter. While the smug expressions on a killer's face might appear sincere enough, what's hidden behind the fake mask that he or she wears tells us a great deal more.

Another thing I hope to reveal in most of the following letters – and this also links to their psychopathologies – is that they love talking about themselves. If they write about their crimes, most often they do so in an off-hand, boastful sort of way. These types are extremely manipulative congenital liars through and through. This makes studying their correspondence even more fascinating when trying to get to grips with their twisted mindsets, especially when they vehemently plead innocence, as we'll see later on with John 'J.R.' Edward Robinson, aka 'The Slavemaster'. One should also be mindful that in cases such as these, and across the lengthy periods of correspondence that I've had with them, the more they put pen to paper the more they forget what mitigation they'd written beforehand. Pathological liars have to have excellent memories, but they do not!

Also nicknamed the 'Bodies in Barrels' serial killer, Pecksniffian to a fault John 'J.R.' Robinson was a 'multiple presenter'; a great dissembler who constantly stole other people's money, with a personality as crooked as a three-card trick, he could change his colours at the drop of a hat. It seems that he truly believed that he'd portrayed himself as an honest, hard-working businessman who had been wrongly accused of serial murder; the very thought of being involved in extreme BDSM (bondage and discipline, dominance and submission, sadism and masochism) activities had never crossed his mind, he claimed repeatedly. Yet when corresponding with a former female FBI agent (who used a fake name and photograph as part of a honeytrap), he played out a very different part of his Dr Jekyll and Mr Hyde mindset, all too soon revealing his true nature. Of course, he was big time into bondage and all other BDSM stuff. He wallowed in it up to his neck – as you'll discover for yourself when you read his letters later on. And what he suggested his female penfriend should do with some golf balls wouldn't go down very well with the stewards and committee of the prestigious St Andrews Golf Club in Scotland, one can bank on that!

Man is not what he thinks he is, he is what he hides.
(Georges) André Malraux

And André hits the nail on the head for while an offender's handwriting might indicate something about his or her character, this can be merely a small part of their psychological narrative. Quite often a killer will reply to different recipients in various ways, and this applies to handwriting styles too. That's not to imply that they have true split personalities or a multiple personality disorder. Rather, this is their cunning manipulation at work: tailoring their letters to suit whomever they are corresponding with, in order to receive in return what suits their own needs best. British serial killer Joanne Dennehy is a prime example. She would write just a couple of grammatically perfect letters to me, great penmanship too with not an expletive on the horizon. Yet when writing to some of her pit-bull-terrier-owning, brain-dead fans, or her imprisoned murderous cohort, Gary Stretch, she wrote bespoke to suit their moral compasses and intelligence – or lack thereof – using language that would have made any 1920s New York longshoreman go blue in the face.

So let's change tack for a moment. Let's take a more detailed look at a subject I raised right at the start of this book. All of us true-crime-minded folk know about Dr Edmond Locard's 'Exchange Principle' which broadly states that any contact between two items will result in an exchange of microscopic material. This certainly includes fibres, but extends to other microscopic materials including hair, pollen, glass fragments, paint, bodily fluids and DNA. In forensic science, this principle holds that the perpetrator of an offence will bring something to the crime scene and leave with something from it. With the great gift of hindsight, this might seem patently obvious, but it was Dr Locard who first figured this out in 1940. I now suggest that we *could*, if we so wished, extend this idea beyond physical forensics and into the world of the killers' writings featured throughout this book. In their letters they are bringing something 'physical' (i.e. their written words) while, without intending to, leaving their conscious and subconscious thought processes concealed between the lines – an alternative 'exchange principle', in other words. Thus, if we take the time to interpret their dual-mix psychological code, and compare it with the 'known facts' about their crimes, it will be of some value to us in understanding more about them – perhaps more about psychopathy in general, dare I say.

Neville George Clevely Heath – a Letter too Far

They're weak and stupid. Basically crooked. That's why they're attracted to rascals like me. They have all the morals of alley-cats and minds like sewers. They respond to flattery like a duck responds to water.

Neville Heath, HMP Pentonville, London,
PRIOR TO HIS EXECUTION

From just those few lines, one can immediately smell arrogance in extremis. The writer is unrepentant. That he's also a narcissist and misogynist is patently obvious. And they come from a man about to meet his doom; he is not trying to eyewash us, as did Bundy.

By way of a brief background, during the night of 20 June 1946, a drunken Heath sadistically beat, whipped and murdered thirty-two-year-old Margery Gardner in his room at the Pembridge Court Hotel in Notting Hill, London.

Even without the 17 lash marks the girl's injuries were appalling. Both nipples and soft breast tissue had been bitten away and there was a seven-inch tear in her vagina and beyond.

Home Office pathologist Professor Keith Simpson

The lash marks had been made by a leather riding whip with a diamond pattern weave; nine lashes were across the back between the shoulder blades, six across the right breast and abdomen and two on the forehead. The young woman's body had been bound hand and foot, the right arm pinned beneath the back. In the pathologist's opinion, the wounds to the vagina were due to a tearing instrument. In the fireplace was a short poker, which Professor Simpson believed may have caused the internal injuries. He surmised that Margery met her death by suffocation, either from a gag or from having her face pressed into a pillow. 'If you find that whip, you've found your man,' Simpson told the police.

Realising that the law would soon be on to him, Heath packed two suitcases into which he put Margery Gardner's bloodied clothing, the scarf he used to gag her and the cloth that had tied her wrists. He washed the riding whip, putting that in too before fleeing to Brighton. And he had very good reason to leg it: already, a wanted notice, along with his photograph, was being circulated to every police force in England. Two days after the murder, Heath sent the following letter to Scotland Yard:

Sir,
I feel it to be my duty to inform you of certain facts in connection with the death of Mrs Gardner at Notting Hill

Gate. I booked in at the hotel last Sunday, but not with Mrs Gardner, whom I met for the first time during the week. I had drinks with her on Friday evening, and whilst I was with her she met an acquaintance with whom she was obliged to sleep. The reasons, as I understand them, were mainly financial. It was then that Mrs Gardner asked if she could use my hotel room until two o'clock and intimated that if I returned after that, I might spend the remainder of the night with her. I gave her my keys and told her to leave the hotel door open. It must have been almost 3 a.m. when I returned to the hotel and found her in the condition of which you are aware. I realised that I was in an invidious position, and rather than notify the police, I packed my belongings and left.

Since then I have been in several minds whether to come forward or not, but in view of the circumstances I have been afraid to [...]I have the instrument with which Mrs Gardner was beaten and am forwarding this to you today. You will find my fingerprints on it, but you should also find others as well.

[Source: *Murder Casebook 15*, Vol. 1 Part 15 – elsewhere with slight variations.]

When we compare this letter, and Heath's attitude to Margery Gardner in particular, to the way he expresses himself in one of the last letters he penned before his execution (*see* the epigraph to this chapter), we find something interesting: he is intimating that the dead woman was of loose morals at once subconsciously revealing that he is also like-minded. Heath is also attempting to paint himself as a hapless victim 'by association'; a jolly decent, hail-fellow-well-met, who was trying to accommodate Margery and who now finds himself in rather a dreadful fix because of it. The police, however, knew that Heath's appalling record of past crimes stretched way back: bigamist; arch-conman; fraudster; thief; wearer of military uniforms he was not entitled to wear; the list was almost endless. The police never received the whip in the post, nor did they believe a word of his bullshit story, so Detective Superintendent Tom Barratt was not impressed with the letter, which had been posted on 22 June 1946, postmarked Worthing, 5.45 p.m.

A taxicab driver named Harry Harter told police that he had dropped off Heath and Mrs Gardner at the Pembridge Court Hotel, where the man was registered as 'Lieutenant-Colonel N.G.C. Heath'. Police knew that Heath held no such rank – and he'd paid the cabbie 2s 2d for the 1s 9d fare. Harter recalled that both were highly intoxicated and they had their arms around each other as they staggered through the front door.

> He stood out from other men, tall, blond proud and arrogant as a Nazi. He played I'm-hard-to-get. So I did. I won.
>
> A woman from Cambridge who refused
> Heath's oily advances

My book *Talking with Psychopaths and Savages: Beyond Evil* contains a detailed chapter on Heath's narrative, but the lady above sums his character up perfectly by describing him as 'arrogant as a Nazi'. This underpins every single line of his correspondence from the death cell and his letter to the police, which he would have been far better off not sending at all –

indeed, why he took away some of the crime-scene artefacts is anyone's guess.

Psychopaths such as Heath are control freaks, and here we find him being stupid enough to believe that elite Scotland Yard detectives would buy into all that he'd told them. But again, it is what is concealed between the lines that should interest us, because there we can see his way of thinking as clear as day. Assuming the moral high ground, he denigrates Margery Gardner, at once giving the police information known only to her killer and themselves, so apart from telling the police more or less what they knew already, he is trying to appear calm and sincere in an effort to convince them that he is telling the truth and to get the heat off his back. However, the police were now aware of his extensive criminal rap sheet that for most of his adult life he had been a con artist with a habit of assuming false identities; yet, so ingrained was his pathological mindset that Heath truly believed that law enforcement would buy into his story as hundreds of people had done before – but the police didn't!

On 3 July 1946, Heath met twenty-one-year-old Doreen Margaret Marshall, then serving with the WRNS, in Bournemouth. Four days later, her body was found in woodland at nearby Branksome Chine. She, like Margery Gardner, had suffered appalling injuries. The pathologist, Dr Crichton McGaffey, noted marks of attempted strangulation. Her throat had been cut twice. One rib had been broken and the others bruised, suggesting that the killer had knelt over her or jumped on the body, all of which shows a total hatred for young women in general. Abrasions on her wrists suggested that her hands had been bound. The hands themselves bore a number of defensive knife wounds, as if she had been trying to deflect the knife blows. Both of Doreen's nipples had all but been bitten off.

When Dorset police started to make enquiries, this arrogant, narcissistic man had the nerve to stroll up to the nearest police station to tell an officer that, in passing, he'd met Doreen the previous day, and that she'd had dinner with him at the Tollard Royal Hotel on the evening that she'd vanished. 'I walked her part the way back to her own hotel,' he told Detective Constable Souter, 'and I have not seen her since.' The sadosexual Heath was arrested that evening. The riding crop and some of Margery's clothing were found in his suitcases in the left luggage office at Bournemouth railway station. Nonchalant to the end, Heath sat calmly in his cell. When Albert Pierrepoint, the public executioner, arrived, Heath reportedly said: 'Come on, boys, let's get on with it.' He accepted the traditional offer of a glass of whisky to steady the nerves, adding: 'While you're about it, you might make that a double,' before, with a stiff upper lip, he strode unassisted to the trap to meet his doom.

The Right Bait

All manner of sin and blasphemy shall be forgiven unto men.

MATTHEW 12:31

Once again praying that I do not incur the wrath of Our Lord –
although I am cast-iron guaranteed forgiveness and redemption
anyway – let it be said that prison ministry pastors, and some
members of the Parole Board good people they may be, all
too frequently become sucked in by these killers who have
suddenly turned to God. These murdering psychopaths, who
have probably never seen the inside of a church in their entire
lives, start attending prison religious services and writing letters
expressing remorse having 'seen the light', with repentance for
their sins jam-packed into all four corners of the prison-issue
notepaper. When we examine the correspondence written by
serial killer John 'J.R.' Edward Robinson later on in this book,
we will quickly realise how these evil men and women are able
to con almost anyone given half the chance. Of course, most

God-fearing folk do, or strive to, seek goodness among their fellow man, and why not? It is natural for us to look for the good in people, not the bad.

> I want to get right with God.
>
> Gary Ray Bowles, kidnapper, torturer, rapist
> and serial killer: letter to the author

Those good people who strive to save the lost souls of monsters such as the sexual psychopath Gary Ray Bowles are on a losing wicket from the outset. They are duped into believing – and they truly *want* to believe – what these born-again redemptionists write and say while not having an inkling as to what is concealed between the lines, or what is actually going through these criminals' manipulating minds.

Kenneth 'The Hillside Strangler' Bianchi, a sadosexual serial murderer – the man who raped and tortured *at least* two twelve-year-old schoolgirls and is now a (self-declared) ordained priest – belonged to so many churches that he lost track of what denominations they were and which pastor was to visit him next. To earn a few bucks, Bianchi even wrote his essay: 'Sociological Theoretical Thesis: My Word on the Word'. What a ream of garbage that was too, yet members of many churches and religious outreach groups read his bullshit and literally queued up to offer succour and spiritual guidance to prepare Bianchi to be greeted by God with open arms 24/7. Indeed, so enamoured with Bianchi's newfound faith were well-meaning Mr and Mrs Dorothy Otter, they wrote to the Parole Board, pleading with deep-seated, holier-than-thou Christian conviction: 'Ken has found The Lord in all sincerity. If he were to be released he would be welcome to stay with us and our two young daughters whom he would get on very well with.'

And, you betcha he would!

I corresponded with Bianchi for a few years before I interviewed him at the Washington State Penitentiary in Walla Walla, Washington State. Then we had a falling-out, with me giving him payback time with some not so diplomatic correspondence of my own. Everywhere I went with my TV crew, I sent him picture postcards from the locations of his killings, along with the words: 'I bet you wish *you* were here.' I even sent him one from Gig Harbor: 'Hi, Ken, just visited with one of your accomplices VerLyn Compton Wallace in the Washington Corrections Center for Women (WCCW). Interviewed her for a TV documentary and bro, didn't she just shit in your nest. Then I went steelhead trout fishing with your assistant governor. She's got a cabin out here, done some varmint shooting ... so how's your day been?'

Sometimes I can be a bit naughty too!

As one might imagine, Bianchi was not impressed. In the good spirit of reconciliation I have since written to him, without even having received the courtesy of a single reply. Yet on 15 May 2021, he sent the following email to a lady pen-pal of his after they'd had a slight tiff:

I'm lying on my 3 inch mattress which rests on a concrete slab. V tired. Busy day, meals, shower, tier porter job morning and afternoon, time to respond to multiple emails from my contact in England who has been working on things for years. Today I'm feeling my age [70]. I get that you get V angry, but what you say is how you feel within. Words cannot adequately express how much I hate and detest Berry-Dee. For you to equate me to him is not only how you feel, but beyond insulting. Plus, it was your contact, Angelique, who most likely caused him to text you. If what you said was not how you feel, you would not have said that during your rant.

You win some and lose some, as the following quote attributed to the poet John Lydgate, and later adapted by President Lincoln, sums up (and my critics should take note): 'You can please some of the people all of the time, you can please all of the people some of the time, but you can't please all of the people all of the time.' So if any reader is of the mind to berate my syntax as shockingly awful, I shall roundly thank him/her because I have been struggling for years to get a smidgen of praise for my syntaxical [*sic*] achievements – allegedly☺.

So, let's look again at Bianchi's email. What does it tell us from what we have learned thus far from the examples of Graham Young and Neville Heath? Bianchi's first few lines are an effort to elicit sympathy. Bless him, he is lying on a three-inch mattress that rests on a concrete slab. I have peered at Bianchi through his bars and seen his cell ('house' in US correctional parlance), so this much is correct. But what about his numerous victims who now lie rotting in their graves and who will never get a chance to get 'V tired', eat meals and have a busy day, let alone ever have the luxury of taking a shower again? Neither will his deceased victims be responding to emails, writing letters or sending tweets.

Then there is a sudden switch in Bianchi's tone. Feeling his age at seventy, he rails against me. He detests and hates me, then he lets rip with this: 'For you, V, to equate me to him is not only how you feel, but beyond insulting.' What an immoral bigot Bianchi is, to then sign off by blaming 'V' and a TV documentary-maker called Angelique for allegedly breaking his confidence. As for his contact in England 'who has been working on things for years', I can tell the reader that this 'contact' is one half of a half-brained tag team trying to overturn his Bellingham murder convictions for the double murder of Washington State University co-eds Diane Wilder and Karen Mandic, even though he has already sunk his own boat – all of his appeals long exhausted. And, this once again proves my point, with 'V' having tried to explain the true facts of Bianchi's rock-solid convictions to those wannabe TV-documentary-making halfwits who are lobbying for his release, and the Bible-thumpers who promise to invite him to live with them and their nubile daughters – they just don't understand that even *if* Bianchi were to be freed from the Washington State Penitentiary, the moment he stepped outside of the gate he would be arrested by LA homicide detectives and extradited to California, where he would serve another life sentence for the 'Hillside Stranglings' that earned him his sinister nickname.

So, what if you decide to write to a serial killer? Well, to start with you will need to use the right bait, simply because quite often it is very difficult to get these people to open up in correspondence – let alone for you to receive a reply – because they are highly suspicious at the best of times. They will only entertain you if there is something in it for them, in the form of money or some other benefit that appeals to their egotistical senses.

If one is writing a book about one of these monsters, or

maybe a chapter within a book, a magazine article or researching a TV documentary, one has to thoroughly research their criminal narratives and their modus operandi as much as possible – even going way back to their formative years. And among all of this info, if you are on the ball, you will find something that might trigger a favourable response.

I look at this 'angling for a response' as a fisherman might; a beach-caster slinging his limpet-baited hook into a roiling surf to entice a sea bass, or a fly-casting laird on the banks of a Scottish river meandering through a heather-carpeted glen. It is all about what bait to use, and how one presents that bait to catch a decent fish, you see. The predatory pike for example: they are greedy SOBs, snatching pretty much anything that swims past, and they'll bite your fingers if you're not careful. Some killers are the same. Tell them straight off that you think that they are innocent. Tell them you intend to write a book about the miscarriage of justice they are suffering; go as far as saying that a major UK TV broadcaster is interested, with maybe even some cash in it for them at the end of the day, and they cannot fail to rise to the surface and take your literary bait as fast as a mousetrap snaps shut. Of course, you are telling them a bucketful of lies, but the easiest folk to deceive are the deceivers themselves. You can take that to the bank, because once locked up in prison these killers become just a number in the correctional system and any attention they can get from the outside world massages their egos.

Other fish are cautious. Carp have to be because they often live to sixty years plus and, just like me, they put on a lot of weight during that time. Another reason carp can become the fish equivalent of a sexagenarian is that the angler who has hooked a specimen has to net it, weigh it, then put it back into the water. Thereafter, the carp slowly dives under a bed of water lily, muttering: 'I really must give up eating those boilies, the scent of fishmeal still drives me crazy.' I really can't see the point in fishing for carp, anyway. They swim slowly around a self-contained lake, are highly addicted to those boilies (flavoured bait) and, providing the angler can drop a load of them on the fish's nose, it is more or less guaranteed to bite. It goes without saying that many serial killers have a similar mindset, especially if they are really (in)famous and have lots of people writing to them week in, week out. Your lure has to be first-rate. These killers are cautious, as was 'J.R.' Robinson, who saw my bait, sniffed at it, swam around it but refused to reply until I eventually figured out his warped mindset and presented him with a tasty bullshit lure he could not resist: offers of money – sacks of it. As you will see later, Robinson took some reeling in. The results were amazing; I was electrified – which, indeed, Robinson should have been – but in Kansas nowadays, they get 'the goodnight juice', aka lethal injection. They stopped using 'Old Sparky' some time back. It may have been because some inmate caught on fire and the witnesses threw up over each other, I'm not sure really, but when you learn what J.R. did to his innocent victims, then read his letters, I am sure that most of my readers would have queued up to pull the switch.

Arthur John Shawcross, aka 'The Genesee River Killer'

Shawcross liked fishing too, especially the Black River at Watertown in upstate New York, and much later the Genesee River, Rochester, 150 miles south-west, and fishing was to become part and parcel of his modus operandi and murderous modus vivendi.

Unlike an elderly carp, Arthur didn't live to a ripe old age. He died of natural causes, aged sixty-three, in 2008, while serving 250 years to life. I spent several years writing to him and trying to get him to agree to be interviewed on camera, my bait being a phoney teaser of some funds coming his way. Eventually I received this blunt response:

Dear Christopher
I WILL SEE YOU.
Sincerely
Arthur Shawcross

91-B-0193
P.O. Box AG
Fallsburg, N.Y <u>12733-0116</u>
<u>U.S.A.</u>

I replied and then came this. As with all the letters reproduced in this book, it's quoted verbatim, including the capitals:

DEAR CHRISTOPHER,
THANK YOU FOR THE LETTER. I WOULD DO THE 30 MINUTE INTERVIEW, BUT CAN YOU TELL ME IF THERE IS A CAMERA INVOLVED OR DO WE TALK TOGETHER? WHICH EVER IS OK. YOU HAVE SPOKEN OF FUNDS AND THEY ARE MUCH NEEDED, MY WIFE IS IN A BAD WAY RIGHT NOW. SHE IS SICK WITH THE FLU-CHEST-COLD. PLUS HER JOB IS UNSTABLE FROM ALL THE PUBLICITY THAT HAS GENERATED AROUND ME. EVERYONE IS TRYING TO GET ME TO SPEAK TO THEM BUT I WAIT. THERE IS MUCH STILL GOING ON IN THE CITY OF ROCHESTER, NEW YORK. PEOPLE WANT MY OPINION. YOU CAN GET IT PLUS WHAT MY THOUGHTS ARE.
WHAT ARE THE QUESTIONS YOU'D ASK OF ME? AS LONG AS MY LAWYER UNDERSTANDS AND WHAT I CAN ANSWER.
NOW THEN, PLEASE HAVE THE FUNDS SENT TO MY WIFE ROSE AND SHE WILL DISBURSE

THEM FOR BECAUSE OF TAXES.

DO NOT SEND ANYONE TO BOTHER HER.

ROSE M. SHAWCROSS

RD #3 BOX 274

ONEONTA, NEW YORK – <u>13820</u>

UNITED STATES OF AMERICA

THANK YOU.

RESPECTFULLY

ARTHUR J. SHAWCROSS.

Reading between the lines of that letter, we can instantly see that my phoney reference to funds coming in his direction paid off. He is also playing the sympathy card with his wife Rose having the flu; that her job is unstable because of all of the morbid publicity surrounding his case. Then he throws in the notion that people want his opinion, but that he will wait. Signally, he fails to mention why people want his opinion, or his thoughts, for here he is spinning hogwash and trying to make himself appear more important than he realistically is. He also mentions that he needs to talk to his lawyer (although he didn't have one at the time) before contradicting himself and forgetting all about Rose's flu, because in truth he wants the cash disbursed to him and for her to dodge paying taxes.

Thereafter, Arthur's letters came thick and fast, all followed in short order by mail from Rose and his long-time lover Clara Neal, whom he was about to bigamously marry, 'no matter what the law is' as he put it to me.

What I found particularly galling, in equal measure to the content of Shawcross's letters to me, were the letters both Rose and Clara Neal penned without any reference to the many women and two little kiddies whom he had previously raped and killed while Rose was living with him in Watertown and him bonking Clara circa the same time. Karen Ann Hill, aged eight, was raped vaginally and anally, after which Shawcross had pushed her body into a drainage pipe on the banks of the Black River. Jack Blake, aged ten, was also killed by Shawcross, who took him fishing along the same river.

Rose stuck like superglue to her husband throughout his fifteen-year prison term and she resumed their physical relationship after he was released and while he was murdering prostitutes in Rochester, New York, and screwing Clara Neal while also using her car during his killing spree. Most of Shawcross's Rochester victims were dumped close to, or in the slow-moving waters of the Genesee River. One corpse was gutted like a fish; he cut out the vagina of another victim and ate it while driving Clara's car. 'It was frozen from the creek,' he wrote in a letter to me, 'so I thawed it under the car heater, chewed on it a bit, then I threw it outa the car window. Went down to Dunkin Donuts and chewed the fat with cops talking about the serial killings [...] Coz I had shiny black shoes, they thought I was an undercover cop. Funny I think.'

It was as if neither Rose nor Clara believed that 'Art' had killed anyone. That surely proves that they had a total lack of moral compass and were plumb-dumb stupid. Both women wanted to get hold of as much money as possible without a single thought or mention in their correspondence about the terrible deaths Arthur had brought upon so many of his innocent victims and the grief he unloaded on their next of kin.

On 23 April 1993, Rose Shawcross dictated this letter to me, which was posted from P.O. Box 453 in Omerta, New York, and the grammar is all hers:

> Dear Christopher.
>
> Please find enclosed a copy of the letter that you sent to Arthur Shawcross
>
> On November 9, 1992.
>
> Art says that he has written to you, but received no answer. I am having a friend of 20 years, write this letter to you. She also take me to see Art, once a month. Recently, we have missed going for 2 months as I have no money. I work in Omerta, N.Y., as a Certified Nurses Aide, doing home care. At first I was getting 50-60 hrs a week until the company found out who I was. They started cutting my hrs until I could not pay my rent or go and see Art. They were giving me 12 or 17 hrs a week, sometimes 20 hrs. I have had to leave the small apartment I had in half of a mobile home, and moved to a room in Omerta.
>
> The busses stopped running, so I had to hire a taxi to take me to work, this I could not afford.

Let's take a breather here to try to fathom out the mindset of this woman, whose husband's killing time was as much concern to her as water off a duck's back. Despite all that he had done, not only to his victims but after having heaped everlasting shame onto her too, she's still complaining that her working hours have been cut down to the degree that she's unable to visit this piece of human scum in prison as often as she'd like to. What follows says it all:

They started offering me jobs 25 miles away from where I lived. I couldn't take them. When I told them I didn't drive, and I couldn't afford a taxi, they said, 'Well why don't you buy a care [*sic*] and learn to drive? Just thing, you could go and see your husband more often.'

My family kept after me to change my name, but, I refused. They are alienated from me.

Art loves to cook, so when I do go down to see him, I take coffee, salad foods etc. Now, if I can get enough money to go see him, I have to go empty handed.

Art has had at least 12 offers for an on-camera interview, but he has refused. He wanted to take you up on your offer, as, we read the Murder Casebook, *Monster of the Rivers*. We thought it was well written. [I did not contribute to the article, although I may have referred to it when I first contacted Shawcross.]

We had a very rough winter here. I had to walk on some of the coldest days. I couldn't breathe, and I fell on the ice. I have a breathing problem. As you know, I am a heavy woman and I have phlebitis.

We would appreciate hearing from you. Thank you
Yours sincerely.
Rose Marie Shawcross.

Rose Shawcross never received so much as a dime from me. A couple of years later, on 4 November 1994, Shawcross's fiancée Clara Neal cottoned on to the possibility of some cash flowing her way. Again, the grammar and spelling are all hers:

Hi, Christopher

How is my Very good Freind doing these days Fine I hope as for myself just doing the same Not yet able to go see ART which you probley know it real hard for me to do only thing I still don't have no car to go in, and he is going crazy to see me before Winter starts. So we can Disguse our Business in person with each other about our money situation and most of all our wedding photos For Spring. Oh yes I ask Art if he would like for your family to bee there at our wedding and he said he would love it too. Christopfer if there is any way for you to bring a camera to make some Pictures O sure would be grateful to you and your Family I am looking Forward meeting your wife and children, yes, Christopher some way the paper here in Rochester got the word out about our interview so they came all the way out here to my trailor they wanted to know everything I said and where you people were from wanted to know where we met and all that JAZZ I told them Plain out no more enterviews ever because everything they even printed was HOG WASH about Art because he never killed anyone. They even ask me if art and I got Married yet I said how he is still married to Rose I am not dumb. They ask me if I still go see him I said yes when I can so did you contact the News Paper when you were in Rochester that they knew about you or did some of my Nosy Neighbors Report to them I don't know [...]

Time for you and me to come up for another gulp of fresh air because Clara, a mother of at least eight children with circa twelve to sixteen grandchildren, hadn't quite finished:

> [...] but there is something offel Funny now the Lady that brought me in for the enterview wont even talk to me now so Iam sorry about the Phone No and that you cant call me. But I hope real soon Arts money From the Service will start coming in to our bank as soon as it does I will get a Phone on here in my own trailor. Then you can call me any time to let me know how things is in your country and I can let you know about me and art how our plan is coming along so all I can say is if you want any enformation from me you will half to rite me a little sorry no phone. Oh yes Christofer what did you do with my pictures I have got them did you take them to England or did you have them here at the Motel if so they said they did not have them Im very unhappy if they are destroyed so please rite and let me know soon.
>
> Your Friend
> Clara Neal
> Ps. Sorry for the miss spelling
> Your name and having to change it.

As mentioned previously, one can get a picture of someone's intelligence, or lack of, through their writings, so I am obliged to tell the reader that this author met both Clara and Rose in the flesh, so to speak, therefore, with my hand on my heart I cannot say that in either case the phrase 'stimulating dialogue' was on the table. Clara's reference to Arthur receiving money from the 'service' proves that she was totally unaware, or too thick to know, that his Army pension had been stopped years ago. As for the photos? Well, yes, I did return them – to the Rochester PD, as a matter of fact. And it was one of those photos with Shawcross wearing a red sweatshirt that helped me and the police close the cold case of murdered Kimberly Logan. My website includes photos of me with Captain Lynde B. Johnston and homicide detectives Billy Barnes and the ever-smiling Lenny Boriello down by the side of the Genesee River where Shawcross dumped so many of his victims' terribly mutilated bodies. So thank you, Clara. Inadvertently you helped clear up one of your lover's murders.

Clara and Rose are, like Shawcross, now deceased, and remain so to this very day.

Phillip Carl Jablonski, aka 'The Death Row Teddy'

The only good woman is a dead one.

PHILLIP CARL JABLONSKI

Thanks for that info, Phil. As an aside, 'Jablonski' is a Polish word derived from the root *Jabłoń*, meaning 'apple tree'. Some say it was originally used as a surname for someone from an apple tree orchard – that would be an 'orchardist', it seems to me. It is also possible that 'Jablonski' was derived from the town of 'Jablonowo' near Mlawa. Polish in root and in origin, but let's see just how far from the 'Jabłoń' Phillip Jablonski fell.

One of the first questions I am always asked while giving public talks, podcasts or during TV interviews, is: 'What makes a serial killer tick?' This is a simple enough, off-the-shelf stock question proposing no definitive answer. Each murderer is as different from another as is a nub of teacher's chalk and one of Poenaru's fountain pens. I can, however, confirm, as will the

FBI, that a grossly dysfunctional childhood can, or will play, no small part in turning some children in thoroughly rotten adults; thenceforth they *can*, over time, metamorphose into serial rapists and serial murderers.

Sticking with the theme of fruit, it should be noted that in many families that have spawned serial killers, and where there are several siblings, usually only one of them turns out to be the rotten apple in a basket of otherwise perfectly good Granny Smiths.

At this point, may I introduce you to a 6-foot 2-inch, 200-pound hulk. The creature we are about to cast our eyes over was thirty degrees below trailer-park trash, yet it would be fair to say that Phil loved writing lots of words, yet nouns such as 'redemption' and 'mitigation' never once existed in his stunted vocabulary. To be frank, this guy could never say 'sorry'.

The correspondence sent to me by Phil from death row in San Quentin State Prison arrived in white envelopes upon which he – or someone else – drew rather cute pictures using coloured crayon: a cuddly teddy bear or some Walt Disney cartoon characters, that sort of stick-down-one's-throat-to-gag-upon yuck. But let me assure you that there was nothing cuddly or endearing about this guy at all, even when he informed me 'and I writ my own biography', but I suppose we can forgive him for that minor grammatical error. What was less forgivable, however, was the number and quality of the psychiatrists called to give evidence in his defence, and those who had treated him beforehand.

And here's the thing; most of the psychiatrists called by Jablonski's defence team to give evidence at his trial would have read (or should have read) the head-shrinker's bible: the

Diagnostic and Statistical Manual of Mental Disorders. For the reader's edification, *DSM* is the go-to reference for psychiatrists and psychologists worldwide.

Time to digress a tad and cutting to the chase, *DSM* (which from time to time is updated – we are now on *DSM*-5-TR) is a sort of trainspotter's guide to every known or yet-to-be-discovered mental illness, malady, unsound-of-mind affliction, round-the-bend, up-the-fucking-pole, sandwich-short-of-a-picnic scenarios that anyone could imagine or even invent. Trust me when I tell you that *DSM* is *the* book for the psychiatrist, the couch head-shrinker, and just about every psychologist, psychoanalyst, psychotherapist, psychologist who can actually understand it. This is Freudian, Jungian, Adlerian, Gestalt psychology versus psychiatry jack-off-hard-on literature. It's about intellect – to be specific to wit the absence thereof. The pages – and there are lots and lots of pages, with lots and lots of very big words – are comprehensively hedge-your-bets explicit about vacuity, brainlessness and up-shit-creek disordered moronic behavioural traits. It is all – or struggles to be – about what goes on inside one's grey matter, because the contributing authors of *DSM* are well into lack of cognition, absence of perception, even an active psychogenesis, ad infinitum, the science – or signally the lack of science – concerning what goes around in the human mind, if very much at all.

And guess what? All of this is *not* a science; it's about as far away from being a 'science' as one can get, unless one calls science a hotchpotch of educated/uneducated guesswork, off-this-planet lateral thinking and flights of psycho-speculation with a handy seasoning of 'dunnos' thrown in for good measure. We will see this writ large in Jablonski's case, as sure as eggs is eggs.

And what I'd like to add here is this scintilla of common sense. If you dear reader had in mind to visit a ~~nuthouse~~ (strike out, insert 'secure mental health facility') and spotted a convicted killer claiming to be Napoleon but mistakenly wearing a policeman's helmet, at once chained to a wall because he bounces off the ceilings during teatime, then you don't need to read any of the edition of *DSM,* to figure out that he isn't right in the head. Alas, much the same thing cannot be said about the many doctors who had professional opinions about Mr Jablonski.

> One day ... just one day ... we might be able to find just two psychiatrists who can agree with each other.
> Prosecution psychiatrist Dr Dennis A. Philander:
> throwing his hands up in dismay following Harvey
> Carignan's first trial for serial homicide

What I am struggling to say here is this: shrinks are not the sort of people us sane folk should barbecue with – nor are funeral directors or accountants, when it comes down to it, at least that's my opinion.

The other thing about these mind-probing folk – as well-intended as they may be – is that not many of them are much ever able to agree with another colleague on someone's state of mind, let alone their own states of mind when it comes down to it.

Many US psychiatrists charge big bucks to entice some person with mental-health issues to lie on a couch for five-and-twenty minutes in what are called 'counseling sessions', which more often than not further car-wreck their patient's life when they're shown the bill – plus tax. And all this while Mr Shrink's own life may itself be fraught with problems. Although I cannot confirm it, I've heard that most American psychiatrists treat other psychiatrists as patients, ad infinitum.

As for psychiatrists being good judges of character, it may interest you to know that while in Los Angeles – and while he was killing numerous young women – Kenneth Bianchi not only applied for a job with the sheriff's department, but using credentials stolen from a psychology student he conned a genuine card-carrying psychiatrist into allowing him to use one of the shrink's vacant offices. That takes the biscuit, don't you think?

It would be very difficult for anyone to find a worse case of psychiatric incompetence than what follows. Did Phillip Jablonski throw the psychiatrists a well-calculated homicidal curve ball that they did not see coming? Was not the writing all over the wall? Were they blind to the fact that they were dealing with a human time bomb? Perhaps a more important question to ask is: were any of these professional men and women held accountable for what later transpired? The answer to the latter is a big countable noun '*no*, not any of them'.

Her boobs had transplants. When I bit into them it didn't taste like milk.

Phillip Jablonski – letter to the author

Schizophrenic to the nth degree, Jablonski was all but sub-human; a sort of hillbilly gone real mean ornery bad. He was not the sort of chappie you'd want a young daughter to date, nor a widowed mother-in-law come to that, nor even your granny if push comes to shove. Can you imagine you and your partner, as responsible parents, arriving home after some evangelical door-to-door knocking/Bible-thumping to find your apple-pie daughter reading a letter. The scenario might go something like this:

You: Hi, Sweetness and Light. Wow, you look so happy this evening. You have received a letter, I see. Have you finally been accepted into the Holy Sisters Order of St Disorder Latter Away-Day Saints?

Her: No, Mommy and Pop, I am thrilled because this letter is from my penfriend Phillip. He tells me he's coming to visit with me. He's just getting out of ...

You: ... out of ...

Her: ... Yes, out of some place called the Atascadero State Mental Hospital. Phillip and some of his buddies found Our Lord in there. I even met Jerry Brudos and Charlie Manson there last week. Very devout is Charlie, he's got something like a crucifix carved into his forehead.

You: Phillip is such a nice name, my child. It's like Philip the Apostle but with an extra 'l'. Is your Phillip the patron of joy and humour?

Her: When he's not sedated, he's a ball of fun. But the doctors say Phillip is much better now because he has apologised for hacking his wife's head off. Besides, he has repented. Can we make up a bed for him in the spare room? He'll be here tomorrow.

Of course, I made all that up, but it is not so far from the truth as we'll shortly discover.

Phil once wrote to me: 'Christopher, do you know John Christie [the British serial killer]? A friend of mine who was in the police, sent me a photo of him. Me and him almost look like brothers.'

What more can I add than this: Phil was not mad in the legal sense, as defined by the M'Naghten Rule which was codified in the 1840s in response to the attempted murder of the British prime minister Robert Peel. The assailant, Daniel M'Naghten, shot Peel's secretary, Edward Drummond, by mistake, but was found not guilty as he was deemed to be insane at the time. A public outcry led to the creation of a more rigorous legal definition of madness. For his part, Phil knew the difference between right and wrong, but by the time you have arrived at the shrinks' so-called professional conclusions, you will have already got this in spades. Why? Because all of my readers are living in the *real* world, not on some planet a million light years from reality.

Let us start with some of Jablonski's back history (or 'narrative', to use a noun that professionals bandy about a lot on TV these days). From there we'll take a look at his correspondence before moving on to his horrific nightmare-inducing crimes. And we'll end – ashes to ashes, dust to dust – with his just place, hopefully in hell.

All women are fuckin' whores.
I ripped off her nose with my teeth. I ate her eyes while I was fuckin' that whore, bitch wife. Are you married Christopher?

Phillip Jablonski: letter to the author

He didn't mince his words, our brown-eyed Phillip Carl Jablonski, who was born prematurely, weighing less than five pounds, on Thursday, 3 January 1946, in Joshua Tree, San Bernardino, California. His parents were Nettie (*née* Miller) and Phillip Jablonski. They'd moved there in August 1945 from Flint, Michigan, while his mother was pregnant with him. There were already two children, Phyllis and Louie.

> The trip took two months [deletion there] because the Chevy's front end was out of alignment and so family had to constantly replace its tires and tires on their trailor [*sic*]. My family arrived in California with no money and had to live in a friend's house.
>
> Phillip Jablonski: letter to the author

As events later transpired, it was not only the Chevy's tyres aka 'tires' that were out of alignment, but Phillip's mind too. And as this book is a 'road trip' of sorts, I feel duty-bound to inform you that Flint, Michigan – and Flint has some import with regard to Jablonski – was *the* go-to place to visit if one's entire family had an overwhelming desire to catch Legionnaires' disease. In 2014, a water crisis began after the city switched its water supply from Detroit's system to the Flint River. A cost-saving, cash-back-pocketing move by a corrupt governor and local politicians resulted in inadequate treatment of the water supply, resulting in foul-smelling, discoloured, off-tasting water being piped into Flint homes for eighteen months. It brought about brain damage, skin rashes, hair loss, itchy skin and pretty much every other ailment known to humankind. Indeed, President Obama – taking only White House-brand bottled water with him – paid a fleeting visit to Flint to try and calm everyone down and met many of the local dignitaries, did lots of grip-an'-grins, then left hastily to allow the County Drain Commissioner, Jeff Wright, to announce: 'See folks, nothing to worry about, the water is fine.'

On a related note, I have visited Russia many times, specifically St Petersburg, Samara and the former mining town of Buzuluk in the Orenburgskaya Oblast. Turn a tap on in Buzuluk and the water has a rather eye-pleasing soft cadmium-orange hue. In Flint, however, the ante went up by a considerably eye-watering amount; colour varying according to which toxic chemicals were in the city's water supply at any given time – anything from phthalo green to shit brown or Prussian blue, along with some teeny-weeny live things bugging around and trying to crawl up the side of one's glass.

And here's the thing. Flint's water woes had been evident for more than a century. The river flowing through the heart of the city served as an unofficial waste-disposal site for treated and untreated refuse from the many industries that sprouted along its shores, from carriage and car factories (including that of General Motors) to meatpacking plants and lumber and paper mills. And that ain't all. The waterway also received raw sewage from the city's waste-treatment plant, agricultural and urban run-off, and toxins from leaching landfills. And yes, not surprisingly, the Flint River caught fire twice. This contaminated water contributed to a doubling – and in some cases the tripling – of elevated blood lead levels in the city's children, imperilling the health of its young generations. To put it another way, Flint's children, and thousands of adults, would be a lot healthier today if they'd upped sticks and trooped en masse to a Thames sewerage outfall pipe to spend a year taking in something far more beneficial.

Lead poisoning damages brains, and without any doubt the

Jablonskis' brains were never much up to scratch at the best of times. And what an interesting road trip the family had, taking two months to cover a distance of 2,200 miles – a journey that usually takes around 30 hours.

According to Jablonski, on the advice of a doctor he was raised on goat's milk, and he volunteers that he didn't start walking until he was sixteen months old. On a more serious note, the official record does show that his father was abusive. Phillip writes: 'He loved to beat his wife and children. My mother loved to be abused physically and sexually,' although that latter comment is most certainly untrue. A sister, Patsy, was born in 1948, a brother, Albert, followed in 1949 and Nettie Jr arrived in 1950.

(Ed note: In a letter to the author, dated 12 March 2008, Phil writes, and the spelling and grammar are all his):

'O-TO FIVE YEAR OLD'

My family first house in California was in Severance Street [it's 'Avenue', bro] in San Bernardino. The area was semi-rural at the time, made up of lower-middle-class of which my family were among the poorest.

My parents sleep in one bedroom and my sisters slept in the living room. Us boys slept in the dining room, which had been converted into a bedroom for us. We didn't have a phone, and my parents raised out own chickens, pigeons, and rabbit for food. My parent would leave me and Patty [it's Patsy, Phil] with a neighbour, Oroll Crum. The neighbor was my parent best friend babysitting for us, while my parent went shopping or went to pay bill.

Shortly after I turn five years old Oroll Crum and his

wife Barbara wus babysitting as normal. But everything was about to change between us and them. Soon has my parents step out of their front door and bearly outside their, a hand was put around our mouths and I was pick has was my sister into a shape bedroom, and while Oroll carry me he whispered in my ear saying: "Nothing to be scared of. Your sister is teaching a adult game between little girls and women. She will be a woman soon and you little boy will soon be a little man. It's normal for a man to teach a boy about being a little man." I heard a loud slap and my sister crying.

Then Oroll Crum pulled my pants off followed by my underwear and his cold hands off over my small butt. And he made me turn over on my back and his hands spreading my butt cheeks.

Then in graphic detail he describes the most disgusting level of child abuse performed on him and Patsy, and how he was anally raped time and again. 'That night we told our Dad what happened. He confront them and Crum said he never touch one of us anyway. So me and my sister was seriously beaten for telling out rages lies [sic].'

The next time the Crums babysat for him and his sister – and this will come as no shock to the reader that there was a *next time* among these families of in-breds – Jablonski claims that he knew he and his sister were in for trouble:

He [Crum] beat us mercilessly until our little butts was bright red and bleeding. And we were made to crawl and was kicked in our butts ... [He added:] ... they tied us up and around our ankles and hung us upside down and swing us back and forth. Sometimes our heads would hit together. We never mention it to our Dad again. If we mentioned it to mother she'd tell our Dad and we would get another beating. One of Crums' favour games was making us play doctor and nurse. Make us play with each other with our hands or licking each other all over.

According to Jablonski: 'They had their way with us for nine months then they moved to another state.' He ends this letter with a dismissive: 'I'll close for now and then start from 6 years to 8 years old. Take care Chris. Phil.'

I have spent eons wading through correspondence from many notoriously twisted serial murderers and sadosexual killers and, for the most part, these offenders have a penchant to make up stories in an effort to mitigate their crimes and try to elicit some sympathy. Yet, somewhat surprisingly, all that Jablonski says turns out to be mostly true. He might have been prone to exaggerated and depraved descriptions, but I have read the case notes for his trial: *The People* v. *Jablonski* (courtesy of Stanford University Law School's library: https://scocal.stanford.edu/ opinion/people-v-jablonski-33578, Harvard School of Law's Case Access Project and other reputable online sources) and can confirm that a number of witnesses corroborated his accounts of an abused childhood. I should add here that I am indeed indebted to the documents arising from the court cases, *The People* v. *Jablonski* and, to a lesser extent, *Jablonski* v. *United States*, for much of the material in the account that follows of Jablonski's multiple murders most foul.

At *The People* v. *Jablonski* his sister Patsy claimed that their father was a bullying alcoholic who abused his wife and children; he called his wife and daughters 'whores', and grabbed their breasts and those of their girlfriends; neighbours called as witnesses confirmed that he was a brutal, cruel man who beat his wife and children – all of which Jablonski quite independently detailed in his correspondence with me. When his parents had sex, his father would beat his wife or try to strangle or suffocate her while the children looked on. This abuse bears all the hallmarks of the way Peter Kürten and Henry Lee Lucas were raised. All three men turned into sadosexual murderers. The British serial killer Frederick West suffered extreme abuse from his father too.

It was Phillip who got beaten the most, because he would come between his parents to try to prevent his father hurting his mother. When Jablonski Sr was in a bad mood, the children would run away and hide from him, their mother signalling them when it was safe to return. There are echoes here in the narrative of the now executed Michael Bruce Ross, the Connecticut serial killer, who sent me a letter while on death row in Somers Prison:

It's hard for me to tell you what was wrong with my family because I don't know anything different. That's how I was raised. I was beaten sometimes but I don't think that was it. It was more emotional abuse, an' like I mean with my dad when we were beaten, we would go out an' pick up a stick from the garage where we had a wood pile. An' what you would do was to go out and you couldn't pick one that broke 'cos if it broke he'd get pretty mad. But, you didn't pick yourself a club. You know, you didn't want to get the hell beaten outa you. An' so I had my own stick put away, hidden away in the back so that people coming in to get firewood wouldn't inadvertently take it. But I mean there is something wrong there when a kid goes to the wood house and picks up a stick; his own special stick for getting beaten. And, he hides it so no one accidentally takes it. And, you know Chris, if you got beat you didn't scream because my father just got madder.

NB: I am not suggesting for a millisecond that what Michael Ross or any of his ilk say or write in a similar vein can be mitigation for the terrible crimes they have committed – far from it. However, innocent kids who suffer such physical and emotional abuse can become hard-wired to seek some form of revenge as they grow older. I do not think that anyone will disagree with me on this. Did Michael Ross express any remorse of his crimes? The answer is 'No'! He revelled in it all during my TV filmed interview with him, and in his letters too. What you got from Michael Ross was as advertised on his homicidal tin. In his filmed interview he said:

Chris, you could show me an array of the girls I raped and killed an' I wouldn't recognize any of them. It's like one of those old black and white flicker movies. Faceless. I feel nothing at all. You ask me what I did with them? I used them, abused them, raped them. I strangled them and dumped their bodies like so much trash. What I got a kinda kick out of at trial was the medical examiner who could not explain the multiple bruising around the dead girls' throats. That because they struggled so much, an' my hands got cramp. I had to stop and massage my hands before I reapplied my grip. What else do y'all wanna know?

Michael then smiled and started to giggle, so much so that the tears rolled down his cheeks.

But back to Phillip. There was violence in the Jablonski family on an almost daily basis. Police were frequently called to the house but refused to intervene. Jablonski Sr was also cruel to animals. He always carried a gun, as Phillip and Patsy confirmed, with which he would threaten them as he berated them for their worthlessness, telling them they had not deserved to be born and did not deserve to live.

Patsy also confirmed that Phillip was sexually molested by a neighbour when he was four or five years old, which backs up Phillip's claim about Mr Crum (the reduced form of McCrum). Crum, she said, also sexually assaulted her. Two local children, Dale and Janice Rearick, were present when this molestation occurred.

A number of the defence witnesses at his trial, who had known the Jablonskis for many years, agreed that the family were among the poorest of the poor in a lower-middle-class neighbourhood. The portrait they painted of Jablonski Sr was grim. One witness described him as 'the meanest man' he ever knew; another said that when he was a child Jablonski had run over his puppy and did not even bother to stop. He shot his neighbours' cats if they strayed onto his property, slaughtered chickens in a sadistic manner and once killed the family pet – a pig – for dinner. A former daughter-in-law affirmed that he had once snatched her month-old infant from her and fed the baby hot sauce.

Witnesses for the defence told the jury that as a youngster Phillip was a 'nice person' who 'was quiet and kept to himself'. He was described as being a very anxious child, 'scared all the time', and as 'a thin, pale, ill-looking and lonely child who cried all the time'. His sister Patsy said that he was a quiet child, and that she and another brother, Albert, used to call him 'Goody-Two-Shoes'. However, Phillip would take out his aggression on Patsy and Albert, and hit them when their mother and father were out of the house, although he would get upset when their parents were gone for a long time, and would dissolve into tears, lamenting, 'They never loved me. They always hate me,' he would say. Phillip 'cried about everything'.

One person called to give evidence, however, recalled that he saw Phillip and his sister Patsy having consensual sex on two occasions when they were teenagers. 'The two bragged about it,' she said, 'and thought it was funny.'

Patsy testified that when she was fourteen years old, Phillip – then aged sixteen – came up behind her, put a rope around her neck, threw her on the bed, and said: 'I'm going to get some of that off of you.' She said that her brother had an erection and that she thought that he was going to rape her, but then he suddenly stopped and began to cry. When she told her parents about the incident, their father beat Phillip.

Such an extremely dysfunctional childhood like that beggars belief. Pretty much from the get-go, he was being psychologically indoctrinated into becoming a very dangerous adult.

Backing up a tad, at the age of six, Jablonski started first grade at Arrowhead Elementary, and walked to and from school each day. 'A rail track ran through part of the neighborhood,' he writes, 'a water train would travel through four times a day. Neighborhood kids would lay pennies on the metal slug on the tracks and came back later to find the flattened coin or metal slug on the track and pick them up.' Searching through Jablonski's letters, sometimes penned in italic script or in bold capitals – sometimes a twixt-mix of both – can dizzy the mind. I really tried to find something of interest regarding his schooling, but my hopes were dashed when he suddenly went off his own rails and started, somewhat undiplomatically, calling the prison mailroom staff 'a buncha fuckin' illiterate incompetent ass holes [sic]', just because they put the wrong stamp on one of his letters.

Having spent more time visiting American prisons than might be considered healthy, I have found that in the main, US correctional officers have very high IQs; circa 70ish I would say tongue-in-cheek, however down in the Lone Star State it's a rare event to find one with an IQ significantly higher, so Phil may have had a valid beef there.

Nonetheless, he writes about those early days, almost as if he were reliving them as a child: playground and class activities; local haunts where he and his kiddie peers liked to spend their weekends and evenings. He mentions his fascination with the fire department, the flood-control department and bulldozers. Then, in a flash, the mood of his writing darkens once again, switching from happy to angry. To me, that indicates a schizophrenic personality disorder, almost as if he is having an angry conversation with himself:

One evening a bulldozer operator ask me if I would like
to take a ride with him on his bulldozer. I said 'sure'. He

gave me a hand up and had his hands on my belt and loosened it and unzipped my pants. I know if I didn't get away he was going to rape me. It was two years since I was raped the first time. I wiggle and twisted but he grab me between my legs and squeeze my balls and I screamed. He told "Stop wiggling or I will squeeze a lot harder", so I stop wiggling and he pulled my pants and underwear down around my ankles and position between my legs and spread my butt cheeks ...

There can be no doubt that Mr and Mrs Jablonski were dysfunctional parents, perhaps even 100 per cent in-bred morally out of sorts, as Phillip hints at here:

My family raised chickens, rabbits and us children were expected to help butcher the animals and during the task our Dad would tease us by slinging blood on us, or pulling the tendon of a dismembered chicken's leg to make the claw move, while he chased us around the yard. We had a pig. We kept it as a pet, not to eat or sell. When it was fully grown we'd ride on it, but then my Dad butchered it and forced us to eat it. Many families in the neighbourhood raised chickens and killed them. My Dad would not merely wring the neck of the chicken, but tearing the head off watching the decapitated body run around the yard until it killed [sic] over.

On the same page, he reverts to some inane writing about playing marbles and mentions the home-built scooters the kids had; how they all made roller skates out of wood and small wheels. Clearly Phillip didn't excel at school, because he was held back from entering the second grade to join his younger sister. When his father learned of this, he thrashed him and sent him straight to bed after dinner, so Phil says.

Throughout Jablonski's letters, he records multiple allegations of rape. In the case below, however, it was one of his teachers (name removed for legal reasons) who was in the firing line. (I note here that this teacher must have moved into the Crums' house after they moved out.)

The teacher who lived next door would come over and set on our porch and drink beer with my Dad and listed to radio and watch us kids play. My Dad mention during one of their communications about my bad grade, and the teacher said all I needed was someone to set down with and take the times to explain to me and just go over my class work and homework, and I would be just fine. He said that he had extra time to tutor me in his free time.

So next night my Dad told me to gather up my books and any class work or homework and he was taking me next door for the teacher.

That evening, Jablonski says his assignment was reading and writing. That the teacher promised he would walk him home. 'The teacher said, "Now that we are alone, I've been eyeing you and like what I have seen. The special way you fill your pants and fantastic how it would be to have you in bed with me."' Once again, what followed in Jablonski's letter is a sickening account of the abuse he suffered over the next two hours. He rounded off this account by adding: 'He [the teacher] said before he was done with me, I would be looking forever in pleasing any man in bed. I would be gay forever.'

Phillip's letters ceased at this point because after several years of sporadic corresponding with your author, sick and tired of the abuse they were receiving from Inmate #C-02477 3EB 84 JABLONSKI. P.C., the prison stopped posting out any more of his letters – his postal sell-by-date had expired, at least to me, it transpires.

Alice McGowan

She [Alice] abandoned me. Like her, her mother was a slut.

Phillip Jablonski: letter to the author

Jablonski met his first wife, Alice McGowan, in high school. He enlisted in the Army in 1966, became a sergeant and served two tours in the Vietnam War, receiving the Vietnam Service Medal. Upon his return to the US in 1968, the couple married and moved to the 'Lone Star State', and it was here while living with his parents that Jablonski started to develop violent tendencies.

On one occasion during sex, he placed a pillow over Alice's face and attempted to suffocate her into unconsciousness. Another time, he grabbed her throat and strangled her until she actually became unconscious. Once, he went into the bathroom while she was bathing and tried to drown her; once, when she was pregnant he began to strangle her until his mother intervened, begging him to stop. Not surprisingly, Alice left her husband. If she hadn't, he would most probably have killed her.

Jane Saunders

That Saunders woman was a whore, like my own mother.

Phillip Jablonski: letter to the author

Tch, tch, Phil, but of course, she was no such thing, however if the truth be told, Jablonski met a Jane Saunders in November 1968 and on their first date he raped her – an offence she didn't report to police because she was afraid of him and felt ashamed. She fell pregnant and when he was discharged from the military suffering from 'schizophrenic illness' they relocated to California in July 1969.

As might be expected, their sex life was marked by Jablonski's violent behaviour. On one occasion, when they were having intercourse and Jane wanted to stop, he pulled out a pistol and threatened to shoot her. He hit her with the butt of the gun and she passed out. When she regained consciousness, he was raping her. The next time, despite her objections, he tied Jane to a bed while they were having sex and left her there before smothering her with a pillow – as he had done with Alice McGowan. Terrified that if he killed her their children would be left alone with him, somewhat belatedly she left him in 1972. Shortly before she fled, he became so angry that he threw a frying pan filled with hot grease at her. The pan missed. She picked it up, knocked him out and then, with her two children, she ran for her life. As might be expected, she never looked back.

Marsha Strain

Strain. Know her? As I recall I have no knowledge of her at all.

Phillip Jablonski: letter to the author

Marsha Strain and her husband became acquainted with Jablonski when they bought some dogs from a company for which this sex beast now worked, training security guard dogs. He delivered the animals to the Strains' home and taught the couple how to handle them. On 17 December 1972, he turned up unexpectedly, even though (or probably because) Mr Strain had asked him not to because he would be at work and his wife would be alone in their house. After wheedling his way into the place, Jablonski and Marsha discussed a problem with the dog. He told her to watch from the bedroom window while he worked the animal outside, then suddenly he crept up behind her, put a knife to her throat and ordered her to undress, threatening to kill her children unless she complied.

The loving mother of two was now subjected to a terrifying ordeal. First, Jablonski raped her at knifepoint. During the assault he struck her in the face with the handle of the knife, fracturing an orbital bone around her eye. Then, with her eight-month-old baby in the room, he tied Marsha's arms and sodomised her. But then the dog started barking. He told Marsha to go and bring it into the house, and that if she didn't return he'd kill her children. Once outside, with great presence of mind, she ran to a neighbour's place. The man of the house grabbed his gun and ran into Jablonski as he tried to leave. The sheriff arrived and Jablonski was arrested. Weakly, he told a detective:

'I don't know why I did it … My wife just left me … I didn't know what I was doing at the time … I just wasn't myself … I figure to myself, under a doctor's supervision that it would never happen again.'

But of course, Jablonski would have murdered Marsha; he could not afford to leave a living witness who could identify him.

Mary McGovern

I have already dug your grave.

Phillip Jablonski: to Mary McGovern

Before we embark on this part of Jablonski's narrative, the reader might wish to sit down and pour oneself a stiff drink, and it goes like this.

Mary became acquainted with Jablonski while he was serving time in prison for the rape of Marsha Strain, and through her participation in a prisoner letter-writing programme organised by her prayer group in Zionsville, Indiana.

Sadly, a multitude of Our Lord's disciples believe that they can redeem these 'lost souls' and help them into 'The Light', even though an ever-growing number of totally verified cases prove otherwise. These good-minded folk really have *no idea* how a manipulating psychopath's mind works; they simply do not have a clue. If one of my loved ones had been abducted, raped, tortured, killed and dumped like so much trash, perish the thought that some Bible-thumper would subsequently visit that piece of human scum, taking him candy bars and other goodies, then read a lot of 'Our Lord forgives all' biblical passages to him so that when he applies for parole, Rev. Goodwill and his wife, from some hick town such as Milton Turdwater, Georgia, can vouch for his integrity. But Mary went one step further.

After Jablonski was released from prison, Mary McGovern accepted his offer to visit him. She agreed on one proviso, making it crystal clear that she wasn't interested in having sex with him and that her stay would all be about the scriptures – and she could do some knitting while she was there too. But he was pulling the wool over her eyes. On the third day of her visit, Jablonski told her that because she was so sincere about helping him to find God, he was going to be honest with her. He explained that the week before he'd dug a grave for her and offered to show her the hole in the ground. She declined – wouldn't you? – and he added, 'but because you are kind to me, I've decided not to kill you'.

How generous of you, Phillip. What an evangelical chappie you turned out to be after all!

God moves in a mysterious way, His wonders to perform.
William Cowper: 'God Moves in a
Mysterious Way' hymn (1773)

I mean, you could not make this up if you tried. When you take into consideration the fact that Mary knew all about Phillip's crimes, that he wanted to show her the grave he'd conveniently dug in advance for her, and with the lecherous twinkle in his eye indicating that he wanted to get his rocks off, one might have thought that any right-minded person would have fled his home faster than a lightning bolt. Not so in Mary's case.

Perhaps with Luke 23:34 ('Father, forgive them, for they do

not know what they are doing') resonating through her mind, she stayed another night and on the fourth day of her visit he woke her up and demanded sex. She refused. Eventually, to placate him, she allowed him to tie her hands and feet together with her knitting yarn, thinking she could break free if necessary. After he tied her up he left the bedroom to return with a glinting straight razor of the type that mafiosi use. Mary thought that he was going to kill her; instead, he shaved her pubic area, then took a photograph before pressing a pillow over her face. She played dead. He stopped and left her alone on the bed. The next day, after Mary came up with the pretext that there was an emergency at her daughter's home, he allowed her to leave.

I betcha that 'Benevolent Mary' never entertained a similar prayer group outreach programme again. 'God moves in a mysterious way, His wonders to perform' indeed.

Melinda 'Linda' Kimball

In February 1977, thirty-one-year-old Jablonski tells us that he met forty-eight-year-old Linda Kimball. By August, they were living together. That December, she gave birth to a daughter they named Meghan; Linda's mother, Isobel Pahls, conveniently lived nearby. So far, so good. But that's about as good as it *would* get.

On the evening of 6 (or 7, accounts vary) July 1978, Isobel Pahls was awakened by Jablonski, clad only in undershorts, lying on top of her. He held a knife to her throat and told her that he had come to rape her but could not because when he'd looked into her face all he could see was Linda's face. Terrified,

Isobel managed to escape and ran to a neighbour's home. She spoke to the police and reported having been receiving obscene phone calls and 'other malicious acts', which the police believed Jablonski was responsible for. Pahls, who later stated that she had spoken to a Dr Kopiloff at Loma Linda Veterans Affairs Hospital after the assault, spoke to the police and discussed the possibility of Jablonski receiving psychiatric treatment, but, out of concern for her daughter, did not press charges against him. Not long after, Phillip agreed to be examined at the Loma Linda VA Hospital. It is here in Jablonski's narrative that the wheels really started to fall off his already unstable wagon.

Taking some initiative, a cop called the hospital to be informed that a Dr Kopiloff had been assigned to treat Jablonski. Kopiloff was unavailable, however, so the head of psychiatric services, a Dr Berman, took the call.

The officer told Dr Berman of Jablonski's prior criminal record, and described to the doctor Jablonski's recent violent criminal behaviour towards Isobel Pahls. He added that, in his view, Jablonski should be treated on an in-patient basis at the psychiatric hospital. Unfortunately, Dr Berman forgot to pass the policeman's words on to Dr Kopiloff, who later stated that had he received the information, he would have hospitalised the mentally disintegrating army veteran, even, if necessary, without the patient's consent.

The omission by a preoccupied doctor to relay just a few words had heart-breaking consequences, for now it was only a matter of time before Jablonski would go nuclear. Let's remind ourselves of how Jablonski had manipulated Mary McGovern with his alleged newfound love of Our Lord. 'Contrition'. 'I've seen the Light,' while pre-digging her grave. Can you see into his warped mindset more clearly now? Because in what follows, you will see him use the same twisted psychopathology to run rings around several highly paid psychiatrists.

I am very concerned about Phillip's behaviour, but I love him.

Linda Kimball: in a private meeting
with Dr Kopiloff

On Monday, 10 July 1978, Linda drove Jablonski to the VA hospital. During the interview, Kopiloff discovered that his new patient had already been imprisoned for five years for raping his wife, Alice McGowan, and that he'd also raped Marsha Strain. Kopiloff also learned that just four days before the interview, Jablonski had tried to rape Isobel Pahls. Jablonski then enlightened the doctor by telling him that he had undergone psychiatric treatment in the past. He refused to comment further, however.

Kopiloff felt that his new patient had an 'anti-social personality' and regarded him as being 'potentially dangerous'. He advised that Jablonski should hospitalise himself. Phillip declined. Kopiloff concluded that there was no urgency in the case, and that it wasn't appropriate to forcibly hospitalise Jablonski. The latter was to return for another appointment in a fortnight's time.

In 1983 Isobel Pahls, on behalf of her young granddaughter, Meghan Jablonski, brought a legal case arguing that the negligence of doctors at Linda Loma VA Hospital in failing to obtain hospital records of Jablonski's prior treatment meant that they wrongly discharged Jablonski who later killed Meghan's mother. The medical records were obtained, and produced, for *Jablonski by Pahls* v. *United States* (transcripts of which may be found online). They revealed that in 1968, Phillip Jablonski had received 'extensive psychiatric care' at an army hospital in El Paso. That hospital's records reported that he had a 'homicidal ideation' towards his then wife (Alice McGowan), that on numerous occasions he had tried to kill her, that he'd probably suffered a psychotic breakdown and that further violent behaviour was highly likely. The icing on this particular slice of fruit cake was that he was 'demonstrating some masculine identification in beating his wife as his father did frequently to his mother'. The diagnosis concluded, in part, that Jablonski had a 'schizophrenic reaction, undifferentiated type, chronic, moderate; manifested by homicidal behavior toward his wife [...] this is a highly dangerous individual, who, if in the future shows such tendencies again, and refuses voluntary psychiatric in-care, must be hospitalized against his will.'

The clock was now ticking. A day or so after Jablonski's interview with Dr Kopiloff, Mrs Pahls telephoned the doctor to complain about the two-week delay in Jablonski returning for his second interview. She threatened to call the police again. Kopiloff persuaded her not to. However, to placate her, he brought forward the date to Friday, 14 July, when Linda drove him to see Kopiloff and his supervisor, Dr Hazle. Although he revealed that he'd experienced episodes of violent anger for as long as he could remember, Jablonski again refused to be admitted as an in-patient. This time Kopiloff concluded that his patient exhibited an 'anti-social personality disorder with explosive features'. Dr Hazle went several steps further. He believed that the man was 'downright dangerous' and stated that his case represented an 'emergency'.

Yet, and only God knows why, *despite all of this* the two shrinks still believed that there was no basis for involuntary hospitalisation. (NOTE: in the UK, Section 3 of the Mental Health Act allows for a person to be admitted to hospital for treatment if their mental disorder is of a nature and/or degree that requires treatment in hospital. In addition (and this is the important part of Section 3) it must be necessary for their health, their safety or for the *protection of other people* that they receive treatment in hospital (author's italics). However, once again, no effort was made to seek out Jablonski's prior medical tests – which could have so easily been achieved by contacting the Army. Instead, Jablonski was scheduled for more psychiatric examinations and sent home, holding a prescription for Valium. A third appointment was booked for Monday, 17 July.

While the second interview took place, Linda Kimball was waiting in the hallway, probably praying that the next time she saw her man he would be wearing a straitjacket and chained to a wall. Upon hearing the quiet discussion through a partly open door, she broke down, as well she might. A third psychiatrist, one Dr Warner – the chief of the mental health clinic – heard her and invited her into his office, where she confessed that she no longer felt safe around Jablonski. Although compassionate, Dr Warner advised the terrified woman in measured tones that if she was frightened about what he might do, and that if the psychiatrists could not establish grounds to hospitalise him against his wishes, she might consider keeping away from him altogether.

Linda took Warner's advice. She left Jablonski and moved in with her mother, who was by now sick and tired of the whole sorry affair. Doubtless she felt that if the police had proved themselves all but useless in dealing with the rages and deviancy exhibited by Jablonski, the medical profession had surpassed them by miles. That she hadn't even filed a sexual assault complaint against Jablonski didn't seem to occur to her.

At about eleven on the morning of Sunday, 16 July, Linda returned to the apartment she had shared with her common-law husband to pick up some nappies and other items for baby Meghan. There, Jablonski attacked and murdered her, and as murders go this one was well below bottom drawer. He beat her, raped her, stripped her, slashed her and – after death had mercifully intervened – he cut off her ears, ate her eyes, and finished it all off by abusing the sexual organs and anus of the corpse (the more lurid details are from Jablonski's correspondence, in which he gloats over his crimes).

A few hours later, Linda Kimball's body was found there. Her shirt had been pulled up, her trousers and underpants pulled down, and her bra ripped up. Her wrists tied together, she had been beaten up and stabbed – and then strangled with a man's belt: the cause of death was found to be asphyxiation.

Eileen Millsap

Now on the run from the police, Jablonski would have been in need of money, and an advertisement he spotted in a local newspaper presented an opportunity to enter someone's property and rectify the matter. He went to the home of Eileen Millsap, ostensibly to look at the stove she was selling, but, finding her there alone with two small children, he took out a knife and, threatening to cut the throat of her three-year-old son, pushed her into a bedroom, and made her undress. In front of the two children, he threw her down and assaulted her, tightening his grip round her neck until she blacked out. When she regained consciousness, he had left, having stolen her card case and purse, later using one of her credit cards to buy petrol for his car (which would have helped police track him down).

Jablonski was arrested in Arizona eleven days later. Police found a note in his handwriting that read: 'Killed to date, Linda Kimball, common-law wife. I told her she would never raise Meghan alone or leave me alive. She begged me not to kill her. You screamed but it was cut short.'

Had the US judicial system had any wits about it, it would have ensured that the US penal system would have gobbled Jablonski up never to see the light of day ever again. But this was not to be, for – wait for it – in 1982, he met and married forty-six-year-old Carol Spadoni after she had answered a lonely hearts newspaper ad he had placed while serving time. Don't these people ever learn? Why can't they find someone half-decent outside prisons instead of shopping for a spouse behind high walls and razor wire? Are they stark raving bonkers?

Nettie (*née* Miller) Jablonski

CDCR recognizes visiting is an important way of maintaining family and community ties.

> California Department of Corrections and
> Rehabilitation: website

While serving his prison sentence for the murder of Linda Kimball at the California Men's Colony in San Luis Obispo, Phillip did some family and community tying of his own: his parents were on a seventy-two-hour family visit in July 1985 and Jablonski lost his temper because Carol Spadoni had not come with them, so in a fit of pique he seized his mother, choked her with a shoelace, put his hand over her mouth and dragged her into the bedroom of the family visiting trailer. She managed to cry out and his father came to her aid.

Despite a momentary lapse of good judgement inter alia attempting to murder his own mother on prison property, Jablonski was released on parole in September 1990 for 'good behavior'. The Department of Corrections prepared a release programme study report in which it was noted that he was a 'Category J psychiatric inmate who had received treatment including medication'. The report also noted that a staff psychologist was very concerned about Jablonski's parole and warned that, although in remission, he could become 'psychotic' at any time. I myself prefer the more professional psychiatric term 'going thermonuclear', as in predicting that Jablonski's brain nuclei would, as so many times before, fuse at high temperatures, and go 'BANG'.

Jablonski's original parole plan required him to seek mental-health counselling, which he eventually did – once more at the Loma Linda VA hospital – and also that he attend a government training course.

A couple of months after his release, on 30 November 1990, a psychiatrist at the VA hospital, Dr Sylvia Winters, undertook an assessment of Jablonski's mental health. He told her during their session that in the previous six weeks he'd been hearing voices and seeing faces, just as he had before he killed Linda Kimball, and added that he'd stopped taking the medication he had been on while in prison. He also told her that helicopters flying above the hotel where he was now living were making him nervous, and that he was having nightmares about a friend who had died in Vietnam when a helicopter, on which they both were, crashed. He claimed a flashback to his time in Vietnam was what led to his attack upon his mother when she visited him in prison, and also blamed his experience in Vietnam for his murder of Linda Kimball, saying, 'I thought my wife was Vietnamese when I strangled her.'

It should have been quite obvious to Dr Winters that Jablonski was a tick, tick, ticking time bomb. She knew all the details surrounding Linda Kimball's murder and that psychiatrists at Loma Linda VA had naively deemed him to be neither homicidal nor suicidal. Despite all that she had heard, however, she believed him when he claimed that he no longer wanted to cause harm to others, and that should the warning signs come back then he would get in touch with his parole officer. Yeah, right!

Dr Winters concluded her examination of Jablonski with a tentative diagnosis of schizophrenia and possible post-traumatic stress disorder, prescribed some medication and referred him to the specialist Post-Traumatic Stress Disorder team at the hospital. Interestingly, however, Dr Winters suggested to Nancy Witney, a clinical social worker attached to the Post-Traumatic Stress Disorder Team, that she 'might take some precautions' for her own safety when Jablonski arrived for his appointment; and she also wrote to his parole officer, telling him to be sure that Jablonski did not sleep in a room with others for fear of his having another Vietnam flashback.

So back to Carol Spadoni.

In April 1991, Carol lived on Sanchez Avenue, Burlingame in San Mateo County with her seventy-two-year-old mother,

Eva Petersen. Carol's relationship with Jablonski had begun after she answered a personal ad he had placed in a newspaper. Yes, you read that correctly – convicted killers in the US can do such things. They were married in 1992 – not in a church with a tall spire, nave, vestry, bridesmaids and some rosy-faced vicar, but behind the grim walls of San Quentin State Prison, where he was, at the time, incarcerated.

Eventually, Carol saw the light and wanted to end the relationship with Jablonski; she'd confided in a friend that she now found him 'weird'. In fact, she was shit-scared of him, and had every reason to be, and by this time he had been transferred to the California Medical Facility (CMF), Vacaville, where he was being treated for schizophrenia.

To claify matters, if one is completely criminally off-the wall, CMF is the place to be. Charles Manson gave his first–ever TV interview in CMF. Bobby Beausoleil, Ed Kemper, Donald DeFreeze and Jim Gordon, among many other unhinged minds, have been housed there. So, if you ever receive a letter from a man giving his address as Vacaville, CA 95696, do exercise due diligence for heaven's sake. Ask, at the very least, for a curriculum vitae; or, as they say in the antique trade, 'good provenance'; or in the parlance of the motor trade, the full service history with receipts and a current MOT.

I am using these two analogies here simply because one does not want to buy an expensive 'genuine circa 1762 Chippendale dressing table' only to get it home and find a well-hidden stamp on its underside bearing the legend 'Made in China, 2020'; neither does one want to buy a 'one careful owner' Jaguar E–Type to have it grunt to a halt in the middle of a motorway. Metaphorically, this is precisely what those who fell for Jablonski *didn't* do. They simply believed every word he wrote to them, that deep down he was a misunderstood cuddly teddy bear.

In the summer of 1990, as the date for his release approached, Jablonski had some of his belongings sent to the address Carol Spadoni shared with her mother Eva Petersen in Burlingame. It was clear from this that he intended to move into their home, and they were very alarmed. Eva phoned Richard Muniz, a friend of Jablonski's and former fellow inmate at San Quentin prison, with whom the women had become acquainted. After his release Muniz, who had settled in Sacramento, had remained on friendly terms with the two women, and Eva, who was scared – I mean *really scared* – of Jablonski and didn't want him anywhere near them, now asked Muniz if he could come to their place and remove Jablonski's belongings. This the obliging Muniz did, storing the items in his garage in Sacramento. Meanwhile, Carol Spadoni had spoken with Robert Paredes, Jablonski's parole officer, and told him how afraid she was of Jablonski and that she did not want him living with her.

Phillip Jablonski was released from CMF Vacaville in September 1990; Muniz was there to meet him, and drove him to Sacramento, explaining that his possessions were now at his place as Carol and Eva wanted nothing more to do with him. Jablonski was not too pleased to hear this, so he spent that weekend with Muniz before going to meet Paredes at his office in Indio, Riverside County, where he would learn the terms of his parole. He was not permitted, Paredes told him, to travel more than fifty miles from his home without permission, and he was *absolutely forbidden* to go to Burlingame or to try to meet up with Spadoni or Petersen. He was also ordered to join a counselling programme at the Loma Linda VA hospital.

That Christmas, Jablonski asked for leave to go to Sacramento to visit Muniz and to obtain a driving licence. Before giving him permission, Paredes spoke to Eva Petersen and explained what Jablonski wanted to do, assuring her that the man would not be allowed anywhere near Burlingame or indeed inside San Mateo County. Petersen raised no objection.

The shit was soon to hit the proverbial fan.

Jablonski spent a week with Muniz in Sacramento, all the while moaning about Eva's influence over Carol, and how they were frustrating his plans to move to the city himself, which he felt had held back his employment prospects. Jablonski returned from Sacramento with a bee in his bonnet, a driving licence and a 1965 Ford Fairlane. In January 1991, he signed up for auto classes at a local community college.

Fathyma Vann, aka Fanny Hansen

Among his fellow students at the automotive course were Fathyma Vann, a newly widowed thirty-eight-year-old mother of two, and a man called Jim Lawrentz, who later told police that Phillip always tape-recorded the lessons and was 'very intelligent', which somewhat speaks for Lawrentz's IQ, too, Anyway, about halfway through April 1991, Jablonski learned that Lawrentz owned a small gun and asked if he would sell it to him – knowing full well that as a convicted felon he was forbidden by law to possess a firearm. Lawrentz demurred at first, but two days later, probably unaware of Jablonski's criminal history, changed his mind and sold Jablonski his .22-calibre RG-14 revolver and bullets.

On 22 April, Jablonski informed his instructor, John

Tamulonis, that he had to go to the doctor's and would miss the next day's class, assuring him that he would be back for the following session. Later on the same day, Tamulonis saw Jablonski with Fathyma Vann.

Jablonski did not return to the college. Nor did she.

That evening, Jablonski gave Fanny a ride home from class. The next day, her body was found in a ditch by a road in the desert outside Indio. It was horribly mutilated with stab wounds in the neck, abdomen, vagina and rectal areas. The ears and nipples had been cut off and the eyes lacerated. On the back cuts and scratches appeared to read 'I [heart shape] Love Jesus'. The cause of death was a gunshot wound to the head.

By way of an afterword, Fathyma's daughter, Yolonda Robinson-Vann, who, with her sister, became an orphan following the death of her mother, later told of having a chilling premonition when, aged nineteen, she met Jablonski for the first time. In an interview with Fox News in 2020, she revealed:

She introduced me to him. And immediately, without even saying 'Hi' to him, I said, 'If something happens to my mother, I'm going to come looking for you.' [Jablonski replied] 'Well, you don't have to worry about me doing anything to her. You should worry about her doing something to me.' And I said, 'Well, we shouldn't have a problem. 'Cause if you don't mess with her, she's not going to mess with you.'

Yolonda added:

Just the way he stood there and was looking at my mother,

there was just something about him that didn't sit right in my stomach [...] My kids always wanted to know about their grandmother. But when you go online and put her name in Google, his face pops up. And you have to remember, I had a conversation with this man. I felt like I was given a warning and I hate the fact that I didn't listen. I still wonder, had I not told him anything about messing with her, would she still be alive today? Or was he already plotting to kill her? I live with that.

Yes, Yolonda. All of my thousands of readers will feel your grief. We are parents too. What *you* saw was something in Jablonski that the shrinks and the cops didn't see — it was streetwise common sense.

Carol Spadoni and Eva Inge Petersen

On 23 April 1991, not even a year after Jablonski had been released on parole, Carol Spadoni and her mother Eva were murdered in their Burlingame home in San Mateo County, California. In fact I would not hesitate to say that they were 'over-murdered in extremis', if it comes down to it.

Carol Spadoni and her mother had been in the habit of meeting a friend, Robert Galindau, regularly for coffee and doughnuts at a coffee shop. When more than once they failed to turn up and didn't answer his phone calls, Galindau became worried, and early in the morning of 26 April he drove round to their house. There was no sign of the women; he noticed several newspapers piled up outside the front door and also a couple of parcels. Round the back he found a few starving cats in a pen, at which his concern became one of serious alarm. He called the police.

When Officer Frank 'Slim' Pickens of the Burlingame Police Department arrived, he first of all knocked at the front door. There was no reply. He checked the windows: there was no sign of a break-in, but he did find that a side door to the garage had been left unlocked and went in, followed by a fellow officer. Across the garage was the open door to the kitchen; on the garage floor in front of him was the body of a woman. She was all too clearly dead. The two officers moved, guns drawn 'tactical style', into the house, where they found, on the living-room floor, a second body, again very obviously dead. The spare, factual prose of the descriptions of the bodies as cited in the trial documents gives a chilling picture:

> The first body found was that of Eva Petersen. A towel had been folded over and pushed into her mouth and a bullet had been shot through the towel. Petersen was naked from her waist down; her sweatshirt and brassiere had been pulled up above her breasts and around her neck. There was another bullet hole above her right breast and a stab wound in her neck. There were also cuts around one of her nipples and around her right eye; the cut to her nipple could have been made with a knife, and the cut to her eye may also have been made by a knife. Blood smears on the kitchen floor indicated that she had been dragged across the kitchen. The stab wound to her throat had been made while she was still alive. The cause of death was the gunshot wounds to her head and chest.

Worse than the state Fathyma Vann's body was left in. And it gets nastier.

> The second victim was Carol Spadoni. Her body was found in the living room, dressed in a nightgown. Her nose and mouth were covered with duct tape wrapped so tightly it would have cut off her breathing except that she had been stabbed in the throat creating a functional tracheotomy. She had a bullet wound behind her right ear and three stab marks in her abdomen. Additionally, half of her right breast was sliced off, exposing a silicone implant. There were also stab wounds to her vagina, and her intestines were protruding from her anus as the result of a laceration. The cause of her death was the gunshot wound with the stab wounds and duct tape suffocation as contributing factors. Because decomposition had begun to set in, the pathologist who examined the bodies could not determine if any sexual assault had occurred.

The hunt now began in earnest for a homicidal psychopathic killer.

Investigators found on the kitchen table a journal, its final entry on 23 April 1991, and envelopes addressed to the women by Jablonski, while a letter addressed to 'Mrs Carol Jablonski' in his handwriting was found in a bedroom.

Back at the police station, a computer check showed that earlier Jablonski had been stopped by a traffic cop in Burlingame for failing to yield right of way. The officer, who was unaware that Jablonski was in violation of his parole terms, reported no signs of intoxication or nervousness in Jablonski.

Further investigations involved a search of Eva Petersen's bank records, which revealed a cheque for $200 made out to Jablonski and purportedly signed by Petersen – the signature, however, did not match that on Petersen's bank card. A cashier at the bank where the cheque had been cashed later identified Jablonski as the individual who had cashed it on 23 April.

Yvette Shelby

Some thousand miles on, on 25 April, now on the run following the Vann, Petersen and Spadoni murders, Jablonski pulled in to a service area in Wyoming. Seeing Yvette Shelby there, who had stopped to let her dog out of her vehicle, Jablonski, for some unexplained reason, reached for his pistol and threatened her with it as he got out of his car. She was fortunate – the gun slipped from his grasp and fell to the ground, and she was able to get back in her car and quickly drive away. She stopped at the next service station and phoned the police. Using a remarkable lack of common sense, the cops who pulled him over didn't even radio the call in. Jablonski, on parole and illegally in possession of a firearm, explained that the gun was for personal protection and had fallen out as he was getting out of his car. The officers accepted his explanation, told him to put the gun in the car's trunk, and let him continue his long interstate drive.

Margie Marie Rogers

On 27 April 1991, the body of fifty-eight-year-old Margie Rogers was found in the service area store where she worked, in Thompson Springs, Grand County, Utah. She had been shot twice in the face with a .22-calibre gun. Her shirt had been pulled open and her bra had been tugged up over her breasts. There was $153 missing from the till – presumably taken by the killer.

This was to be Jablonski's last kill.

The next day, a Kansas Highway Patrol Trooper spotted a car with its bonnet up in a service area in McPherson County, Kansas, and stopped to check on its driver. Not satisfied with the driver's response, he ran a quick check on the vehicle's registration, learned that there was a warrant out in California for Jablonski, and, calling for back-up, arrested Phillip Jablonski.

When they searched him, the police found $710 cash in his wallet, alongside a cheque for $90 drawn on Eva's bank account and a credit card in her name. There was also a small address book in the wallet, in which Jablonski had written the names, addresses and dates of birth of Eva Petersen and Carol Spadoni. Beneath each name were the words 'Death, April 23rd, 1991'. At that time, the dates of the murders had not been publicised.

In Jablonski's car, officers found a loaded .22-calibre revolver beneath the driver's seat, and a box of .22-calibre cartridges. Bullets removed from Eva's body matched the rounds in the revolver; the bullet recovered from Carol's brain was too damaged to be conclusive, but it did match the rifling characteristics of the revolver. The police also found in the car duct tape similar to that used to gag Carol; an electric taser; homemade wire handcuffs, and a sheath from which the knife was missing; the latter showed signs of what seemed to be blood. Also recovered was a holdall containing blue trousers stained with human blood and semen. There was a black leather belt found in the car, on the inside of which the words 'Carol

Jablonski 4-23-1991, Burlingame, California' and 'Eva Petersen 4-23-1991, Burlingame, California' were written in ink. The handwriting was later resolved by an expert to be Jablonski's, as was the writing in the address book.

What makes these terrible homicides even more horrific was a cassette tape found in the car, on which Jablonski had recorded what he did from his arrival at the victims' house: he described shooting Petersen, fondling her breasts, sodomising her, having sexual intercourse with her and trying to gouge her eyes out. He described shooting Carol through the brain, binding duct tape around her mouth and nose, stabbing her in the throat, slicing open a breast and stabbing 'her ass and pussy'. According to his taped account, he then moved their bodies, had something to eat and a shower, and then, before departing, fired a shot through a towel he had stuffed into Eva Petersen's mouth.

So back to Jablonski and your author. One of his pen-pals wrote to ask if I would correspond with Phil as he was writing a book. My interest piqued, I dropped Jablonski a line. That said, having met and corresponded with so many manipulating serial killers over the years, one kind of gets a sniff of something being not quite right when someone claiming to represent a convicted felon sends one a letter out of the blue. Death-row inmates, or those serving extremely long tariffs for committing the most awful crimes, are not allowed by their respective departments of corrections (DOCs) to go fishing for any kind of money-making venture, so they are cute enough to get someone on the outside to do this for them.

Jablonski was straight out of the starting blocks in replying. His correspondence was written on both sides of lined, buttercup-yellow prison-issue paper, sometimes using quite neat capitals throughout, at other times flowing italic script, sometimes a mix of both. Unlike so many inmate correspondents he did not cram his writing onto the page. He justified his text, with paragraphs short and to the point, all in all making for an easy, albeit disjointed, read. Overall, on the face of it I *quite* liked his style. The envelopes in which he placed his correspondence featured very well drawn, crayoned cartoons. Assuming they were his work, in better times perhaps he could have found his calling as a children's book illustrator, even for a Teddy Bear story, but, alas, Phillip opted for a different route, taking five lives and committing a string of dreadful sex offences to boot.

My suspicions increased with the different style of writing Phil used. Furthermore, even a blind forensic document examiner would have noted that *before* the envelope was addressed to me the cartoons, which always took up at least one-third of the paper, were drawn and coloured first with Jablonski's address on the left-hand-side, noting the different styles of penmanship. It's all very confusing so maybe Phillip Jablonski is a Dr Jekyll and Mr Hyde. Maybe he didn't draw the cartoons after all!

Phillip JABLONSKI, C-02477 3EB 84, San Quentin State Prison, San Quentin, CA, 94964, USA

While the envelope was addressed to me in capitals on the right-hand side, below is an earlier letter from 28 January 2008 that he sent to me, penned in reasonably competent script and in which he feigns surprise that I'd written to him at all. As cunning as foxes these guys and gals are. Published verbatim is a taster, so see if you can smell a rat here:

Dear Christopher.

Received your surprising letter. I am only acquainted with a few true crime authors in the states. I had a newspaper reporter write a autobiography about my crimes and it wasn't in the market long. Maybe at the most less than a year. Its first appearance for sale in Australia and then in the States. Many of my pen pals who read it thought it completely boring and a lot of shit, full of half-truths and numerous lies and crap. There was little investigative work done by him. He got most of his information from Court reports. I did do an interview with him on paper and not a thing I wanted appeared in the book.

What are the titles of some true crime books you writ [*sic*]? Are any of them in book stores in the States? Do you know John Christie? I believe he is a famous killer in the U.K. I believe he killed his wife and prostitutes and burned the bodies. A friend of mine who was in the police, sent me a photo of him. Me and him almost look like brothers.

Having told me that he looked like John Christie's brother, and that some unnamed newspaper reporter had written his autobiography when he should have said 'biography', and adding that it 'was full of crap', he upped the ante a bit with:

Will be glad to assistance you in writing my side of the story. Your letter was wrote on Jan 3, 2008, my birthday by the way. With all the work I am going to be putting into the project, what am I going to get out of it? Just curious!' I would seriously like IWC Media to do a TV documentary about me.

Nice try, Phil. Subtly fishing for a few bucks already. Goodness gracious me, now it's a TV documentary you want too – you're no shrinking violet, are you? And all that work you are going to have to do. Such a shame to put you out while you lie on your bunk twenty-three hours a day. But please go on:

> Have you ever heard of the 'Death Row Survey' here in the State. They publish a magazine titled 'Stuff'. My interview was selected to be published in the 'Stuff' magazine and I was to receive a copy of the magazine with my interview in it. It's called 'Maxim' in the U.K. I was wondering if you ran across the magazine and read the interview?
>
> By the way I have son name [*sic*] Christopher, who is doing time in Michigan for child rape. I guess you could say he is following in his father's footsteps.
>
> I have no remorse for murders, rapes or pumping young adolescence boys and girls I did [*sic*]. I am proud of raping my slut sisters and mother. Maybe my slut mother will rot in hell. They died in 1986. Beside the murders you might have read about what I committed. There is a few that are unsolved at this time. And a few are over twenty years old.
>
> I'll be looking forward to working with you on this project.
>
> Take care
>
> Phil.

Let's take a breather here shall we, and maybe have a cup of tea. I really wanted to tell him that *Stuff* magazine is for electronic geeks. In no way is it associated with *Maxim*, either. Why an electronics mag would do a death-row survey beats the hell out of me, unless they were advising electric-chair operators and refurbishers on how to service 'Old Sparky', or Alabama's 'Yellow Mama' or 'Old Smokey' (New Jersey and Pennsylvania), that is.

The same letter now went on a bit more, this time underneath his previous and most courteous sign-off (we can call this an addendum), starting in script followed in capitals dated 2/28/08, and here things go grammatically downhill faster than former ski-jumper Eddie 'the Eagle' Edwards. I reproduce it here, verbatim:

If you cant read the handwriting, I'll be glad to PRINT MY PREPARED TO YOUR INTERERDUCELY LETTER ON DATE OF THIS LETTER BUT OUR ASS HOLE MAIL ROOM PUT I INCORRECT POSTAGE ON THE ENVELOPE SO I HAD TO BORROW A STAMP TO RE MAIL THE LETTER TO MAKE SURE THIS LETTER REECH YOU. I REAL KEEN ON WRITE MY SIDE OF THE STORY. I HOPE YOU STILL INTEREST IN ASSISTANCING ME.

I AM A INDIGENCE INMATE SO I HAVE TO DE PEND ON THE PRISON FOR MY POSTAGE, WRITING SUPPLIES, ETC, ETC.

We are not quite out of the woods yet, because guess what? He then reverted back to script, with:

Just some information you possible haven't seen on the inter-net, there is a book write about my crime entitled

'DEADLY URGES' by BARRY BORTNICK. Also enclosed is a poem wrote about one of my murder victims. The nigger I torture and brutally tortured and rape, sodomy and shoot to dead. Anything about me on the internet is I am Bisexually and proud of my sexually originally (Miasspelled [*sic*]). Again I hope that you my reply [*sic*] to your letter I received on February 19.2008 that you mailed on January 21, 2008.

I again like to express that I am really keen on getting my side of story out to the public with your assistance, and I hope you didn't think I am pulling a con for on about asking for $50.00 to cover postage and for writing paper, etc, etc. Kindly try to understand our mail room is must [*sic*] of uneducated and inefficient ass holes. I would sent you the envelope the return to me that the mail room put incorrect postage on. But I am filing an appeal to get the matter corrected if they can read before I am contacting my lawyer about the matter.

Take care Phil.

As you will have now gathered, with serial killer Phillip Jablonski there is some very good news and buckets full of bad news; the former being that he died, of 'unknown causes', aged seventy-three on 27 December 2019, in his San Quentin State Prison death-row cell. However, as late as 1994, he was still using a website asking for men and women to write letters to him, in which he described himself as a 'Death Row Teddy Bear'.

Now comes the fun part. Jablonski's actual words in describing himself on this website are detailed below:

I ask your indulgence male and female and promise to he as brief as possible allow me to introduce myself as 'Death Row Teddy'.

I am 58 years old. My DOB is January 3rd 1946.

I have been on death row for 11 years ((Aug. 1994).

I am seeking for a female/male Teddy Bear.

I once lost my heart scarcely used by one careless owner.

As I last saw it was thubbing [*sic*] in your direction.

Caucasian male – seeking an open minded male/female for unconditional correspondence on mature and honest level, that has a caring heart to create a special friendship build from the heart.

Why choose me?

I am a professional artist, photography, amateur poet, writer, masseur, college educated, not a rude person, like to party, travel. My home town is Joshua Tree, CA. I am very understanding and loving. I believe in giving a second chance. People describe me as a gentle giant.

I love cats, dogs, parrots and teddy bears.

What I like in a friend? I like to travel, party. Someone who is mature and wants an honest friendship. Someone who is able to discuss personal issues on a mature level and is not scared of Frank [*sic*] discussion.

Jablonski would not be travelling and partying with anyone, anytime soon. As for discussing personal issues on a mature level, he signally failed to mention that five of the women with whom he 'discussed personal issues' ended up mutilated and in their graves.

At this point in Phil's love-seeking soliloquy, I would like to stop for fear of boring my readers; however, I simply cannot resist what follows:

> What I miss the most: Traveling, photography male and female company, giving massages, partying, walking in the rain, romantic walks along the beach, romantic candlelight dinners, cuddling in front of a roaring fire.
>
> Lets share our thoughts and feelings (good or bad) lets learn about one another freely and watch our friendship bloom like a rose and be as strong as a castle wall which can't be broken.
>
> A loving heart is worse then a mountain of gold [*sic*]. Love communicates on any subject or issue. Write me please you won't be disappointed.
>
> Don't let my situation stop you from writing me. Pick up your pen and pay me a visit ... if possible, please send me $50 for my stationary [*sic*] and stamps, and you will get a guaranteed response ... sincerely, Phillip.

But here's the rub. Scores and scores of women answered Jablonski's ads, and all as a result of an effort by him and some scammer on the outside to hoover up as much cash as they could. Indeed, while his hideous rap sheet was readily available on the CDCR's death row website, along with his mugshot, so enamoured with our Phillip were these ladies that he actually received several offers of marriage. I tracked two of these halfwits down.

'Miss A' (name removed for legal reasons) is from Hastings – the once genteel Edwardian/Victorian, silver-spoon-born-in-one's-mouth seaside resort, not far from the *original* Brighton, which for American readers is in the UK. An *extremely* substantially built woman, 'Miss A' writes to countless serial killers and mass murderers, using her social benefits for airmail stamps, many biros and lots of stationery to court at least one of these homicidal maniacs in an effort to entice him into wedlock. What funds she did have left over she sent to Phillip Jablonski – a total of circa £600, all told – and she was broken-hearted when he passed away. 'Christopher, don't be heartless. You don't even know how much I adored Phillip,' she wrote in a letter to me. 'We thought in exactly the same way. His letters touched my soul. But don't let my grief upset you or your work; I am now writing to [serial killer] Gary Ray Bowles. With a reverse twist on the late actor and comedian Benny Hill, she finished with, 'He likes big women so he tells me. Do you?'

Next up was 'Miss B' (name removed for legal reasons at my publisher's lawyer's advice and *not out of choice*). She hailed from Wisconsin, and *actually* visited Phillip while he was still in CMF Vacaville. Obviously, 'Miss B' had the upper hand in the courtship stakes over 'Miss A' because she met him in the flesh. Love at first sight was the order of the day. But let me ask you – and you can check this out for yourself when you take a look at his photos online – would Phillip have been suitable for casting in *Baywatch* or even as one of the Chippendales strippers, come to that? C'mon my dear lady readers, pretty please take a peek at the now late 'Romeo Phillip' and drop me a line with your thoughts. I'm easily found on Facebook Messenger, so, God's truth, I would love to hear your opinions.

I don't know how old 'Miss B' was back then. I don't even know whether or not she wore high-power spectacles, either. I don't know if she had any religious leanings. I have not a *single* clue as to how many dollars Jablonski fleeced out of her – though I would hazard a guess that it was a tidy amount going by how easily these women get fleeced– even though she lived way up in Oregon, some 670 miles distant from California. Well, love conquers all obstacles, or so they say. She did confirm that he was the 'most handsome man I have ever cast my eyes upon and his poetry [shown and dated 2000, with a cartoon of some chap looking through a mirror, by Jablonski, text verbatim below] entered my heart.'

Phantasm
I have dreamed a dream
A dream of wisdom and pain
Where all in this made up world seems right
I know what I have done
And yet, I can take comfort in those acts
As they have set me free,
Free like a bird in the dream
Drifting to places unknown
Always searching
Always looking
For answers
To questions
That others are afraid to ask
But not afraid to answer.

Detalles de la sepultura desconocidos
('grave details unknown')

Melanie Lyn McGuire, aka
'The Ice Queen'

Beauty lies in the eyes of the beholder.

PARAPHRASE OF A STATEMENT MADE BY THE
GREEK PHILOSOPHER PLATO

There is something magnetically alluring about femmes fatales, including the killer breed. Especially the more intelligent and better-bred women – although among the homicidal criminal ranks they are a rare species indeed. For further reading, my book *Talking with Female Serial Killers: A Chilling Study of the Most Evil Women in the World*, might give the guys pause for thought!

In the US, any up-market partners that these up-scale gals put into a grave are mostly for double-indemnity insurance purposes; tending to be dentists, doctors or other well-paid professionals with life insurance policies the size of the Federal Reserve. By contrast, British female killers rarely murder their spouse or partner for monetary reasons; it is far more common for them to do so out of jealousy. And, again, only a very small proportion of those women who commit murder are serial killers.

And so to Melanie McGuire, who is not a serial killer, but could be said to be a serial letter-writer. And that is my excuse for including her in this book.

On 23 April 2007, thirty-four-year-old Melanie Lyn McGuire was found guilty of murdering her husband some three years earlier, by first drugging him and then shooting him, dismembering his body and disposing of it in three black rubbish bags, placed in three identical suitcases and dropped into Chesapeake Bay. She received a full life sentence.

This is a defendant who puts on a face and shows the people before her whatever it is she wants to show. I don't know who the real Melanie McGuire is.

Assistant State's Attorney Patricia 'Patti' Prezioso
at Melanie McGuire's trial in 2007

With so many letters from killers in my collection, choosing which, and written by whom, to select for this book has been no mean task. The now executed serial killer, Robert Joseph 'Bobby Joe' Long a distant cousin to Henry Lee Lucas, penned dozens of porn-driven filth to my confederate 'Kate' in a honey-trap sting set up by me and her. (I am still working with Kate even today; the choice of name is hers.) But as I am sure my publishers would agree, putting this disgusting material – even with the heaviest of edits – into the public domain would be a bridge far too far. For my own purposes, it certainly gave me a very detailed picture of this man's utterly depraved mind.

If it is a case of judging a person's character by the quality of the material that they are reading – which would make my readers not only astute, highly intelligent but dear friends of mine for life – it would be fair to say that Melanie McGuire was more eclectic in her reading than some other killers I could name: she favoured a mixed bag of stuff, including some conspiratorial literature, as we will see in due course. But the same cannot be said of Bobby Joe Long. In his letters to 'Kate', he promotes *Bizarre Magazine* and *Draculina*, graciously listing an entire catalogue of his must-reads, while also recommending suppliers and giving her the addresses and zip codes for the websites QSM Mail Order, Redemption, *Rose Comics* and *Centurion* magazine. After that, he prints in bold black ink – and it should be noted that this was his first letter to 'Kate', who'd merely asked if his crimes had a sexual element to them, mentioned that she would be interested in him as a person and asked about his literary preferences:

… AND BE SURE TO SIGN AN AGE STATEMENT, AND I THINK THEY'LL ALL SEND YAH SOME CATALOGES YOU'LL FIND … INTERESTING ☹. WHO KNOWS, MAYBE EVEN SOME 'STUFF' YOU'VE <u>NEVER SEEN BEFORE!</u>
HAVE YOU NEVER WATCHED A HARD CORE XXX RATED, GRAPHIC 'FUCK-VIDEO'??? IF SO, WHAT DID YOU SEE THAT <u>MOST 'INTERESTED'</u> YOU? IF NOT, WOULD YOU LIKE TOO?

At this point I am sure my readers will know 100 per cent where Bobby Joe Long is going next. Among the varied subjects up for discussion are:

WHO WOULD YOU LIKE TO "TORTURE AND
RAPE ... KILL? ... KITTEN, XOX. I WILL CALL
YOU "DARK KATIE" . I FIND THIS EXTREMELY
INTERESTING. I HOPE YOU WILL SHARE IT
WITH ME, AND NOBODY ELSE. THAT'S MEAN A
LOT TO ME, PEANUT!

From here on in his perversions plunged downhill, to rock-
bottom into an abyss of sexual depravity. Kicking off with:

I LIKE SHOPPING FOR WOMENS' CLOTHES.
I HAVE A LOT OF OUTFITS – AND SHOES
TO WEAR, THAT I'D REALLY LIKE-REALLY-
REALLY LIKE TO SEE YOU IN ... CAN YOU
CUT OFF A LOCK OF YOUR HAIR ... 10-15
STRANDS UP ABOUT 2 INCHES FROM YOUR
HAIR LINE AT THE NAPE OF YOUR NECK ...
BUT I'M 'DISAPPOINTED', BECAUSE I THINK
THAT YOUR LITTLE PUSSY IS STILL 'CHERRY'
... MY TITTIES ARE I THINK BIGGER THAN MY
VIRGIN PUSSY KATS.

Former nurse Melanie McGuire, in contrast, stands almost atop
so many others for she has oodles of wit and humour in spades.
She can be blatantly flirtatious, calling me 'Christopher', 'Chris',
'Chris my darling' and 'my love', as suited her mood. She almost
weaves a spell. One cannot help but like her because she can
have oodles of charm and style, too.

SBI #00319833C McGUIRE, Melanie, corresponded for
many months. She is enigmatic to a fault; even her handwriting

seems to beguile the reader. Her penned words have a rhythmic sequence that flows easily onto the page with not a grammatical error to be found. One could say that her syntax is nigh-on perfect, unlike mine, so some of my critics say. So I was soon able to imagine – just from her correspondence – why men found this petite nurse so attractive. Scores of her female patients adored her too. And, as will soon become apparent, for 99.99 per cent of her life Melanie never put a step wrong. She wasn't a drinker and would never have failed a field sobriety test. But for 0.01 per cent of her life she went bad, and I mean ape-shit, flying well over *The Cuckoo's Nest* seriously bad!

For this once pixie-faced, 5-foot 3-inch, 121-pound mother of two killed and then chopped up her husband. The media dubbed her 'The Ice Queen' because she appeared so cold and emotionless throughout her entire trial proceedings. In her heyday, no one could have said that Melanie was unattractive. Today, however, after more than fifteen years behind bars, life has chewed on her.

There is an old saying that 'one should never judge a book by its cover'; similarly, 'all that glitters is not gold' and 'beauty is only skin deep'. You might apply all three to Melanie McGuire, in different ways. Let's take 'one should never judge a book by its cover' first.

She has been judged by some – such as newspapers local to her – to be one of the most notorious femmes fatales in the criminal history of New Jersey (the 'Garden State'). That is the cover of her life's narrative that we see at first blush today. But if we were to read into her history, perhaps we might discover a decent person, albeit one who has now become a lost soul. I will let my readers decide on this.

'All that glitters is not gold?' As mentioned, for the vast majority of her life she did glitter. Most of those who knew Melanie felt that she sparkled from within, from her heart even. We can't take this away from her either.

'Beauty is only skin deep?' Physically, Melanie McGuire modestly says, she had no outer beauty; her manner is self-effacing, but it was what lay beneath the surface that drew people to her. 'Little Melanie was a powerhouse of energy,' one of her former patients explained. 'She would do anything for us. She was so loving, sweet . . . made me feel like I was her sister.'

Shortly after her conviction on 23 April 2007 for killing her husband, Melanie cropped up on my radar. She had become a media sensation, with journalists and authors clamouring for her exclusive red-top story. If I wanted a piece of this better-baked all-American homicidal pie, I had several obstacles to overcome:

1. Melanie was incarcerated in New Jersey, 3,500 miles from my home on England's south coast.
2. She was in mega demand from writers and journos far closer to her than I would ever be.
3. There would be every chance that if I did arrange to visit her she would cancel the meeting at the last moment, leaving me and my film crew high and dry – as had happened while making a TV documentary with another incarcerated killer from the 'Garden State', the now deceased James Allen Paul, who committed three murders in New Jersey, Vermont and Connecticut:

Yeah, so what. I did agree for you to interview me. Now I've changed my mind. So fuckkk off.

James Allen Paul: to the author,
Trenton State Prison, New Jersey

Actually, I did get to meet James Paul for a moment. We had been filming a TV documentary with my late, dear friend, Connecticut state homicide detective Mike Malchik – the lead cop in both the Michael Bruce Ross and James Paul serial killings. I had hauled my film crew all the way to Trenton (now New Jersey State Prison). They parked up outside while I went inside to sit down on the right side of a bullet-proof glass screen, only for this pasty-faced serial killer to tell me to 'Fuckkk *off!*'

Absolutely no class at all. We made the programme without him.

As for Melanie McGuire? Finding myself in a bit of a quandary about the distance involved, and also considering that I am related to Scrooge, I decided that some thinking time was needed. So, after dinner I put on my Sherlock Holmes houndstooth deerstalker, lit my calabash pipe, sat back in my captain's chair, took a swig of Sherlock's favourite tipple – the 'Gloria Scott' port – and did what they call 'musing' before the shrill ring of my telephone rudely brought me to sensibility.

Okay, I made all of that up, but I did have what some people call a 'eureka moment'. If I were to even stand a chance of catching and landing this little fish, I needed the right bait. I did a little bit of research and discovered that not only did she try to feed her murdered husband to some bigger fishes (in that she chucked the suitcase containing his dismembered body into the Chesapeake Bay), she was well educated. In point of fact,

Melanie had graduated from Middleton High School South in the top 50 per cent of her class. She went to Rutgers University, graduating with a bachelor's degree in 'statistics' as she called her double major in mathematics and psychology, then went on to get a nursing diploma. This was when the dime dropped. Unlike James Paul, 'Our Mel' would appreciate a classy approach, so it was time to do what some university students do – as in carry out some thorough preparation.

Being the true-blue parsimonious tightwad that I am, I nipped down to my local stationers, where I asked the young assistant to remove three sheets of Conqueror laid cream paper from an unopened ream, and place them in a brown paper bag along with a matching envelope and a stick of red sealing wax. Then, with a, 'May I have a receipt please ... it's for tax purposes, you know,' I hastened out to flash my bus pass for the ride home. Back at my PC, I typed a short letter to Melanie, leaving her name and my signature to be added in ink. I smugly admired my handiwork. All that remained was to impress my family seal ('D') in wax below my signature, include photocopies of several of my book covers, along with a generous spray of Chanel 'Égoïste', and an airmail stamp. Into the post it went – and I didn't expect a reply until hell froze over.

As my grandfather, the very late solicitor Oscar Berry Tompkins, used to say while peering over his half-moon spectacles and nodding a head of the finest silvery spun hair: 'You'll learn, my boy, that you can wait ages for a bus then half a dozen all come along at once.' He was a tightwad too: tight-fistedness runs throughout our familial DNA. Oscar defended William Henry Kennedy, who, in 1927, with accomplice Frederick Guy Brown, shot to death a PC 489 George William

Gutteridge at Stapleford Abbotts in Essex. His client was hanged, but he was right about the buses. I didn't have to wait too long for Melanie to reply and soon her letters began popping through my letter box, often several at the same time.

'Glancing at a piece of handwriting for the first time is rather like meeting someone new,' writes Margaret Gullan-Whur, in *Discover Graphology: A Straightforward and Practical Guide to Handwriting Analysis*. She adds: 'We are bound to be aware of a unique essence: we receive impressions which, because they are unconcerned with reason or cause, evaporate quickly on further acquaintance.' Here, specifically with regard to Melanie McGuire, Gullan-Whur hits the nail right on the head. If one is *really* interested in graphology, then her book is a must-read. Intriguingly, she advises at first we should consider handwriting as a picture, and ask ourselves: 'Are its component parts well-blended, or do some aspects seem harshly exaggerated [...] is there one movement which regularly spoils the flow? Is the penmanship well-proportioned and clear, or is there a sudden contraflow testifying to a lack of harmony within the mind of the writer? Is it gracefully simple or fussily embellished?'

Then comes into play grammar. 'Is the person educated or lacking a fundamental grasp of English?' Margaret asks. Think back to when we studied a few of the letters from Phillip Jablonski. Aside from his totally screwed-up script, we most certainly witnessed a mentally disturbed mind using a pen. This is the lack of harmony that Margaret alludes to. There are regular moments where Jablonski spoils the flow, almost as if he is two characters, and this is confirmed by the psychiatric assessments he underwent – the shocking results of which were treated by doctors in an offhand way, resulting in them more or less giving

Jablonski a licence to kill. Yes, Phil was schizophrenic, but pathologically he was much more than that, was he not? To me, he brings to mind the image of a boxer in a ring fighting himself, something all too evident in his writings.

Not so with Melanie Lyn McGuire. Her handwriting seems completely at odds with the horrendous nature of her crime; that said, her letters show no genuine regard for her children, who adored their dad. The other thing worthy of note is that she avoided like a pinprick of sarin any discussion about the crime for which she received a natural-life prison term. When I eventually pressed her on the subject, she stopped writing to me altogether. This rejection may have been because at that time she was still pleading her innocence and appealing her sentence, even though the evidence against her was overwhelming. Perhaps she was (indeed, is) living in a state of pathological denial.

Melanie's first letter to me was dated 26 January 2008:

Dear Christopher.

I apologize for not responding to your first letter. While I am indeed interested in telling my story and the events totally, and in depth, to a reputable news outlet, I am currently involved in appealing my conviction and sentence. As a result, I must defer to my appellate counsel and their advice regarding the matter.

At this time we are having some difficulty with our telephone communications, and I've not been able to contact them directly. I realize that contacting me via conventional mail is less than expedient – as a result, I'd like to provide you with the contact information of one of my closest friends, Allison Li Calsi, as I speak to her daily, and she might function as an intermediary.

Thank you for contacting me – again, my apologies for not responding sooner.

Warm regards

Melanie McGuire.

As I am sure the reader will agree, a polite, measured letter, that was too. So I replied, pointing out that I was *not* a 'news outlet' – just a minor italic slap from me to put her in her place, so to speak.

Considering Melanie's alleged reluctance to say very much because of her upcoming appeal, she replied much faster (indeed, by return of post) than I'd anticipated. Dated 8 February 2008, here's her next letter, at once proving that a splash of Chanel 'Égoïste' can work a treat – with the ladies only, I stress!

Dear Chris.

Thanks so much for your letter. I continue to be amazed that your correspondence seems to find me with greater expediency than that of my own family, who live a mere few hours away. I also smiled when I read your comment (and the postman's) about my penmanship, imagining the conversation: ('... yes, but this incarcerant can write'). I should warn you that I have what many consider a fairly caustic sense of humor – it's proven itself to be a good coping mechanism, especially in my current environment.

You needn't have pondered my astrological affiliation – my birthdate is on my DOC 'factsheet' where you obtained my contact information ☺. I was born Melanie Lyn Slate on 8 October 1972. My parents divorced when I was 5. My mother remarried shortly thereafter, to a gentleman named Michael Cappasaro, and I have a younger brother called Christopher. My biological father and I had sporadic contact before he died on 26 Feb 1987.

Melanie then went on to explain that having graduated in 1994, she waited tables, during which she met another waiter, William T. 'Bill' McGuire. 'I was attending the Rutgers School of Pharmacy at the time,' she writes, 'ironically housed in the same building as the Stats Dept.' She had been 'less enthusiastic about the major' she had chosen, even 'taking a number of psychological and educational courses', so at the age of twenty-two she had made the decision to enrol in the Charles E. Gregory School of Nursing in the autumn of 1994.

It is now that Melanie hit her stride. She tells that she excelled there, graduating, second in her class, in 1997. Not long after, she befriended all-American hunk James 'Jim' Finn, who would soon become a famous American football fullback playing for the Chicago Bears. To add some spice to her story she says: 'We had a bit of an on and off relationship.' I tentatively wrote back to ask Melanie what had attracted her to James Finn. In reply, she wrote: 'I am not the football type – being more of the conspiracy theory/science fiction type.'

Subliminally here, Melanie was giving us a clue to what would follow later, so take note of those words, then think about what is so often hidden between the lines of a letter and the thought-processing system – in her case her modus cogitandi, for here she is making a teeny-weeny slip of the tongue as will become apparent later. Football or not, she and Finn kept in touch – and he would become a state witness in her subsequent trial.

Melanie also told me that she was from the 'shore'. Seafood was her favourite, 'French cuisine the more the better and foie gras I can die for.' She also likes her books – certainly a better class of literature than that of the aforementioned Bobby Joe Long who was up to his neck in hard-core porn reading material:

My favourite authors are: Stephen King; Janet Evanovich (selected works); P. G. Wodehouse; Martin Amis; Haruki Murakami; Hugh Laurie, and Matt Beaumont, he's so hilarious. I intend to read 'Duma Key' by Stephen King, 'The War against Cliché' by Amis, and 'The Gnostic Faustus' by Ramona Fraden [*sic*]. That's quite a few, I know.

Alas, time for group therapy, so I'll close for now (and before, somewhere in my DC, my appellate attorney has a grand mal seizure). Let the healing begin (yes, that's sarcasm you smell). This should all be duplicative anyway, as I've channelled to your mailman all I wanted to say (the poor bastard).

Love, Melanie.

Now you're talking, Melanie. (I'll vouch for Janet Evanovich; she's the bee's knees. Sir Pelham Grenville Wodehouse was the creator of 'Jeeves', the supreme 'gentleman's gentleman'. Ramona Fradon's book is way above my own head but I do get Hugh Laurie, as in *big time*. These are Melanie's words, not mine; Ramona Fradon is a graphic-novel artist.

To be totally honest with you, I was getting to the point where I started thinking: 'Why should I allow a damned good Agatha-type murder mystery get in the way of developing a lifelong, loving relationship with Melanie? Maybe Bill had gotten some well-deserved comeuppance?' Her correspondence came across as amusing, witty, well-read, with a *very* dry sense of humour, which is most refreshing in my line of work. I stress 'refreshing' because usually when trying to communicate with femmes fatales – perhaps a 'Black Widow' who has killed in quick succession three of her spouses by giving them drinks laced with antifreeze – I get something along the lines of: 'Before we start, how mucha yo's gonna pay me for my story. If not, yo go fuck yrseleves, an' wassat smell on the paper, it's stinking out my cell.'

> Melanie McGuire is just a powerhouse in a tiny petite little body. And she makes you feel like you're her only patient.
>
> Former fertility clinic patient on
Melanie McGuire

> You felt that she was, you know, almost a girlfriend.
>
> Another former fertility patient on
Melanie McGuire

While at nursing school, Melanie responded to an advertisement for ovum donors, and by the time she graduated, Melanie had undergone three such donations: 'treatment cycles which were anonymous at the St. Barnabas Medical Center', she wrote to me, adding, 'and in talking to the staff and head nurse there, they knew that my licensure exam wasn't far off, and they offered me a position as an ovum donor coordinator'.

Melanie tells us that she and Bill were by then an item (with Jim Finn being a fullback in the background so to speak), and it was Bill who encouraged her to accept the job offer. They became engaged in 1998, after which she had two more ovum donations – this time 'solely for research purposes'. The couple married on Sunday, 6 June 1999. She was twenty-seven, he was thirty-four. A week before the wedding, she learned that she was pregnant:

> I'd suffered a very early miscarriage about six months before that, I was thrilled but nervous. Later that year, the physician I worked with left St. Barnabas to form Reproduction Medicine Associates (RMA). I would eventually come to meet and work with Dr Bradley T. Miller there, and he still runs a successful practice in Morristown today.

And I'd put money on it that you are going to guess what happened next. Dr Miller was also an all-American hunk, and with three children, none of which proved an impediment, and he and Melanie soon indulging in some extra-marital bonking on the side. As for husband Bill, he was also having a bit, or even a few bits, on the side, too. Sadly, unbeknown to him he had less than five years left to live before becoming the contents of three brown suitcases that were *intended* to sink into the depths of the Chesapeake Bay – but oops-a-daisy, they floated.

During my correspondence with Melanie, and reflecting back on her formative years, I asked her whether she thought that the break-up of her parents' marriage when she was aged just five may have had any negative impact on her. She replied:

I wouldn't necessarily say that my parents' divorce troubled me – I barely have a recollection of it, and I consider myself infinitely fortunate that my mother subsequently remarried to a wonderful man, who I truly consider to be my "real" father. However, I can and do acknowledge some pervasive abandonment issues – it would be disingenuous of me to say I wasn't affected by my natural father's absence (and occasional re-entry) into my life. I am reluctant to reflect on that and assign blame – I am an educated woman, and if it has power over me, it's because I allow it to.

At this point in our pen-pal relationship, it was becoming obvious that Melanie liked the attention of men. She liked her feathers stroked too – and who doesn't, I suppose? (She once wrote to me: 'Oh, I knew the Chanel immediately I opened your letter. It's my favorite men's cologne. You must be psychic.') So to reel her in just a tad further, I put it to her that she must be proud of her academic achievements. She responded in her typically humble fashion. Indeed, when I read what follows I wondered where, and at what point, she came up for air. She started with: 'Chris, dear Chris, my academic achievements are anything but interesting. You fascinate me. We could become soulmates. We could spend so much lovingly intelligent time, walking and talking about the finer things to be had from our lives,' ending with 'I must go now. It's lunch time. I wish I had a plane to catch.'

If Melanie had left it at that I would have been a happy man. But next came: 'but, I'll run through them if you like?'

'Oh, shit, here we go,' I mused once again. Throwing my bottle of 'Gloria Scott' port, calabash pipe and replica Sherlock Holmes deerstalker into a bin and replacing them with a twelve pack of Carlsberg Special Brew, two hundred Philippine rip-off Marlboro Reds and a pink papier-mâché hat that I'd kept from the previous Christmas, in a waste not, want not, sort of way. So here is the *exact* wording of what Melanie wrote to me:

When I was in the second grade, someone thought it would be helpful to test my IQ. As a result I was placed into what was called a 'Gifted & Talented' programme (how politically incorrect – smile).

[...] I was in this programme throughout grammar/middle/high school, where I excelled even in a fairly competitive school system [...] I was amazing at stats, was a member of both the Spanish Honor Society and the National Honor Society and a drama club [...]

[...] I was selected as an Edward Bloustein Distinguished Scholar intended to recognise the highest achieving graduating, high school students in or from New Jersey and to reward them with awards that are granted regardless of need [...]

[...] then I went to Rutgers University, and got a 1.0 on the GPA scale my first semester to the acute distress of my parents. I discovered unchecked freedom – and parties [...]

[...] I think I pulled a 3.0 or better each semester after that: Statistics major, Psyche minor, Religion Mini, but my initial fall from academic grace doomed me to mediocrity. I decided in my senior year that I wanted to pursue nursing, but I didn't have the credentials to switch majors at this point, so I completed my BA first at my parents' insistence.

She did not explain, however, how she killed and dismembered Bill, nor did she mention the three suitcases that she packed him into and threw into the Chesapeake Bay. Did I not explain from the outset of this book that corresponding with killers can be like wading through molasses?

In 2002, Melanie was pregnant; her second son would be William 'Bill' McGuire Jr. Meanwhile, her relationship with Dr Miller had evolved from two co-workers who flirted into a full-on *Sunday Sport*-type of affair. Indeed, Bradley would later tell the trial court that he bought two pre-paid cell phones for them to communicate and that they called each other ten to twenty times a day, 'even when we worked together' – although in different treatment rooms, we hope!

Now giving it the full *Fifty Shades of Grey* tin of beans, Nurse Melanie and Doctor Bradley fell deeply in love and started planning on how to leave their respective spouses, or so she says. Then, dammit, in 2004, just when Melanie decided to move out of their deluxe apartment and divorce Bill, her totally in-the-dark husband had just closed a deal on a more upscale home with a big yard for the kids. Then, to thank him for his alleged loving devotion to their marriage, Melanie killed Bill in what would ultimately become a cause célèbre.

The state claimed that Melanie's motive for killing Bill was so that she could start a new life with her boss Dr Miller without a messy divorce. During the seven-week trial, prosecutors relied on evidence of the affair along with testimony from a forensic expert. The latter stated that the black garbage bags containing the victim's remains that were found inside the three suitcases bobbing around in the Chesapeake Bay were microscopically consistent in every respect with the bags, filled with Bill's clothing, that were later discovered with one of Melanie's friends after his death. Despite all of her wit, intelligence and cunning, she had failed rule no. 1 in the *Murderer's Handbook*: get rid of every single piece of physical evidence involved in *any way* with the crime.

> He's charismatic. Bill has a sense of humor, a lot of *'Saturday Night Live'* type sense of humour. [...] He could pick on you but make you feel good about it at the same time.
>
> Jon Rice: Bill McGuire's best friend

Jon Rice had known Bill since they'd met in the Navy during the 1980s. When Bill and Mel married in 1999, the Rices were happy to take the newlyweds with them on holiday to the Bahamas. Then, in 2004, Jon and Susan Rice picked up on the bizarre story of suitcases containing parts of a dismembered corpse turning up in the Chesapeake Bay. At the same time, they were also engrossed in another strange tale, one that concerned the McGuires.

The Rices had just heard about the beautiful new home the McGuires had bought in New Jersey. Yet a few days later, Melanie phoned the Rices to say that she and Bill had had a terrible argument about their dream home just hours after signing on the dotted line. Melanie told them that Bill had got physical with her and stormed out of their apartment. Thus she broke rule no. 2 in the mythical *Murderer's Handbook*: attempting to transfer blame while not considering what the Rices might make of it. To them, Melanie's story simply did not add up. They knew that Bill loved his two sons, and had just signed up for a house with a spacious yard for them to play in. Jon was immediately suspicious. But Melanie insisted that he had left after hitting her and that she'd obtained a restraining order in case Bill slunk back.

In an effort to add weight to her phoney story she told a family court judge: '[Bill] told me I was stupid, and slapped me, uh.' The judge asked: 'Where did he slap you, ma'am?' Melanie replied: 'In the face.' The judge then asked a pointed question: 'Has your husband got a firearm or is there a gun in the house?' Melanie replied: 'No, ma'am,' to which the judge responded: 'That's fine. You are safe here.' However, what does not add up is the fact that immediately after the alleged assault, Melanie had failed to make an official complaint to the police, an issue that the judge completely overlooked. Moreover, she lied to the judge about that firearm, because just a few days earlier she had bought a gun. Mel loved tales of duplicity and deception, as suggested by her letters, but failed to differentiate between tales and realism.

While the Rices were unconvinced by Melanie's allegations, others were not. Speaking to NBC News in 2007, Melanie's friend Selene Trevizas, who had known Melanie for many years, said of Bill, 'I don't think he was a good husband . . . I don't think he was a great father.'

For years, she said, she'd thought that Bill was stressed by all his responsibilities. The good-natured banter between them had degenerated into verbal abuse from Bill. 'She was no longer fighting back. The arguing – it wasn't back and forth. It was more one-sided. She was just tired.'

Soon enough, people were starting to ask where Bill was. Selene and another friend, Allison LiCalsi, told NBC that Melanie had told them that Bill was a heavy gambler – so might he have gone to glitzy Atlantic City, lost a fortune he didn't have, got involved with the wrong people? 'Well, she knew that Atlantic City had always been a monkey on his back,' Allison said. 'But she also wasn't sure the extent of what he was involved with.'

The Rices thought it quite possible that their missing friend was in Atlantic City, perhaps gambling in the many casinos. When speaking to NBC News, they later mentioned that he used to go on trips to Atlantic City, and spoke of one occasion when he treated the Rices to a weekend there, and still returned home several thousand dollars better off. They were adamant, however, that Bill did *not* have a gambling problem or hang about with unsavoury characters. His chosen game, Jon explained to NBC News, was blackjack, and he was good at it.

With Bill now missing, the Rices began telephoning hotels in Atlantic City to see if they could get any information about his movements. As time went on with no news of Bill, they became more concerned. They did not immediately connect his disappearance with the strange story that was on the news – the one about the three suitcases found bobbing around in the Chesapeake Bay with parts of an unidentified man inside them. But one day Susan's attention was drawn to the television news and heard the reporter saying that the police had released a sketch of the dead male. 'I looked at the picture, and something about the military-style haircut looked familiar, so I compared it to a photo I had of Bill,' she recalled. 'I just remember that my heart just sank to my stomach.' She told Jon and they rang the Virginia Beach police.

When corresponding at length with convicted killers behind bars, I've noticed that over time they become trapped in their own way of thinking – more often than not they inadvertently reveal insights into their state of mind through slips of the tongue, or indeed in what they write. Over time, patterns of conscious or subconscious thought processing emerge. Let's focus on the modus cogitandi once more.

To all intents and purposes, the way we work and live our lives is inextricably bound by our modus cogitandi – it is human nature. Indeed, all animals desire to live within the confines of what makes them feel comfortable. Step out of our comfort zone and life becomes more uncertain – we are never truly happy when doubt enters our cosy lives. Everything we do, say or write, whether it's MO or MV, must, to my mind, spring forth from MC. Would you disagree? In that light, modus cogitandi is an issue that we should keep in mind as we read the letters penned by these evil people.

Let's return to Melanie's expounding on her academic achievement to the point of tedium. By relating that she is a dedicated bookworm of sorts, one fascinated with conspiracy theories, I suggest that she is subconsciously telling us – dressed up with a seasoning of pathos – just how clever she is. Her psychopathology does not permit otherwise, for she is trapped within her own learning-from-experiences. In reading the works of great storytellers, she becomes one of them in her own fantasy-driven world, a place where *everything* is possible for an educated woman like her – conspiracy theories into the bargain, for criminal psychopaths are the greatest control freaks of all. Along with zero feelings of guilt and exhibiting zero remorse, Melanie's true, manipulating mind will be revealed at the end of this chapter – and also her inability to be realistic – so I hope you'll enjoy every bit of the big reveal.

In a letter, Melanie writes:

> Did I have a 'bad' marriage? Yes. Was my husband abusive, be it emotionally, and/or physically? Yes. But I am responsible for staying and bending to his will on issues that I should have remained firm on. So, while I think things like a battered woman's syndrome do, indeed, exist and are appropriate affirmative defenses in some cases, I do place some degree of accountability on the 'victim', albeit limited. In my criminal case, I never waged an affirmative defense – my defense was always that of actual innocence.

That all seems very plausible, does it not? Although Melanie freely admits that her marriage was far from happy, suggesting elsewhere that 'Bill had a few problems – drink, gambling, and women on occasions', she was also quick to point out: 'I am not entitled to any righteous indignation about this as I, too, was unfaithful.'

If one were to take on its face what Melanie says as being sensitive and totally honest – which she wants us to believe – then one might sense that a *crime passionnel* might have taken place;

that in the heat of the moment, while trying to defend herself from an abusive husband, she had killed him. This could have been construed as second-degree homicide, or manslaughter as we have it in the UK. And, *had* this been the case and *had* she called the police with the body still in situ, then a state's attorney would have been extremely hard-pressed to charge her with premeditated murder. However, by now Melanie had already sunk her own boat with indirect admissions of guilt along with the three suitcases containing her husband that had remained floating on the water's surface, rather than obligingly sinking. It would become only a matter of time before motive, coupled with premeditation to commit murder most foul, was established. Attorneys for Melanie McGuire would later aggressively contest these allegations, arguing that their client had no motive to kill her husband – a man whom, they claimed, was involved in an extramarital relationship too.

And didn't Melanie say that she loved conspiracy theories?

So what had happened to Bill McGuire? He was last seen alive by Melanie on Thursday, 29 April 2004 – the day the couple had closed the sale on a $500,000 up-market house in Asbury, Warren County. Shortly after he disappeared, and over a period of days, three suitcases were found bobbing around in the Chesapeake Bay. Shock Stephen King horror: on opening, they revealed black plastic refuse bags containing a dismembered Mr McGuire.

In a case (excuse the pun) built entirely on circumstantial evidence, prosecutors theorised that Mrs McGuire had served her husband a celebratory glass of wine spiked with a sedative, then shot him to death – there were two bullet holes in him, after all. In a previous phone conversation with a friend, she had let slip that she had purchased the gun just two days before her husband disappeared. And of course, when she'd applied for a phoney restraining order she told the judge that the couple did *not* possess a firearm. Oh, Melanie, you really should have superglued your lips on that issue, as in when to speak and not to speak!

Police initially believed that Melanie had cut Bill up into four pieces in the shower using a saw. This caused a problem because investigators were unable – even using all the forensic CSI techniques available to modern law enforcement – to link the man's murder to his home in any way whatsoever. In her defence, Melanie claimed that the last she saw of her husband was on the morning of 29 April, after an argument over their new home. She said he drove off in his car and that that was the last she ever saw of him. At her subsequent trial, the defence suggested that his death may have been related to gambling debts. A letter (*see* later) allegedly written by a mobster from a major organised crime family in New Jersey had been sent to the DA; in it, the writer claimed that Bill McGuire owed a $90,000 debt to a Mafia family. This is why he was fed to the fishes in the true Cosa Nostra style, so the letter claimed.

In my opinion, she's a lousy actress.
Virginia Beach Detective Ray Pickell
(sometimes spelt 'Picalle') on Melanie McGuire

Now that the detective was able to confirm the identity of the dismembered body, he could try to find out who had so much wanted the man dead and had gone to so much effort to cover their tracks – a bit like covering over cracks with wallpaper which, when peeled off, reveals the flaws beneath.

Cherchez la femme: as in all such investigations the officer was particularly interested in speaking to the victim's wife, Melanie McGuire, for she was, he felt, best placed to help him. She must surely be able to tell him something that would give him a clue, he hoped.

He quickly dismissed Melanie's notion that Bill had been the victim of a gangland hit. From what the Rices said, Bill McGuire knew what he was doing and incurred no debts, or so they thought, so any suggestion of a large, unpaid gambling debt was ruled out. Pickell was more interested in the body itself: the almost surgical dissection of Bill's body was plainly the work of someone with medical knowledge, and this, the cop reckoned, was significant. What's more, it turned out that a blanket found in one of the suitcases was from a hospital; Pickell did some digging and discovered that Melanie was a nurse. 'She works at a doctor's office and those types of blankets were being supplied [there]?' Pickell asked NBC, rhetorically. 'Yeah, there's a lot of suspicion there.'

A week later, the sleuth was again interviewing the 'Black Widow', this time in her attorney's office with not just one lawyer present but two. The detective found it strange that she would need two lawyers present when all he wanted was to ask a few simple questions such as 'Did you ever own any brown matching luggage, which is now missing?'

In a knee-jerk reaction, she bluntly replied, 'No!' But to throw the detective off the scent, she volunteered that her husband's car might be in Atlantic City, New Jersey, and soon after that's just where police found Bill's blue 2002 Nissan Maxima. After

CSI examined the vehicle, they handed over to Detective Pickell a phial of white liquid – it was chloral hydrate – found with a syringe in the glove box. These items, along with the blanket, were significant finds. Chloral hydrate is a 'hypnotic', used among other things as a sedative prescribed in the short-term treatment of insomnia to help one fall asleep and stay asleep for a proper rest. When taken with any form of alcohol, this can lead to decreased mental and motor function. Symptoms may include excess sedation, confusion, loss of coordination and consciousness. Knock back a glass or two of wine spiked with this stuff and within twenty minutes one is living in the land of many, many fairies.

Police now searched the McGuires' home. It was spotless – and unfurnished, as Melanie had now vacated. As for Bill's clothing, Melanie told Pickell that she had, perhaps with somewhat indecent haste, passed them on to a friend. Pickell soon found them packed in black plastic bags identical to those that contained Bill's dismembered corpse.

As for the suitcase: the day after her interview in her attorney's office she told the detective that she and Bill *had*, after all, owned a matching three-piece set of brown Kenneth Cole luggage. 'I showed her a picture of one piece of luggage that was recovered from the Chesapeake Bay,' Pickell told NBC. 'And she identified that as the family luggage.'

But despite everything, there was no watertight evidence to pin Bill's death on his wife. The only thing Pickell felt sure about was that Bill had been murdered in New Jersey, not Virginia. So he opted to kick the can down the road. It was now someone else's problem, some other law enforcement's jurisdiction, to solve, to wit: New Jersey.

At the end of the day it's a horrible, gruesome murder.

> Detective David Dalrymple,
> New Jersey State Police

Dalrymple was the lead investigator in New Jersey, and opted to start with a different line of enquiry. He searched gun registration records and popped into gun shops, in the hope of picking up a trace of someone who knew Bill and had purchased a firearm. Bingo. He discovered that Melanie had bought a .38-calibre handgun on 6 April, just days before the murder. There was more to come. Police tracked down James Finn, the former on-and-off again boyfriend of Melanie's, who told them she'd been in touch to say she was worried about Bill's deteriorating state of mind and wanted advice on buying a firearm. Finn, a gun enthusiast, had informed her that she could get one within twenty-four hours from the neighbouring state of Pennsylvania. The cops got Finn to call Melanie and taped the conversation. Here is a short extract of that recording:

> Finn: Throw me a bone. Where's the gun?
> Melanie: The gun was in the lockbox when [Bill] first left ... I put it into the storage unit ... Of course, I went later and looked and it's not in there.

Which, of course, worked out well for her: no one could run forensic tests on a missing firearm. But hadn't she told the family court judge that the couple didn't have a gun? Indeed she had, so she was lying again, this time to James Finn, and inadvertently also to the cops listening in.

So what was the possible motive for killing her husband? In the course of their enquiries, the police contacted Dr Bradley Miller, Melanie's boss at the RMA fertility clinic. This turned out to be more informative than they could have hoped as they learned that Miller and Melanie had been conducting an affair for three years. And the doctor told the cops a lot more; relating an unconvincing story that Melanie had told him about how after the row with Bill, and her getting the restraining order against him, she had driven all the way to Atlantic City, where she had somehow managed to find his car and, out of vindictiveness, moved it to the out-of-the-way motel's car park. 'A security camera may have caught me doing it,' she told Miller. Tired out, Melanie said, she had taken a taxi home, and then, the next day, had taken another back to Atlantic City to fetch her own car, she said, and it was all smoke-blowing, all lie after lie, so now a sceptical Dalrymple checked with all the local cab companies and not one of them had a record of taxi rides to and/or from Atlantic City, a long journey that would have cost hundreds of dollars. Besides, if she was so exhausted, why didn't she simply book into an Atlantic City hotel that night? It just didn't add up. Melanie had also told Dr Miller another unconvincing story – that she had, coincidentally, happened to have been shopping for furniture in Delaware – which is not far from Chesapeake Bay – the day before the first suitcase was found.

Detective Dalrymple persuaded Miller to confront his lover in another secretly wired conversation, as reported by NBC News:

Dr Miller: The trip to Delaware. They [the police] want to know what you were going there for and what furniture stores you were looking for there and seem to believe that you went with your father.

McGuire: There was nobody else in that fucking car with me ... I think that they're ... when it comes to, like, the mythical second person. I think they're talking shit.

Dr Miller: I think they're either gonna come down on me or come down on your father. That it was, you know, the one that helped you do the murder.

Circumstantial though it was, the evidence looked damning: an affair; a string of lies; indirect admissions of guilt; missing gun; rubbish bags; unlikely trips; implausible explanations; wadcutter bullets, a syringe, a phial containing traces of chloral hydrate and a hospital blanket. What exactly did it all add up to? Would it all end with an arrest?

Let's start with the .38-calibre special. She had bought this handgun just two days before Bill's murder. He was shot by a firearm – once in the head, once in the body with wadcutter bullets – and the gun, according to Melanie, had conveniently gone missing from a locked storage locker *after* Bill had allegedly driven away from their home. She had told friends about the pistol after Bill's death; even then she shifted stories, saying that it was actually Bill who wanted the gun. Hadn't she told Finn that she wanted it for her *own* protection against her husband?

Forensic scientist Tom Lesniak carefully examined the McGuires' apartment and its few contents (for Melanie had moved out with her children) and also the rubbish bags that Melanie had with undue haste used to dispose of Bill's clothing. On examination, the forensic team's conclusion was that all the bags, those used for Bill's clothing and those the body parts were found in, were manufactured on the same production line *and* on the same extrusion run. Most suspicious, however, was what the forensics team did *not* find in their rigorous search of the apartment. It was dust-free, there was not a hair, no trace of blood or minuscule particle of skin – indeed no DNA material whatsoever – nothing at all to suggest that the McGuires, or, come to that, any person, had ever lived there before the McGuires' visits to the property and after it had been vacated. The obvious conclusion would be that the apartment, known to have been occupied by people until recently, must have been *very* thoroughly cleaned – a conclusion supported by a witness who stated that when she went round to the apartment there was a very strong smell of cleaning fluids and bleach.

'Who scrubs a bathroom wall when they're leaving an apartment?' the prosecutor, Patricia Prezioso, asked the jury, a question that she could have more forcibly put to them, for after all was said and done: wasn't Mrs McGuire a nurse who was an expert at cleanliness and hygiene, and this being the case she would be 'forensically aware'.

Melanie, however, was not out of the woods: more concrete evidence was found during the meticulous forensic search of Bill's car. Sifting their way through the particles of dust and bits vacuumed up, Tom Lesniak and his forensics team found microscopic traces 'that to me look[ed] like it could be possibly human tissue,' said Lesniak, as reported by NBC News. DNA testing showed them to be from Bill McGuire; and the medical examiner identified the particles as skin with associated fibrous connective tissue – and therefore from deep layers of the skin which would not normally be shed by a live human being.

This was a very significant find. The reader will remember that Melanie had already admitted moving the Nissan to the car park at the Flamingo motel that night. Prosecutor Prezioso said that it all added up. Melanie had picked up traces of Bill's tissue on the soles of her shoes before she had cleaned up and, that the particles had been transferred to his car when she had driven it to Atlantic City.

At the trial a computer expert told the jury about incriminating internet searches that had been made during the days before Bill's death. 'The search history, which was extensive, included searches for such items or topics as 'undetectable poisons', 'state gun laws', 'instant poison', 'fatal insulin doses', 'instant undetectable poisons', 'how to commit murder', 'chloral hydrate', 'neuromuscular blocking agents', 'sedatives' and 'Nembutal', *and* a local Walgreens (a major American pharmacy store chain). Chloral hydrate – a powerful but uncommon sedative – was of particular interest to the police because, as mentioned earlier, a phial of the stuff was found in Bill's car. Moreover, the Google searches led police to a branch of Walgreens and a prescription for chloral hydrate in the name of an RMA patient in the clinic where Melanie worked. It had been filled at the pharmacy just a mile from the day care centre where Melanie dropped off and picked up her children on 28 April.

With the noose tightening around her neck, the prosecutor pointed out that Melanie had access to the prescription pad and would certainly have in the past written out prescriptions for her boss, and sometimes signed them on his behalf. The prescription in question featured the signature of Dr Bradley Miller – Melanie's boss and lover. He was also the state's star witness. Under examination:

Prezioso: Sir, did you write that prescription?

Dr Miller: No, I did not.

Prezioso: Are you familiar with the handwriting on those two prescriptions?

Dr Miller: Yes.

Prezioso: And whose handwriting do you believe it to be?

Dr Miller: It appears to be Melanie's.

Melanie McGuire glared at her former lover. Her face crumpled up and the corners of her mouth dropped. Despite the fact that she had obviously forged Miller's signature on a prescription for chloral hydrate, in a letter to me this devious woman wrote: 'Bradley betrayed me. There is no decency in him at all.'

But the jury must have been privately asking themselves what had motivated the defendant to commit such a brutal, calculated crime. The answer was not long in coming.

In his testimony, Dr Miller told the court that he and Melanie had spoken of getting married and having children in the future but – possibly because Melanie was afraid that if she filed for divorce Bill would take their two sons and 'disappear' with them – they did not have immediate plans to divorce their spouses. Future plans, the prosecutor insinuated, that Melanie felt would never come true while Bill was still alive, at least.

Despite a spirited defence that revealed a few snags in the state's case, especially regarding the computer searches and the black plastic garbage bags, after deliberating for four days the jury foreperson announced that they had reached a unanimous verdict. McGuire was guilty of six of the ten counts. She was sentenced to two life sentences plus ten years for desecration of human remains and five for perjury. Her later appeals were unsuccessful, so she will die behind bars; most likely ruing the day she hadn't gone down the second-degree route, that she had shot Bill in self-defence, afterwards panicking and stupidly disposing of the body in the manner that she had.

The question we might now ask ourselves is: does Melanie Lyn McGuire really deserve to be dubbed 'The Ice Queen'? I reiterate: for the vast majority of her life – all but a week of it – she was a dedicated nurse who cared passionately about her patients and who wanted to bring children into this world. No one could fault her for any of that.

Melanie was unhappy in her marriage. As we have read from her letters, she admits that she should have left Bill way back. I also sense that here we find a well-educated young woman who was seeking the perfect husband – a stable professional man, whom she finally found in Dr Miller. Had she played it more sensibly, left Bill much earlier and played things with a straight legal bat, then that would have been the right thing to do. What would have been better: a messy divorce or a natural-life prison term?

It doesn't bode well to speak ill of the dead, but two issues have come to my mind over the course of this chapter. The first being that while a couple's relationship might seem all rosy to outsiders, one usually never knows what marital tensions exist behind shuttered windows and closed doors.

Every failure teaches a man something, to wit, that he will probably fail again next time.

H.L. Mencken: *A Little Book in C Major*, 1916

On Bill's gambling? Several of his friends were contradictory – one minute saying that Bill was not addicted to gambling then saying that he was a fanatic at blackjack; a 'high-roller' who fluttered with sometimes as much as $10,000 during a trip to Atlantic City, where he was considered a favoured client to the degree he gambled to such an extent he was awarded 'comp points' by his favourite casino with free perks thrown in. It would be right to acknowledge that he did win big *sometimes*, but we have no idea of his losses either for we all know gambling is a mug's game.

Whether or not Bill McGuire was a 'compulsive gambler' we will never know. In her letters to me, Melanie McGuire doesn't really touch on the subject. They were not a wealthy family by a long chalk and more than a family's financial health is at stake when gambling problems enter the picture. I know from my own research that Bill McGuire was ducking and diving, trying all sorts of shady business schemes and scams to make an extra buck. More to the point, thousands of gamblers live in a fantasy world, always dreaming of hitting the jackpot while losing their shirts at the same time, all of which can cause much domestic stress. So I believe Melanie when she claims that Bill was becoming more agitated and paranoid by the week. Perhaps some physical violence came into play. Melanie says that she was not sure if Bill knew about her affair with her boss, adding: 'very possibly he did'. She also claims that she placed her children first; that she adored her two young sons, that she wanted to raise them 'not losing a father at such early ages, just as I had done aged five'. But that is a somewhat strange statement to make when she did exactly the opposite in blowing away the kids' father; to deprive them of their dad and herself for the remainder of their lives.

151

Yes, she had been having an affair with the married Dr Miller. It would be fair to say that what both lacked in their respective homes *might* have been found in each other's arms. No terrible sin here, either – at least not unless one spends one's life living a puritanical existence, with one's nose stuffed into the Holy Book every minute of the day.

And what of Melanie McGuire's guilt? This chapter does not judge her, because a jury of her peers has already done so, with the state of New Jersey confirming that she committed a most heinous crime and without meaning to be crass here, a murder is a murder whichever way we judge such a crime. As is par for the homicidal course, this case bore all the hallmarks of sensationalism, which guaranteed headline-grabbing print. The petite 'Ice Queen' had shot her man, chopped up his body and thrown his remains off a bridge into the ice-cold Chesapeake Bay. It is almost too horrible to think about, is it not? However, as mentioned earlier, I believe that had Melanie come clean from the outset – confessed that she had shot Bill after a violent argument, had bought the gun a few days beforehand because she sensed he was going to hurt her, that she had obtained the chloral hydrate to calm him down, make him sleep, but then panicked, killed him and disposed of the body as she did – then she would have received a lighter sentence. In so many ways, Melanie dug her own grave using a treacherous spade of her own making, so what does my reader make of that?

Her defence argued that within twenty seconds either Melanie *or* Bill could have searched the internet on their home computer for information on gambling in Atlantic City, followed by a search for poisons. C'mon guys and gals, we can plain as daylight see that any suggestion that Bill was looking up Atlantic City's gambling venues does not hold water. He'd have known them and the locale like the back of his hand. Furthermore, it makes far more sense that Melanie, having checked out gambling venues her husband might be frequenting in Atlantic City – perhaps with a view to taking his car and then moving it to a different venue – should also then look online for a drug she could use to knock her husband out.

There are said to be thousands of individuals who painstakingly plan the perfect murder. However, they fail – to their cost – to plan the perfect getaway, for the devil is in the details. Melanie McGuire was too careful but plumb-dumb stupid at the same time; lacking streetwise common sense, she left a trail of circumstantial clues, none of which would have pointed to her guilt if they had stood alone. Instead, she left a trail of links that formed a chain of evidence so strong that no one could ignore their significance. Cold-blooded premeditation to kill was writ large over each blood-splattered page of her testimony.

If we follow the State's theory, then Melanie drugged her husband senseless while he was celebrating the purchase of their dream home with a glass of wine while their two boys were asleep in their beds. The next morning, after dropping off the kids at school, she returned home, placed a pillow over her still-sleeping husband's head, took out the revolver, shot him dead and then cut him up. Somewhat unfortunately, however, all of that leaves us with some other questions. Where was the blood splatter, if indeed he was shot in their home or even in their garage? Perhaps a pillow might have stopped the blowback, who knows? Could her thorough scrubbing of the apartment really have left not a single clue? Did she shoot him someplace else? How did this tiny woman drag her large, deadweight husband, dead or alive, into his car? And where did she dismember the body? For my part, there are a whole set of questions one cannot pair with answers, and this, as I am sure you will agree, sums up the dreadful enigma that still surrounds Melanie Lyn McGuire.

Oh, what a tangled web we weave,

When first we practise to deceive!

Sir Walter Scott, *Marmion:*

A Tale of Flodden Field (1808)

Letters from killers are the central raison d'être for this book's existence, so I leave you with a lengthy letter typed by Melanie McGuire in the guise of a mobster and received by the State's attorney while she was on bail. It purports to explain why Melanie could *not* have killed her husband, so enjoy it because it gives us a unique and rare insight into the mind of a devious and twisted woman weaving together truths, half-truths, downright lies and a whole mile of crap into a narrative that exposes her for who she truly is. We will also learn a lot more about the relationship between Melanie and Bill McGuire than she would ever say out loud, and this I am obliged to tell the reader was originally reproduced in my book *Talking with Serial Killers: Dead Men Walking*:

Mr Harvey,

Your office and the media have reflected on the life and the death of William T. McGuire, and you've made it obvious that you intend to prosecute his wife. You and the media have exalted him as a decent person and a victim. He was a victim, all right. Of his greed, his big ego, and his even bigger mouth. I first met McGuire because we knew a lot of the same people. He was friendly enough at first, and loved to talk about himself along with anything and everything else he could claim to know anything about. He talked about work. He talked about AC [Atlantic City]. He talked about a house. About Virginia. About his wife. His sister. His ex-wife. You couldn't shut the guy up, which was part of his own undoing.

McGuire bragged about his position at NJIT [New Jersey Institute of Technology]. Said he had the placed [*sic*] wired and that the boss man had no idea what he was up to, which is how I imagine he got out and got away as much as he did. He talked of his connections at the local and state level, in various departments of state. How they could and would play into his consulting business. He talked of corruption at the health departments, and how it was given a pretty face by NJIT. He bragged about he once worked two full time jobs, at NJIT and at a local health office, and how even doing that he still had enough time to get in all his side action [women] and get home without the wife being any wiser. He talked about all his scams at work, the anonymity the access to some of the technologies could give him, to do almost anything he wanted at work or outside of it. He talked about blackmailing some of the higher ups at the state level who were doling out grant work to people collecting unemployment. He seemed to be unfazed by the stink his confrontations could raise in the office, stating it was their own fault for putting themselves in a compromised position to begin with. He talked of overthrowing his boss at the college, and about overthrowing the state level boss with the help of a guy named Ray. Did your office bother to note any of that during their thorough investigation? I think not.

He also loved to gamble, loved to flash card. I'd see him in AC, and at some private games to [*sic*]. The funny part is that he was a pretty good player but his ego wouldn't let him lose. He won a lot, but when he lost, he lost big and chased the money as hard as he chased some of the tail [women] that hangs around those places. He blamed everyone when he lost, the house, the dealer, even his wife, if you can imagine that. I personally find your observation that his death could have nothing to do with gambling one of the most hilarious things you've said publicly. Have you ever BEEN to AC?

Don't believe me? Ask his wife about the Stakehouse in North Jersey, and about an unfortunate accident coming home from work there late one night. What he didn't tell her was that he wasn't working, and he had lost a bundle. I heard him talking about getting pulled over on top of it that night, and how it was her [Melanie's] fault. I laughed. You can't be serious, man. She takes that from you? That and more. She likes it, is what he said and that put me off. You want to screw around on your old lady? Fine. You want to gamble away the family nut? That's fine to [*sic*]. But saying she likes it and seeing that he believed it blew me away. No wonder she ended up in bed with some doctor. Of

ARTHUR SHAWCROSS
91-B-0193
P.O. Box AG
FALLSBURG, N.Y. 12733-0116
U.S.A.

Dear Christopher,

I will SEE you.

Sincerely

Arthur Shawcross

The letters and other documents shown here and on the following seven pages are all from the author's extensive private archive of correspondence, over many years, between him and numerous convicted killers.

Arthur John Shawcross (1945–2008), 'the Genesee River Killer'.

INTERVIEW CONSENT FORM

N.Y.S. DEPARTMENT OF CORRECTIONAL SERVICES

I ARTHUR J. SHAWCROSS · 91-B-0193 hereby grant permission to the
Inmate Name and Number

New York State Department of Correctional Services and CHRISTOPHER BERRY-DEE
Name of newspaper,

to make use of my name, comments, still or
publication, radio/TV station

motion pictures, voice recordings and/or video tape of me for any legitimate purposes.

Including publication in news media and for professional and institutional purposes.

Signature Arthur J Shawcross Date 1/5/93

Witness Charles Gramlich Facility Sullivan

CHARLES A. GRAMLICH
Notary Public, State of New York
Sullivan County Clerk's #2086
Commission Expires September 5, 1993

NOTICE: inmates who are a party to any pending or anticipated legal proceeding are
advised to notify their attorneys prior to conducting a media interview.

DEAR CHRISTOPHER,
THANK you FOR THE LETTER.
I would do THE 30 MINUTE INTERVIEW, but
CAN you TELL ME iF THERE is A CAMERA INVOLVED
OR do WE TALK TOGETHER? WHICH EVER is OK.
you have SPOKEN oF FUNDS AND THEY ARE
MUCH NEEDED, MY WIFE is iN A bAd WAY RIGHT
NOW. SHE is SICK WITH THE FLU-CHEST cold.
Plus heR Job is UNSTABLE FROM ALL THE Pubicity
THAT has GENERATED AROUND ME. EVERYONE is
TRYING To get ME To SPEAK To THEM but I
WAIT. THERE is MUCH STILL going on iN THE
CITY oF ROCHESTER, NEW york. people WANT MY
opinion. you CAN get iT plus WHAT MY THOUGHTS
ARE.
WHAT ARE THE QUESTION's you'd ASK oF
ME? AS long AS MY LAWYER UNDERSTANDS
And WHAT I CAN ANSWER.

Now THEN, pLEASE have THE FUNDS SENT
To MY WiFE ROSE And SHE will disburse THEM
FoR bECAUSE oF TAXES.
Do NoT SEND ANyoNE To boTHER heR.

ROSE M. SHAWCROSS

UNITED STATES oF AMERICA

THANK you.

P.S.
How is THE LITTLE oNE doing?.   RESPECTFULLY

Arthur J Shawcross

2-19-08

Dear Christopher,

Recieved your short note. Your letter you wrote me on January 3, 2008. Dont go adrift. I recieve the above mention letter on January 28, 2008.

Cause of the ass-hole mail-room staff who sit on their ass picking their nose or whatever.

Has I express I am more then well to write a book about my crime and express my side of the story.

You mentioned that IWC, are very keen to work on a T.V. documentary which is rubber-stamped by me, and with a view to interview me. Only trouble is California has a law now that forbid the media from interviewing dead row inmate on camera. Only way they prison allow interview is in visiting room and the reporter can would bring in pen and paper. No tape recorder.

I would like do the book in stages. Like a foundation of a house.

Like ① Basic information like information about my parents, How or they were went I was born. Date of my birth to age 5.

② the age of 6-12 - covering school years, any crimes I committed

③ 13-19 How I was treated and how I treat people

④ 20-40 informing about my crimes else.

Carl Phillip Jablonski (1946–2019), 'the Death Row Teddy'.

Dear Christopher,   26 Jan 2008

    I apologize for not responding to your first letter. While I am indeed interested in telling my story eventually, and in depth, to a reputable news outlet, I am currently involved in appealing my conviction and sentence. As a result, I must defer to my appellate counsel and their advice regarding the matter. At this time we are having some difficulty with our telephone communications, and I've not been able to contact them directly. I realize that contacting me via conventional mail is less than expedient — as a result, I'd like to provide you with the contact information of one of my closest friends, █████████████, as I speak to her daily, and she might function as an intermediary. Thank you for contacting me — again, my apologies for not responding sooner.

Warm Regards,
Melanie McGuire

Melanie McGuire
#584496 / Smith Hall S-9
EDNA MAHAN
CORRECTIONAL FACILITY FOR WOMEN
PO BOX 4004
CLINTON NJ 08809

Air Mail

Chris Berry-Lee
█████████████████

00144X1000

Melanie Lyn McGuire (1972–), 'the Ice Queen'.

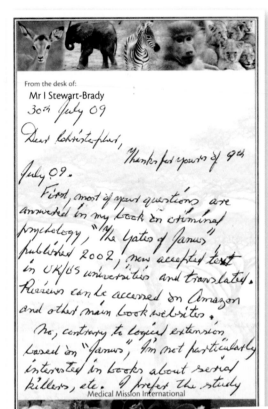

30th July 09

Dear Christopher,

Thanks for yours of 9th July 09.

First, most of your questions are answered in my book on criminal psychology, "The Gates of Janus" published 2002, now accepted text in UK/US universities and translated. Reviews can be accessed on Amazon and other main book websites.

No, contrary to logical extension based on "Janus", I'm not particularly interested in books about serial killers, etc. I prefer the study

of major criminals, such as Blair, Bush and their profiteering henchmen. As I've always stated since teenage years, you can't beat "decent, honest, respectable people" when it comes to global serial slaughter, theft, greed, treachery and hypocrisy. Which is why they exploit petty, underclass crime and criminals to distract attention from themselves and their threadbare pretensions / claims to moral superiority. Nothing new or profound in any of this, of course; just generally convenient to ignore such unpopular juxtapositions. // Please acknowledge receipt.

Best wishes,

IS Brady

PS: The current satirical gall of Cherie Blair lecturing the nation on the "horrors" of "knife crime", highlights the absurdity and arrogance of the class. Greed has replaced vocation in the professions.

Ian Stewart Brady (1938–2017), 'the Moors Murderer'.

HAL KAREN 03-A-3087
GREEN HAVEN CORRECTIONAL FACILITY
P.O.BOX 4000
STORMVILLE, NY 12582-4000

CHRISTOPHER BERRY-DEE

14 DECEMBER 2009

Dear Chris,
I hope it's O.K. to call you Chris. It's always nice to get a letter from a former
soldier. Under different circumstances I'm sure we could down some pints and exchange
stories. Anyway I was kind of surprised when I got your letter because I feel that my
case was not really a big deal and they put my military experience into the picture to
elevate the picture inorder to get a conviction. I have never been able to tell my
story before and I don't think it's anything what the T.V. shows had portrayed and if
Dr. Baden would not have testified for the DA as he did, I would not be here and if I
would have had money enough for a better defence I surely would have been able to
prove my innocence of murder. So with all that I'll give you a quick gist of what
"REALLY" happened. I meet Tammy at a topless bar outside of FT. BRAGG N.C. I had just
returned from Haiti after a six month deployment and needed some winding down. I ended
up getting her pregnant so we went to las Vegas and got married. She used drugs when I
meet her but during the pregnancy she did not. When Hunter was born she starred using
drugs again and that's when everything went down hill. I could not get her to stop and
she did not want to. One day I came home and found her dead in the bathroom. For a
long time I covered her drug problem from people, it was embarrassing. So I took the
body and I got rid of it and I told everyone she left because she has done this before
with her first child which she left with her mother and took off. But I did not hide
it good enough. I know what I did was wrong but I had my reasons and if you are still
interested I will tell you them. But I feel that after you read this letter you are
not going to even want to use this story. And as the investigator that you are I'll

Hal Karen (1960–).

bring up just two points that you can check out for yourself. 1. How can someone go
into a court room and tell a jury that this person died from strangulation when you
only have some bones and not even any neck bones. 2. After almost 3 years of the body
being in the woods and they still managed to find a piece of liver from her body which
this alone is incredible and they test it for drugs and it comes up positive with 30
nanograms of cocaine byproduct, How can you say that that is not enough to kill
someone. You would think that there had to be a awful lot to even show anything after
3 years. if you know a forensic pathologist ask him or her what they think. Anyway I
don't think I'm being much help to you. Like I said before once you read this letter
you'll just back away because its not the story everyone thinks it is. I tell you this
and I have no idea what they said in the T.V. shows which I believe there are several
That I'm not the person they made me out to be. I never hurt anyone in my life without
a reason. I don't know how much help this letter is to you and your book but I do have
a lot to say, its probable just does not help you. Actually I'm the one who needs
help. Sometimes I wish there were more veterans with special skills that can help
other veterans out with out charging a arm and a leg but that would be asking to much.
Well if your still interested write me back or write me back even if your not, its
nice to get a little mail, I don't have a lot of people who write me because when
things go wrong people tend to turn their backs on you and just forget you. If you can
I would like to read your books, I do a lot of reading. So if you can and if you want
please send me copies of your books

Take care and good luck with your books.

Best Wishes

Hal

HAL (aka RAMBO) (aka HALANATOR)
(Thats the name the guys gave me)

Ronald DeFeo 75A4053
Box 338, Eastern C.F.
Napanoch, N.Y. 12458-0338

Christopher Berry-Dee
The Conifers
Botley Road
Shedfield
SO3 2JH
Hampshire
England

(June 2, 1993)

Dear Christopher, I will get right to the point okay. After Talking to My Attorney ███████████ (After Reading) All Your Letters, Promise's Deal's, etc.(And seeing Now How its going on Two Year's Yes, "We" have come to the conclusion that you have been selling us a dream and trying to make money off of me and my case behind our back as Your Last Letter with the tape recording You wanted me to do said it all.

If You Cant or Won't Send Some Type of Money in Good Faith, then We Are Requesting the Immediate Return of Every thing I sent to You as Well As Letter's ███████████ ████████████████ sent to you as well Because I Asked them to. (So the Choice is Now Your's As if this is not done one way or another, then the correct action will (Be Taken with the U.S. Attorney's Office etc.

Very Truly Your's
Ronald J. DeFeo
Ronald J. DeFeo

:copy to ███████████ /

Ronald 'Butch' Joseph DeFeo Jr (1951–2021), 'the Amityville Horror'.

Ronnie DeFeo 75A4053
Drawer B.
Stormville, New York 12582-0010

Christopher Berry-Dee, The Conifer's, ████████ ████████ England.

(March 13, 1994)

Dear Christopher, I hope my letter finds you in the best of health and the Best Of Spirit.

To This Day Why I was Transfered To the Worse As I was in The Best Max Prison in the State, NO ONE KNOW'S and Above is my New Address.

"NOW" Did You Ever Recieve the Tape's As ███████████ And Mr. ███████ Springer what are all Witnesses in My Case and who know ███████ Personally Told Her to Mail you the Tape's Five Week's Ago Yes.

I CAN TELL You There is A Problem Now with ███████████ "Attorney" As She is Blaming ███████ And I am in the Middle. Could You please let me Know what's Happening so I Know what to do As Chris its Going On three year's with "US" You and I As we have Come A long way my "Friend" As the Word Friend is Very serious As they are Very few in My Life. Well I will close and Await Your Reply /// My Friend, Thank you and Take Care,

My Best Wishes
Ronnie

9-16-09

Dear Christopher,

Hi?, I hope this letter finds you doing well, and I'm sorry it has taken me so long to start to answer your letter.

It was good to hear back from you (20 mins) and I want to thank you for taking the time to write back to me. I also want to thank you for taking an interest in me and my story. I'm not sure what it is you plan to do as far as the writing goes, but all I want is to tell my story and maybe it will help someone, somewhere. As Victoria might of told you it's not about the money, and I would never ask someone to pay me. I didn't do that with her, and I won't do it with you. Besides I'm not allowed to profit from my crimes. :)

If you wanted to help me out I would be very thankful for whatever you did or do. At the same time this is not something you have to ~~do~~. If you want to send me money for stamps and other things enclosed is some slips that show you how to do that. You can also use J-Pay and Western Union to send money right to my account. If you have any questions just let me know, or maybe Victoria can help you.

As to what you said in your letter I will tell you what I remember and know as best as I can. This was a long time ago, and some things you just can't remember.

It all started in Rupert, West Virginia. That is where I lived, but I was born at the nearest hospital which was in Clifton Forge, Virginia.

NO LETTER
ONLY SLIP + MONEY ORDER

1. Use black or dark blue ink.
2. Print CAPITAL letters and numbers in block style.
3. PRINT all requested information.
4. Money Order, Cashiers Check, or Certified Bank Draft MUST be payable to "INMATE TRUST FUND" and include the inmate name and number. ALSO MY NAME
5. Mail Money order, Cashiers Check, or Certified Bank Draft and completed form to the Bureau of Finance & Accounting/Inmate Trust (address below).

Florida Department of Corrections   (866) 209-7250   IF QUESTIONS CALL
Inmate Trust Fund
Centerville Station
P.O. Box #12100
Tallahassee, FL 32317-2100

CHRIS,
MAIL SLIP AND INTERNATIONAL MONEY ORDER OR CASHELS CHECK TO THE ADDRESS SHOWN

Gary Ray Bowles (1962–2019), 'the I-95 Killer'.

Christopher Berry-Dee   January 10, 2008

████████ ████████
██ █████ █████
█████ ██, ███ ████

England

Christopher,

I received your 2 January letter. At first I was simply going to forward it to my attorney to place in the file of vultures flying overhead wanting to pick my bones for personal profit. I also often get crackpots who write claiming to be someone else, offering friendship and financial support. The last two, a woman named ██████ █████ from Fort Lauderdale, Florida who was moving to North Tonawanda, NY to go to college. The address in Florida was a phony and the address in NY is a pizza restaurant. Shortly after that I received some kind of release agreement which was seized by the prison mailroom (prisoners are not allowed to sign contracts except through their attorneys) from someone named ██████ █████ postmarked Colorado. When your letter arrived my first reaction was to laugh. It seems the past few month period has brought out those named "Chris." Please understand, for my protection, my attorney must first check you out.

I decided to respond, possibly wasting the precious postage, and send you one letter setting out

John Robinson 45690
E.D.C.F.
P.O. Box 311
El Dorado, KS
      67042
     USA

WICHITA KS 672

20 FEB 2008 PM 1 T

Christopher Berry-Dee
████████ ████████
██ █████ █████
██████   ███ ███

England

00144*1000

John 'J.R.' Edward Robinson (1943–), 'the Slavemaster'.

course, you could say it was her own fault for marrying him, more her fault for staying.

More laughter from me when you leaked to the papers that this doctor friend of his wife's turned 'state's evidence'. There was nothing that man could of [sic] said that would hurt her for the simple reason that she didn't kill him. So that either makes you a liar, or him a coward who makes up stories to save his own sorry skin. Either way. I guess she never learned her lesson about choosing men.

Also, if you haven't figured out yet that his sister knew more of what he was up to than what she ever let on, you have had your head further in the sand than I imagined. He talked about her a lot, and I think they had a weird relationship, those two [Bill and his sister]. The guys used to joke about it a lot. She [Bill's sister], did something with real estate – he bitched about paying for her license, and he got her to give him access to one of those agent only sites. He would plug away on there for days at a time, looking up houses, looking up tax records of people he knew. She [Bill's sister] had a husband who owned some kind of pharmacy, and he talked a lot about all the scams there, and cash to be had. But in the same breath he [Bill] would complain how selfish she was not to want to put her ass on the line, whatever that meant. I tuned out a lot after I figured out how he lacked a certain amount of follow through with some ideas. He shrugged it off, saying there are all kinds of strings that get set up around stuff like that. He wanted the cash, but didn't want to get his hands dirty where anyone could see, was more of what I thought. As for the other sister, I guess the apple didn't fall far. He played us a phone message she [Melanie] left him, laughing at what a crazy she was. The message had said she would sue him and he wouldn't get his house he was buying. Christmas must have been something at their house.

We kept McGuire close because he was good for certain things – obviously things you'll never find out about. But in time he developed a drug habit. He even tried dealing. Then he decided he wanted a piece [of the action] to [sic]. We privately agreed against putting one in his hands. He tried Camden, Trenton, even Newark, but his problem was that he looked like a cop. No surprise the wife bought it, even if she was a damn fool for not knowing better. He always complained about how stupid she had gotten. I even asked him, wasn't she stupid when you married her? He said no way, his first wife was stupid but good in bed. The second he said was a lousy lay, but pretty. He claimed she had been smart but let herself go to hell after having kids. Which is why he felt completely justified in sticking it in anything [women] that walked. Personally, I thought he was either gay or sexually bent. He said his wife was so stupid he come home high one night, and when she asked him why his eyes were blood shot he told her he had taken viagra [sic]. When she asked why he got pissed and told her even that couldn't help him get it up for her. Nice guy. My point being that Billy Mac [Bill McGuire] liked an altered state of mind. I'll bet you twice your pension that the toxicology report showed more than a little viagra [*sic*] How about [it] H? Do you believe yet that I'm more than some random psycho writing to harass you? If not, you will.

Pausing to take a breath, and perhaps have a cup of tea, we can see Melanie's vitriolic mind working at full speed here. Not only is she giving her husband a post-mortem shit storm thrashing, she is dumping all over the State's attorney at will.

There is no doubt in my mind that she was under immense stress, her once stable life falling around her like an upscale house of cards. With nobody willing to talk to her – closest friends shocked at what had happened to Bill, her doctor lover leaving dust in his wake like Road Runner in the *Looney Tunes* cartoon series – Melanie had become persona non grata, someone to be avoided at all and *any* cost.

This 'Mafia' letter is nothing more than an hysterical, conspiratorial rant, with Melanie letting off steam while in the drink. When I compare the lengthy correspondence she sent to me with this letter, if there were invisible subtext between the lines we would see Melanie McGuire's psychopathology as clear as if it were written bold with one of Donald Trump's Sharpies. Even more fascinating are the references here in which she deliberately belittles herself in the 'second person' just as she does in her 'first-person' letters penned to me. It is her way of trying to show that she has her own weaknesses; attempts to show that she is a fair-minded individual – a cunning ploy, indeed.

But, let's move back to the letter in hand. And here Melanie's conspiracy theories are given full rein, for it seems that Bill McGuire had *her* death in mind, not the other way around if one was to believe all that this wannabe 'made man' would have us believe:

Here's a question for you, Mr Harvey. McGuire was talking about the life insurance he was going to get. A mill [million] on the wife. Two on him. He talked about Virginia, and how that was where he was going once he made his money here [New Jersey]. How the wife hated it. When I asked him how he was planning on convincing her to move, he smiled and said he would be rid of her by then. Did [it] dawn on you that Mrs McGuire, in her 'selfish' plot to kill her husband, didn't bother to wait for him to actually purchase the insurance? Oh, she got the boyfriend with money, she didn't need it. First, I don't know anybody who would pass on two mill, money or not. Second, even if she coaxed that boyfriend away from his happy home, how much do you think it would leave for her after he paid out his old lady? I'm telling you that I don't know what he meant when he said he'd be 'rid' of her by then, but I have a couple of thoughts. And two mill on him and one on her casts a little doubt on his motivation should anything tragic happen. Did any of you in the midst of your 'dogged detective work' even ask her about it? Or are you going to sit there with a straight face and tell me McGuire meant he wanted a divorce?

Enough already, Melanie. We have all cottoned on by now that you have lost the plot. Actually, Mel, the good doctor probably never had any intention of ever leaving his wife and three children. It was all pillow talk, Mel. He was putting you in the 'Promised Land', Melanie, just so he could give you a good bonking whenever he felt the need – in between treating patients, if needs must. Moreover, and as you have a literary bent, perhaps you might have acquainted yourself with this quote from American author, John Bytheway: 'Sometimes you have to go through the wilderness before you get to the Promised Land.' Precisely, Mel, and the correctional wilderness is *exactly* where you are right now. Oh, sorry, you were saying?

Don't get me wrong. I'm not going for sainthood myself. But what got to us about him was that he eventually turned on everyone. He talked about going to the press about a lot of money the college spent on equipment for a terrorism database that no one bothered to use. He talked about getting 'rid' of his old lady. He talked about turning in his sister's husband to the pharmacy board. Even blood wasn't thicker than water with this guy. And he wouldn't shut up. Didn't matter if he liked you or didn't or even if he owed you. He feared no payback from anyone. I don't even think he wanted the piece out of fear. Not a guy like that. He wanted to intimidate people with it. What intimidated people more was his running mouth.

Hey, Melanie, or mafiosa John aka 'Teflon Don' Gotti, or 'Cadillac Frank', or 'Ice Pick Willie' from the New Jersey outfit, or whoever you are, put down that bottle of whatever you are drinking and focus. Pray tell us what the prosecutor *should* have done. Please?

You shouldn't care that the wife bought a gun. You shouldn't care that the suitcases were hers. You shouldn't care that the garbage bags match. I'm telling you that you shouldn't care if there's a video footage of her smiling and waving from the docks of Virginia Beach. Know why? Obviously you don't, so I'll make it simple. And it's not because she couldn't physically have done what it took two – and at one point three men to do.

To do what, Mr Joseph 'Joe Bananas' Bonanno, 'cos you're certainly not a sidekick of Joseph 'Joey Brains' Ambrosino, are you? As you 'made guys' should know, 'Mel the Moll' pumped iron in a gym as well as pumping other chappies. A petite but a strong lass.

It's because Billy Mac brought everything that was needed to do him, and more. Not on purpose of course, but it was easier than anyone could believe. And the fight with his old lady? Probably he saved her life leaving her that morning, even if all he was doing was looking to get the hell out of Dodge for a few days. I'm guessing you didn't find any of his cell phones – the ones that weren't traceable, anyway. Point is if it was necessary, if she was with him, she would have been done the same as him. Probably worse, if you catch my drift, even if she was a lousy lay like he said. She ended up helping us, but not in any way you or your dogged detectives think. Her bad luck was our good fortune. And Billy Mac left the door wide open.

So why write this? Well, I can tell you now to abandon the print analysis, and even analysis of the type [of this letter]. This will be photocopied and handled in a manner you couldn't trace even if you did your job. So it's not hurting me any. And I've got nothing for the wife, or against her. But I read about the kids. The father they're better off without, but they don't need a Ma on death row. So now it's up to you to figure it out. She can't help you much, but did you ever even ask her? I know, you think this is a hoax. Well, allow me to part with some facts that should finally convince you otherwise:

1. I'm taking the liberty of sending this to the media, in case you want to close your eyes to this same as you have everything else in this case.

2. I'm sending it to the wife's lawyer.

3. The way the articles read last year, it made it seem like his arms were cut off. They weren't.

4. He was wearing nothing but purple briefs when you found him.

5. Ever figure out where the weights came from?

NOW DO YOU BELIEVE ME????

I *don't* believe you, Melanie. Nor, dare I say, will a single one of my readers worldwide. If only you had been as forensically aware in the killing and dismemberment of 'Billy Mac' as you were in sending out an untraceable photocopy of the aforementioned letter to the DA, you'd be down at the shore right now enjoying helpings of your favourite foie gras. So, Melanie, I guess that we can now part company with a large au revoir, along with a seasoning of bon appétit. However, I challenge anyone to find similar correspondence sent to any prosecutor in history typed out by a Mafia mobster whose bear-paw writing skills might stretch to: 'Yeah boss, ya wanna me to go feed Anthony 'Big Tuna' Accardo to the fishes?'

As I said before, Melanie was an intellectually smart woman but she was *not* streetwise. She undertook a course of action – murder – which was evil, wrong . . . and stupid. Then she proceeded to dig herself in further and further with her fantastical lies and subterfuges, flailing in her tangle of deceit.

What a Novel Idea!

It's a good binding, you see, and I thought they'd be all good
books . . . But it seems one mustn't judge by the outside.
This is a puzzlin' world.

GEORGE ELIOT (MARY ANN EVANS),
THE MILL ON THE FLOSS (1860)

Taking a breather here; a short break from blood, guts and
murder most foul and into what amounts to some trivia, as is
my wont occasionally, 'don't judge a book by its cover' is the
expression warning us that one should not judge the worth or
value of something by its outward appearance alone and is one
that appears in many guises – 'appearances can be deceptive',
the many variants of the aphorism 'all that glitters is not gold',
'beauty is but skin deep'. Often in my books, on TV, or during
lectures, I use a similar analogy with regard to the outward
normality of the serial killers and mass-murderers whom I have
interviewed. The different masks they wear to conceal the beasts

sleeping and breathing deeply within. Moreover, my *Talking with Serial Killers: Stalkers* offers some terrifying examples of how we often misjudge these 'human books' by their socially acceptable covers.

With letters typed or handwritten, or any form of electronic correspondence, be they the inane tweets spewed out by sociopathic 'influencers', or an email from a business associate, or an actual handwritten letter from an old friend, most of the time we read and believe what is intended to be conveyed. As Margaret Gullan-Whur says in her aforementioned graphology study, glancing at a person's handwriting (or even a page of their typing) is a bit like meeting someone for the first time. Not until we have read more of their correspondence, or met the person several times, do we start to see their true character, good or otherwise, and form our own opinions about them.

With individuals such as those included in this book, we already know who they are and the grim reasons why they are in prison. So, in this regard we do know something about them from the get-go. Their correspondence tells us a little more, yet it is what they don't say, or refuse to say, that hopefully tells us a great deal more about that person's psychopathology.

Donald Trump's signature tells us what sort of man he is. What is the point of slamming his Sharpie signature across a page? What is he trying to prove, who is he trying to impress? We know a great deal about this man's over-inflated self-narrative up until the present date. Being the brash, unrepentant sociopath that he is, his signature echoes his mindset perfectly, and most graphologists agree that the overall significance of large writing, is that the writer *needs* or *demands space to protect himself*. Impulse stemming from pride, vanity, enthusiasm, dynamism, strong feelings or vigorous activity may cause this need – the need to protect a basically weak ego. Indeed, every time we see 'The Donald' his face is the colour of a Valencia orange and he didn't get that from sunbathing either. However, I betcha that once he takes his clothes off his skin reverts to the colour of plaster cast from neck down to his toes.

Without wishing to be as impertinent, as others are far more qualified to discuss the subject than myself, to me it seems as a general rule of thumb that very small writing hints at a shyness in character, while large writing denotes quite the opposite.

Here's another perspective. One cannot help but be stunned by the masterful oils painted by Richard Dadd, an English artist of the Victorian era. Dadd was noted for his depictions of fairies and otherworldly folk, depicted with an extraordinary (one might say obsessive) attention to detail. We admire the beauty of his creations yet never, *ever*, do we wonder from where his ideas came. At first glance, we would never know what made this superb painter's mind tick, and so would doubtless be shocked to learn that his mind was severely unbalanced, to the extent that he knifed his father (whom he believed to be Satan) to death, then escaped to France. There, while travelling to Paris, he tried to despatch a fellow passenger with a razor, however, and was swiftly subdued and taken into custody. He suffered from paranoid schizophrenia and died on 7 January 1886, aged sixty-eight, in the Broadmoor insane asylum, where he completed his most famous works. We behold the beauty of the artwork now brushed onto a once pristine white canvas, beauty being only skin deep – *as is the oil paint.*

Dadd was a man possessed by a dreadful insanity behind the scenes, and the same applies to another long-serving

Broadmoor patient, one William Chester Minor. While heavily sedated, and often chained to a wall, he became an important contributor to the *Oxford Dictionary*. Next time you thumb through it, look for the meaning of the word 'syndrome' and think of the Canadian comic-book creator and producer Blake Leibel, co-author of the graphic novel *Syndrome*, who was convicted of first-degree murder, aggravated mayhem and torture of his fiancée, Iana Kasian, in 2016. Kasian had given birth to their daughter only weeks before her murder. It was proved that Leibel used his graphic novel as a blueprint for the gruesome slaying, something described by prosecutors as 'a case of life imitating art'. It is believed that Kasian was kept alive while she suffered at least six hours of torture. Her body was then mutilated, and pieces of it were discovered in the trash. The novel that Leibel co-wrote featured depictions of bloodletting and when Kasian was found, nearly all of the blood had been drained from her organs.

Many of us have read at least one of Anne Perry's sixty novels, all the while totally unaware that she'd committed a terrible crime aged fifteen. In 1954, when she and her parents were living in New Zealand, she went by the name of Juliet Hulme. Her parents split up, and plans were made to send her to South Africa. Her best friend, Pauline Parker, wanted to come along, but her mother wouldn't allow it. A few days after Pauline was denied the opportunity to move, the two girls went on a walk down a trail with Parker's mother and bludgeoned her to death.

And I would be remiss in failing to mention William S. Burroughs, or María Carolina Geel, Krystian Bala or James Tiptree Jr (pen name of Alice Sheldon). If you have ever watched the true-crime Netflix docuseries *The Staircase*, then look up Michael Peterson. Then there is bank robber Albert Nussbaum, and E. Richard Johnson. And there are more – writers and creators, all of whom have taken the life of another human. For those who read their books, it can be hard to reconcile the storyteller and entertainer with the killer. However, the majority of writers do not kill, and the majority of killers do not write – as we have witnessed – very well at all.

Harvey 'The Hammer' Louis Carignan, aka 'The Want-Ad Killer'

I knew that she was going to falsely accuse me of rape, and as
I tried to talk sense into her she jumped out of the car
and bolted. Unintentionally, I picked up a tree limb and threw
it at her. It hit her one time and she fell down dead.
I hate people accusing me of rape when I have never raped any
woman. She should have kept her mouth shut so it
was her fault, not mine.

HARVEY LOUIS CARIGNAN: TO THE AUTHOR AT INTERVIEW

Author's note: I make no apology for including material about Carignan from my 2009 study of killers I have interviewed, now republished as *Talking with Serial Killers*. This chapter draws upon my previous published writings but used here in a different context; that of his letters to me and what was written, or not written, between the lines. The research I carried out at the time, and subsequently, remains valid.

Getting to the Minnesota Correctional Facility (aka MCF-Stillwater) took some doing. Especially if one is bringing in a TV documentary crew from London, then having to road-trip in a couple of Mitsubishi Shoguns across to snow-bound Minneapolis, stay for a few days interviewing cops, filming some POVs (points of view), then drive twenty-seven miles north-east up to MCF itself, tucked right up close and personal to the Wisconsin state line.

An industrial prison, MCF is the state's largest close-security institution for adult felons, with a population hovering around 1,320. I corresponded with one of its inmates, Harvey Carignan, for several years and finally interviewed him during a full-contact visit (i.e. unshackled) in March 1995. This was the first and only interview ever granted by 'The Hammer' since his arrest for multiple rape and homicide on 24 September 1974.

> The guy's the fuckin' Devil. They should have fried him years ago, period, an' they would have queued up to pull the switch. When he was dead, they should have driven a stake through his heart and buried him, digging him up a week later to ram another stake in, just to make sure he was fuckin' dead.
>
> Detective Russell J. Krueger, Chief Investigator
> on the Carignan case, Minneapolis PD:
> to the author at interview

Top tip: beware of bears wearing a cop's uniform because Russell Krueger, of Irish descent, is built like one and he's as mean as a grizzly whose home has just been destroyed by some lumberjacks. Then Russ added: 'And you're gonna film that asshole. He's a big mother [...] built like an ape, looks like an ape. Even now, in old age, he can still do one-arm pull-ups without breaking sweat.'

'No problem,' I replied. 'I've been writing to Harvey for ages. He's good to go with me. Any chance of us guys getting hold of the Carignan files? We love the Irish, I'm into Guinness, you know. Just a glimpse of the files ... we will give them back ... honestly.'

That Berry-Dee. He convinced me to go get the files and my supervisor gave me deep shit, but he did get to interview Harvey. God bless Chris. If it were St Patrick's Day I'd buy him a drink, but it ain't.

Detective Russell J. Krueger

If there were ever a label tagged 'amoral monstrosity', it would suit 'Harv' the Hammer' extremely well. We always think of Theodore 'Ted' Robert Bundy as being the numero uno in the world's sadosexual homicide top-of-the-pops league of over-the-top murder most foul, yet by my reasoning, as far as sheer brutality goes, Carignan is on a par. I say this because Bundy never once admitted his crimes, let alone told us what terrible depravities he enacted upon his innocent victims, prior to and during his killings, nor his disgusting post-mortem degradation of so many beautiful young women. Indeed, no one knows how many murders Bundy actually committed. As for Carignan, he was responsible for *possibly* up to fifty kills – and you should take that number with a pinch of salt. After Carignan was arrested, one of America's most vicious serial killers would never use his hammer again. And here's the thing: Harvey spilled many of his beans to me, at once blaming all of his victims, telling me that it was *their* fault that he raped then bludgeoned them to death. So let's meet 'The Hammer' and try and get into the head of a man who literally destroyed the heads of so many women.

> Even now, it sometimes seems my childhood was short, only a few days long. There is nothing about it I cling to and nothing to look fondly backwards towards. From where I sat then, and sit now, it was and it is truly a pit of despair.
>
> Harvey Louis Carignan: letter to the author,
> 14 April 1993

Born on 18 May 1927, on the wrong side of the tracks in Fargo, North Dakota, Harvey (like Ted Bundy) was an illegitimate kid who never knew his father. His unwed twenty-year-old mother, Mary, was ill-equipped to care for her sickly boy, who failed to thrive and, in 1930, during the lowest point of the Great Depression, she started farming him out to anyone who would look after him. Thereafter, the youngster was moved from pillar to post, school to school, unable to form family roots or enjoy a solid education. He was passed around his mother's family from Fargo to Cavalier, North Dakota, back to Fargo then to Williams, North Dakota. As the FBI will confirm, this really ain't the best start to any kid's life.

Very early in his formative years, Harvey developed a facial twitch and suffered from bed-wetting until he was thirteen. He also suffered St Vitus's dance – or childhood chorea – which manifests itself in uncontrollable spasmodic jerking movements.

And, not unlike the serial killer Kenneth Bianchi, Harvey had an imaginary friend. Harvey called his invisible buddy 'Paul'.

Around the age of eleven or twelve, Harvey says he was sent to the ND Training (Reform) School at Mandan, North Dakota, where he remained for some seven years. During this time, he alleges that he was constantly bullied and sexually assaulted by a female teacher. There may be some truth in what follows, for that reform school was little more than a human warehouse where any concept of love was alien.

In a letter dated 12 June 1993, Harvey writes:

I had a teacher who used to sit at my desk and we would write dirty notes back and forth. I was either 13 or 14 at the time – and just show me a 14-year-old boy anywhere who wouldn't willingly and happily sit in a schoolroom and exchange porno notes with his teacher. I never got to lay a hand on her without getting slapped, but she would keep me after school and make me stand before her while she masturbated and called me names and told me what she was going to make me do – some of her threats she even kept, damn it! The bitch wouldn't even let me masturbate with her! I took my penis out and she beat the living shit out of me! She had enormously large breasts. She was truly a cruel woman [...]

I have always been quite unsure why Harvey was telling me this. I suspect much of it comes from his overheated sexual imagination. Perhaps he was actually saying: 'What I would have *liked to have taken place* at Mandan – but didn't.' The flip side of this unedifying coin, of course, is that he is truthfully recounting some of the events that occurred at Mandan, where child abuse was all too common. Reading between the lines and combining what we find there with what we know as absolute facts about his killing times might give us a deeper insight into what made this depraved serial killer tick.

Am I being a tad dismissive about Harvey offering that sordid information? Maybe I am, for there is another very subtle clue here, presented right at the start of his many letters to me, and much like Melanie McGuire gave to us when she mentioned her fascination with conspiracies. This was no slip of her pen; it came from her subconscious. In other words, what flowed onto the page came from deep within her psychopathology; an unwise slip as later events would prove. With Harvey's letter above, I believe that his psychological makeup *demands* that he tells us this sordid information, in very much the same way as Phillip Jablonski did. When we read some of Harvey's letters later, we will see exactly the same thing again and again – a complete inability to stop himself from writing what one might say is homicidal pornography, although nothing close to the vile porn that dripped from the pen of Bobby Joe Long.

By the time Harvey reached eighteen, he was no longer the weedy runt who had allegedly suffered mental and sexual abuse since the age of four. The high-carb, well-balanced diet at Mandan had helped him to grow into a strapping, quite articulate, well-nourished, immensely powerful young man. With few family ties, he went straight into the US Army. He was stationed at Fort Richardson in Anchorage, Alaska, and it was here that this man exploded.

Laura Showalter

The killer was so strong, with one punch he [Carignan] blasted a hole through her skull like a rocket slamming into a tank.

> Anchorage police officer: on Showalter's murder

At about nine in the evening of Sunday, 31 July 1949, a time of year when Anchorage was bathed in sunlight for most of the day, Carignan killed fifty-seven-year-old Laura Showalter during an attempted rape in a small Anchorage park. Her body was found early the following morning – he had smashed her head in with his fists. Between her forehead and her chin, her face was completely shattered. Her face was virtually destroyed from chin to forehead; bone, tissue and brain crushed to a pulp under the battering. Carignan walked away covered in blood; later he would be charged with this homicide.

Christine Norton

He turned into something from hell. His fury came out of nowhere.

> Christine Norton: reliving the attempted
> rape by Carignan

Less than two months later, early in the morning of 14 September, Christine Norton (also known, presumably to protect her privacy, as Dorcas Callen) was accosted outside a tavern in a street in Anchorage by a tall and well-built young soldier who seemed intoxicated despite the hour. He was persistent, trying to claim acquaintanceship with her, and offered to give her a lift in his car. When she declined, he grew angrier and angrier. She thought of how a woman had recently been horribly killed in the area and was frightened, but before she could move off, he had caught hold of her and was dragging her away from the empty street. As she struggled, they fell into a deep ditch at the side of the road, the soldier on top of the young woman, tearing at her clothing, hitting her furiously, tugging at her limbs. He was heavy, extremely strong, in a rage, and intent on raping her. Yet somehow, strengthened by her terror, she managed to wriggle free and scramble up the crumbling dirt wall of the ditch (which bore her weight better than the hulking soldier's) to run back up the road to the safety of the tavern, bruised, blood-stained and in tattered clothing. From there she phoned the police, to whom she was able to give a clear description of her assailant, and it was just a matter of hours before they found and arrested Carignan.

In the meantime, it transpired that the man who on 1 August 1949 found Laura Showalter's body had seen Carignan with her the evening before his horrifying discovery but had not at the time realised anything was amiss. Both he and Christine Norton identified Harvey Carignan in a line-up on Friday, 16 September.

Carignan was charged with murder and assault with intent to commit rape. He pleaded guilty to the assault, and a written confession to the murder of Laura Showalter was obtained from him. He stood trial for the first-degree murder of Laura Showalter in early 1950 in the District Court for the Territory of Alaska, Third Division, Justice George W. Folta presiding. It should have been simple: he was pronounced guilty on both charges. He was then sentenced to hang – and this is where justice was turned on its head. Carignan had been led to believe that if he confessed he would not receive the death sentence, and while he was prepared to spend time in jail, he felt that he had been deceived and appealed. In October 1951, his sentence for the murder was overturned on a technicality – his confession, which he made of his free will, was nevertheless ruled inadmissible because it was obtained during his detention for the assault on Christine Norton, whereas he had not yet been arraigned before a magistrate for the murder.

So Harvey escaped the hangman's noose by a whisker while perhaps as many as fifty women lost their lives. Thereafter, prisoner #22072 Carignan was transferred from the Seward Jail in Alaska to the US federal penitentiary on McNeil Island in Puget Sound, Washington State. The prison would hold several notable convicts in its lifetime, including: Robert Franklin Stroud, later aka 'The Birdman of Alcatraz'; Vincent Hallinan, a presidential candidate in 1952; and Mickey Cohen, the 1930s Los Angeles gang leader. And as this book is all about writing, I am also obliged to mention fellow inmate James Fogle, published author of the autobiography *Drugstore Cowboy*. There is a brilliant movie of the same name – well worth a watch.

At this point in Carignan's narrative, and before we examine his correspondence in more depth, it is worth pausing to reflect on the deep-rooted hatred of women that resides within the psychopathologies of killers such as Carignan, Neville Heath, Bobby Joe Long, Ted Bundy and Peter Sutcliffe. Outwardly, they may present to the world as being normal people. They often are good-looking and charming to a fault, but this is merely the mask of normality that I mentioned earlier. These people have very fragile egos; they pen in their inner fury often for weeks and months on end. Then, for one reason or another – often simply because of a minor slight – they emotionally explode.

It *could* be the case that the abuse he suffered at Mandan, and which Carignan told me about, was a contributory factor. He once told me that later in his life women played mind games with his head, giving us a subliminal clue as to why he inflicted so much damage to heads, brains and bodies. Peter Sutcliffe learned early on that his allegedly devout Catholic mother was cheating on his father; he grew to despise her. Perhaps the fact that he was unable to have children was a contributory factor in the awful stabbings and mutilations to his victims' stomachs and vaginal areas after he'd rendered them unconscious with blows to their heads. Theodore Robert Bundy is much easier to understand. Ted was jilted by a beautiful young co-ed, his first true love. Her parents had seen right through Bundy's oily, shallow façade and convinced her to unceremoniously dump him which did nothing to assist his already fragile ego. Thereafter, his chosen victims were lookalikes of his first amour – he was punishing her through them.

Joanne Dennehy's motive for the three stabbing homicides and two attempted stabbing kills is documented in my book *Love of Blood*. By her teens Jo had developed a pathological hatred for men. Later, married with two little babies, which she never touched or even cared for them, she viewed her husband as merely a convenient tool to look after her children and do the housework, while sometimes she'd bring men back to their home and have rough, degrading sex in front of him.

We can apply similar criteria to Neville Heath. A narcissist to the nth degree, he despised women – witness the godawful injuries that he inflicted upon Margery Gardner and Doreen Marshall.

So many more vile killers still live among us, yet we never suspect a thing as to their deep-seated intentions. We take them at their face value – the visible ink on the page – but it is what is hidden from view – between the lines, so to speak – that is most terrifying of all. We'll see proof of that as we move on through Carignan's life, and on to the rock named 'Alcatraz'.

Alcatraz

Laura Showalter ... Dorcas Callen? Those names mean nothin' to me. [Callen, sometimes Callan is on his rap sheet and confirmed by investigator Russell Krueger in my TV series *Serial Killers*.]

Harvey Carignan: to the author at
interview MCF-Stillwater

Alcatraz is the old Spanish word for 'pelican' (now it means 'gannet') and the island was named after the hordes of seabirds that made the island their home. In 1775, the Spanish explorer Juan Manuel de Ayala became the first to sail into what is now known as San Francisco Bay, and his expeditions mapped and named one of the three islands La Isla de los Alcatraces – 'The Island of Pelicans'. Over time it became the briefer 'Alcatraz'. After a century or more of use as some kind of fortified establishment, detention centre or various types of prison, it was bought by the US Department of Justice and from 1934 to 1963 was designated a federal prison. With most attempted escapes being met with either death by drowning or shooting, or by recapture, the island jail gained the reputation of being inescapable from. And that was where Carignan was transferred, on 13 September 1951, to spend the next nine years. On 2 April 1960, aged thirty-three, he was paroled. Except for his few years in the Army, he had not really been at liberty since he was a kid.

After landing at San Francisco's waterfront jetty wearing a cheap prison-issue suit, and with a bag containing his few belongings, Carignan boarded a train for Duluth, Minnesota. As Harvey explained in one of his letters to me: 'In Duluth I moved in with one of my three half-brothers but, on 4 August 1960, just four months after my release, I was arrested for third-degree burglary and assault with intent to commit rape.' No shrinking violet is Harvey, I'm sure you'll agree. The rape charge was dropped through lack of evidence, but for the burglary and parole violation, he was sentenced to 2,086 days in the US Penitentiary Leavenworth, Kansas.

Carignan was paroled in 1964, moving swiftly to Seattle where, he told me: 'On 2 March I registered as Parole Convict #C-5073.' On 22 November that year, he was arrested for second-degree burglary and, again, violating parole. On 20 April 1965 he was sentenced to fifteen years in the Washington State Penitentiary (WSP) Walla Walla, in 'The Evergreen State'.

Don't worry, guys. My husband is the pilot. He's flying blind right now. He knows where Mount St Helens is. If he doesn't, he and I might have a problem.

Air stewardess: to me and my TV documentary
producer, Frazer Ashford

If you want to visit the WSP, you have to truly like flying. As the crow flies, the distance is 212 miles between SeaTac and Walla Walla. But en route, the pilot has to navigate around the 2,500-metre-high, semi-dormant volcanic Mount St Helens, which occasionally has a bad-hair day. For the record, this is higher than the plane Frazer Ashford and I flew in, made all the more exciting as the volcano was blanketed in clouds of mist – or was it steam?

Walla Walla

Walla Walla – I am reliably informed by Keith Hunter Jesperson, aka 'The Happy Face Killer' – is *not*, as I previously mentioned in one of my books, one of the tri-state cities along with Richland and Kennewick on the south-east border of Washington and Oregon. 'Walla Walla is 40 miles east of the tri-cities ... you must be totally correct 100 per cent of the time,' screams Keith in one of his letters to me, adding: 'Pascoe [*sic*] is the third of the tri-cities.' Let's give him his due, at least Keith was correct on the latter.

Now locked up in one of the oldest and most notorious prisons in the United States, Carignan applied his mind; taking a high school diploma, enrolling in many college courses including sociology and psychology; he also submitted papers on sexual psychopathy, the paranoid personality and the well-adjusted individual. He read constantly, gaining top marks; and studied journalism. All of this impressed his tutors, who stated that: 'Mr Carignan's cognitive thinking processes allow us professionals a greater understanding of the first-hand experiences that only a man like Mr Carignan can offer us,' adding possibly with tongues in cheeks: 'Presently, however, more correctional adjustment is needed before we can recommend he be paroled, *if* ever.' Yes, the italic *'if'* really does appear in Carignan's psychiatric reports. Good gracious me, there *are* psychiatrists in the US who have a dry sense of humour.

While the shrinks at Walla Walla praised Harvey for his academic achievements, they were also well aware that when talking to his fellow cons he was constantly fantasising – and at night, masturbating – about nubile young girls. We see pre-echoes of this mindset in his letter about Mandan. Harvey freely admits that he has a fixation about young flesh, which is mirrored in his victims. In a letter to me he explained: 'Young girls have to be my ultimate choice. It would be very unhealthy for me to go with a much older woman than me.' About two decades ago his pen pal was a youngish mother serving a life sentence for beating and smothering to death her baby in its cot while her partner looked on. The love letters they exchanged are enough to make one cringe.

Then in his early forties, a hulking giant of an ex-con, Harvey's chances of dating a teenager were non-existent, so he hooked up with Sheila Moran, a divorcee (some accounts say a widow) with three children. She had her own house in Ballard, the Scandinavian district of Seattle, and there he settled down with her.

As mentioned earlier, sexual psychopaths can *never* be cured, but with all those years behind bars and all of the psychiatric counselling under his belt, let's at least give Harvey some moral support here, with: 'Go for it, Harvey ... you be a good ole boy now, y'all hear. You got it made, bro. Move in. Getcha your feet under the table. Become the man of the house and let ya homemaker do the rest.' But Sheila soon got wise to her newly betrothed's character. Coming from a decent family, she was left under no illusions about the real personality of her husband, who hung around with a bunch of villains. He was always out until the late hours, tearing around in his car at breakneck speeds. He was sullen, uncommunicative, would frequently get up at night and drive long distances 'to be alone and think', he told me; sometimes he was away for days on end. After he had, without provocation, launched a vicious attack upon her aged uncle, she decided his violence and unpredictability presented too great a threat to her children and herself, and took her children and left. When Harvey found them gone, he decided to kill her. He waited in vain through the night, a hammer clutched in his hand. Sheila did not return home and they never saw each other again.

Harvey bigamously remarried on 14 April 1972. Widow Alice Johnson, a somewhat naïve soul in her thirties with two children, fell for him and thought she had met her 'Mr Right', unfortunately she'd met her 'Mr Wrong'.

Later, in his lengthy correspondence with me, Carignan avoided mentioning Sheila Moran, Alice Johnson, Laura Showalter or Christine Norton/Dorcas Callen in any meaningful way – it is as if these four women had never ever existed in his worthless life. However, and this may not come as a surprise, he did highlight this: 'Alice had been married before, had a son called, Billy, aged eleven, I think, and a very, *very* pretty young fourteen-year-old daughter called Georgia. What man wouldn't lust after that?' Of course, there was no need for him to say anything about Georgia. But he can't help himself.

At around this time, Carignan managed to lease a Sav-Mor

gas station from the Time Oil Company. He needed staff and advertised in the local papers. Soon Alice noticed that he had a string of young girls working the pumps, and that no sooner had one started than she left to be replaced by another pretty lass. This aroused Alice's suspicions, and local gossip led her to the conclusion that her husband was totally obsessed by teenage girls. He would approach any girl he saw making obscene suggestions and uttering smutty remarks. When Alice confronted him about his behaviour, he shouted and swore at her. He beat her son, and skulked about, leering at his stepdaughter Georgia, which made her feel decidedly uncomfortable – so much so that she ran away from home. Not surprisingly, the marriage collapsed soon afterwards. 'That not so innocent Georgia was begging for it. They all do at that age,' Carignan wrote to me.

On 15 October 1972, the body of nineteen-year-old hitchhiker Laura Brock was found near Mount Vernon, Washington State. She had been raped and murdered. The cause of death was found to be repeated crushing blows to the head – Carignan's favoured MO – but the killing was never pinned on him. Several witnesses apparently claimed to have seen Laura get into a silver-topped truck – like Carignan's – but nothing was ever proved.

Katherine 'Kathy' Sue Miller

You really want the truth from me? You're dead right, Chris. Yes, I smashed their heads to a pulp. Why? Because women and young chicks always played mind games with me. Not even the psychiatrists have figured this out.

> Harvey Carignan: to the author at interview,
> MCF-Stillwater

The world owes Harvey Carignan nothing, as in zilch, but he does give us some murderous ideas on how depraved criminals go about luring young women to the most terrible of ends. So, if Carignan has any value at all, it is that he is inadvertently warning us – the amoral bigot that he is – that young girls should *always* heed the advice of their parents and never, ever get into a car with a strange man. And 'strange' Carignan most certainly was; that and a damned sight more.

Kathy Sue Miller's case offers a prime example. She was born a beautiful, healthy baby at the French Hospital in New York, on 23 May 1957. Her mother, Mary, later gave birth to her brother Kenny. Sadly, Kathy came to a dreadful end after she read a 'want-ad' in the *Seattle Times* dated 1 May 1973. Help was required at a local gas station. Fifteen-year-old Kathy wasn't looking for a job herself, but her boyfriend, Mark Walter, was.

The notice had been placed by none other than Carignan – who would subsequently be dubbed 'The Want-ad Killer' – metaphorically sitting in the shadows, trawling for young prey. At this point, I would ask the reader to recall the words of Christine Norton/Dorcas Callen: 'He turned into something from hell. His fury came out of nowhere, like he was suddenly switched on with evil.' Now imagine, if you dare, what Kathy went through soon after meeting 'The Hammer'.

The next morning, Kathy rang the number advertised. She was, remember, acting on her boyfriend's behalf at the time, but when the man who answered the phone said that he also employed girls, she excitedly thought she too would apply. Unwisely, she gave him her address and telephone number and agreed to meet him after school. They arranged that he would pick her up in his car – a maroon one, he told her – outside the

Sears Building on Utah Avenue South, and would then drive her over to his gas station to fill out a job application form.

Mary was worried, as any mother would have been. She didn't like the fact that her daughter had given her telephone number and address to a stranger. She felt uneasy about the way the interview had been arranged; in particular, the thought of Kathy getting into a car with someone she had never met before concerned her deeply. Running through her mind was a recent news article about Laura Brock, who had been raped and murdered while hitchhiking – most probably killed by Carignan, police later said.

'I mean it, Kathy,' Mary warned. 'Don't even think about meeting him!' Kathy promised not to and left for her classes, a stack of schoolbooks under her arm.

Mother and daughter rode the same bus that morning. Kathy alighted first near Roosevelt High School at 1410 NE 66th Street. Mary watched through the grimy window as her lovely daughter hurried away, turning once with a smile to wave back. The story of what followed has been compiled using police documents and details from none other than Carignan in his letters to me.

After school, Kathy flagrantly disobeyed her mother's orders and met Carignan as arranged. In his correspondence this sexual predator recalled, with unexpected lyricism that made him all the more repellent, that he had been waiting with 'growing impatience', that 'my heart skipped a beat when I saw a tall, athletic girl walking in my direction. Her blonde hair was darkened to a burnished butterscotch colour and fell to the middle of her back in thick waves. Kathy had green eyes, and just the faintest suggestion of freckles sprinkling over her fair skin. The all-American sexy lass, she was to me.'

Kathy paused opposite his car to cross the street and he looked on as the teenager, sporting a navy-blue blouse, blue-and-white jumper and blue-tinged tights, waved to him.

In a letter to me, Carignan explained that he leant across the front passenger seat and pushed the door open. However, Kathy walked to his side of the car and spoke to him through the open window. Her first sight of Harvey would have been unappealing: an unattractive man with a peculiarly domed forehead and a receding chin. Carignan looked years older than his true age of forty-five, with his skin deeply lined and wrinkled bags beneath his eyes – a deep scar running over one of them. His usual expression was a glowering frown. To smile, he had to make a concentrated effort, so he turned on all the charm at his disposal.

'Hi, you must be Kathy?' he asked, with a broad grin beaming across his face.

Kathy would have noticed the dimple on his chin, then smiled back. 'Sure, that's me.'

Motioning her to get into his car, he said, 'We need to fill in the application forms and they are back at my office ... just hop in. I'll drop you off home when we've finished.'

Carignan recalls that it was obvious to him that Kathy felt uncomfortable. 'My mom isn't too happy about this,' she explained to him, so he moved up a gear.

'Can't say that I blame her. I've got children of my own. Married, too. Nice house. Lovely woman. Yep, we can't blame your mom for being careful.'

Kathy was almost convinced by the man's reassurance. 'You sure this is OK?' she asked.

'Absolutely. Tell ya what, I'll even introduce myself to your mom when I drop you off. Everything will be fine then.'

Kathy was never seen alive again. In the wake of the crime, Harvey, whose violent record was known to police, was questioned at length, his movements watched 24/7 for weeks. But there was insufficient evidence to arrest him and charge him with abduction let alone murder.

On Sunday, 3 June of that year, two sixteen-year-old boys riding their motorcycles through Tulalip Reservation just north of Everett, found a naked body wrapped in black plastic. The corpse had decayed so badly it was initially impossible even to tell its gender. During autopsy it was found that the teeth matched Kathy's dental records. It was clear from the damage to the skull that death had resulted from a brutal battering: there were holes in it the size of a hammer head or tyre lever. Carignan writes that he also raped Kathy using his hammer handle.

Of course, we cannot know much at all about what happened after Kathy climbed into Carignan's car. Throughout his correspondence with me, although he says nothing about the actual killing of this fifteen-year-old, he recalled that his patience had been wearing thin as he'd waited by the kerbside for her to appear, if she was to appear at all. This was a man quick to anger, a man who had clearly been struggling to control his sexually driven, pent-up fury as he waited and waited. Then, when Kathy finally appeared, he switched to a 'Mr Nice Guy'; all he had to do was to persuade her to get into the car and sit beside him.

Rapid flicks of the mental switches from 'Mr Nice Guy' to something hellish is not unusual in the dread annals of criminal history. Aside from Harvey Carignan, examples include 'nice', all-American bookish Michael Bruce Ross, whom I interviewed on death row in Somers Prison, Connecticut, and smooth-talking Ted Bundy. Such men do *not* waste their time when a victim is under their control. Their perverted sexual psychopathology does not permit small talk. The moment Kathy cautiously edged up to Carignan's car, she was already a dead girl still walking. So let me repeat this: do not, under any circumstances, get close to a stranger's car if he, or she, asks for directions or uses any other pretext to lure you in.

Having studied Carignan's modus operandi, modus vivendi and modus cogitandi more than, I suggest, any other commentator on 'The Hammer', I conjecture that he would have driven Kathy some distance, then when the chance seized him, smashed her in the face to render her helpless. This was his MO – one almost identical to that of Ted Bundy – and one that would be played out again and again in Harvey's future murders; poor Kathy would never have seen it coming. Now that she was unconscious, he would have taken her out into the deep woods that night, and done what his urges told him to do. At one time in my letters to Harvey, I pressed him on Kathy's murder and he had this to say: 'Chris, those details are what I call my "string of pearls". They are secrets I share with no one not even you. These *pearls of wisdom give me intense pleasure* but as you are not a man like me, why should I waste my time revealing them to you?' [Author's italics.]

Let's consider his 'string of pearls' and this 'intense pleasure', that he shares with no one. Earlier, I mentioned 'trophy-taking', and that this can also mean a killer's sexually gratifying memories of their murders. We know from Carignan's previous prison psychiatric reports that he, like Bundy, Bianchi and Ross, masturbates constantly to these sick memories, all the while

191

boasting to his fellow cons about his preference for young girls. Given which, Carignan's words can only mean one thing, and I am sure that I do not have to explain further.

But what of Kathy's legacy?

I admire Mary Miller more than almost anyone I know. She has survived unbelievable tragedy, but rather than spending her life mourning her losses, she has devoted herself to helping others who have lost beloved family members to murder.

Ann Rae Rule, author (1931–2015)

Kathy's mother, Mary, went on to dedicate her life to humanitarian work. In a nomination letter to the Red Cross, the well-known writer Ann Rule talked about Mary's experiences escaping war-torn Latvia as a teenager after World War II, then suffering the loss of her daughter, Kathy, and raising her developmentally disabled son as a single mother. If that is not heart-breaking, I do not know what is and, when Kathy was just four months old, her mother had a nightmare that haunted her through the following years. Mary Miller described how, 'I dreamed I had a daughter with long, dark hair. She was fourteen years old in my dream, and someone had hurt her. There was blood all over her face. I couldn't tell if she was dead, but I knew that she was terribly hurt. There was so much blood, and try as I might, I couldn't help her.'

Throughout Kathy's childhood, Mary kept a close eye on her, checking more frequently than was normal. But as her daughter retained the long hair of childhood, Mary began to relax. And when she passed the age of fourteen, Mary finally felt the danger was over. Before another year had passed, however, her nightmare came true.

Eileen Hunley

After Kathy's body was retrieved from the forested Tulalip Reservation, Seattle detectives, Billy Baughman and Duane Homan, both big men in their thirties, with each of them having a teenage daughter of about Kathy's age, and who knew of Carignan's grim criminal record, watched and hounded him with such determination that he left Seattle with the intention of going to Denver – to end up in Minnesota after first driving through California. A speeding ticket from Solano County on 20 June 1973 placed him in the vicinity where half a dozen women had been murdered in the previous two years, but there was nothing definite to connect him to these crimes. To this very day, there is still only circumstantial evidence to link Carignan to these brutal murders.

Having escaped Seattle and the clutches of the seven-man team of homicide cops assigned to the Miller case, Harvey now made his way to Minneapolis, Minnesota, and moved in with his half-brother, and here he initially bombarded his estranged wife Alice promising his eternal love. While blaming her for their separation, he continually assured her he was willing to forgive and forget. They were, Harvey announced, 'poor tormented lovers, with a love as great as Abelard and Heloise, Antony and Cleopatra, and Romeo and Juliet'. He also went to great lengths to portray himself as a peace-loving man. He described how the children had laughed to see a bird killing a snake in a television programme. He told Alice that he was horrified to see how anyone could 'so intensely enjoy the sight of killing'.

So now one can see how duplicitous 'The Hammer' was, portraying himself as being life's constant victim. He wrote how much his rent cost him; how he only made $7.60 an hour, and that was his pathology way back then, and we see it in his letters that follow as plain as day.

Further playing the victim card and that everybody was out to get him, in another letter to Alice he described how he had been set upon by a gang of five youths and beaten so severely with a claw hammer that he feared he might lose the sight of his right eye. If that attack ever happened, and of course it hadn't, Harvey never reported it to the Minneapolis police. Even if he had done so, it is almost certain that little would have happened, for the cops were far too busy investigating his own assaults.

In Minneapolis, on 28 June 1973, Marlys Townsend was standing at a bus stop on a street corner when she was suddenly knocked unconscious by a hammer blow from behind and dragged barely conscious into the perpetrator's vehicle. She came round to find herself in a pick-up truck with a huge balding man, who demanded that she touched his genitals. As Marlys scrambled for the door, her assailant grabbed her hair. Luckily she was wearing a wig, and after falling out onto the pavement she ran off down the street and managed to escape. She gave police a description of her attacker that would later match Carignan exactly.

Two months later, on 9 September 1973, came a sickening attack on a child. Thirteen-year-old runaway Jerri Billings was thumbing for a lift in north-east Minneapolis when Carignan stopped. She soon noticed, however, that Harvey – or 'Paul', as he called himself – was not heading to the address she had given, but instead was driving out into the empty spaces of Hennepin County. There, Carignan struck her on the head with a hammer and dragged her off into a cornfield where she was forced to perform oral sex on him. Jerri was convinced that the man was going to kill her but to her astonishment he let her get dressed and drove her back to Crystal, a small town just north-west of Minneapolis. 'Get out,' he said, 'and don't tell anyone, ever.' Luckily for 'The Hammer', Jerri heeded his threat. She did not report the assault until 29 October, by which time she was in reform school and it was only after seeing someone in the chapel who looked just like her assailant that she decided to speak out. The unfortunate man, Karl Olafson, bore an uncanny resemblance to Carignan and it was to take a full year to eliminate him entirely from their enquiries. In one of his letters to me, he made a passing comment about Jerri Billings: 'She was a cute kid and she reminded me of my niece.'

In the meantime, there was a lull in Harvey's attacks; the reason being that he had sidled back to Seattle in February 1974 to attempt a reconciliation with Alice and still with a leching eye on her daughter. When this failed, he struck up a relationship with Eileen Hunley who was hitchhiking and a member of 'The Way', a fundamentalist sect that Harvey soon joined too. It seems that at first Eileen felt sorry for him. He seemed like a decent, devout, hard-working man, who was trying to overcome the rough hand life had dealt him; however, he soon returned to type. By the summer she was becoming disillusioned – he was drinking hard and his violent temper began to flare up with increasing frequency so she tried to get away from him. *Murder Casebook* Vol. 80 has it that Eileen was last seen alive at her home in Minneapolis on Saturday, 4 August 1974. She did not appear at church the following day, nor did she show up on Monday at the childcare centre where she worked. Carignan turned up at the latter, claiming that she was ill and had sent him to collect her latest pay cheque, but Eileen's employers were suspicious and refused to hand it over to this big, scowling man. Instead, they notified the police of their concern. Weeks later, her body, the skull caved in, was found on 18 September, in Sherburne County. In response to my questions about Eileen's murder, Carignan had little to say, dismissively commenting: 'She was my common-law wife an' I thought she was seeing a black man so I stopped her in the street … I ran her head into a lamp pole, and I stamped her face into a drain cover until she was dead. Then I tried to feed her to some pigs.' Whether or not his account is true or not, Eileen's skull had indeed been crushed, as Detective Sonenstahl later claimed with a hammer, but it is known that a tree branch had been forced into her vagina, which, as might be expected, is denied by Carignan.

Returning to Carignan's homicidal narrative, a string of brutal sexual assaults on girls and young women throughout Colorado and Minnesota during the latter part of 1974 all bore his stamp. At least seven of the victims died; the survivors were scarred for life, mentally and physically. Those who could, mostly described their attacker as a large man, middle-aged, balding, wielding a hammer. On 8 September 1974, a pair of teenage girls, June Lynch and Lisa King, were hitchhiking, and were picked up by Carignan. On the pretext of needing some help picking up another vehicle he drove them to a rural area near Mora, Kanabec County, Minnesota. Asking one of them to wait in his car, he took the other into some woods to, they thought, give him a helping hand with this fictitious car. When the teenager left behind heard screams from her friend, she ran as fast as she could to get help. Carignan fled. His victim was alive but severely injured and traumatised. She had been beaten about the head with a hammer and sexually assaulted with its handle. The girls were able to give a description of the assailant and the vehicle he was driving: a pea-green and black Chevrolet Caprice.

The Later Victims

On 14 September 1974, Carignan picked up a nineteen-year-old Gwen Burton, a student nurse whose car would not start in a south Minneapolis car park. After he'd tinkered with the car briefly, and using his usual ploy, he told her he needed more tools and persuaded her to accompany him to fetch them. He took her instead to an area of wilderness in Carver County, sexually assaulted her several times, including forcing a claw hammer handle into her vagina. He beat her about the head with the hammer (which he was later to insist was a lug or wheel nut wrench, as though this would somehow exonerate him), and left her in a field to die. It is to be noted that to all intents and purposes Carignan was impotent, meaning he couldn't get it up unless his victims performed oral sex on him. Nonetheless, Gwen did not die and managed to crawl up an embankment on to a road where, three hours later she was found, seriously injured, and rushed to hospital. She, too, was able to give a description of her attacker and his vehicle – a four-door Chevrolet Caprice, light green with a black interior, and with Minnesota licence plates – and of some of the car's contents – down to the brand of cigarette he smoked.

Five days later, on 19 September 1974, two teenage female hitchhikers reported that they had been picked up by a man and driven in a green Chevrolet into the country where he threatened to rape and kill them. To make his point, Carignan struck one across the mouth, breaking one of her front teeth. Both were eventually able to escape by jumping out of his car when he stopped to fill his vehicle with gas. Their descriptions of the man matched those given by the previous victims.

The very next day, seventeen-year-old Katherine Jane Schultz set off for school in the morning. She never got there. The following day, 21 September, the body of a young woman was found by pheasant hunters in Isanti County, an area 40 miles north of Minneapolis. She had been sexually assaulted and had sustained horrific and fatal injuries to the head. Two days later the body was identified as that of Katherine Schultz.

Carignan had cunningly taken each of his victims into a different county in order to hinder the investigations, reasoning that law enforcement jurisdictional limits would mess the cops up. However, this latest atrocity stung law enforcement into action and, very much like Mike Malchik earlier in this book, Detective Archie Sonenstahl started to coordinate their efforts.

The attacker was described as a huge man with balding, greyish brown hair, a dimpled chin and wearing work clothes with the trousers tucked into his boots. He smoked Marlboro cigarettes, used obscene language, was incredibly strong and had driven either a green Chevrolet with a black interior or a silver-topped pick-up. This provided Sonenstahl with his first solid lead: the Isanti PD had taken a cast of brand new Atlas tyre treads found in the ground near Kathy Schultz's body, and if they could match them up a with a suitable silver-topped pick-up or green Chevrolet, they could have some hard evidence at last.

A few days later, Carignan was arrested. When I was filming in Minneapolis years later I was lucky enough to be able to interview the arresting officers who recollected for me how Harvey's arrest went down.

The idiot got too complacent.

Serial killer Keith Hunter Jesperson:
commenting on Carignan

It was 24 September 1974 and early morning in Minneapolis. The sun was up and patrolmen Robert Nelson and Robert Thompson were cruising along 1841 E 38th Street when they spotted a 1968 black–over–pea-green Chevrolet Caprice. It was parked across the road from a diner. Thompson made a slow circuit of the block, while his partner checked the police bulletin details issued the day before.

'That's it,' said Nelson. 'That looks like the car. All we gotta do is find the driver. He's a big guy and, according to this BOLO [Be On the Lookout], he's built like a gorilla.' The two cops peered through the Caprice's window to scrutinise the interior. Sure enough, there was a red plaid car rug, pornographic magazines and a Bible, all as described by several of the victims. By the gear lever were several packs of Marlboro Red cigarettes.

While Nelson telephoned his precinct requesting assistance, Thompson wandered into the diner and asked the owner if he knew who was driving the Chevy.

'Yeah, sure,' came the telling reply. 'He just saw you guys and hightailed it out back.' Minutes later, the two cops spotted

Carignan strolling casually away from them. They questioned him briefly, then arrested him and took him downtown, to be read his Miranda Rights and booked on charges of homicide and multiple rapes.

A police search of Carignan's belongings uncovered a number of maps with some 180 red circles drawn around locations, some isolated, in both the United States and Canada. Some of the circles marked places where he had gone to buy vehicles or apply for jobs; others, however, seemed to link him with a string of unsolved homicides and assaults involving women.

Suspected of up to fifty kills, one of America's most vicious serial killers would never use his hammer again. In separate trials conducted in 1975 and 1976, Carignan was convicted of just two murders, those of Eileen Hunley and Katherine Schultz, and a number of other offences. His defence was that God had told him to humiliate and kill all harlots and whores, and he was only following orders ... That did not hold water, though he was later diagnosed with antisocial personality disorder. He received prison sentences amounting to one hundred years plus life.

What follows is part of a charge relating to five counts regarding offences committed against a thirteen-year-old girl. Her name, as with those of others likely to be still alive, has been omitted to protect her identity. The document has been supplied courtesy of the Minneapolis and Hennepin County Prosecutors:

The said –, was hitch-hiking in Minneapolis when the defendant, driving a truck-camper, stopped, picked her up, engaged her in conversation as to where she was going, stated that he would take her to her destination directly, forced her to commit oral sodomy upon him with the threat of hitting her with a hammer which he picked up from a compartment between the seats of his truck, compelled her to remove her clothes by threatening to 'put a hammer through your head', attempted to shove the handle of the hammer up into her vagina, struck her several times in the area of her buttocks with the hammer, when she resisted the advances of the defendant, again compelled her to commit oral sodomy on him, drove to a corn field where he compelled her to lie on her stomach where he attempted to have intercourse with her through the rectum then, for the third time, again compelled her to commit oral sodomy on him. That the defendant then permitted the victim to dress and drove her to home of a friend situated in Lakeland Avenue, Crystal, Hennepin County, where he allowed the victim to get out of the truck-camper; that, in addition to the foregoing, the defendant told the victim that his first name was 'Paul' and that his last name was 'Harvey'.

Because individuals like Harvey Carignan have traversed such sickening extremes, their souls have become like locked rooms hiding mysterious secrets. Therefore, it takes a certain sensibility to draw them out. For each case, I adopt an in-depth approach, spending an enormous amount of time getting to know the unique qualities of each killer, rather than depersonalising them with generalities based on the heinous crimes. Furthermore, while I develop a false empathy with my subject, I always take care not to sympathise to the extent that their dramas start playing in the theatre of my own mind. It is a constant balancing act between identification and analysis.

To learn anything from these evil people, you must try to put yourself in their place; follow their train of thought and feel their emotions. However, while you follow the often dysfunctional thinking processes of your subjects to some extent, you take care to remain yourself. You may draw close for a while, close enough to get a sense of these often repellent, outlandish ideas and emotions, but you must always pull back to restore the integrity of your own moral and psychological boundaries.

There have been occasions when I've interviewed serial killers that I've sensed they are seeking to shock me, make me recoil in disgust. Many do the same in correspondence, as Phillip Jablonski and Bobby Joe Long did. But if you are almost at one with their thinking, at the same time you are immunised from all they say or write. It is difficult for me to explain. I cannot really put it in any other way. And although some of the letters in this book might make you feel sick to your stomach, please try to study them as one would a blowfly preserved in amber through a microscope. Try to understand their rationale, their modus cogitandi: what makes these monsters tick. This is why it is important for those with a deep interest in criminals of this type to always read between the lines of their correspondence, which is usually where the true beast resides.

On that note, I'm reminded of words written by German philosopher, Friedrich Nietzsche. It's worth repeating them now: 'Whoever fights monsters should see to it that in the process he does not become a monster. And when you look into an abyss, the abyss also looks into you.' That's precisely what one of Harvey's psychiatrists was getting at when he told me, 'Yes, you will get to interview Mr Carignan, or something living inside his head. You'll get to interview him, and pure evil will get to interview you.'

> Most killers I talk to try to act as if they are the worse [sic] people I'll ever meet. In turn they tell people that I don't sound like a killer.
>
> Serial killer Keith Hunter Jesperson:
> letter to the author

So let's now meet this killer in the flesh and it is March 1995, and I need to make a strong point here. Even the strongest, ever-so intimidating sexual psychopath will very rarely lash out at a man. You see, they are bullies and cowards at heart, even weak-willed, and even the likes of Ted Bundy would never pick a fight with a guy for fear of having his teeth knocked out. The same applies to the hulking Keith Hunter Jesperson, Arthur Shawcross, Douglas Daniel Clark, Peter Sutcliffe, Kenneth Bianchi and Angelo Buono, or even Ronnie DeFeo Jr who bravely shot to death his entire family of six at point-blank range with a Marlin hunting rifle as they slept soundly in their Amityville, Long Island home. So, when meeting this human pondlife in the flesh, if you have done your homework, as any homicide cop will tell you that you control the game through mind control, you will win.

Harvey's personal pager summoned him for our interview at the Minnesota Correctional Facility. One's first impression will be of a lumbering hulk – when I met him, he weighed well over 240 pounds (109 kilograms) – standing over 6 feet tall, although slightly stooped because of his age, with heavy brows overhanging piercing blue eyes beneath a balding dome, huge hands attached to long arms hanging from immensely powerful, sloping shoulders. He talks in a low, husky voice. At face value, he is no beauty, yet his overall persona presents a gentle giant of a man. You could see why his 'grandfatherly' voice might easily overcome his ugliness and reassure impressionable young women and girls and lure them into his clutches. Appearances, as we know, can be deceptive.

Except for exchanging the usual pleasantries, three minutes dragged by without either of us saying very much at all, while all the time his eyes stared into my face. Harvey was summing me up. It was as if there were some alien creature, an invisible insidious force, gently probing into my mind using long, squirming tentacles of enquiring thought, exploring, touching, sensing with taste and smell. Some of the killers I've interviewed – Kenneth Bianchi, for example – radiate hatred, pure evil as hot as a kitchen stove. You can smell it. It's like foul breath. Each killer is different. Some are calm and beguiling; others are 'amusing' in a strange sort of way, as was Douglas Clark, aka 'The Sunset Slayer', whom I interviewed on death row in San Quentin State Prison (SQ). With Harvey, he was just a big dude psyching me out. He was reading me while I was reading him. But having come to know this man through several years of correspondence, and with a good knowledge of his life of crime, I knew – and *he* knew that I knew – 'The Hammer' better than anyone else, because I had been closely studying him and his letters for so long. Then, suddenly, as if a switch inside his head flicked off, a secret but twisted smile started to play around Harvey's mouth. His lips, moistened with saliva, were slightly open, but otherwise his face was without expression.

Now, try to put yourself in my shoes, because this stone-cold serial killer is insidiously fascinating to observe at such close quarters. His plate-size hands were resting just inches from mine on the table. (It is all very well writing about these beasts, or lecturing to others about them, but one never gets the true picture unless one is sitting just a touch away and able to sense their distilled evil.) For up close and personal, Harvey is the wolf in sheep's clothing; almost part-human, part-Antichrist, the stuff of our worst nightmares come true. Then he spoke his first full sentence, low, almost husky and contradictory from the get-go: 'Ya know, Chris, never did I commit a crime then commit another to keep it quiet. I committed murders to ensure that false accusations of rape would not occur.' We will see this denial attitude in some of his following letters.

The ice was broken.

My previous belief that Harvey lived in a continual state of denial – existing in a world where he admits some guilt all dressed up in mitigation while not taking total responsibility for his brutal and heinous crimes – was confirmed.

Pausing for a moment, he looked deep into my eyes. Most of the serial murderers I have interviewed are shifty and cannot maintain eye contact, but not for a single second did Harvey take his eyes away from mine. He was seeking my reaction to what he'd just said, but nothing came back from me – my blank expression telling him everything: his manipulative 'game-playing' wasn't working on this Brit. I wasn't playing by *his* rules, I was playing by *my* rules, and he was starting to realise it.

'Were you scared, Christopher?' is a question I am often asked. My reply is always the same: 'Nope! Killers like Carignan are cowards who prey on the weak and vulnerable. Did Bundy,

Bianchi, Sutcliffe, Shawcross or any of their ilk ever attack a man? Of course not! Neither did Carignan. They are gutless at heart.

As the interview progressed, it was as if this self-alleged font of all known serial killer knowledge was quietly lecturing me. Whenever Harvey admitted that he had raped and killed young women, it was always, so he claimed, as a result of 'their provocation'. He said that it was always the victim who brought up the subject of sex when he offered them a ride in his car, and the reader will see this writ large in his correspondence to me. When we think back to fifteen-year-old Kathy Sue Miller, can one imagine that innocent girl raising the subject of sex with this mega-ugly man? I can't, that's for sure. In fact, nowhere can this be better illustrated than in his written account to me of a ride he gave to a perfectly respectable nineteen-year-old nurse whose car had broken down.

The truth is, according to her police statements, that he offered to fix her car, but beforehand he explained to her that he needed to fetch his tools. This was his well-practised ruse. He then forced her into his car, drove her into the country, then brutally raped and attempted to kill her by smashing into her head with a wheel wrench. He pathetically argues in mitigation that she got into his car of her own free will; his story comprises a smattering of the truth and a bucketful of lies, something not uncommon when sexual serial killers give their accounts of their crimes. They weave fact into fiction, so that once you've checked out certain facts, which turn out to be true, you might be duped into believing that their false accounts also pass muster. All of which is proven by what follows.

This is at once disturbing and disgusting, yet the following account from 'The Hammer' offers a fascinating statement from the mind of a homicidal sexual psychopath. It does not make for pleasant reading, but let's see what you can discern between his rambling lines. As always, I quote verbatim:

She got in and may have been somewhat nervous, but she did not seem afraid. During the ride we talked about another girl I used to see, one who had left me because I had not given her $30 I had been giving her every each and every week. It was not payment for anything, but a gift. The girl [the nurse] riding with me said she would never exchange sex for $30 – making it seem she believed the other woman had, and that herself despised her for what the first woman had done. I tried to enlighten her thinking, but she was adamant in her statement that she would not have sex for $30 because those were her words and not that she would not have sex for money, which was my thought at the time.

It was then that I got the drift; that she thought I was offering her the same amount for sex and she was turning down the offer – but I am not saying she wanted money to have sex at all. The way the conversation went it could have been either, that she would not have sex for $30 or she would not have sex for any amount of money. It was no big deal to me at that time, so the conversation had no special meaning to me until much later when I tried to remember everything that was talked about and how it was said.

At this point the reader will sense that here Carignan is already starting to build some mitigation for what was to come. Let this opportunist serial killer's transference of blame begin.

When we got to my friend's place where the tools were supposed to be, I stopped the car, turned around, and immediately drove away. My friend told me if his pick-up, a 1973 ¾ ton Chevrolet, was not in the yard, to not hang around because his sons did not like me. This was a surprise because I did not know his boys. I had never met any of them [in fact, Carignan did not have any friends; he was a fantasy-driven loner]. Anyway, I drove away and stopped the car just before driving onto the main road. I put my arm around her and, although she hesitated, she did move over closer to me when I indicated with arm pressure that is what I wanted. It was not a pressure that forced her to move, not a hold that would have moved her head had she declined. Instead it was an indication of what I would like her to do, and she complied.

I can remember my thoughts as plain as it was yesterday: 'She wants it!' This in spite of the fact that I wondered why she had been so adamant in denying she would have sex for $30, which in my mind could have been any amount at the time. I slid my arm behind her head, put a slight, almost gentle pressure on her neck behind her head, and she bent down – not because of the pressure but with her own strength – unbuttoned my pants, took out my penis, and stroked it while we kissed, until I indicated with the same kind of pressure that I wanted her to suck it. She did.

When she finished, I told her, 'Spit that damned stuff out' when I saw her sitting there holding the semen in her mouth. She did – but I did hold on to her in case she wanted to jump out and run away. I was not satisfied that she was not going to say I had forced her to do what she had done. She looked at me, giving me a strange smile – like I was a fool for thinking she would run – closed the door, and I drove on.

One can almost hear Carignan's low voice talking there. Everything to his compensatory, warped mind, is gentle, caring, trying to understand; an effort to portray himself as a victim more than anything else. But, there is more going on here, is there not? Although unable to have actual physical sex with a woman, he resorted to oral sex; it is known that when recalling his crimes, Carignan is a compulsive masturbator even today. The late Michael Bruce Ross was too – multiple times a day, until he had sores on his penis. Kenneth Bianchi constantly masturbates to the memories of his crimes, and in Harvey's correspondence we see this sexual fantasising too; his 'pearls of wisdom' correspondence reliving, like some mental 'trophy', the terrors he put his victims through.

In her book *Discover Graphology*, Margaret Gullan-Whur talks at length about the extraordinary variety of handwriting regularly committed to paper. And it is true that 'Handwriting's genesis lies in electrical impulses originating in the brain' and 'The hand and the pen are its tools, and inky traces.' She goes on to say that reading someone's handwriting for the first time is a bit like meeting them in person for the first time; that the more you read, the better you get to know the person putting pen to paper. I'd say that this could apply also to those who type their letters, even though the appearance of each letter remains constant. Gullan-Whur says to look for breaks in a writer's 'flow', and we can see this in the sudden changes of mood in the written words that all of the killers discussed thus far have exhibited. The 'Mafia' alter ego presented by Melanie McGuire, the schizophrenic penmanship of Phillip Jablonski, and now Carignan, whose subconscious, his unconscious mental programming, compels him to retell his sex crimes and treat his perverted memories as mental trophies.

Carl Gustav Jung represented a certain kind of psychologist – three kinds, in fact: (1) he was a psychiatrist, i.e. a doctor practising psychology as a branch of medicine; (2) an analytical psychologist using the method of free analysis to draw out the contents of the unconscious mind; (3) a psychotherapist, one who helps clinically disturbed people to reach an autonomous understanding of their problem, thereby emphasising the individual's own role in his or her recovery. Of course Jung would not have been able to use (1) (2) or (3) with homicidal psychopaths, because they could never have accepted such mind-probing; they are far too streetwise to do this.

Psychologists such as Jung and Sigmund Freud believed that the feelings, fantasies and attitudes buried in the unconscious are all part of the truth about a person's real character, and could not be neatly cut off from what was observable, be it through the written word and/or physical behaviour. And as you'll know by now, in this book we are trying to fathom not only what is observable in ink but also what is invisible. Let's apply this to the facts about a few offenders' case histories.

From the crime-scene interchanges we've already explored in Locard's Exchange Principle, many serial killers deliberately take away something physical from the 'event'. It could be a lock of the victim's hair, underwear, an item of jewellery. By way of example, we need look no further than former Canadian Armed Forces Colonel Russell Williams, who not only video-recorded his crimes and took still photos but stole his victims' underwear and shoes as trophies. These he kept at his home, often dressing up in his victims' stockings, bras and panties and taking selfies. And he was the commanding officer of Canada's largest air force base; with the highest security rating. He had once ferried the Queen around. Holy shit. You could not make this up if you tried; go check him out on Google. If the circumstances were not so serious, it would be a real hoot seeing him all dressed up like that; a complete prat. But did he stalk and kill men? Of course not!

American serial killer Joel David Rifkin, now serving 203 years in prison for murdering nine women (but suspected of up to 17 kills between 1989 and 1993), took away from his crime scenes locks of his victims' hair, jewellery and other intimate items. These he kept in his cluttered bedroom. He touched them while recalling his sex crimes during his regular masturbation sessions.

Kenneth Bianchi is an arch-manipulator and who also kept many of his female victims' jewellery items to give to his common-law wife Kelli Kae Boyd, who believed his yarns that he had bought them for her to wear. When he was finally arrested in Bellingham, Washington State, police found these 'trophies' on her dressing table.

Of course, 'trophies' need not be physical items; they can be memories too. Jablonski relives his crimes in his letters. Melanie McGuire is gloating and metaphorically urinating over her husband's grave in her 'Mafia' letter to the district attorney. Graham Young relived his lethal poisonings and the agonising suffering he caused his victims by expounding to all and sundry about his knowledge of toxic substances. Michael Ross, Bianchi, and so many others, including convicted killer paedophiles such as Arthur Shawcross, Colin Pitchfork and, in extremis, Bobby Joe Long, use these 'sex memories' almost like snuff material, with no shame or repentance for their crimes. This reflects the true nature of evil. So, when we have a killer boasting about his crimes in correspondence, it effectively represents an incarcerated man's 'jack-off' material. The following passage, taken once more from Carignan's correspondence with me, illustrates the slow build-up in his mindset as he relives a crime on paper; as ever, he reveals as much by what he doesn't say as by what he does:

While we were starting out, I told her, 'I want to fuck you. I know a place where we can go.' She asked, 'How long will we be gone? I must be back by one o'clock.' It was then about 10.30.

I did have a place in mind but it was miles away. So I drove along and pulled in next to a lake. When I stopped I saw a house in the distance in the midst of some trees and a man walking our way from another direction. I turned around and drove away. During this, the girl did not make any attempt to open the car door and get out.

Directly across the road from the lake a road led into a glen. It was about 500–600 feet from the main road. When we got there, I went to the trunk and took out a blue plaid blanket [subsequently recovered by police] and threw it on to the ground, and I told her, 'Get ready!' I was not happy with her for some reason, but she was a very sexy woman, about 20 years old, and I wanted to have sex with her, especially since we already had after a manner of speaking. She took off my jeans and her panties and laid down on her back with her feet in my direction. The whole of her pudendum was pointing towards me – and it was beautiful, as was herself, a very pretty woman. Now, I do not know what other men look for or how they act, but I generally always look at the vulva, play with it. The prettier she looks in her genital area, the more I want sex.

Now, I only stopped to help the girl get her car started. When she climbed in, I only had in mind to get the tools to fix it. Sex was not on my mind, and I did not kidnap her. Everyone assumes these women and girls as innocents. They generally are not. Each and every one of them wanted something from me, either money, to drive one of my cars, or something they would not divulge. I never kidnapped them, or forced them to come with me. She is no different from the others. I am not a rapist, and the word itself is revolting to me it turns my stomach.

Yes, yes, Harvey, we get it now, but all of my readers across the world are extremely astute. It must have been terrible for you. All those girls and young women wanting something from you, 'Mr Innocent', and you accused of being a 'rapist'. Shocking, eh, Harv? But please go on. What happened next?

Despite what anyone says, we had a delightful time in that clearing until she accused me of taking money from her purse, and then I thought, 'Here we go again.' I became much more angry than the moment called for and acted out within the content of that anger rather than against the accusation which called for no more than an explanation that I had not taken her money. The right rear tire on my car had gone flat and I was changing it when she screamed out at me. She kept screaming that the money was not hers and almost insanely demanding that I return it. Then, in a wink, her tone changed and she told me how she wanted to trade her car for another. That I should give her $200 for the trade or she was going to say I had raped her.

Wow, Harv, this wasn't a good day, then. Flat tyre (tire). Wrongly accused of stealing money from the nurse's purse. Unwarranted demands with menaces for two hundred greenbacks. Gosh, Saint Harvey, this ain't going down too well, is it?

Until that instant, I had gone on with the business of replacing the lug bolts on the hub; but in that instant when she made that threat, I became what I see as being uncontrollably angry and I hit her with the lug wrench – and not with the hammer as she later testified, and what is generally believed. She was fully dressed and I can see it now as plain as it was happening even now. She fell to the ground as if she had been pole-axed and she slid slowly down a 12-to-14-foot incline into a ditch, feet first, with her brown sweater rolling up under her armpits. I did not panic, but put the lug wrench in the trunk and the remaining lug bolt in my pocket, got into my car, and drove away. At about 15–20 minutes down the road, maybe 15–20 miles, I realized I could not leave the dear woman there to die if she was only wounded, and I had to know, so I turned around and went back to try and help her. As I drove by, there were several cars and a tractor with a wagon behind it stopped on the road, and all of the people were bending over someone that I knew was her, so I kept on driving.

Following up his letter, I reminded him that he had left the young nurse for dead in that ditch. That she had regained consciousness several hours later, lying in a pool of blood and suffering from almost fatal brain injuries. It was practically nightfall and, in dreadful pain, she crawled over a mile through ploughed fields to a road where a farmer discovered her and summoned help that morning. 'That rather shoots out your lie about returning within about forty minutes of hitting her, Harvey?' I suggested.

In his later face-to-face interview with me, he said:

I hope that you treat me right if you write about me. I have friends in your country who look after me. They've seen your house. Long track up to it, right? You drive a silver Mercedes. Pretty young wife and two little daughters. Just treat me with respect and all will be fine for them.

In fact, Carignan saw the ambulance at the crime scene as he was returning to it not to save the nurse's life, but, concerned that she might have survived and would describe him and his vehicle to the police, to finish her off. By then, however, she had crawled to safety and been found. The only thing that kept the young woman going was that her sister had told her the previous day that she was expecting a child – and she was determined to stay alive to see the baby.

Throughout my correspondence with Harvey Carignan, he made much of what he calls his 'string of pearls'. In effect, he implied that these 'pearls of wisdom' are priceless details that he will release only when he judges the time is appropriate for him. 'The truth is my pearls of wisdom,' he bluntly stated. 'I am *not* going to release the pearls of this part of the truth at least for years,' he added, before clamming up and refusing to answer any more questions in our interview or in correspondence about the nature of his crimes, however during the early part of my interview with 'The Hammer', he devoted his 'valuable time' to presenting himself as a man of considerable knowledge. It is true that he has studied philosophy, among other subjects, during his incarceration, so one might imagine that his opinions are worth hearing. But within this beast there is a fatal flaw.

> If the truth hurts, change it.
>
> Serial killer Keith Hunter Jesperson:
> commenting on Carignan's persona

Despite having spent the better part of his worthless life behind bars, Carignan is totally unable to come to terms with his guilt. This is a trait he shares with many other serial killers. Even with the evidence being consistent and overwhelming in every case of sexual assault, rape or murder attached to him, Carignan is psychologically compelled to transfer most of the blame for his crimes onto his luckless victims. Thus, not only is he an opportunist serial murderer but a compensatory killer, for when he is exposed with all of his excuses staring him straight back in his face as complete untruths, he retreats to the trench used by so many offenders: the refuge from which he can blame the entire law-enforcement and criminal-justice system for fitting him up. Indeed, if the gravity and number of his offences were not so serious, one might be forgiven for regarding his excuses as merely laughable. Some may even say that his letters are the ramblings of a madman and, as such, should be dismissed or, at best, ignored. However, Harvey is not mad by any definition. What he refuses to say – hides between the lines of his correspondence or conveniently chooses to forget to say, or answer for when pressed – is ultimately of some interest, if we want to try and figure out how such deviant minds work.

But was this the end of what Harvey 'The Hammer' had to say for himself? It was not. It seems that my face-to-face confrontation with him had an impact; let's remember that for much of the time we were alone, with him unshackled, unpredictable, and quite able to slam me up against a wall and tear my head off in an instant. The reader will recall his veiled threat to me, about where I lived; 'The Hammer' had looked inside my mind as I had looked into his. For an instant, I recalled how his huge hands and his hammer had smashed into his prey's heads; what damage could he do to me right there and then, if he suddenly flipped? You might also recall his psychiatrist telling me: 'Yes, you will get to interview Mr Carignan, or *something* living inside his head. You'll get to interview him, and pure evil will get to interview you.'

For some reason – a reason for which I will never fully understand – my meeting with Harvey produced the most unexpected of results, which I will now share with you for the first time. Although he had promised me a tele-filmed interview, when we arrived at MCF-Stillwater he'd abruptly changed his mind, much to the chagrin of Frazer & Co. It was to be me, Harv and a tape recorder – that was it. In so many ways this was a good thing, for when they're being filmed, these monsters play to the camera. They revel in being the sole centre of attention, as did Michael Ross. Some killers want 'special treatment': a little powder on their faces; their hair groomed; candy or a cold, fizzy drink. The TV crew make them feel important, you see. The crew are stroking their feathers to inflate their egos, so that they can return to their cells and tell their fellow inmates: 'Hey, guys, I am going on the BBC.'

To be fair to Harvey, he wanted none of that malarkey. He wanted our meeting to be personal. To him, we had been penfriends for some years. He had never given any sort of interview before I met with him, and he has not done so since.

Realising that he had threatened me, by alleging he had friends in the UK that looked after his interests, he apparently felt ashamed of himself. He had, to his mind – although the veiled threat was empty and uttered in the heat of the moment – potentially cost himself the only male 'friend' he'd ever had in his life. He knew that I was a former HM Royal Marines 'Green Beret' commando; that I had always treated him with great respect; that my crew and I had travelled hundreds of miles across the US at great expense to see him, so he knew that he had let us all down big time. Yet, not once did I complain to him. I took it on the chin and I guess that he respected that.

After I had returned to the UK, the postman delivered a letter. Dated 17 March 1995, it was from 'The Hammer' and it contained all of his 'pearls of wisdom', as if this was a gift to apologise for his behaviour when I had called him out. It is a deeply personal letter, almost a 'compensatory letter' from him, and one that I have never made public before. It is typed, not a grammatical error anywhere, obviously written with deep thought and attention. So, as you are now pretty much fully aware of least a few of the bestial crimes he committed, I let you judge the following. It's one of the most remarkable letters from a homicidal maniac. However, for the sake of decency, and out of deep respect for the victims' next of kin, I will not publish here those 'pearls of wisdom' that relate to the humiliations and agonies he inflicted on them – nor, I suggest, would my readers expect me to, as they are his truthful confessions to the most awful crimes imaginable:

Dear Christopher, your beloved family and the Cat.
Greetings from the Colonies and may St Patrick's Day, which is an anathema in England this year, be good to you. Chances are you are still in The States and up to something or other [serial killer interviews]. I was too full-minded to ask when you were here; which, by the way, was great and could have only been more wonderful had I been able to see your wife and the kids as well as you, Christopher, and if only we could have had a more equitable bargain. In all truth, I did not want to do as much as I did, but I could see you were exceedingly upset and genuinely concerned, so I went as far as I thought I could without offending my attorney who, by the way, would 'eat my ass out royally', if you are familiar with the term. In English, he was as mad as a wet hen and made all

the noises appropriate to his demeanor. The price is right for his services, but other than that he and I do not agree on much. His fee is free, which is hard to beat in this day and time, but the crap I have to take is just a little much, if you know what I mean?

At this point, I would like the reader to consider the comment I made much earlier with regard to Harvey and his typewriter, 'Clyde'. It is important to note that he used this machine to communicate with me until it broke. For a while he wrote in longhand. Almost unreadable to be sure, and I told him so. But in this letter he is, to his mind, sharing something special to him, and he is not *overtly* giving me 'intimate' details that are intended to manipulate. In that context, one might see evidence of *some integrity* here – let's say the building blocks of a sincere letter – although, I stress once again, none of which must be interpreted as any mitigation for his crimes.

Anyway, meet Lazarus who was brain dead and I had to send to a Typewriter Savior for his Resurrection. He used to be Louis, who replaced Clyde, but I thought Lazarus more appropriate being he had actually become junk and had to be completely resuscitated. It cost me $261.15, or $185.00 more than if I had bought a new Personal Word Processor of comparable quality. I would have bought the new one except I was not allowed to. Those of us who have this style and of comparable quality can keep them, but we cannot replace them except with heaps of junk that cost no more than about $150.00, which is the [as written] equivalent to bacon and eggs for a breakfast for a family of five. He [Lazarus] tells your Cat he is going to have to steal his mouse next time he sees him with one. There, that ought to sufficiently scare the little critter and cause him not to sit in your window with a mouse in his mouth and laugh at you. (Yah, and watch the damned cat be a she and catch me with my genders down!)

What can I say other than I wish you a safe and speedy trip home. I do not know how much of The Colonies you saw, but I am sure that in driving from Seattle to Minneapolis, which is about one-half way across the bloody place, you got some idea of just how enormous, big and wide the place really is. Also, I hope you enjoyed yourselves when you saw the country. You told me how lucky you were in evading the storms so you saw our season called Winter at its best. It can be a beautiful time of the year and there are so many wonderful and happy things to do. Have you tried skiing, sledding, snowmobile riding, cross-country skiing, wind sailing on the ice, hay rides, walking in the snow up to your butts, or throwing snowballs at each other? I have. Also, there is something special about getting in a sleigh and going to Grandmother's house for Thanksgiving Dinner, a holiday that once upon a time really meant something and was shared by all, Native Americans and we Interlopers from Europe, mostly 'Meanie Olde Englande', as I think it might have been spelled then.

Of course, Harvey did none of those 'romantic' things. Most of his time while on the 'out' he was running amok, tearing around in his cars, burning rubber, mixing with his crooked cronies, thieving, leching, raping and bludgeoning, but at least he's trying to imagine what life should have been like and not face the reality of the unfortunate fix he's in right now. Once again, here's that dissociation between reality and fact, but oh so subtle.

> Well, my friend, you have seen where I live, probably mentally measured the extent of my physical world, and I imagine you were chilled by the sight, but the size is not what bothers me: I am not fazed by it. What scares the ever-loving crap out of me is being done not to me so much as to others, especially the younger men with so much of their lives left to live, whose wishes are those of children and whose hope are being taken from them. All of them, Whites, Blacks, Latinos, and Others as the next Cro-Magnon specie [sic] is called, with their ethic chatterings, their pathetic makings which they hope will distinguish themselves from all others, and the steely-eyed rage they show in return for their maniacal ravings of some of the staff.

Steady now, Harvey. You were doing okay, so let's not go into a hyper-rant, please.

> It is not our persona, our outer beings, I fear for, but our futures thinking and feelings, theirs and mine, which are being taken away from us, futures we give away freely and almost innocently according to the hate and vindictiveness we feel for and perpetuate against each other. [Here, Carignan is back-handedly referring to his hatred towards women in general because, as he has stated many times, 'They played mind games with my head.']

If only we could redirect this wasted energy in a common direction, toward some common goal, there would not be anything we could not achieve. We would be men and seen as human beings instead of as names society so conveniently foisted upon us to set us apart and to place us at the lowest part of the human junk heap. If only we would not wear our deficits like badges and our social scars like medals of honor, we would no longer be White Trash, Niggers, I-ties, and Slant-Eyed Motherfuckers, but fallible human beings fulfilling our human aspirations, a contributing forces [*sic*] to be reckoned with, pulling together instead of apart, and a group united together instead of a mob pulling every way and having to form gangs and to seek protection from behind the lines of their limited parameters.

. . . Just once, if only for a Limited [*sic*] while, we might inhale the scent of freedom instead of breathing in the odors of each other's sweaty bodies and the lingering nausea of human excrement that prevails over even the pine smell of industrial-strength deodorizing disinfectant used liberally and to no avail, and be more than the ignorant animals we are thought to be, treated like, and people think we might have become due to the smell of our stinking thoughts that are inwardly boiling away our self-esteem, our caring for ourselves as individuals and as a whole, and the dreadful odor or our dead Loves we suffer over through the darkest hours of the night instead of sleeping and steeling ourselves for our tomorrows. Dear God! What do we teach each other?' [Spelling and punctuation as written.]

'The Hammer' went on and on for another eight double-sided pages, and I simply cannot put you, dear reader, through any more of his literary purgatory. I mean, I would love to, of course I would, but you might either need to seek psychiatric counselling (not recommended, for the reasons mentioned earlier) or turn to the drink then throw yourself off a cliff (certainly not recommended either). Yet after his rant into his world where elephants fly, lead balls bounce and fairies reign supreme, his 'words of wisdom' were signed off with:

I hope you had a magnificent trip on the way back and splendid times away from home and a safe and satisfactory trip on the way back. My heart is with you, each and every one. Take care of yourselves. I cannot afford to lose even one of you, I need all of you to care for and to love.

Your friend, Harvey.

Phew, I wonder what you make of that lot? It seems very much as though there are two characters living inside Harvey's head – one good, the other deadly evil. Both totally inconsistent with each other. As my late friend, the former Lord Chief Justice Geoffrey Lane, Baron Lane, AFC, PC once wrote to me: 'There is good in the worst of us. Oddly enough, prison sometimes serves for that fact to be proved', but in Carignan's case he can never learn nor will he be able to: aged ninety-five, he died of natural causes within the walls of MCF Oak Park Heights, 5329 N. Osgood Avenue, Minnesota, on 6 March 2023.

Ian Stewart Brady, aka
'The Moors Murderer'

*We do whatever we enjoy doing. Whether it happens to be
judged good or evil is a matter for others to decide.*

IAN BRADY, *THE GATES OF JANUS: SERIAL KILLING
AND ITS ANALYSIS* (2001)

Along with tag-team accomplice Myra Hindley, Ian Brady ranks
among the worst serial killers in British criminal history. Little
further introduction is required here because all that you will
ever want to know about this murderous couple is extremely
well documented elsewhere.

Two sadistic killers of the utmost depravity.
    Mr Justice Fenton Atkinson: on Brady and Hindley

The span of their crimes, which became the subject of extensive
worldwide coverage, ran from 12 July 1963 until 7 October

1965, when Brady and Hindley were arrested. Their victims were: Pauline Reade; John Kilbride; Keith Bennett; Lesley Ann Downey and Edward Evans – aged between ten and seventeen. At least four of the children were sexually assaulted. Two bodies were discovered in 1965, in shallow graves dug on the bleak, grey Saddleworth Moor, an area of the Peak District National Park, in north-west England, that bears the suitably ominous name of the 'Dark Peak'. In 1987, police uncovered a third grave on the moors, that of Pauline Reade. Keith Bennett's body is also believed to lie there, although the whereabouts of his final resting place remain unknown, despite several searches over the years. Both killers were given a full life tariff. Hindley died of bronchial pneumonia on 15 November 2002. Brady died by natural causes, his sell-by date expiring on 15 May 2017.

I have not read Brady's book *The Gates of Janus: Serial Killing and its Analysis*, for what I believe is a sensible reason: this diagnosed sexual psychopath's opinions and analysis on serial homicide are, quite frankly, neither here nor there. More of interest to me is the never-before-published correspondence that Brady sent to me while he was incarcerated at the high-security psychiatric hospital Park Lane, now named Ashworth, in Maghull, ten miles to the north-east of Liverpool.

Before we begin, let's remind ourselves of Mr Justice Fenton Atkinson's description of Brady and Hindley, while also bearing in mind that neither of these two monsters ever exhibited a shred of remorse. Myra Hindley tried to curry some mitigating favour with a bunch of left-wing do-gooders – including Long Longford, famed for championing social outcasts and unpopular causes and especially notable for his lifelong advocacy of penal reform. Whether Lord Longford had it in mind to try to reform

Brady and Hindley is something else, but the Lord Chief Justice Geoffrey Lane does not seem to have been in agreement when he wrote: 'This is the case if ever there is to be one when a man should stay in prison till he dies.'

Brady's biro-written letters to me were upon 'Medical Mission International' 11 x 12-cm cream notepaper, featuring coloured photos – one each of an antelope, elephant, zebra, baboon, white cuddly bear cub, monkey, giraffe and some people pushing a rubber boat through some water. These were, of course, very small postage-stamp photos, as you will have gathered. His notepaper had been designed for him bespoke: atop the front page had been personally printed for him: 'From the desk of: Mr I Stewart-Brady'.

If that is not obsequious from a man of his ilk, I don't know what is.

Mr I. Stewart-Brady's first letter to me from his 'desk' is dated 30 July 2009, kicking off with 'Dear Christopher, Thanks for yours on 9th July 2009'. As he had a lot to say within so small a page, written on both sides, his handwriting was neat and readable.

First, most of your questions are answered in my book on criminal psychology, 'The Gates of Janus' published 2002, now accepted text in UK/US universities and translated. Reviews can be accessed on Amazon and other main book websites.

No, contrary to logical extension, based on 'Janus', I'm not particularly interested in books about serial killers, etc. I prefer the study of <u>major</u> criminals, such as Blair, Bush and their profiteering henchmen. As I've always stated since teenage years, you can't 'beat decent, honest, respectable people' when it comes down to global serial slaughter, theft, greed, treachery and hypocrisy, which is why they exploit petty, underclass crime and criminals to distract attention from themselves and their threadbare pretensions/claims to moral superiority. Nothing new or profound in any of this, of course; just generally convenient to ignore such unpopular juxtapositions. Please acknowledge receipt.

Best wishes,

Ian Brady.

PS: The current satirical gall of Cherie Blair lecturing the nation on the 'horrors of knife crime', highlights the absurdity and arrogance of the class. Greed has replaced vocation in the professions.

Which strikes me as a lot of 'Speakers' Corner' set-the-world-straight, top-of-a-ladder blathering. And what's more, did you know that Brady, who was pathologically obsessed with the Nazis, actually received German language lessons from a senior university professor while in the nuthouse? He was tipped to land a job as a translator if ever he were to be released. When future prime minister James Callaghan – then the Home Secretary – popped in to visit Brady at his desk, this paedophile praised the Nazis for their 'efficiency'. Actually, that last point stuck with me, and I started wondering if I had missed something.

My editors are always informing me that I have missed many, *many* things. Some of my readers and critics say the same thing. And my publisher's lawyers are always telling me not to write certain things. So I asked myself: Was Brady really being groomed for a job as an ambassador in Berlin within some future Callaghan government? Because not-so-long-ago-released prison records now reveal how prison governors, and a welfare officer, praised Brady's intelligence and excellent use of Hitler's oratories 'with a cracked grin', stating that they hoped that the German classes would end with him leading a 'healthy normal life in society'.

Then I woke up in a cold sweat: German language classes for Brady? C'mon, are these leftie clowns kidding us, or what?

My crimes were no different to massacres being carried out by US troops in Vietnam.

Ian Brady: to a prison chaplain

After which came this utter fantasy-driven drivel from the chief education officer at Durham Prison: 'If Brady continues to come along well in his German I see no reason why he should not make a living one day as an interpreter or translator,' adding: 'The tuition given to Brady has given a new interest to him in life, begin [*sic*] to pull him out of himself on the long hard road to *a healthy normal life in society*.' [Author's italics.]

By now the reader will be thinking, 'What the fuck are these fools going on about? This is taxpayers' hard-earned money being thrown at a sexual psychopath who still refused to reveal the locations of his victims?' It may be of some interest – although to whom, I simply don't know – that Brady also passed courses in English literature, maths, psychology and was encouraged to pursue a university degree – at the taxpayers' expense, once again, of course. Then comes the juicy stuff. Brady, who strangled some of his victims with string or a shoelace and buried them on Saddleworth Moor, was given lessons – wait for it, wait for it – in knot-tying while in jail, by a young female therapist who became infatuated with him. A prison spokesperson commented: 'Reluctantly, we had to separate them because of our fears their bond was becoming unprofessional.' You really couldn't make this up if you tried.

So back to I. Stewart-Brady's desk and the contents of his letter to me. It occurred to me to look up some online reviews of *The Gates of Janus*, and they are a mixed bunch. Whether or not his claims that the book is 'accepted text in UK/US universities', especially those with large Jewish campuses, seems at best debatable. It all comes across as a lot of over-egging-it, if you ask me. As for any knot-tying – may I be so blatantly crass in suggesting that the best knot of all would have been in the form of a hempen noose tied around his scrawny neck?

Poisoned Nibs

My fellow-prisoners [...] seemed to me in no way morally inferior to the rest of the population, though they were on the whole slightly below the usual level of intelligence, as was shown by their having been caught.

THE AUTOBIOGRAPHY OF BERTRAND RUSSELL,
1951–69

A dry wit, had Bertrand.

NOTE: what follows was not, I stress *not* penned by a serial murderer but it does earn its place in this book because it was written at the behest of one of the most evil men in US homicidal history, and although one short note from a pretty much nondescript prisoner might not amount to a hill of beans, the following account has more twists and turns than fiddling with a Rubik's cube. It proves that corresponding with dangerous criminals can be a risky business indeed – as authors far better than me will agree, even more so when a letter that at first blush seems innocuous enough, harbours cunning most foul between the lines.

Miguel Langebeck was not a criminal big-hitter by any stretch of the imagination, but he did earn himself a fifteen-year stretch as inmate #192103 J2S3 at Florida State Prison (Main Unit) in Starke. In August 1995, I received an unsolicited letter from Langebeck, which started: 'Dear Christopher. Receive my greetings and best wishes. We haven't been formally introduced, but a mutual friend asked me to write to you. Gerard Schaeffer [sic], as you know a fellow litigant for prison reform and prisoners' rights, is the mutual friend I speak of.' Now that other name I knew. He was one of America's most heinous serial killers: Florida ex-cop, Gerard John Schaefer Jr.

One can instantly sense 'flowery' prose, perhaps along the lines of Graham Young's letter quoted earlier, or one from Mr I. Stewart-Brady. I soon got a sniff of a jailhouse lawyer here too − (another Ian). Miguel's penmanship was okay, grammar reasonably good, yet for the life of me I was certainly *no* mutual friend of Schaefer, nor Langebeck for that matter. The former I had no interest in at all, the latter I had never even heard of, so this letter came right out of the blue.

Curious to a fault, I looked up Langebeck's details on the Florida Department of Corrections website, to learn that he had been arrested in Miami-Dade County on 1 February 1990 for cocaine trafficking. He was released on 1 October 1998 − his present status 'unknown'. Small fry when it comes down to it, most certainly not in Schaefer's bestial league, yet why would Langebeck write on Schaefer's behalf. I sensed some naughtiness going on here.

Let's deal with the remainder of Miguel's letter first:

He has informed me of your interest in his plight and being somewhat of a litigator myself, I was drawn by our mutual views on prisons today.

I hope you overlook my boldness in writing you, but it's also to offer my time and services if needed since Mr. Shaeffer [sic] has closed a book deal which he'll be working on, withdrawing himself from any further legal work until his completion of his project.

I'm currently undergoing some research for some Virginia prisoners, for them to attack Virginia's Parole Board's new stringent guidelines. I'm trying to demonstrate an Ex Post Facto clause violation. Hopefully when completed it'll be entertained by the courts with merit [...]

Straight off the bat, I knew that at the time of Langebeck's letter, Schaefer had grievously annoyed several authors who were now treating him like a literary plague. And the first thing the reader will notice will be the utter hypocrisy of the letter. Langebeck could not even spell Schaefer's name correctly, moreover; plus, I didn't give a jot about Schaefer's plight either. Here we have Mr Langebeck, a convicted cocaine trafficker by profession – a trade costing tens of thousands of lives a year – using typical jailhouse shyster legalese while banging on about a number of subjects: Schaefer, a sadosexual serial murderer who didn't give a damn about his many victims' rights; something about a book deal; fellow prisoners' rights; and something to do with an 'Ex Post Facto clause violation'. To be honest with the reader, I hadn't a clue about this 'Ex Post Facto' stuff; you probably don't either, then, straight out of Brady's and Carignan's playbook. Langebeck rails on:

I've been amazed, at how the prisons in this country, abuse and outright disrespect the rights of the inmate body. They're the first to criticize other nations in human rights issues, yet they are probably the biggest culprit of human rights violations. I believe, that the major problem has been the media portrayal of crime offenders, that have the general public appalled of being victimized, causing a general disconcern for prisoners only enhancing the public's views toward harsher sentences, focusing more on punishment rather than rehabilitation and education.

And, Miguel, the point of your letter is ... what? Please get on with it.

Like all typical capitalist nations, their expertise in maintaining a façade impression on the world, always point a finger, instead of deal with reality, keeps its people blind of the facts. Yet, there's always hope, as long as a few care and bring it to light.

Yours Truly,

Miguel Langebeck

I am not sure if Miguel had studied at the 'Professor Ian Stewart-Brady Berlin University of Schwachsinn', so I haven't a clue if he had received a Doctorate in Flannel. I can't even confirm what the Virginia Parole Board made of Langebeck's *ex post facto* submissions. However, I am 100 per cent sure that the Virginia Supreme Court justices would *not* have messed their pants if they'd ever got as far as flicking through it all. Moreover, I am 200 per cent positive that if convict shyster

Langebeck's 'inmate clients' chose him to represent them, their sentences would have been quadrupled for wasting everyone's time, with any of them serving six months for shoplifting ending up in the electric chair. I was starting to think that 'Miggie' was yet another member of 'The Complicated Surreal Club' – a jerk-off who rode around the prison on a pink, three-wheeled Toy Town bike with a shiny ding-a-ling bell – and turned the last fragments of my dwindling attention to Mr Schaefer. I will trouble the reader little with this serial killer's narrative – Wikipedia is pretty thorough in this regard and there are several TV documentaries and interviews available on YouTube. Nonetheless, what follows *did* interest me.

There are plenty of narcissistic jailhouse attorney wannabes (think Ted Bundy and Kenneth Bianchi, for instance) – a litigious bunch of halfwits who get a perverse thrill out of wasting millions of dollars of taxpayers' money firing off lawsuits to all and sundry. Most of the time they use lined, yellow prison-issue stationery, although I once received a short note written on toilet paper from one prisoner. Sadly the text was all unreadable, so I replied thanking the chap for his ingenuity and enclosed several sheets of one of our better-known, softer, perfumed brands featuring a puppy should he feel the need to write again or have a sudden need to do something else.

Despite the fact that all of Schaefer's appeals had been rejected, off he went filing meritless lawsuits. First in his firing line was true-crime writer Patrick Kendrick, who described Schaefer as: 'an overweight, doughy, middle-aged man who preyed on victims who were psychologically and physiologically weaker than him'.

Patrick, congratulations. That portrayal is right on the nail.

Further down range came litigation aimed at other authors: Sondra London; Colin Wilson; Michael Newton; and former FBI Special Agent Robert Ressler (whom Schaefer targeted for describing him as a serial killer). Indeed, Schaefer sued Ressler all costing the former cop a fortune to defend, because at that time Schaefer had only been convicted of two homicides – although more charges were being loaded into the DA's magazine. The FBI's *own* criminal lexicon defines a serial killer as having murdered three or more victims with a cooling-off period in between events, so Schaefer had a moot point.

Sondra London, an old girlfriend from high school, collaborated with Schaefer in writing and publishing crime fiction but soon learned that his 'fiction' was rather closer to fact than was comfortable, and ended her association with Schaefer, repudiating his story that he was merely a 'framed ex-cop' who wrote lurid fiction. When she stated that he was indeed every bit the serial killer he simultaneously boasted of being, he repeatedly threatened her life and filed suit against her for calling him a serial killer in print.

In support of her defence against the lawsuit – which was costing her time and money to defend, of course – Sondra London compiled an exhibit of photocopies of 500 incriminating pages of Schaefer's handwritten correspondence; the judge dismissed his case without further ado. In a further turn of the screw, she generously provided Newton and Wilson with the same 500-page exhibit too, so his lawsuits against them were also kicked out.

Up until his death, Schaefer continued to threaten Sondra London. He also wrote letters to Kendrick, suggesting that he had willing agents who would do his bidding and that he 'would hate to see something happen to your family'. Unfazed, Kendrick went on to write novels often describing brutal murders that he relates to his experience with this former police officer turned *really* bad. So Schaefer got himself screwed once again. These psychopaths never learn, do they?

It was at this point that I twigged on to the fact that Langebeck's letter was even more full of garbage than I'd first imagined. Why? Before 1995, all of Schaefer's efforts to have his *own* book published had been blown away. Since then, he'd been fishing for authors to write his story and, being the obnoxious control freak that he was, he blew them out every time. Then, I recalled that Sondra had edited a 1993 book called *Knockin' on Joe: Voices from Death Row*, and I vaguely recalled that she and I had spoken a couple of times on the phone. Somehow Schaefer had gotten wind of this, so *via* slippery Langebeck, he was trying to draw me into his web of deceit.

Gerard Schaefer was one of those up-his-own-backside prison idiots who never learn to shut up so, not unsurprisingly, he was making enemies fast and furious. Not only was this litigious, pseudo-religiously bigoted loudmouth a former cop who had abducted, tortured, raped and hung up to strangle to death at least two (although probably around thirty) of Florida's precious little darlings, he'd pissed all over the law-enforcement agencies who had hired him in all good faith to 'Protect and Serve'. He had used his uniform and his shield as a means of luring these trusting girls to their deaths. Now this smug, filthy little man was courting TV interviews and litigating against anyone who said a word against him. He had become a snitch in an attempt to curry favour with the guards, and using his status as a 'death-row law clerk' to get confidential information from prisoners that found their way to the prosecutor's office, only to be used against his fellow inmates. It is no wonder that in the year before his own murder he had human excrement thrown over him several times and his cell was twice set on fire. Now almost under siege, he made another fatal mistake by grassing on an inmate who was well respected in the prison. Bad move, Gerard.

At this point, please look up some of the TV-taped interviews of this fat bespectacled creep on YouTube. See for yourself what sort of man he was. Look at his eyes. His sickening grin, the obsequious piece of work only a sexual serial killer can be. I also strongly recommend the book *Knockin' on Joe*, edited by Sondra London, and published by Nemesis Publications. Strong stuff. Highly recommended, no-punches-pulled accounts. Not intended for a bedtime read.

US penitentiaries are not nice places in which to set up home. 'Newbies' chain-shuffling through the gates are entering 'The Belly of the Beast', especially the younger lads. Pretty boys are soon exploited – if you catch my drift – with the older cons being streetwise enough to keep their mouths superglued tight and snitches summarily dealt with; the correctional officers usually turn a blind eye. So Mr Schaefer really should have known better, but his psychopathological mindset was so ingrained, that he, like so many other psychopaths, never learned the error of their ways.

The pen is mightier than the sword.

Edward Bulwer-Lytton, Lord Lytton,
Richelieu; or The Conspiracy, 1839

On 3 December 1995, less than a month after I had received Langebeck's letter, Schaefer was found stabbed to death and trampled upon in his cell. One eye had been gouged out by a pen – prison punishment for snitches, or grasses – giving a new meaning to the above famous metonymic adage created by Bulwer-Lytton. All of which made for a most fitting end to a monster who was pathologically addicted to making everyone's lives a misery by using pen and ink to cause a stink. His writings to Sondra London were homicidal porn, he was reliving his crimes in ink, but in making his so-called 'book' a novel, and hoping to make a fast buck, he was gloatingly memorialising in the third person, and using Sondra London as the one to catch the heat.

Official sources put out the story that inmate Vincent Rivera killed Schaefer over an argument about a hot cup of water – it might have been coffee – but after attending the murder trial and debriefing Rivera, the admirable Sondra London, I believe, exposed what amounted to a cover-up, saying that the hot water story was implausible, noting several little-known facts:

- A full palm print in blood was found on the wall of Schaefer's cell, which in lab tests failed to match those of either Schaefer or Rivera – unconfirmed evidence that was thrown out instead of being presented to the jury.
- Expert testimony at Rivera's trial also established that the patterns of the footprints on Schaefer's corpse matched those of prison service issue, worn by prison officers but not by inmates.

Already serving a life sentence for two previous homicides and robberies, Vincent Faustino Rivera was sentenced to an additional 53 years and ten months for killing Schaefer. He never confessed to the crime, or to having had a motive to kill Schaefer. But he *did* write to Sondra London and tell her of a similar incident in that prison, claiming that he'd been an 'ear-witness' to the prison murder of death-row inmate Frank Valdes by prison officers. Valdes was on death row for his part in the fatal shooting in 1987 of a prison officer during an attempt to help an inmate escape. (A fellow inmate also involved in the shooting was executed in 2013.)

In his letter to London, Rivera alleged that he'd written a complaint to the prison authorities about an earlier assault by prison staff on Valdes, who occupied the cell next to him. Rivera's claim was ignored and he was still being held in a cell next to Valdes's when the second, fatal beating took place. Rivera knew what was happening – he had heard it before.

In the trial that followed Valdes's death, prosecutors stated that the attack on him was to prevent him discussing 'mistreatment of prisoners and writing letters' to the press. The defence's story was that Valdes had threatened one of the officers, leading to an extraction team being called to his cell. He had then, they alleged, killed himself – by the unlikely means of taking a nose-dive off his bunk into the bars of his cell. The autopsy showed that a number of Valdes's ribs had been broken and there were 'prints of correctional officers' boots' on his skin, therefore the Florida Department of Law Enforcement (FDLE) ruled that Valdes died as the result of a beating, and nine officers were arrested. The officers, who were fired from their jobs, refused to talk; four were acquitted and three years later all charges against the remaining defendants were dropped.

And here I return to the title of this chapter: 'Poisoned Nibs'. There is a common thread running throughout all of the aforementioned characters: an almost overwhelming, pathological desire to write countless letters, protesting about their communal welfare and prison rights while ignoring their victims' rights, attempting to sue all and sundry, at once poking their criminal noses into the business of others when they would have been better advised not to have put pen to paper at all. Have we not seen so much of this with the other killers featured within these pages thus far?

Endnote: before we move on, I'd like to address a point often claimed in articles, that Ted Bundy admired Gerard Schaefer: 'We often spoke together about our crimes, and Ted thought of me as his equal,' Schaefer boasts. 'We are both attorneys at heart fighting against the downtrodden.' All of which conveniently ignores the fact that Bundy was housed on death row while Schaefer was in the general prison population with no access to 'The Green Mile' remotely possible – apart from in Schaefer's wildest wet dreams.

As for Miguel's letter to me, guess what? I didn't reply.

Hal Karen and Ronald 'Butch' Joseph DeFeo Jr, aka 'The Amityville Horror'

There is no fire like passion, there is no shark like hatred, there is no snare like folly, there is no torrent like greed.

SIDDHARTA GAUTAMA

As regards the following case, the epigraph above defines the subject of this chapter to a T.

One more pertinent quote before we get going, this one relating to egotism. It's from Publilius Syrus's *Moral Sayings*, *c.*50 BC:

A cock has great influence on his own dunghill.

All of which seems most fitting for the subject of this chapter. I'll open with a bit of trivial travelogue.

A hamlet in the town of East Fishkill in Dutchess County, New York State, 'Stormville' is named after the siblings Jacob and Rupert Storm, a pair of settlers. According to the town's own website, the area is located at the intersections of 'Dutchess County Route 216, Old Route 52 and Seaman Road', and 'was begun as early as 1739'; Derick Storm is noted as the earliest individual to 'take up land' here. The website adds that the Storm family were slave owners and that a 'slave cemetery' can be found on Phillips Road. And this will excite my readers even more: Stormville's flea market is reportedly well worth a visit although, alas, 'pets are not allowed' to the event.

As you will have gathered by now, I love my etymology. The term 'flea market' may well have originated with the French 'marché aux puces' ('market of the fleas'), a reference to the sales of used merchandise, quite possibly flea-infested. And the reason that pets aren't permitted? Apparently because if an animal hasn't got fleas when it goes into such a market, it will most certainly have some when it leaves. For more information about the Stormville Airport Antique and Flea Market, including the dates, hours and rules, check out their website.

As this book is all about writing, you'll be delighted to know that East Fishkill was the birthplace of one Mr Platt Rogers Spencer – the inventor of the leading US business-handwriting style of the nineteenth century – in 1800. For those of my readers more inquisitive than me, one can take it as gospel that Platt was the originator of the Spencerian script – a popular system of cursive handwriting. To add to his bona fides, he was a teacher and active in the business school movement. So, if you care to ask me, it's a damned shame that there is *no* pigeon-shat-upon statue of him *anywhere* in Dutchess County, although there is the Platt Rogers Spencer Monument in Geneva, Ohio, where he lived and died.

Spencer's elegantly flowing copperplate-style script was adopted Stateside from the mid-nineteenth century to the mid-1920s for business correspondence. Think Coca-Cola's logo, still bearing a strong resemblance to its 1880s manifestation, or Ford's logo, dating from 1911, and you will get the idea.

But we are not in Stormville to discuss its history, or, indeed, calligraphy in general. Nope, we are going to visit a place called Green Haven, which is not – as one might at first imagine – an exclusive retirement home with lush gardens, or an exclusive private hospital or expensive health-and-fitness spa. Green Haven, on Route 216, is in fact a maximum-security facility near the town of Beekman. Behind its grim walls are warehoused circa up to two thousand highly dangerous offenders. It opened in 1949.

This prison, one of the last 'big houses', contained New York's execution chamber during the time the Empire State briefly had the death penalty. Indeed, New York's notorious 'Old Sparky' was moved here from Sing Sing (the former Ossining) Correctional Facility in the early 1970s.

I mention this glittering, highly embroidered criminological trivia because no fewer than 614 men and women were fried in Sing Sing's 'Old Sparky'; and believe this or not, I have sat in it. It's antiquated, sure enough. Some traces of the cables still exist, but it was the head piece I found morbidly fascinating. It was falling apart and going rusty. While I was sitting comfortably in 'Old Sparky' and examining the 'Hot Hat', my TV producer Frazer said to the warden: 'There is something wrong with that chair.' A look of confusion crossed the warden's face and he replied, confused, 'Oh, sir, and what is that?' With a smug smile, Frazer replied: 'It ain't switched on!'

With a TV producer like that, who needs enemies? But did you know that the first design for an electric chair was drawn up by a dentist, with an electrician adding the wires shortly thereafter? Well now you do, so give this some thought when you next open your mouth to *your* dentist. Or maybe not.

Hal Karen

In late December 2009, a letter dated the 14th of that month, from Hal Karen – DIN #03-A3087 – of Green Haven Correctional Facility, dropped through my letter box. It was typewritten and Hal was replying to my initial interest in his case. There was nothing spectacular about him. He was not a serial killer or anything like that, but I wanted him to tell me his side of the story of why he was convicted of killing his wife. And then, without him knowing, to compare his written 'story' with the official file.

The reader might be asking: 'Christopher, why did you select Hal?' To be straight with you, I really don't know the answer to that very sensible question. I get a lot of very sensible questions from my very sensible readers for which I have no sensible answers, but somewhere sleeping at the back of my mind was the vague memory that testifying for the state in Karen's case was none other than the world-renowned Michael M. Baden, MD, an American physician and forensic pathologist who was at the time director of the NYS Police medicolegal investigations unit. An impressive if at times contentious figure, Dr Baden has been involved in the investigation of a number of high-profile deaths and cases, including the assassination of John F. Kennedy; the O.J. Simpson trial; Phil Spector and his role in the death of Lana

Clarkson; the shooting of Michael Brown; and, more recently, the deaths of George Floyd and of Jeffrey Epstein (he does not share the accepted view that Epstein committed suicide). Although highly controversial, Dr Baden knows his stuff and his books are a fascinating read. A Dr James Gill testified for the defence. I've digressed. In a nutshell, Hal Karen wrote to inform me that, to his mind, the medical examiner, Dr Baden, made a mistake. I quote verbatim:

Dear Chris,

I hope it's O.K. to call your [*sic*] Chris. It's always nice to get a letter from a former soldier. Under different circumstances I'm sure we could down some pints and exchange stories. Anyway I was kind of surprised when I got your letter because I feel that me [*sic*] case was not really a big deal and they put my military experience into the picture to elevate the picture in order to get a conviction. I have been able to tell my story before and I don't think it's anything what the T.V. shows had portrayed and if Dr. Baden would not have testified for the D.A. as he did, I would not be here and if I would have enough money for a better defence I surely would have been able to prove my innocence of murder. So, with all of that I'll give you a quick gist of what "REALLY" happened.

I meet Tammy at a topless bar outside of FT. BRAGG N.C. I had just returned from Haiti after a six-month deployment and needed some winding down. I ended up getting her pregnant so we went to Las Vegas and got married. She used drugs when I meet [*sic*] her but during the pregnancy she did not. When Hunter was born she started using drugs again and that's when everything went downhill. I could not get her to stop and she did not want to. One day I came home and found her dead in the bathroom. For a long time I covered the drug problem from people, it was embarrassing. So I took the body and I got rid of it and I told everyone she left because she has done this before with her first child which she left with her mother and took off. But I did not hide it good enough. I know what I did was wrong but I had my reasons and if you are still interest [*sic*] I will tell you them. But I feel better that after you read this letter you are not going to even use this story. And as the investigator that you are I'll bring up just two points that you can check out for yourself.

1. How can someone go into a court room and tell a jury that this person died from strangulation when you only have some bones and not even any neck bones?
2. After almost 3 years of the body being in the woods and they still managed to find a piece of liver from her body which this alone is incredible and they test it for drugs and it comes up positive with 30 nanograms of cocaine by-product. How can you say that that is not enough to kill someone? You would think that there had to be an awful lot to even show anything after 3 years.

If you know a forensic pathologist ask him or her what they think. Anyway I don't think I'm being much help to you. Like I said before once you read this letter you'll just back away because it's not the story everyone thinks it is. I tell you this and I have no idea what they said in the T.V. shows which I believe there are several. That I'm not the person they made me out to be. I never hurt anyone in my life without a reason. I don't know how much help this letter is to you and your book but I do have a lot to say, its probable just not help you. Actually I'm the one who needs help. Sometimes I wish there were more veterans with special skills that can help other veterans out there without charging and arm and a leg but that would asking too much.

Well if your [*sic*] still interested write me back or write me back even if your [*sic*] not, its [*sic*] nice to get a little mail. I don't have a lot of people write me because when things go wrong people tend to turn their backs on you and just forget you. If you can I would like to read one of your books, I do a lot of reading. So if you can and if you want please send me copies of your books.

Take care and good luck with your books.

Best Wishes

HAL (aka RAMBO) (aka HALANATOR)

(That's the name the guys gave me).

I don't know what you make of that letter, full of [*sics*]. On its face it is polite, respectful, fairly well written, almost self-effacing. My only gripe would be that he only referred to his wife's name, 'Tammy', the one time; elsewhere it is 'it', or 'the body'. Regarding the post-mortem issues, however, he may have raised something of interest. The downside it seems to me is that there is some transference of blame, with Tammy being at fault because she, according to him, was a drug addict. He was a serving soldier, yet had any man arrived back home to find his wife dead on the floor, I suggest that he would have dialled 911, got paramedics to the scene asap, then gone searching for her will or any existing paid-up life insurance policies and a list of local undertakers. But Hal didn't.

As has been my wont throughout this book, I'll try to consider the subtext of this letter. One cannot fail to note that although the couple had a baby, Hal had no respect for the mother; he simply took her corpse out some place isolated and dumped it. 'But I did not hide it good enough,' he says – 'it' meaning the mother of his child. That he signs off with 'HAL aka RAMBO' aka 'HALANATOR' – the name the guys gave me', I suggest, is a figment of his imagination.

Green Haven is one of the toughest penitentiaries and it still houses some of the worst of the worst, and I know this because I have been in there – not as a convict it goes without saying. That these extremely hard Yardies, Crips, Bloods, American Front (white supremacists), Tongs, Triads, Mafiosi of pick 'n' mix all-sorts including the Gulf Cartel, along with outlaw motorcycle clubs from the 'Bandinos' through to the 'Warlocks', serial killers beyond counting, would have nicknamed Hal 'Rambo' would be side-splittingly funny if it were not so serious a matter.

The long and the short of it is that, in 2003, Hal Karen was, in legalese, 'convicted of murder in the second degree, offering a false instrument for filing in the first degree and perjury in the second degree in connection with the death of his wife in June 1999 and his subsequent efforts to conceal her death'. His sentence was an aggregate term of 26⅓ years to life.

Tammy was last seen on 27 June 1999. According to Hal Karen, a former Special Forces paratrooper, his wife had said goodbye to their child, taken some of their belongings from their home and taken off in a stranger's car not to be seen again. A month later her sister reported her missing to the police; for his part, Hal had filed for divorce and sought a protection order against his wife in the Family Court. That all smelt a bit fishy but the stench got even worse when, almost three years later, in March 2002, decomposed human remains were discovered in a garbage bin tied into two rubbish bags at the bottom of a steep 80-foot embankment in a wooded area a few minutes' drive from the couple's home.

Forensic investigators examining the find were able to establish through a DNA test that the body was Tammy's. In such cases a spouse is frequently the first suspect, and what clinched the killer's identity for the police were the military appearance of the cord used to tie the bags onto the bin, and, specifically, the knots used, which were used by Special Forces paratroopers. When Hal was confronted by police and shown the evidence he changed his story about Tammy's departure. He told police that he found her dead of a cocaine overdose in the bathroom of their home and admitted that he had placed her body in the bin and rolled it over the embankment. At his trial he maintained that he had disposed of his wife's body and concealed her death because he feared that her use of cocaine would result in his loss of the custody of his child. The thought that he would lose his child if he ended up in prison apparently never crossed his mind, as it didn't with Melanie McGuire.

Hal's defence was that his wife died as a result of a cocaine overdose. A second medical examiner testified that while *some* evidence of cocaine was found in the victim's remains, the amount would have been 'insufficient' to cause Tammy's death. And it is here that Hal raises his moot point. So: how long does cocaine stay in one's system, bearing in mind that Tammy's remains had been found some three years after she had gone missing? Well at no charge to the reader, it goes like this:

How long cocaine remains in the system
- Blood: two days
- Saliva: two days
- Urine: four days
- Hair: ninety days

If one is a long-term and/or heavy drug user, traces of the drug can be found many months or even years after complete cessation, and this is how the second pathologist formed his opinion – while forming no conclusion either way as to whether Hal Karen was right or wrong. Hal's beef is that the pathologist gave the impression to the jury that on this issue alone he, the defendant, was lying. Yet the medical examiner at the same time inadvertently confirmed what Hal Karen had claimed from the outset – that his wife was a hardened drug addict.

So, was Hal Karen's defence team fast asleep?

I'd argue that the defence team *was* asleep, if not in a coma. In hot and humid conditions, or under water, a body will completely decompose within weeks or less, especially if insects and other forms of life are about; in the frozen Arctic, it can take years; in temperate conditions, it can take from a few weeks to several years for a body to decompose into a skeleton, depending on factors such as ambient temperature (it would decompose faster in hot summer than in winter), humidity, the presence of insects, and so on. By now, after rotting for some three years after her tragic death, Tammy would have become all but bones and a liquefied mass; that she died of traumatic asphyxia would have been a matter of some highly speculative guesswork, yet somehow the defence team didn't pick up on this. Supporting evidence offered to the jury by the State's attorney's investigating officer established that, according to the official case notes from the trial *People* v. *Hal Karen* from July 2005, 'given the position of the toilet and sink, it would have been impossible for the victim to have been in the position as described by the defendant when he allegedly found her body in the bathroom.' Well, guys and gals, we all know how allegedly bent some cops can be, do we not – 'a light touch can hang a man', 'tis true.

According to the same source, another piece of hearsay evidence produced by the prosecutors was that, according to her sister, Tammy was planning to leave her husband, and that Hal told police that 'his wife had ruined his life he had been angry with her for stealing cash from his wallet'. But does this prove motive for murder most foul? Of course not.

I'm no Lieutenant Columbo, but retrospectively I believe that Hal Karen truly messed up from the get-go. Did he deserve an aggregate term of 26⅓ years to life in prison? I'll let you decide, but as the New York Department of Corrections website confirms, he is no longer behind the grim grey walls of the Green Haven Correctional Facility in Stormville. Indeed, where he is these days no one seems to know – not even him, I'd hazard a speculative guess.

Ronald 'Butch' Joseph DeFeo Jr

DeFeo, on the other hand, is definitely dead. He was found guilty of the 1974 killings of his father, mother, two brothers, and two sisters in Amityville, Long Island, New York. Condemned to six sentences of 25 years to life at the Sullivan Correctional Facility, the previously mentioned maximum-security prison for men at Stormville, Fallsburg, New York – making a minimum sentence of 150 years. Given the notoriety of the case, his whereabouts were not always easy to discover, but when Ronald DeFeo and I finally started corresponding he was incarcerated, according to the address he gave, at the Eastern Correctional Facility in Napanoch, Ulster County, New York, another maximum-security men's prison, and one of the oldest such institutions in the Empire State. Then, in about March 1994 – if another of his letters is anything to go by – DeFeo was, to his extreme annoyance, transferred to Green Haven Correctional Facility, Stormville, New York.

My aim was to make a television documentary about 'The Amityville Horror' and interview him on camera. My homework informed me that DeFeo was a litigious mass-murderer; a money-greedy little guttersnipe who bathed in his notoriety. Knowing this, I cast my hook well baited with goodies that would appeal to him: some of my CV; copies of my previous book covers; promises of money, international TV fame and a book deal – all false – and waited for him to respond.

Butch jumped at it. I mean he *leapt* from his bunk and started writing letters, sending documents, giving me just about everything he had access to. Initially, therefore, everything was all rosy in the garden. In reality, however, he had fallen foul of several of the deadly sins, namely 'greed' and 'lust' (for money), 'wrath' (to get some revenge for being, as he saw it, wrongly convicted), misaligned egotistical 'pride', and I will add 'sloth' because he was, until his death from natural causes on 12 March 2021, an amoral gluttonous weasel. He was also a pathological liar and, in my humble opinion, one of the worst letter writers in American criminal history.

It soon became obvious that 'Ronald the Impatient' thought that Rome actually was built in a day, for on 2 June 1993, using a biro, he frantically wrote the following letter on lined, yellow prison-issue stationery. I include it verbatim in this book because: (1) it has never been released before; and (2) it shows what an obnoxious, narcissistic piece of work he was. As always, I quote verbatim, grammatical warts and all.

Dear Christopher,
I will get right to the point okay. After talking to My Attonrey FRANCEL TROTTER BELLINGER, After Reading All Your Letters, promise's Deals, etc ANd seeing Now How its going on Two Year's Yes, "<u>WE</u>" have come to the conclusion That you have been selling us a dream ANd trying to make money off of me and my case behind our back as Your Last Letter with the tape according You wanted me to do said it all.

If You Can't or Won't send some Type of Money in Good Faith then We Are Requesting the Immediate Return of Every thing I sent to You as Well as Letter's the Nonnewitze's, Springer, Davidge sent to you as well Because I asked them to. So the choice is Now Yours as if this is not done one way or another then the correct action will be Taken with the U.S. Attorney's Office etc.

Very Truly Your's
Ronald DeFeo BOX 338, Eastern C.F.
Napanoch, N.Y. 12458-0338.
Copy to Francel Trotter Bellinger/7442 9th, Street, NW.

The reader should understand that throughout his several court proceedings, indeed, right up until the day of his departure to hell, DeFeo had been trying to profit from the godawful point-blank shootings of his parents and four siblings. He'd despatched all of them via the trigger of his .35-calibre Marlin rifle as they slept warmly in their beds.

Aside from his nothing-to-read-between-the-lines scrawl, the attorney he mentions – Francel Trotter Bellinger – was apparently so concerned about her client's complaint that *not once* did she contact me. There was a very good reason for it, too: DeFeo 'pro-bono lawyer-shopped' as fast as a Monday morning quarterback vainly scrambles for a touchdown, enjoying a very singular lack of success, as each lawyer dumped him until one shyster called William Weber saw a pot of gold at the end of the rainbow and milked the murders for all he could back-pocket. So, now fully aware of this man's psychopathology, I replied with:

Dear Ronnie.
Thank you for your letter, 2 June. Noted. My film crew and I will be on Long Island circa September 1994. Lt Robert Dunn and Det. Dennis Rafferty, Homicide, Yaphank Police HQ (who gained your confession for multiple murder with the assistance of a Long Island telephone book smacked around your head), His Honor

Mr Justice Stark, Chief of Amity PD, Greg Greguski, two
of your former attorneys plus the State's attorney, and
your best friends Mr Nonnewitz and a Barry Springer,
along with others have already agreed to appear on
camera for our documentary programme.

I have been to your former home, 112 Ocean Avenue,
LI. I have examined and handled all of the exhibits inc:
the murder firearm a .35-cal Remington lever-action
rifle, victims' clothing, ballistics – bullets and cartridge
casings – CSI photos.

We respect your desire not to work with us. We all
wish you well in your endeavours.

One day, when it is convenient to me, and I am a
very busy man, I will return all you have requested. Please
advise whomever attorney you are now instructing.
Thank you.

Christopher.

Job done and dusted. However, if the truth be known I was
still trying to entice 'Butch' to appear on camera; to become
one of the killers Frazer Ashford & Co. and I were making in
the aforementioned TV documentary series, hence the two-
year back-and-forth correspondence and my stalling tactics as
we hoovered up all Frazer needed to make the programmes.
The book idea didn't come along till much later; the chapter
on DeFeo originally appearing in my 2003 book *Talking with
Serial Killers,* and the reason I selected 'Ronald the Impatient'
was that, much like all of the other killers within my brief, he
had never been interviewed for a TV programme before. I was
intent on becoming the first to meet-and-greet the man who

had spawned more 'based-upon-a-true-story' horror movies, books (factual, fictional and floating between the two), over-heated magazine and hyped-up press articles than one can count – with William Weber's assistance that is.

Getting 'The Amityville Horror' on camera would be a scoop.

I have included that letter from 'Butch' in this book because it sums him up in a nutshell. There is nothing concealed between the lines of his letter that should concern us; it is all writ large. Ronnie was too dumb to try to covertly manipulate anyone. Thick as a plank was our Ron, making it ever so easy for me to get him to conform to my wishes, while allowing his ego to think that he was the shot-caller, with all of his imaginary legal advisors behind him. We will see the same fondness for legalese when we meet John 'J.R.' Robinson later. An evil man J.R. certainly is, but there are moments in his letters when even he becomes a real hoot.

Just a few weeks before we were due to fly to America, I received a letter from Ronnie dated 13 March 1994. It had all come about as me having previously dismissed him out of hand; I had told him that we had enough interviewees, as well as Ronnie himself, on audio tape anyway so we were going to make the programme without him. He had got wind of this through one of his pals on the outside and, not wanting to lose out, he penned this:

Dear Christopher,
I hope my letter finds you in the best of health and the Best of Spirit.
To this Day Why I was Transfered To the Worse as

I was in The Best Max Prison in the state NO ONE KNOWS and here is my New Address.

"NOW" Did You Ever Recieve the Tapes as Lin and Roger Nonnewitz and Mr BARRY Springer who are all Witnesses in My Case and who know Bellinger Personally Told Her to Mail you the Tapes Five Weeks Ago Yes.

I CAN TELL You There is A Problem now with Francel Bellinger "Attorney" As she is Blaming Paul Woods and I am in the Middle. Could you please let me know whats Happening so I know what to do as Chris its Going On three years with "US" You and I as we have come A long way my "friend" As the Word Friend is very serious As they are very few in my life. Well I will close and await You Reply My Friend, Thank you and Take Care.

Ronnie DeFeo 75A4053

Drawer B.

Stormville, New York, 12582-0010.

I've been fuckin' waiting for two hours for you. Who ya think I am? I got better things to do.

> Ronald DeFeo's less-than-welcoming greeting
> prior to his TV interview with the author
> at the Green Haven Correctional Facility,
> Stormville, New York

Ronnie's ego was mega big, as big as the entire Empire State, I think, but therein lay another of his flaws. He kept boasting to fellow inmates, correctional officers and any lawyer whose ear he could catch that none other than the BBC were coming all the way from the UK to interview him. He was confident that the world-famous broadcasting station believed that he was innocent and that he would be paid a handsome fee for his time, for which any attorney acting in his interests would receive a fat bung. When I started contacting the authorities, stating categorically that we were *not* from the BBC, DeFeo still kept fishing. By then, however, the more enlightened of his lawyers had dropped him flat having realised that their client, nor they, would receive not a dime.

As it is, there are many TV documentaries on DeFeo and the Amityville murders freely available on Google (a search for either 'Ronald DeFeo' or 'Amityville Horror' will suffice). Gruesome crime-scene photos can be found elsewhere if you have the stomach to view them. And of course the many books and articles I mentioned above – including my own *Talking with Serial Killers*, my colleague Ric Osuna's *The Night the DeFeos Died: Reinvestigating the Amityville Murders,* Jay Anson's book *The Amityville Horror,* which inspired shelf loads of books, many having nothing to do with the actual case, but much to do with supernatural horror. Similarly with films: a single act of mass-murder led to a web of money-spinners for everyone except Ronnie.

I will leave you with this. The weapon used in the DeFeo slayings – a .35-calibre Marlin 336C lever-action rifle – is one of the choice firearms for taking down deer, bear, elk, even moose. Most .35-calibre rounds travel at around 2,100 feet per second and this load generates circa 1,900 pounds of energy. To get a sense of the power of this firearm and the noise it makes, look up 'Marlin 35 Remington Range 2' online, or something along those lines, then imagine these shots being discharged at point-blank range into two sleeping adults and four kids inside a relatively small house in the dead of night. Yet despite all of this, DeFeo was twice married while behind bars, to women who wanted to have children with him, who provided him with funds, built a website to which thousands of his sicko fans could contribute and inanely chitter-chatter among themselves like monkeys in a zoo.

Ronald Joseph DeFeo Sr (forty-four), Louise Marie Brigante DeFeo (forty-three), Dawn DeFeo (eighteen), Allison Louise DeFeo (thirteen), Marc Gregory DeFeo (twelve) and John Matthew DeFeo (nine) are buried in the Saint Charles Cemetery, East Farmingdale, Suffolk County, New York.

Ronald 'Butch' Joseph DeFeo Jr died aged sixty-nine and was cremated. I think that he is still dead to this very day.

Gary Ray Bowles aka 'The I-95 Killer'

I hope my death eases your pain. I want to tell my mother that I am sorry for my actions. Having to deal with your son being called a monster is terrible. I'm so very sorry.
I never wanted this to be my life. You don't wake up and decide to become a serial killer. I'm sorry for all the pain and suffering I have caused.

GARY RAY BOWLES: LAST WORDS BEFORE

HIS EXECUTION

Azure peepers earned Frank Sinatra the popular nickname 'Ol' Blue Eyes'. He led a colourful personal life, often becoming involved in turbulent affairs. Of course that useless titbit of information has nothing at all to do with the now deceased #086158-P-3226-S Gary Ray Bowles, formerly of Florida State Prison (FSP) in Raiford, except that the letters I received from him always bore two Frank

263

Sinatra postage stamps and this serial killer had brown eyes anyway.

Executed on Thursday, 22 August 2019 by lethal injection, Bowles had been nicknamed the 'I-95 Killer'; he'd murdered six gay men, the majority of whom had lived within the vicinity of the East Coast's Interstate 95 highway, between March and November 1994. He encountered most of his victims in gay bars, offering them sex in return for money and a place to stay, then strangled or bludgeoned them and made off with their cash and credit cards. Police found Bowles's fingerprints and probation records at the scene of his first victim's death in Daytona Beach. CCTV footage also caught him using the man's ATM card. So desperate were cops to catch Bowles, he appeared on *America's Most Wanted* programme multiple times and made the FBI's 'Most Wanted List' just three days before he was brought in for questioning in connection with the murder of his final victim, Walter Hinton, whose head was bashed in with a 40-pound concrete block. Another victim was found with a dildo jammed down his throat.

> Each of the murders was brutal. It was not an instant death, like somebody getting shot and dying from that gunshot … It was a life-and-death struggle.
>
> Bernie de la Rionda, Jacksonville prosecutor:
> to the *Daytona Beach News-Journal*

In mitigation before sentencing, Bowles's attorney brought up his client's troubled childhood. Gary's father had died of black lung disease before he was born, and he and his older brother were raised by their mother and a series of stepfathers – some of whom were abusive. After fighting back against the last stepdad, Bowles left home aged fourteen, making money as a male prostitute. Despite several appeals, and spending twenty years in a 6-foot by 9-foot cell, Bowles was never reprieved. Florida Governor Ron DeSantis, probably doing the only sensible thing in his entire GOP career, signed the death warrant on 11 June 2019. His last meal consisted of three cheeseburgers and a side of French fries.

I wanted Gary's story in his own words, and here it is, never published before, scant though it may be. In the original letter his handwriting is neat and he used small capital letters throughout. Moreover, each letter contained two Inmate Trust Fund Deposit Forms – one which he filled out as an 'example', just so that I didn't make any mistakes. Let's call it a letter from a 'Dead Man Walking, Talking and Writing and On the Hunt for Cash'.

DEAR CHRISTOPHER.

... I'M SORRY IT HAS TAKEN SO LONG FOR ME TO GET BACK TO YOU TO ANSWER YOUR LETTER. IT WAS GOOD TO HEAR FROM YOU AND I WANTED TO THANK YOU FOR TAKING THE TIME TO WRITE TO ME. I ALSO WANT TO THANK YOU FOR TAKING AN INTEREST IN ME AND MY STORY. I'M NOT SURE WHAT IT IS YOU PLAN TO DO AS FAR AS WRITING GOES, BUT ALL I WANT IS TO TELL MY STORY AND MAYBE IT WILL HELP SOMEONE, SOMEWHERE. AS VICTORIA [Redstall, a British-born American actress and true-crime writer who has interviewed such killers as Gary Ray Bowles and Keith Hunter Jesperson]

MIGHT HAVE TOLD YOU, ITS NOT ABOUT THE MONEY, AND I WOULD NEVER ASK SOMEONE TO PAY ME. I DIDN'T DO THAT WITH HER, AND I WON'T DO THAT WITH YOU. BESIDES I'M NOT ALLOWED TO PROFIT FROM MY CRIMES ☺.

IF YOU WANTED TO HELP ME OUT I WOULD BE VERY THANKFUL FOR WHATEVER YOU DID, OR DO. AT THE SAME TIME THIS IS NOT SOMETHING YOU HAVE TO DO, IF YOU WANT TO SEND ME MONEY FOR STAMPS AND OTHER THINGS ENCLOSED IS SOME SLIPS THAT SHOW YOU GOW TO DO THAT. YOU CAN ALSO USE J-PAY AND WESTERN UNION TO SEND MONEY TO MY ACCOUNT. IF YOU HAVE ENY QUESTIONS JUST LET ME KNOW, OR MAYBE VICTORIA CAN HELP YOU.

What a nice man one might think, yet does one not sense at least some impertinence in him enclosing two inmate trust fund deposit forms from the get-go? Anyway, being a 'Mr Penny-Wise', I had accidentally misplaced these forms until I started writing this chapter some time ago. (God moves in a mysterious way, His wonders to perform.) Gary ditched the capitals and henceforth used script:

AS TO WHAT YOU SAID IN YOUR LETTER I WILL TELL YOU WHAT I REMEMBER AND KNOW AS BEST AS I CAN.

IT ALL STARTED IN RUPERT, WEST VIRGINIA. THAT IS WHERE I LIVED, BUT I WAS

BORN AT THE NEAREST HOSPITAL WHICH WAS IN CLIFTON FORGE, VIRGINIA. [Here Gary ditched the capitals and henceforth used script.] I had one older brother, William Franklin Bowles, Jr. who was born Feb 2, 1960, and my mother was 6 months pregnant with me when my father passed from black lung disease. He was a coalminer. I don't know, not from my first few years, but my mom moved us to Kankakee, Illinois. When we were young there was a few stops along the way to there but I don't know the name of the towns. I was raised by my first stepfather, William Otto Fields, who had two kids later with my mom (Pam & David). I thought he was my dad till of was 6 or 7 yrs old. We took a trip to West Virginia to visit my grandmother just before she passed away. I found out then who my dad was. After our return home things got bad. My mom worked nights at Ford Motor Company, and my dad worked days. After work my dad would drink and the kids got no help from him. When I got into trouble he would beat me with a belt, leather strap, fists, and we had a willow tree and he would use a whip like branch from that. It was bad and my brother also got beat a lot. His kids were younger then.

When I was 8 yrs old I played a lot of sports. In little league baseball I was a catcher, pitcher, shortstop. I was really good, and I wanted to be a baseball player. I was, and I am still a big clubs fan. I also played football with all of the kids from my neighborhood. We lived in a small 3 bedroom house, and most of the houses in my neighborhood were all the same. It was three streets with a total of about 400 to 500 homes altogether in the whole area.

We had a high school and a baseball field as part of the neighbourhood. It was a nice place to grow up. I just have a normal family life. We never ate together, and no-one helped with homework. I was not very good in school, and my highest grade completed was 6th Grade and I was in my 7th Grade when I left home. I went to school called Martin Luther Kids Jr. High.

When I was 9 yrs old I was smoking pot, not a lot, but some. When I was 10 yrs old my mom left my dad, and we moved to Joliet, Illinois. We moved a few times before she met Chester 'Chet' Hodges, and they got married when I was 12 yrs old. I was not even allowed to go to the wedding. He drank a lot and so did my mom. I was forced to live in the basement, and by 13 yrs old I was kicked out of the house and was living in the garage. There was no heat, and I had had enough. I didn't know if Chet was home and I went in the house. He was drunk and started beating me. We ended up in the driveway, and I grabbed a brick and I started hitting him in the face and head. Looking back I think I really wanted to kill him but my mom came home and she pulled me off saying just that, that if I didn't stop I would kill him.

That was the breaking point for me and I told her we did not have to live this way. She took her share of beatings as well with a broken arm and other things. I told her it was either him or me. I will never forget her words: "Don't make me choose". I put what few things I had in a bag, and I left. I didn't say anything to her. That first night I stayed in the back of a U-Haul moving truck.

I find myself reading a well-written letter from a death row inmate who has committed six of the most brutal and sickening crimes imaginable, yet nothing jumps from these pages that even hints at psychopathy. No bullshit – à la Melanie 'Ice Queen' McGuire, Harvey 'The Hammer' Carignan or Kenneth Bianchi – from Gary Ray Bowles at all. Or is there? For although he appears to be telling it as it is, quite obviously he is leaving a heck of a lot out, as will soon become apparent.

The next day I went to one of my friend's house and he hid me in his garage. It had heat, and a bed ☺. A week later the two of us took a bus to Buras, Louisiana, to go and stay with his dad. His dad worked off shore on an oil rig. I was 14 yrs old now, just turned, and his dad got us a job working with him. We had to say we were 16 yrs old, the legal age to work then. It was a really small town, and everyone worked off shore. We would work for two weeks and then be off for two weeks. My first pay check was over $700. I wrote my mom and sent her a copy of the check. She never wrote back and I didn't see her again until after I was 18yrs old. We ended up getting busted for being under age and I was only able to work for 6 months or so. My friend stayed, and I was off on my own. I hitched to New Orleans, and on the way my first ride is how I got started in the gay hustling business. The guy offered me $20 to suck me off. He was surprised by how big I was and if I want, he told me I could make a lot of money doing this kind of thing and that is how I became a hustler. I did this in New Orleans, and I even met a woman who took me in for the same thing. I had sex with her, and her friends, and boy did I learn a lot.

All for now. I'll write again next week to tell you more. Take care ... let me know what you think.

Gary Ray.

This litany of non-useful info was almost unbearable to read and certainly not as exciting as watching grass grow, but I did write back to never hear from Gary Ray Bowles again – most probably because I didn't send him any cash. Or perhaps because he had some explaining to do about his arrest in 1982 for beating and sexually assaulting his twenty-year-old girlfriend, for which he was previously sentenced to six years in prison, because, you see, it's often what is not written on the page which matters the most.

Even more explaining for him to do in 1991 when, after his release from prison, he was convicted of unarmed robbery during the theft of an elderly woman's purse, a crime for which he was sentenced to four more years behind bars, which was signally another omission in his correspondence. He was released after serving two years. But we should primarily concern ourselves with Bowles's first confirmed kill. At the time of the discovery of the body, he became a suspect but was nowhere to be found – as a result of which five more men are known to have been murdered in the most godawful ways.

On 15 March 1994, Florida police found the body of fifty-nine-year-old John Hardy Roberts at his Daytona Beach, Volusia County home. He had been beaten about the head and strangled. His car and wallet were gone – his credit card was later used in Georgia and Tennessee. Bowles had been staying at Roberts's home, and had left fingerprints and even some documents in his own name. He was immediately and unsurprisingly a suspect – but there was still no sign of him. The missing car was later found in Georgia.

On 14 April 1994, the body of thirty-nine-year-old David Alan Jarman was found at his home in Wheaton, Maryland: he too had been beaten and strangled; his credit cards, keys and vehicle were gone (the vehicle was found a week later in Baltimore). On 4 May, Milton Bradley, seventy-two years old, was found dead behind a shed on a golf course in Savannah, Georgia. He had sustained a blow to the head and been strangled. On 13 May, forty-seven-year-old Alverson Carter's body was found at his residence in Atlanta: the MO was the same as in the previous killings. And on 18 May, Albert Morris, who was thirty-eight, was found dead in his trailer in Hilliard, Nassau County, Florida. He had been hit on the head, shot and strangled. It later transpired that Bowles had lived with him for about two weeks.

Then came the murder of forty-seven-year-old Walter Jamelle 'Jay' Hinton, whose body was found on 18 November 1994. By now Bowles was already a suspect in five other, similar murders, and on a wanted list; it was only a matter of time before he would be found. He was arrested on 22 November. Under questioning, he eventually confessed to the six murders, but was arraigned on that of Hinton. He was indicted before a grand jury in December 1994.

Documents available from the Supreme Court of Florida (Gary Ray BOWLES, *Appellant* v. *STATE* of Florida, Appellee. No. SC96732. Decided: October 11, 2001), quoted below) give details of the trials (first and subsequent hearings).

Summarising the case as presented at Bowles's indictment, the appeal courts stated:

Appellant [Bowles] met Walter Hinton, the victim in this case, at Jacksonville Beach in late October or early November 1994. Appellant agreed to help Hinton move some personal items from Georgia to Hinton's mobile home in Jacksonville. In return, Hinton allowed appellant to live with him in his mobile home.

On November 22, 1994, police arrested appellant for the murder of Walter Hinton. During subsequent interrogation, appellant gave both oral and written confessions regarding Hinton's murder. Appellant stated that upon returning home from going with Hinton to take a friend [Richard Smith] to the train station, Hinton went to sleep and appellant kept drinking. Appellant, Hinton, and the friend had drunk beer and smoked marijuana earlier. At some point in the evening, appellant stated that something inside 'snapped'. He went outside and picked up a concrete block, brought it inside the mobile home, and set it on a table. After thinking for a few minutes, appellant picked up the block, went into Hinton's room, and dropped the block on Hinton's head. The force of the blow caused a facial fracture that extended from Hinton's right cheek to his jaw. Hinton, now conscious, fell from the bed and appellant began to manually strangle him. Appellant then stuffed toilet paper into Hinton's throat and placed a rag into his mouth. The medical examiner testified that the cause of death was asphyxia.

The pathologist later 'observed on Mr. Hinton's body five (5) broken ribs, abrasions to the front and back of his right forearm, and more abrasions on the outside of his left knee'. His findings tied in with Bowles's own confession that Hinton had struggled desperately with him, despite the injuries to his face. The court found that 'The victim was strangled while conscious for a time sufficient to suffer a physically and mentally cruel and torturous death'.

The account continues:

Mr. Hinton was found inside his locked home on 22 November. His sister and her then fiancé became concerned when he failed to respond to telephone calls and knocks on his door. After several days went by without word from Mr. Hinton, the fiancé broke into his mobile home and found his dead body wrapped in sheets and bedspreads.

Mr. Hinton's watch, car keys, automobile and stereo equipment were missing from the home. His wallet was found on the floor next to the bed. The Defendant was seen after the murder driving Mr. Hinton's car.

At his appeal hearing, Bowles weakly explained that his theft of Hinton's property was an 'afterthought' and not 'the motivation for the murder'. This directly contradicts his earlier claim during the FBI interrogation, when he said that he had expected to find money in the victim's trailer home or on Hinton. There seems no reasonable doubt that the murder was committed in the course of an attempted robbery.

In imposing the death penalty, the trial court identified five aggravating circumstances. Whether the reader is an anti-death-penalty advocate or pro–death–penalty supporter, they make for sombre reading. I quote verbatim:

(1) Bowles was convicted of two other capital felonies and two other violent felonies; (2) Bowles was on felony probation in 1994 when he committed the murder as a result of a July, 18, 1991 conviction and sentence to four years in prison followed by six years' probation for a robbery in Volusia county; (3) the murder was committed during a robbery or an attempted robbery, and the murder was committed for pecuniary gain (merged into one factor); (4) the murder was heinous, atrocious, or cruel (HAC); and (5) the murder was cold, calculated, and premeditated (CCP).

Perhaps now we are beginning to see Gary's letter to me in a different light. Getting into the nitty-gritty of this man's criminal past, we learn that on 27 September 1982, in Hillsborough County, he was convicted of sexual battery and aggravated sexual battery. He had subjected his girlfriend to a brutal sexual assault of such violence that, as reported in the case notes, she suffered 'contusions to her head, face, neck, chest, as well as bites to her breasts. She also suffered internal injuries including lacerations to her vagina and rectum'. For this he was jailed for six years. A couple of years after his release, Bowles pushed an elderly woman to the ground and stole her purse. He was apprehended and, on 18 July 1991, a Volusia County court convicted him of unarmed robbery.

During his incarceration for the murder of Hinton, Bowles was convicted, on 10 October 1996 in Nassau County, of first-degree murder for the slaying in May 1994 of Albert Morris; and on 6 August 1997 he was convicted in Volusia County of first-degree murder and armed robbery. This was for the March 1994 killing of John Hardy Roberts. Bowles pleaded guilty to both.

What I found particularly interesting were the two mitigating factors put forward by Gary Ray Bowles following his death sentence for the Hinton murder – and this provides yet another bullshit example of a defence attorney trying to get a client if not completely off the hook, then at least to blow some smoke into the jury's yard to cause doubt that the well-deserved death sentence would be inappropriate. The suggestion was that at the time of the crime Mr Bowles was suffering 'extreme emotional disturbance', thus he was of 'substantially diminished capacity to appreciate the criminality of his acts at the time of the murder'. In a nutshell, he was claiming temporary insanity. I would argue that's all very well if it had been applied to the Hinton murder *alone* – an isolated case of temporary insanity without any of the mitigating factors present. But for Bowles to use this defence in the context of *six* homicide cases is too ludicrous to even think about – it cuts no ice at all, would my reader agree?

To put a legal slant on this issue, and to keep it brief, an 'aggravated murder' is a killing made more serious by its violent circumstances. Unfortunately, in the UK although these offences carry a natural life term, many monsters who commit such acts are later released back into society, such as homegrown Brits Graham Young and Colin Pitchfork. Our American cousins see it differently, however: over there, murdering someone in furtherance of another serious felony – say a robbery, rape or killing a cop or a public official such as a prison officer or while trying to evade arrest – carries a mandatory natural-life term with zilch chance of release. Better still, in my opinion, in multiple/serial killings, as with Bowles, a damned good execution.

The mitigating factors kick in when defence attorneys (mostly in the US) attempt to reduce their client's sentence by bringing up something trivial – let's say bad potty-training, or the defendant having been denied breast milk and forced to wean off green-top instead of full-cream up until the age of fifteen.

Before we move on with Mr Bowles, as a side note – and to make this issue of bullshit psychiatric mitigation more interactive for the reader – look up the 2008 YouTube documentary *Interview with a Serial Killer* about Arthur Shawcross, who featured earlier in this book. It's a damned good programme featuring Captain Lynde B. Johnston, the prosecutor Charles J. Siragusa and others whom I met during the making of my own TV documentary. In particular, I would ask you to listen to the defence's psychiatric mitigation put forth by forensic psychiatrists Dorothy Otnow Lewis and a colleague, and how their evaluations of Shawcross were basically shit-canned – not only by common-sense police officers and FBI criminal profiler Gregg McCrary, but none other than prosecution psychiatrist Dr Park Dietz, whom I admire greatly. And, have we not seen examples of this psychiatric mitigation smoke-blowing before with the examples of Messrs Colin Pitchfork, Graham Young, Phillip Jablonski et al? Yes, we have; indeed, even with Harvey Carignan and Peter Sutcliffe, psychiatrists for the defence vehemently argued that their clients truly believed that they were following the Word of God.

As well as his alleged state of 'extreme emotional disturbance', another suggested mitigating factor was that Gary Bowles was a 'gay-hater'. This is based on his remarks to some of his pen friends, to whom he wrote: 'A gay raped my mother.' He also tried to claim that his girlfriend, who was allegedly expecting his child, had an abortion when she learned he was a sex worker whose clients were gay men – a tenuous bit of logic. No mention of this came up at his initial trial; when the judge was subsequently told that he was a hater of gay men, the death sentence was reversed, and another hearing called. Indeed, Bowles was to appeal several times. The claim that he hated gay men was, sensibly, not accepted as a mitigating factor. The fact that he targeted such men – those men to whom he willingly prostituted himself – must surely be because he saw that he could weasel himself into their homes and benefit from their hospitality.

So, let's cut to the chase here. A controversial subject it is indeed, but having read his letter, we cannot say that this man was so mentally upside-down that he did not realise that his offences could well earn him the death sentence, if caught. Yet he sailed on regardless. As his Honour Mr Justice Thomas M. Stark once told me during a 1994 filmed interview at his Riverhead, Long Island courthouse:

Society makes the rules. People have to live by them or anarchy breaks loose. Most know what punishment might await them if they step over the red line. It is their decision. In states where the death penalty applies, society merely supplies the rope, the electricity or the drugs to execute them. Christopher, if it were one of your own children who had been raped, butchered, then killed, tell me that forgiveness would be in your heart?

And there would be no chance of that!

So, I might well ask all of my readers Judge Stark's open question, but what I will say is this: didn't Gary Bowles live a well-fed, well-watered life behind bars at the US taxpayers' expense? He enjoyed free accommodation; food, Medicare and he racked up several million dollars of public money with his pathetic appeals to save his own worthless life. Meanwhile, Mr Hinton's agonising appeals to Bowles – and those from his other murder victims, including his former girlfriend, whose womb he destroyed – all fell on deaf ears.

For a stone-cold serial killer, his signature being shoving leaves, toilet paper, even dirt, socks and sex toys into the mouths of his victims, and unlike serial killer John Wayne Gacy, whose last words were reportedly 'Kiss my ass', Bowles did have something to say after he was strapped down onto the execution gurney:

> I'm sorry for all the pain and suffering I have caused. I hope my death eases your pain. I want to tell my mother that I am also sorry for my actions. Having to deal with your son being called a monster is terrible. I'm so very sorry. I never wanted this to be my life. You don't wake up one day and decide to become a serial killer.

After his death warrant had been signed by the state's governor, Bowles was moved to a 'Death Watch' cell that measures 6 x 9 feet wide and 9.5 feet high, and he was able to order a last meal, the cost 'not to exceed $40'. He opted for three burgers, fries and bacon. As the lethal drugs were administered, he went white, coughed once and died.

John 'J.R.' Edward Robinson, aka 'The Slavemaster'

In seeking truth you have to get both sides of a story.

WALTER LELAND CRONKITE JR,
AMERICAN BROADCAST JOURNALIST

Although what I am about to say might offend some of my readers, let me be blunt: if anyone deserves a painful lethal injection it has to be 'The Slavemaster'; nevertheless, what if there are three or four sides to a story, or even more? What if there were a person who has so many sides to his personality that, like a chameleon, he could change his outer persona – his social camouflage – at will, and had multiple personalities hidden beneath that could change in a heartbeat too?

Meet 'J.R.' Robinson, without doubt the most psycho-pathologically complicated serial killer I've ever dealt with.

The first question you'll ask is doubtless: 'Where is Robinson right now?' Actually, he is on death row at the El Dorado

Correctional Facility in 'The Wheat State', aka Kansas. He is on the 'Green Mile' for killing eight females, leaving five of their bodies to decompose in their own juices in barrels on his property and in a lockup he'd rented.

Dumb move, J.R., especially considering that at one time you were telling the world that you were hyper-intelligent. May we remind you that you are residing on 'the row' because you first pleaded 'not guilty', then flipped, changing your tune to 'guilty' to avoid the death sentence out of state, then back to 'not guilty' as soon as you were extradited to Kansas?

While hoping not to be accused of plagiarising my own writings about J.R. (I covered him in my book *Dead Men Talking*), I will summarise his story as briefly as I can, as we are more concerned here with the letters he wrote to me. Letters in which he categorically denied being a sadosexual pervert. 'BDSM?' he wrote, incredulously. 'What does that mean [...] what does Slavemaster mean [...] and NEVER EVER tell me that I said that golf balls can give a girl sexual excitement. I have NEVER played golf in my life.'

This Mr Robinson is someone to behold. To be fair to J.R., it isn't particularly unusual for a tenant of death row to spend years protesting his innocence of the crimes for which he stands condemned. After all, when faced with the prospect of execution, who wouldn't make some effort towards self-preservation? And, wow, J.R. once, way, way back when he was a thirteen-year-old Eagle Scout, stood before Queen Elizabeth II, and later was on a charities board and received a bogus award of 'Man of the Year', as reported by the *Kansas City Star* (to their subsequent extreme embarrassment). He became quite adept at forging letters and documents to help him along, did J.R.

Despite having no qualifications whatsoever, J.R., you were once employed as an X-ray technician by none other than retired Brigadier General Dr Wallace Harry Graham, who for many years was the personal White House physician to President Harry S Truman and his wife, Elizabeth. You fleeced Dr Graham and bankrupted his medical practice, did you not?

J.R., my readers are now well impressed and anxious to know more.

'Manager of a TV rental company' appears on your richly embroidered CV. But no mention of you tuning into the firm's funds and stealing thousands of dollars. And you were a contemporary Saint Albertus Magnus OP: scholar philosopher, patron saint of the natural sciences thrown in too. Goodness me, J.R., my readers would never have guessed that it was you who first invented hydroponics. In this regard, your glossy, sixty-four-page brochure promoting your (bogus) hydroponics modestly claims it was you who trail-blazed and pioneered this mouth-watering subject; that would come as a *big* surprise to the ancients, who somewhat thought that this had been their idea – witness the Hanging Gardens of Babylon and the Aztec nation's *chinampas* ('floating gardens') of Mexico, to take just two examples. So, it should not surprise my readers to hear that your company, Hydro-Gro Inc., consulted NASA on growing plants in outer space. If you say so, we believe you, John. And I sympathise with you that Richard Branson has *still* not replied to your proposal that he offer you a $2-million cash-up-front book deal for you to 'tell all'. Not so long ago, Richard was a tad busy launching his mega-sized cruise ship, *Scarlet Lady*. When it leaves my city's port, I watch it go by. Long it is, bro: the bow goes by on Monday, the stern a month later. The height is 66 metres. That's tall, J.R., as tall as your phantasmagorical stories.

So, John, this sadosexual stuff. Are you sure that you never trawled the World Wide Web's BDSM chat rooms to entice young women and their kids into your own homicidal web? Because you see, I have all of the perverted letters you wrote to a former female FBI special agent. Pretty lass, wasn't she? As cute as Agent Clarice Starling in the movie *The Silence of the Lambs*, yes? Ever heard of the compound noun 'honeytrap'? No, I didn't think so.

At this point in J.R.'s narrative, I should remark that he signally fails in his CV to flag up that he thieved from everyone he came into contact with, including in 1985 conning his brother into adopting a baby – for a hefty fee, of course – from a young woman he 'rescued' from a battered mothers' home and then beat her to death. In short, with John Robinson we have one of history's most complicated serial killers, but when we read between his lines, perhaps he isn't too complicated at all. Yet cruelly he didn't give a damn about the disgrace he heaped upon his devoted wife and children. He did not blink an eyelid when he persuaded an acquaintance to invest in one of his crooked businesses on the promise of a swift, high return, so the guy could get his wife, who had cancer, the palliative care she needed during her final days. J.R. fleeced him too.

For the record, Robinson had spent several previous stints in prison for fraud. Once while behind bars, he seduced a governor's wife. Upon his release she moved in with him; he killed her, drawing upon her funds until they were exhausted. In the main, bespectacled J.R.'s murderous MO was simple. Especially once he had discovered the internet, which in those early days, and more so today, presented so many possibilities of committing nefarious deeds. Posing as a very successful businessman and using the best type of calm, reassuring patter known only to shady used-car salesmen, he trawled the internet's BDSM websites searching for easy prey. Places where lonely young women swam in shoals, seeking either a 'Slavemaster' or a better way of life, using the prospect of 'hope' as bait, a lure to catch prey.

Mr Robinson promised everything, with assurances of financial rewards too. In one instance, he offered a mother with a mentally retarded daughter a well-paid position as a carer on his non-existent millionaire grandmother's non-existent yacht. As soon as they were in his clutches, he battered both mother and daughter to death, then carried on drawing upon their state and disability allowances using forged signatures. They ended up rotting in barrels.

It came as no surprise to your author when J.R. penned a letter to me, dated 20 February 2008, making unreasonable demands straight off the starting blocks:

I was represented by court-appointed attorneys who did NO INVESTIGATION, hired no experts, tested nothing and admitted in court a day prior to my trial that they had not read any discovery documents.

Before I enter into any form of correspondence with you, I want $400,000, although that amount may be adjusted depending on need. My attorney will control all information and distribution of funds. Don't blow smoke! I don't have time for meaningless delays. I will await word from you.

For unadulterated arrogance that takes the biscuit, wouldn't you agree? And, John, it's no wonder your attorneys did nothing, because you pleaded guilty from the get-go, and is it not so that most of the bodies were soon found on your property and in a secure lockup rented in your name? And scores of documents police found in your house linked you to all the dead women. What about all the internet searches you made for the girls, who wound up dead in the barrels you bought – along with the receipts the police have – and mountains of paperwork showing how you enticed victims into the world of BDSM?

At this very early stage in our correspondence John was totally unaware that I knew all about his criminal antecedents. And he had plenty. Between 1969 and 1991 he was convicted four times for embezzlement and theft. While some of his thefts could be considered trivial – he once appropriated $300-worth of postage stamps from the company he worked for – mostly he went for more significant hauls. In 1980, doubtless with the help of forged credentials, he was appointed director of personnel at a firm. Very soon he zeroed in on the company's cheque book and funds, using the former to direct quite a lot of the latter into his own bank account. More often than not he seems to have earned nothing worse than a fine and probation (which he was not averse to violating) and when he was sent to jail – for instance, when he laundered $40,000 into one of his fraudulent paper companies – it didn't slow him down. He did, however, get barred for life by the Securities and Exchange Commission from engaging in any kind of future investment business. Excellent credentials I'm sure you will not agree?

Between the mid-1980s and 2000, Robinson was incarcerated several times for embezzlement; he also spent time online, usually in BDSM chat rooms. And he devised a new and thoroughly unpleasant way of gaining money. A number of women, mostly young, vanished, but their families did receive the occasional letter from them, with, at least, authentic signatures, and their bank accounts continued to be drawn on, and cheques sent to them cashed. The bodies of five of them were found in barrels near or on Robinson's land. Once detectives had cause to obtain search warrants (following separate complaints of theft and assault from two women), they found the bodies in the barrels and arrested Robinson.

One of the women who had come to him had had a young baby with her: she was never seen again, but, as touched on earlier, J.R.'s childless brother and sister-in-law, in exchange for hefty 'legal fees', found they had adopted an orphan baby through him, Robinson having beaten the mother to death.

Robinson is known to have killed at a minimum eight women, three of whose remains have not been found, and it is thought he is guilty of further murders of women who mysteriously vanished. He stood trial for theft, fraud, kidnapping and murder in both Kansas and Missouri, and was convicted of capital murder on two counts in Kansas, for which he received the death penalty, and convicted of first-degree murder on five counts in Missouri, for which he received life without parole.

> He had no real employment, unless you consider figuring out ways of scamming people out of their money to be real employment.
>
> District Attorney Paul Morrison:
> at J.R. Robinson's murder trial

Returning to my correspondence with Robinson, my carefully baited hook to entice him into my world of criminal literature was now in his mouth. The phoney deal I offered was that he could write what he wanted to say, for reproduction, verbatim, in a single chapter for a book. In fact, I then generously went further: he could even have his *own* book if he most graciously agreed.

The reverse psychology I was using with this particular piece of over-the-top, low-life narcissist is not rocket science. Your author was playing upon John's over-inflated ego, because the easiest people to lead up the garden path are the ones who have been doing pretty much the same thing to themselves from the day they could walk. If you can convince them that a fast buck is to be made, then you can lead these pathologically greedy people almost anywhere, as with Ronnie DeFeo in an earlier chapter.

J.R. had become so ensconced within his narcissistic mindset that this would become his downfall. The prospect of his having the platform of a complete book on the cards was an offer he could never have refused.

With tongue in cheek, I also offered him the opportunity to be interviewed by one of the UK's leading top-end television producers, ostensibly giving him the chance to say what he had to say to prove his innocence, all of which embedded my hook even deeper into his gullet.

Note: to put it mildly, J.R.'s letters are exhaustive. For the most part, they might seem to be the inane ramblings of someone who should be chained to a padded cell wall and only allowed to walk, wide-eyed and dribbling, through some nuthouse garden escorted by some very large men wearing whites. But John is not like someone who lies down on the grass and starts having an in-depth discussion with a daisy about Darwin's theory of evolution. Actually, he is very intelligent in a totally cooked upside-down sort of way.

By reverse engineering J.R.'s MO, I made him an offer he could not refuse. He replied:

Yes, I will agree to your offer so *I will allow you* to go to the next phase, the expert phase, photos and testing. Then to complete the necessary testing that has never been done. Each step of the way, *we* will evaluate and adjust *our* investigation or approach as required. [All author's italics]:

Can you see this podgy-faced, short-sighted, sweaty, overweight lump of lard right now? He added this:

The proposed budget is fairly simple at this point but may have to be adjusted depending on need:
- Database: $100,000.
- Investigator: $150,000.
- Travel: $20,000.
- Experts: $60,000.
- Attorneys: $50,000.
- Communications, copies, supplies: $10,000.
- Equipment: $8,000.
- Misc: $2,000.

TOTAL: $400,000.

He continues seemingly quite oblivious to the fact that no inmate, condemned or otherwise, can receive bags stuffed with money, or have it sent to another party; it's against the rules, you see:

> My first letter to you was perfectly clear about the possibilities available to you. Yet you responded with a request for information about my formative years, assuming it would be no threat to my future legal status. Unfortunately, that is not the case. When I win a new trial, it will be necessary to prepare a 'mitigation case' containing the VERY information you now seek. My attorneys did NOT investigate or provide any mitigation at my first trial.
>
> I did offer you a smidgen of palpable researchable material right there in England. It is very, very valuable information. In November of 1957, I was a 13-year-old Boy Scout who travelled to London to appear in the Command Performance for the Queen. No one has yet recovered the newspaper articles of that trip. As you see, everything is tied together [...]

Correction, J.R.: just a minute's search on the internet brings up a press cutting of you and your fellow scouts in London talking to our late queen. In any case, who, or what, is 'tied together'? For a convicted serial murderer who rarely comes up for air, I struggled to not start hyperventilating and collapse on the floor in carpet-rolling hysterical laughter as J.R. continues:

> I offered you the opportunity to do a real-life true crime book and documentary. One that would expose blatant police and prosecutorial misconduct, fairly present the

real evidence including complete details of the lives of the victims, and perhaps unveil the real killer. You could of course simply go for the titillating, sensationalized products based on the fiction story already out there. That decision, of course, is yours.

The 'titillating products' J.R. refers to are the official trial and appellate court documents, which I already had in abundance. You can get these documents too. Many are available online; if not, the Americans are very agreeable to send you most of what you will need under The Freedom of Information Act, courtesy of the US Treasury.

In many respects, John 'J.R.' Edward Robinson is much like John David Guise Cannan and John Wayne Gacy – sadosexual serial killers who pose as businessmen with all the apparent trappings of integrity and unlimited wealth. They use a hunter's skills to trawl and entrap their prey. However, whereas bisexual Gacy tortured then murdered young lads for sexual perversity, J.R. searched the internet for his victims, motivated both by BDSM urges and financial gain.

If I may, I'd like to draw an analogy between J.R. and the legendary wreckers who were said to have used lanterns to lure sailing ships onto the rocks. In a modified form, this is precisely what he was doing in his correspondence – it's an opportunity of a lifetime for you, grab the opportunity while you can, he is suggesting. Thus, this predator, this human parasite sent out attractive signals that were intended to entice the vulnerable towards him, rather like a female firefly that fools males from another species into approaching her by using a flashing code. Once the intended prey does so, it is summarily eaten.

We all want the good life, do we not? Each of J.R.'s victims was searching for something – some kind of dream perhaps – and along comes a knight in shining armour. It might be that friend who was tempted into investing in one of J.R.'s businesses so that he could soon pay for his dying wife's medical care, or offering to adopt a baby for his own brother because the couple could not have a child of their own. But underneath this façade is a monster – rather than a gateway to your dream, he turns out to be your worst nightmare come true.

J.R. was, and still is, a salesman – a purveyor of faulty goods and piles of bullshit. When you read his letters he comes across as almost a cartoon character (if the context were not so horrific). Yet one can clearly perceive his warped psychopathology shouting out as he puts pen to paper.

I am a fair man, and if any credit is to be given to J.R., it is that he is determined. He says that for the past years he had been 'tireless [in his attempts] to locate individuals, companies or organisations willing to assist in the completion of the necessary investigation, testing, etc. To fully disclose the real story.' I pressed him often about his use of internet BDSM chat rooms, but he always responded vehemently that he was fitted up by the police; that never once in his whole life had he ever been into bondage or been a 'Slavemaster'. Let's return to his correspondence with me:

Determined to prove my innocence or die trying I began writing letters to anyone I could think of for both the UK portion of my case as well as those who might possibly help on this side of the pond. I wrote to Alan Hayling – head of documentaries at the BBC, in March 2007, and received not even a courtesy reply. I recently wrote to Mr Felix Dennis, owner of *Maxim* magazine who lives in Stratford–upon–Avon, and have no word yet.

My basic offer has been very simple. If they would provide the initial funding [the $400,000] for the investigation and testing, along with the equipment necessary, I would give them access to the results no matter the outcome as long as everyone agreed that nothing would be made public until my attorney, acting upon my instructions, authorized release.

Quite what J.R. means when he mentions 'the UK portion' of his case, God only knows because all of his murders and scams came under American jurisdiction. The reader will have now come to the correct conclusion that J.R. is a fucking idiot, and if the matter were not so deadly serious, one would be forgiven for sticking up two fingers to be followed by F**k off. No doubt that the BBC and *Maxim* were likewise bowled over by the generosity and once-in-a-lifetime opportunity offered them by J.R Undeterred, and indeed moving up a gear, J.R. wrote on:

The cost of putting all discovery information onto a searchable interactive data base, investigating, testing, travel and equipment will be about $400K and will require at least twelve months to complete. The investigator will need some specialized equipment, video and digital recorders capable of two concurrent recordings. All funds would be disbursed by an attorney. I would receive nothing but an allocation to cover supplies and postage.

But J.R., you don't have an attorney because anyone with half a legal mind has washed their hands of you, so my readers do not really need to read between the lines here, do they? By now, this homicidal clown who resides in La-La-Land with his already distended ego is inflating faster by the minute, for J.R.'s verbosity all but bursts into song:

> We are starting from scratch with a thorough methodical investigation of everything. Every document, every photo, every video, every witness, testing every item and utilizing acknowledge experts to evaluate to calculate every person or object.
>
> To facilitate this investigation we [the royal 'we', I guess] have obtained every page of material connected to my case, some 300,000 more or less. Here is how we anticipate proceedings:
> a) data base will be designed with unlimited search capabilities. All documents will be scanned, cross-referenced with new documents as developed.
> b) full time investigator will be hired under the supervision of my attorney. He/she will complete the legwork required to secure records and documents previously ignored, and conduct video interviews with all witnesses.

Perhaps J.R. felt that he needed a little extra incentive to lure me in, for he continued:

> I may be able to up the ante for you. For several years I have been in contact with a person who befriended Denis

Rader, the confessed BTK serial killer of 10. This person visited him in jail and corresponded with him regularly. This individual claims to have details and information never before revealed and has been working on a book. The person who has the information, wants to do a book, but has no industry name. The two of you should be able to do a great 'insider' true crime book and a documentary about BTK. You and your publisher could end up getting two for the price of one. I will await word from you.

Yes, J.R., I am sure that my publisher would literally leap at your suggestion of me co-writing a book about BTK with a fucking halfwit. My editors are already at their wit's end with me sorting out this chapter, you homicidal clown. Nevertheless, J.R. then returned to a well-trodden path – the plaintive theme of the wrongs he'd endured:

I was embezzled out of over two hundred thousand pounds over a three-year period. To that end I have received preliminary word that a non-profit organization – Reprieve – operated by an attorney Clive Stafford-Smith [sic] OBE has agreed to help. My attorney has replied to a letter I received from them, by email, and we are still awaiting a reply [...] Finally I must tell you that I am working with a group of college students to publish a book of my poetry and short stories. An attempt to raise money for the required investigation. No credit would be given – no author named. The book will, if published. Simply be written by 'A CONDEMNED ON KANSAS DEATH ROW'.

Great idea that, J.R. A knockout title, to be sure ...

> ... for the record, I will explain exactly how the Kansas Department of Corrections mail system works. When a letter is received it is automatically date stamped on the outside of the envelope. Then the letter is opened by the censors, date and time-stamped, read and all the letters to the inmates in segregation copied.

And so he goes wittering on and on and on for another ten pages of excruciating drivel. It was at this point in our 'business relationship' that I demanded that J.R. give me, at the very least, his attorney's name so that I could check out some of his claims, at which J.R. lost the plot.

Point of fact: no pro-bono attorney would touch J.R. with the proverbial barge pole. He snapped back with: 'YOU, BERRY-DEE, have wasted my valuable time.' Backtracking, he then ranted on:

> I have never asked you for $400,000. I have never asked anyone for $400,000. I didn't say I was going to use students, and if you print this I might sue you. I fucking told you that I never used the internet, and I was never into BDSM and I was never into kinky sex. I was a happily married business man with many awards. FUCK OFF!

Psychopaths, such as J.R., never learn from the errors of their ways. Even as I write he is, when he can afford some postage stamps, trawling for gullible folk and enticing them to send him 'donations' so that he can start up another nefarious scam. He is still asking people to send in their own poetry so he can claim it as his own work, get the crap printed and sold through a friend to raise funds for his prison commissary to buy a few luxuries, such as extra chocolate cookies, candy and the like.

We should be mindful, however, that this scumbag still hasn't revealed the locations of several more of his victims' bodies, thereby denying closure to their grieving next of kin, and this is why your author cooked up the idea of a 'honeytrap' by introducing a woman who has had hands-on, blue-chip experience of dealing with serial killers for years. If anyone could get inside the head of John Robinson it would be the woman we'll call 'Annabel Leigh'. This ex-FBI agent had a degree in criminal justice and I asked her if she would study J.R.'s life and crimes. Thereafter, we set him up. We turned the tables on this evil man who has, for decades, been turning the tables on just about everyone he came into contact with. The results were both disturbing and electrifying. And when J.R. twigged on that he had been conned, I am sure that he was not best happy.

So, let's meet 'Annabel Leigh'. As the reader will see, this extremely clever lady taught me more than a lesson or two about approaching and writing to serial killers. She put me in my place from the get-go, although we both agreed that we each brought our own skill sets to bear. So enjoy.

Annabel Leigh, aka 'The Honeytrap'

'A sprat to catch a mackerel.' We all know that this means something along the lines of 'a small investment of some form or other in the hope of a larger gain'; the idiom goes as far back as the mid-nineteenth century. Enter Annabel Leigh, who subtly worked her way into John 'J.R' Edward Robinson's sensibilities while I was feeding him my own bait. I think we were a great double act. We'll proceed to J.R.'s letters to Annabel (all previously unpublished) but first, this slap to me from her:

In trying to get inside the heads of serial killers, any attempt to appeal to the better side of a psychopath's better nature will be judged by these master manipulators as a sign of weakness, for conscience is something they do not possess, and one's efforts will fail.

Christopher, you should be using their own 'victimology' against them. It is the strongest weapon of all. You would have achieved much greater success with John Wayne Gacy had you presented yourself as an attractive young man when you wrote to him – falsify a 'pretty' photo if needed be – so that Gacy could have sexually identified with you; in his subconscious you becoming a possible victim, and a photographic image that he could masturbate over while locked up in his prison cell.

You, like so many criminologists and psychologists, miss the obvious. With respect, you guys fail to think outside of the box. If you're writing to a female killer, you should use a multi-sensory approach: the written word which has to appeal to the inmate's way of thinking; photographic stimuli that will conform to their victim type or previous lifestyle and, finally smell – the latter being the most important. A spray of expensive cologne will linger in her cell long after the written word has been absorbed, making your letter stand out, and bring back memories of her better days long past [it was this same

TOP TIP that helped me hook Melanie McGuire, the reader will recall]. The same approach works even better with men. If it fits with his MO, a sexy photo, a splash of perfume, and they have to reply, and this is why I adopted this approach with J.R. Robinson.

While this may seem very unprofessional from me, I think that your thousands of dedicated readers will appreciate my no-nonsense approach, being: Mr Robinson's thought-processing system seems, for the better part of his life, to have been hung between his legs at the same time folded up in dollars in his wallet. For my part, I see no reason why nothing much would have changed today. Therefore, I hope that you, and your readers, will find the results of my correspondence with J.R. of some interest.

Annabel Leigh.

Sadly, Annabel's own correspondence with J.R., is not for publication, and for professional reasons I understand why. However, although it might now seem an obvious plan, its very simplicity was its beauty. Annabel was setting a honeytrap and he walked right into it. In a neat and educated hand, she wrote to him posing as someone interested in him as 'a person'. Insisting that she was not interested in his criminal offences, she enclosed, with her first letter, a photograph – not of her, of course, but someone she thought he might find appealing. She told him that she was fascinated by BDSM; she liked controlling, mature, strong, businesslike men. Considering that J.R. had recently blown me out, one would have thought that he would have been very careful about whom he wrote to next. He wasn't. True to form, he replied with this:

> Annabel,
>
> I received your letter. First of all let me explain that I have some simple rules for anyone that I write. You must realize that all kinds of people write me. It usually happens when some story is run on TV. All claim to want to 'be my friend' when actually all they want is to receive a letter from a death row inmate. My attorney located a blog that tells people how to write to me to receive a response. If that was your goal, here you are.

In truth, at this time Robinson had no attorney; moreover, no such blog existed. What he's claiming in his own overblown way is that he has a lawyer who at no charge trawls the internet on his behalf. In fact, anyone can look up Robinson's full details and address by visiting the Kansas Department of Corrections website, then clicking 'Inmate Locator'.

That notwithstanding, off he went again:

> I laughed when you said you were into true crime, if you have read either of the books written about me, you just read a media created fairy tale. 85% of the material is false, but people like to read crap so that's what they write. The DA who prosecuted me had his wife, who runs a media company, create quite an evil persona of me.
>
> OK, the rules Annabel – first, if you really want to communicate with me you MUST send me a copy of your driver's license and a photo ID that shows who

you are, your birth date, address. Second, don't ask me about my case. I have maintained my innocence from the beginning. My case is on appeal and I don't need to discuss it. Third, if I detect any phoney BS I won't respond again. Fourth, you must guarantee me that anything we write remain completely confidential.

The reader will observe Robinson's psychopathology working flat out once more. Denigrating the DA and Mrs DA, pouring scorn on well-known, highly respected authors, laying down his ground rules from the get-go, and about to leak a whole shed-load of perverted BDSM garbage, which – had he actually been appealing his sentence – would have had his imaginary attorneys in seizures. As for maintaining his innocence from the beginning – oh, no. He had admitted all of his crimes to escape the death sentence in one state only to be extradited to Kansas where he now sits a short, stumbling walk to the death chamber.

He continued:

Annabel, if you write me here is a way to do it. On the front of each page write a very normal letter. If you want to write other information about your BDSM experiences, fantasies, etc, write them on the back of the pages like a separate letter. The censors only read the front of each page.

Your list of lifestyle interests like you copied it from [as written] the alt.com website questionnaire [the website where he found one of his victims, Suzette Trouten]. If you are seeking, tell me but understand I am very demanding.

I am enclosing information that tells you what can and cannot be sent in ... actually it's a list of don'ts. Look good at the information about photos, "sexually obscene material or nudity". Yes, I want you to send pictures but they have to get past the censors so use your head.

I'm enclosing you information about how you can help out financially. I live in solitary confinement, I don't work (they won't allow it) and I have very limited funds. If you want to help out with postage and supplies you need to follow the directions.

You say you have two degrees, in what, from where and when?

How involved do you want to get? Are you interested in helping if I need typing complete, computer searches, light investigation? Tell me about your computer literacy, etc. I will give you the opportunity to tell me all about yourself and I want you to be very frank about what you're looking for! I need someone who will be committed to help me. If I'm ever going to prove my innocence I need a person on the outside I can really trust.

Goodness gracious me, J.R.; Annabel isn't applying for a job, bro ...

So, there you have it. The beginning, where we go from here is up to you ... I mean everything!!!

What type of animals do you have? Are you willing to take this to whatever level?'

There may come a time when I need to ask a favor, are you willing to help?

Thanks for the letter and the picture. I hope it's just the first of many. You are very pretty. I will be not only a Master to you but a father too ... Oh, last rule – if we're going to do that you have to commit to write at least once a week.

JR

P.S. If you have experience in setting up websites or blogs, let me know.

From here on, the completely off-the-wall Robinson didn't waste any time in returning to his over-controlling ways. He said that he was in a 'foul' mood because someone was 'attempting to sell an envelope' supposedly written by him on the internet for $40. 'I hate that kind of exploitation and crap,' he told Annabel, adding, 'and that's why I'm careful about writing to people. They use me and I hate it!! Your first assignment is to go online and see if you can find out who it is for me.'

Despite being told by Annabel that she wasn't interested in his criminal case history, J.R. volunteered that his 'conviction was more than a miscarriage':

I was framed, and that's what I have to prove. My appeal when filed, will result in a new trial. But, when that happens I have to do everything necessary to prove my innocence. Your degree might come in handy if you are to work with me ... help me investigate what needs to be done, etc. In time I will reveal what has to be done ... I do have attorney's [sic] provided by the state for my appeal. One is a young woman who I trust. She tells me I will get some relief either a new trial or convictions reversed. If

301

not, there are more appeals and whatever the case it will require heavy investigative efforts. This is not a game!!! We believe we know who set me up, why it was done and how. Now we have to prove it.

Isn't J.R. Robinson morbidly fascinating? Here he is totally embedded with an imaginary frame-up scenario, writing about an attorney who does not exist, while previously he mentions 'light investigative work' but now it's 'heavy investigative efforts', that are required. So by means of the written word and the concealed subtext of his letters, he is allowing us to venture deep inside his mind. Ever the authority on BDSM – although of course he categorically denied to me he'd ever heard of the subject – J.R. goes on to tell Annabel, 'Submission has to be a total commitment without reservation.' Then, completely contradicting himself, he adds: 'Obedience is voluntary and must be given, accepting the Dom as her Master, following his instructions. Tell me about any fantasies you have, how, why, what. I also need to know what you think I can offer you.'

Jumping from one subject to another, he returns rapido to funding and empire-building:

Annabel, check out how difficult it is to set up a web site. I've had an idea ... for a long time now to set up a non-profit organization specifically to help death row inmates with $s for investigators, lawyers, etc. Yes, there are a lot of anti-death groups out there, but none actually help the inmates. They protect, hold vigils and raise funds to pay big salaries. Hell, with your smarts we might just do ... Of course you would probably have to move here [to

Kansas from her supposed home in California] when it really got going. So the web site would have to be very professional, able to accept donations, tax free, etc. I've been working up the idea for a while. Interested ...?

Reading between J.R.'s lines we find echoes of the murderous hunting techniques he used on his many victims and how he managed to fleece pretty much everyone he came across. I mean a lot of these folk were blessed with high intelligence, but perhaps not. However, then, this monster's mind now switches back again to perverted sex as if he cannot resist the subject with this unhealthy missive, so close your eyes if needs be:

I like my submissive shaved and able to complete simple tasks ... like masturbation. I want her to be able to begin, just to get to the point of release and stop. Wait a moment, begin just until she is ready and stop again, repeating this four times, it takes practice, then on the fifth time feeling the massive release ... Do it. Write about it. How did it make you feel ...?

I have no idea what Annabel's husband may have thought about J.R.'s sex lessons, but having continual back-channel access to his letters to Annabel made me wonder what the prison censors were making of it all. One gets the impression that he's almost all but out of control when he writes: 'You say you like poetry. Do you write it? What kind?' And: 'Send me something you have written. I too like poetry and would you like to do a book of it but not identify the author of a book and short stories from an anonymous death row inmate. Hell, with self-publishing it should be easy! Just need someone to type up my poems, locate pictures on the internet to go with them and go. You MUST type it out for me.'

Bear with me, dear reader. I guess that by now you'll be thinking that voluble J.R. is stark raving bonkers. But no, J.R. is sane; not perhaps completely sane as he reminds us that:

> I just finished a two-year project and wrote a disertation [*sic*] on the history of the death penalty in Kansas. From territorial days to today. A reference librarian at the Kansas Historical Society got me the research information. It's pretty good ... needs to be typed out also, so you can do this as well! Can't send it out, no money ...!

To check out J.R.'s claim, I contacted the Kansas Historical Society. Surprise, surprise, they can't find a trace of his 'disertation' enquiries anywhere, although the history of the death penalty in Kansas can be found on their website. Then, without drawing breath, he suggests to Annabel:

> One letter a week, photos that will please me. Now, in your next letter at the end of it under your name, I want you to put something make-up color on your erect left nipple and make a print of it. A nice, small, round print, and you will enjoy 'it'...

John also generously educates Annabel about his leisure activities by explaining that he loved to play golf, although it would be fair to say that he would not know the difference between a putter and a driver. However, he does tell her that he likes golf balls (again please close your eyes now, ladies):

> Also next time you're out shopping, pick up a package of golf balls. 3 balls in a package, and locate some really small tiny rubber bands. Insert them into your vagina when you next go dancing. You will find that I am demanding, but reasonable. I want you to be all you can be and still commit. You'll understand more about that later ...

If I had been Annabel I would have asked J.R. what specific brand of golf ball he is promoting, maybe with his proposal that this brand sponsors him and helps him get off death row. Hey, John, now that's a damn good business idea if there ever was one.

I have to stress with a wry smile that I am not making light of this man's terrible crimes. I am, however, suggesting that the Kansas Department of Corrections are, to say the least, somewhat lax by letting him write then post garbage like this out. And he's still raking in cash. I imagine myself as the parent of one of J.R. Robinson's victims who were enticed into his web, bludgeoned to death and ended up as a stinking black mucky mess in one of his barrels. The quicker he's strapped to a gurney and executed the better it will be for the still grieving next of kin and society too.

Meanwhile, still he rants on to Annabel, boasting that he draws 'sarcastic cartoons about politics, my case and prison', adding:

> My attorney keeps the originals but I have sent some signed copies to certain individuals. One [copy] was sold

with my permission by a local battered women's shelter for $750. When I found out that a guard's wife bought it I had a great laugh. I do hate it when people write to me and con me and then sell envelopes, etc, for personal gain.

When I asked the Kansas Department of Corrections to confirm whether Mr Robinson was indeed such a popular and accomplished cartoonist, a spokesperson *eventually* replied: 'It is the policy of the KDOC not to comment on an inmate's custodial details, so I am afraid I cannot answer your question. I can tell you that this inmate does not attend any art-related activity because of his security status combined with his inability to draw a straight line.'

That was, perhaps, the best letter I have *ever* received from *any* department of corrections. It shows that Kansas has a dry sense of humour after all.

After all of our work in drawing him out, Annabel and I eventually agreed to pull the plug on J.R. In his last letter to her, he finished off with:

I AM expecting one letter a week from you. I want to know everything about you. And you must sign the Slave Contract and send it back to me instantly. I want to know your body measurements. How it reacts to my directions to what turns you on, how intense your reactions and release. What kind of experiences have you had, your most memorable that left you completely quaking and exhausted. Do you enjoy doing it and why. How complete do you envision your submission to be. Where did you grow up? What kind of brothers and sisters ... what was your first experience with sex? Were you abused? Do you really understand what total commitment means and are you ready? Now that I guess that you're a bit moist you may have some works to do! You might look for some padded tapestry hangers ... PS: Perhaps the nipple imprints should be in something light ... now do the right one ... Lemon juice?

J.R., you have come unstuck. The tapestry hangers, what the hell is that all about? Perhaps we will never know. As John Steinbeck wrote: 'There are some among us who live in rooms of experience we can never enter.' I suggest that the room inside John Edward 'J.R.' Robinson's head is one of them. His appeal was flat-out denied. At the time of writing, sadly – for me, at least – no execution date has been set. If the reader wishes to become more interactive with J.R., one can easily find his DOC number and location on the internet – although I'd leave aside the BDSM stuff, and do not mention my name or he won't be a happy bunny.

Go on, make his day.

Summary

To bring this book to a conclusion, I must stress that every-thing I have written here represents my own thoughts and conclusions. If I have made any grammatical errors, technical mistakes, or if any reader takes issue with what I've written or even if my syntax is a bit up the creek, I will take it on the chin in good spirit.

As I've explained, I have files of letters from serial killers, mass murderers and other homicidal killers in my possession. Deciding which of these to include in this book has been a very difficult task. On that note, I'd like to add that a sequel has been commissioned in which I'll include some of the extraordinary material I've been obliged, because of word-count restrictions, to leave out of this title. On the menu will be:

Viva LeRoy Nash

Until his death from natural causes (he was ninety-four) in 2010, LeRoy (one of the longest-serving inmates in the US, and the oldest on death row) penned hundreds of letters to me. Riddled with arthritis down to his fingertips and using just the plastic infill tube of a biro, he struggled valiantly with every single word, and without complaint, to document his life's narrative. LeRoy was one of the original 'Angels with Dirty Faces' throughout the Great Depression. His story would make a great movie.

Michael Benneman Sams

This individual is easily one of the most devious, sick and twisted kidnappers, extortionists and one-off killers in British criminal history. No one of his ilk had ever been seen before and no other offender has yet matched Sams's guile and cunning. His correspondence with me, my visits with him in prison and his taunting letters to police all illustrate 100 per cent exactly why this sequel came into being: my fascination with the written page versus the subtext; the subjective mindset of the killer versus the objective facts.

David Mulcahy

This convicted serial rapist and killer preyed on women in tandem with the notorious British 'railway rapist' John Duffy. Mulcahy's exclusive letters to me are a real mind-bending whatdunnit, whodunnit, whereabouts-dunnit. And he raises some questions about the integrity of his conviction, so is what he writes all phoney-fake or is he telling the truth … that is for my readers to decide?

Douglas Daniel Clark

Doing himself no favours, if anyone could find a man who looks like a crazed, foul-mouthed serial killer, Doug fits the bill, yet he is quite a funny guy in a strange kind of way. Also known as 'The Sunset Slayer', Clark is probably innocent of most of which he's been sent to death row for, yet he sits there today as a condemned man, while efforts are afoot to overturn his conviction. I found that he was a fascinating man to interview on death row at San Quentin State Prison; probably a patsy, who was fitted up by the cops and a devious woman, he most certainly was.

Bobby Joe Long

This serial killer dubbed 'The Classified Ad Rapist' reeled off multiple pages of the most sickening material I've ever had to stomach. This chapter could easily ruin your appetite so be warned.

Charles Lannis Moses Jr

Dubbed by the media 'The Lonely Fugitive' and 'Outlaw Mosey Wales' – the latter after a well-known Clint Eastwood Western – Charles was a fugitive drug dealer who did anything to avoid capture. He barrelled along from Nebraska to Wyoming, with the authorities in hot pursuit, in a desperate flight fuelled by drugs and punctuated by gunfire. As with LeRoy Nash, Charles spent hundreds of hours carefully, and I might even say beautifully, writing his fascinating life's story.

And in truth, I have not even touched the tip of the literary iceberg when it comes to the countless monsters who have written to your author to date.

There's a saying that 'truth is stranger than fiction'. By presenting in this, the first of two books, a selection of correspondence from some of the most dangerous criminals convicted in recent years, I hope I've offered you the chance to appreciate the disparity between the fiction of what they've written and the true facts. To gain a little more understanding of the nature of psychopaths and sociopaths who believe that your property, your life and the lives of your children are theirs to do with as they please. And as for any remorse from them – forget it.

I'll end as I usually do. Happy days. No nightmares, please and God bless ☺.

christopherberrydee.com

Christopher Berry-Dee's
TRUE CRIME WRITING
MASTERCLASS

WELCOME TO THE TRUE CRIME MASTERCLASS

Join Bestselling author Christopher Berry-Dee on a grim road trip to murder most foul. For the first time ever, Christopher reveals how to write an intriguingly dark book about murderers and the mayhem they ignite. Offering his unique insight, and delving into the minds and crimes of extremely violent killers, this series reveals the secrets to uncloaking the most evil people on earth.

Christopher draws on his experience as a world-renowned investigative criminologist, he offers advice on how he has gained the trust of killers across the world, entered their high security prisons and encouraged them to discuss in detail their shocking crimes. Across the series Christopher provides unique tips and tricks he has picked up over his years as a Best-Selling true crime author and gives viewers all the know how they need to write a book of their own.

From choosing who to write about, how to research and conduct interviews, the writing process and how to get published…

The True Crime Writing Masterclasses are a must for any budding writer.

Seven-part series available to stream:
www.picturethistv.co.uk/shows/video/masterclass/
Readers can claim 50% off the entire series with code
truecrimemasterclass

'A powerful story about love and obligation . . .a persuasive novel, very well written.' **John Burnside**

'Moving, poetic and quietly provocative.' *The Independent*

'Take any aspect of the novelist's art and you'll find it exemplified here to perfection.' **Bill Kirton**, *Booksquawk*

'Heart-warming, realistic and page-turning.' **Lorraine Kelly**

'Beautiful – lyrical and sensual by turns.' **Hilary Ely**

'Blisteringly eloquent.' **Joyce Macmillan**, *The Scotsman*

PRAISE FOR CATHERINE CZERKAWSKA'S WRITING:

'A romance of Scotland's great Romantic. There is a pastoral beauty . . .their courtship is drawn gorgeously. *The Jewel* finally gives voice to Jeany Armour, the girl who sang as sweetly as the nightingale, who was muse, mother, wife and lover to Scotland's national poet. This is her song.' *Sunday Mail*

'Uplifting . . .does much to put right the wrongs of historians. The characters come to life beautifully on the page . . .Serves as a superbly researched biography of a deeply admirable woman who until now has been . . .unjustly neglected.' *Undiscovered Scotland*

'Beguiling and enchanting . . .Czerkawska is an excellent storyteller . . . Full of suspense . . .and lush sensuality, so you can almost feel the grass brushing against your skin, and smell the honeysuckle on summer evenings.' *Scottish Review*

'A beautiful historical novel.' *Edinburgh City of Literature*

'Czerkawska tells her tale in a restrained, elegant prose that only adds to its poignancy.' *Sunday Times (season's best historical fiction)*

'A compelling read, with a satisfying blend of history, nature and romance.' **Amanda Booth**, *The Scots Magazine*

Also by Catherine Czerkawska

THE
CURIOSITY
CABINET

Catherine Czerkawska

Saraband

Published by Saraband,
Suite 202, 98 Woodlands Road,
Glasgow, G3 6HB,
Scotland

www.saraband.net

10 9 8 7 6 5 4 3 2 1

ISBN: 9781910192603
ISBNe: 9781910192610

Typeset by Iolaire Typography Ltd.
Printed and bound in Great Britain by Clays Ltd, St Ives plc.

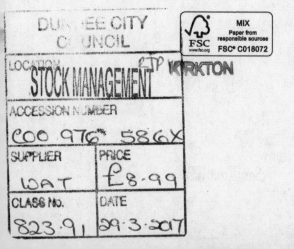

PROLOGUE

People tell an old story upon the Hebridean island of Garve regarding one Manus McNeill, sometime laird of the place and a younger son of the Clan McNeill, this small island being the whole of his inheritance, that Manus had in his possession a great treasure which he subsequently lost. None, however, would claim to know whether it was gold or silver or the bejewelled haul from some Spanish wreck, and certainly nothing of great value has ever been found among the stones and profuse flowers of the island in the years that have passed since Manus ruled over it.

The tale is also told upon the island that this Manus married the daughter of a lowland lord who was disposed to be favourable to the Stuart cause. He brought her home to his house at Achadh nam Blàth, or Auchenblae, which name means Field of Flowers, but she died young and left him a widower. Thereafter he turned to the two vices of drinking and gambling in about equal measure, occasionally interrupting these pursuits to dabble in the politics of the time, which were precarious. But he was a canny man and able to suit all sides, trimming his sails to the prevailing wind, as befits an islandman born and bred.

Whether he won his treasure at the gaming tables of Edinburgh or whether it was freely given as a reward for a favour, or the booty of battle, the stories do not relate. But in due course this extraordinary man is also said to have taken to himself a 'bride from the sea'. Again tradition is disappointingly silent with regard to whether or not she came complete with selkie tail and pearls stolen from her father, the Sea King. Oral histories go on to relate that ultimately Manus lost his treasure, but by what means is all unclear.

There seems to be a superstitious dread among the people of these parts with regard to this same Manus. Half-tales and snatches of old song are the most that can be gleaned by the assiduous collector. Islanders profess 'not to know' or to have 'forgotten', in the same breath declaring it to be 'all nonsense. Just nonsense anyway.' Then one remembers that these are people who can keep a secret for a thousand years, and one suspects that this is exactly what they have done and will go on doing for as long as their chieftain, the fearsome Manus, is remembered.

From *Island Tales,* by the Rev. Bartholomew Scobie (Edinburgh, 1900)

ONE

The island crouches long and hilly on her horizon, like some mysterious hump-backed animal. Already she can smell it, the scent that is somewhere between land and sea and has something of both in it. The island is full of flowers. Ashore, Alys knows that honeysuckle will clutter the hedgerows like clotted cream, weaving a dense tapestry with marching lines of purple foxgloves. Earlier in the year there would have been clumps of thrift, a wild rock garden defining all the bays. Later, meadowsweet will fill the hedges and ditches. But now there will be pink roses and yellow irises. There will be nut-brown boats drawn up on the pale sand, and dress-suited oystercatchers patrolling among the seaweed. As the ferry comes to shore, she notices that the sea around Garve is still that shade of turquoise she has seen nowhere else. The light is different here; the colours are brighter and more luminous. None of that has changed. It is the same as it always was.

The hotel is only a short walk from the ferry. They have sent a car to meet her and to fetch her bags. She lets the Australian chauffeur – who, he tells her, is also the barman – load her suitcases into the boot, but then asks him to go on. She will walk the short distance, so that she can adjust to the island, breathe in clean air, be silent. She misses Ben, bouncing beside her, tugging at her jacket, talking. She trusts his father and stepmother to look after him. Well, she trusts his father, but still her imagination conjures

1

horrors. She tries to put them from her mind, think about the pleasure of a week's freedom, but Ben's absence is a constant low-key worry.

Oddly, the hotel looks bigger than her memory of it: an elegant stone building, facing the sea, Georgian, in all probability. When they used to come to the island on holiday, when Alys was seven, and eight, and one last time when she was ten, it wasn't a hotel at all; it was called the New Laird's House. They had stayed in a holiday cottage on the estate. The current laird was a brown-sauce manufacturer from Warrington in search of peace and quiet. He was not a bad landlord, the islanders said. He did his best. You could walk in the grounds, but you had to ask permission in those days. As a child she had found gardens boring, preferring the haphazard fascination of the wilderness. She still prefers it, though recently she has also begun to understand her mother's interest in growing things, particularly flowers.

The sauce manufacturer is long gone and there have been a number of more or less satisfactory successors, a few much less so, but now large parts of the island are community-owned, and the house has been a hotel for some time. This is her first visit in twenty-five years. They had always come back to the same rented cottage down by the seashore: her parents, her brother, herself, but now her parents are dead, and her brother Robert is living half way across the world. She booked the holiday on impulse a few weeks ago, because eight-year-old Ben would be spending a fortnight in Italy with his father and stepmother, and she couldn't bear the thought of the empty flat in an Edinburgh crammed with tourists. Then she found herself wondering if she had done the right thing. How would she occupy her time on a small Hebridean island: a grown woman, with a wardrobe full of unsuitable shoes? So she made a special shopping trip for flat lace-ups, tough sandals, a waterproof jacket. Her friend Sophie came too and laughed at Alys, who had never before set foot in any of those alarming shops dedicated to the Great Outdoors.

'Oh God,' she said, 'look at you, Alys.' Sophie is tall and skinny and goes hillwalking or even cycling from time to time. 'Just look at you. I never thought I'd see you here among the gas burners and the hand warmers!'

The hotel smells of polish and pot pourri. Her bedroom is high up, looking out towards Scoull Bay. She unpacks, finds the bed to be firm and the linen to be crisp, showers in a gleaming bathroom, and then descends in search of gin. The residents' lounge is the source of yet more pot pourri and polish but the windows are open. The sea is palest turquoise and there is the little lozenge of the ferry, zig-zagging back across a rock-strewn sound. The air outside smells of honeysuckle and roses and seaweed.

In the bar she drinks gin and tonic, eats salted peanuts, looks at the dinner menu (heavy on seafood), smiles at the barman, who carried her cases and drove them up from the ferry.

'Just having a wee break?' he asks. He uses the word 'wee' self-consciously.

'That's right. I used to come here on holiday when I was a kid. I always promised myself I'd come back some day.'

'Good for you,' he says absently. People keep telling him this, but he can't quite understand it. He has been here for a month and already he is bored. What do people do here? he wonders. How do they stand the rain?

The bar is quiet. The other residents are either changing or still out and about on the island, golfing, sailing, fishing, walking.

She can hear footsteps pattering across the wooden floor of another room. Somewhere a child is running about the hotel. Fleetingly she wishes it were Ben.

'Excuse me?' says the barman. 'Do you want another?'

She holds out her glass, smiling at him, then turns again to look out of the window. Small clouds are strung out across the sky like

3

sheep. Their shadows fall on the water below. Suddenly it feels like a homecoming.

Presently she takes her drink and finds the residents' lounge again. It is still empty, so she moves about the room examining pictures. They are large oil paintings, grim death rather than still life: birds, their feathers tumbled and bloody, hunks of meat, overflowing platters of fruit and vegetables. There is the inevitable stag, on a heathery hill. There is a grimly handsome highlander, staring pensively into the distance. There are a few portraits of bald-headed, pot-bellied, self-satisfied old men, so dark as to be almost indistinguishable from each other.

And then she comes upon a display case of mahogany and glass. There are objects, neatly arranged on three shelves. But the casket is central. The casket has raised, heavily embroidered panels on a wooden base and little gilded feet. The scenes are biblical. A woman stands breast high amid the growing corn. She is Ruth. 'Whither thou goest I will go . . . thy people shall be my people,' thinks Alys, surprised by her own knowledge, remembering the words from some long-ago reading, a school service perhaps. She hasn't been to church in years. There are birds and flowers too: long-necked swans and plump seagulls, honeysuckle, wild roses with their centres formed of tiny seed pearls, drooping foxgloves.

The embroidery has faded over time but only a little. The two front doors are open to reveal five drawers, two wide and three narrow, also embroidered with flowers and birds and beasts. There is a tall house in grey silk, with fragments of mica for windows.

She can still hear the child pattering about, giggling.

Other objects, presumably the contents of the cabinet, are spread out on the shelves above and below it. Here is a miniature shuttle, prettily inlaid with gold, and with a few discoloured threads still attached. Here is a needlelace collar, very fine and floral. Here is a tiny pincushion, a painted silk fan and a coral teether. On another shelf is a hand mirror, intricately decorated

4

with semi-precious stones in the shape of flowers: forget-me-nots and pansies. Alongside these precious keepsakes, she is puzzled to see a little collection of pebbles and shells and swansdown. Finally there is a scrap of yellowed paper, with a few words of incomprehensible writing: a letter? A poem? Alys is enchanted by these things and suddenly possessed by the need to know more about them.

She wants to talk to somebody about the cabinet and its contents, but there is nobody in the room. I should have brought someone with me, she thinks. I should have got Sophie to come. She is distressed to find that she has a lump in her throat. The absence of her son is a dull ache inside her.

The barman passes the door with a couple of big bottles of wine and a bag of ice. 'Are you looking at our curiosity cabinet?' he says, grinning.

'Curiosity cabinet?'

'Well, that's what they call it here.'

'It must be very old.'

'Seventeen hundreds. Something like that,' he says vaguely. 'Maybe older. Sixteen something?' He shrugs. 'I wouldn't know.'

'Where are they from, all these things?'

'Not sure. You'd have to ask Mr Cameron, the manager. I think somebody lent them to the hotel. Must be worth a fortune.'

After dinner, she goes out and walks down towards the sea. Grey clouds veil the mainland. There has been a shower of rain, and all the fuchsia hedges are festooned with spiders' webs and hung with droplets of water. Alys finds herself glancing back at the spine of the island, behind the hotel. It was what they always did as children; looking west to see where the weather was coming from. The sky is clearing. The island reminds her of those magic painting books. The shop here used to sell them. You would dip your brush in water, and pale, clear colours would emerge from the page, as this green and blue landscape is emerging from the mist. She will never tire of seeing the transformation.

She heads for the wooden jetty in Scoull Bay and walks along it, looking at the water. She has not been so alone for years; not since Ben was born. She still misses him, but the peace of this place tempers her homesickness. Its familiarity, after all this time, is comforting. She is relieved to discover that the catwalk has not been replaced by anything bigger or more ostentatious. She used to come here, she and her brother Robert and a local boy. She tries to remember his name but she can't call it to mind. He fetched an old creel from home and showed them how to bait it, and they suspended it below the catwalk, trying to catch crabs. They caught several, much to their excitement: small, inedible creatures that they always threw back into the water.

The boy knew about the sea. He was a great hero to Alys. He could handle a boat, all by himself, and he told them stories of fierce conger eels that lurked in holes in the rocks and would bite your thumb off if they got half a chance. It had obsessed them for two summers: catching crabs on Garve. And then the third summer, when she was ten, Alys invited a friend, a girl called Honey ('We had a golden retriever of that name,' her father said), and it wasn't the same. It was a rainy summer and Honey didn't like the island much. She didn't like the mud and the wind, and she certainly didn't want to go trapping crabs. 'Yeuch!' she said. 'Crabs!'

The island boy looked at her in astonished disgust, and Robert followed suit. Nothing was the same. Robert, thirteen by then, got crabby himself, and went off with the island boy, telling Alys to get lost. They didn't want her. And then the boy's father took them out on a real fishing boat, but Honey wouldn't go because she was afraid of the water as well as the crabs, so Alys couldn't leave her. She and Honey fell out. They were barely on speaking terms by the time they got back to Edinburgh, and after that Alys's mother said she wanted to holiday somewhere 'where we can be sure of the weather'. They never went back to the island again.

'I must bring Ben here,' she thinks. 'He ought to get to know the place.'

Alys walks back up to the hotel, finally driven indoors by the midges, which are beginning to bite. Mr Cameron, balding and cheerful, is behind the bar now. The place is busier. Locals, fishermen mostly, lean on the counter, chatting and drinking beer. Several parties of yachtsmen and a few women are eating bar meals and taking up lots of space with their inevitable yellow and red oilies. The room smells of chips. The locals look at her with polite but silent curiosity. The yachtsmen smile faintly. 'Hi. Oh, hi there,' they say. She finds a seat at the other end of the bar and Mr Cameron, recognising her as a resident, comes over to talk to her.

'Everyone comes back sooner or later,' he tells her comfortably.

'Do they?'

'Oh aye. It's that kind of place.'

'Twenty-five years ago. That's when I was last here. I was a little girl. It doesn't seem to have changed much.'

'Oh but it has. We're all masters of our own fate now, you know.'

The island had been the subject of a community buy-out some years previously. She had followed the story in the national press, intrigued.

'But that's a good thing, isn't it?' she asks.

'Oh, a very good thing – on the whole. But we're used to having a laird in these parts, you know. So many hundreds of years of tradition. It's very hard to let all that go. Still, it had to happen. It's all well and good when your laird takes his job seriously, when he realises that there's more than just a business or an investment at stake.'

She senses a 'but' and waits for him to continue.

He shrugs, unwilling to embark on local politics. 'Different times call for different solutions. We're in uncharted waters. We have to find a new way of handling our fragile places and people if they're to survive.'

She agrees with him. 'Well, they have as much right to life as any other endangered species.'

He chuckles, pours her another drink and goes to attend to a group of yachtsmen. 'You'd think so, wouldn't you?' he says, over his shoulder. 'In these environmentally conscious times.'

'Can you tell me anything about those things in the lounge?' she asks, when he comes back. 'I mean the embroidered box.'

'Ah, our treasures. They belong to Iain McNeill from Ardachy. He lent them to us so that visitors to the island could see them.' Mr Cameron looks around. 'He and his son Donal come in here most days. They could tell you more.'

'Donal's on the mainland,' says one of the men at the bar. 'Taken his dad to the hospital for a check-up. Should be back tomorrow morning.'

'So he donated them?' asks Alys.

'Lent them to us. Donal tells me the cabinet and its contents were all packed away in an old blanket box in his loft. We've been offered thousands for the things. We pass all the enquiries on to Iain but he always says no, not for sale. Nobody knows who they belonged to.'

'What about the locals? Doesn't anyone here have any ideas?'

'Well, if they do know they aren't saying to me. But then maybe they wouldn't. After all, I'm an incomer like yourself, my dear. Only been here ten years. That's no time at all on this island.'

That night, prompted by fresh air and gin, she falls asleep almost instantly. But she wakes up in the small hours, with a suffocating sense of loss, and wishes desperately that she was at home, that she could go into Ben's room and plant a kiss on his cheek. She can almost smell the scent of his skin. She knows that he would wrinkle his nose and turn over with a sigh, clutching his toy dog closer to him.

When she falls asleep again, she dreams that Ben has gone missing. She is crying uncontrollably.

'I want my son!' she wails in her sleep. 'I want my son. Where is he?'

It is a horrible dream, and she struggles to wake up from it. At last, she sits up in bed with her heart pounding. Fully awake, she switches on the light and listens. The hotel is quiet. She puts the light off again, gets out of bed and pads over to the window. She can hear the faint, sporadic swish of water on sand and the peep of wading birds, but nothing else. It strikes her how, at home in Edinburgh, you can always hear the muted background roar of traffic, day and night. The profound stillness here is almost unnerving, magnifying each sound. It never grows completely dark at this time of year. This is equally true in Edinburgh but the sky is always artificially light there, anyway. Here, she sees a dim twilight and a comforting smudge of brightness in the eastern sky. So she goes back to bed, and back to sleep, and her dreams are untroubled.

She spends the next morning following the narrow road to the north of the island, wearing her new shoes and her new waterproof jacket, until it makes her far too hot, in spite of its promise of 'breathable fabric', and she has to carry it tied round her waist. She has brought a picnic lunch supplied by the hotel kitchen, and around one o'clock she finds her way down a track through bracken and heather, to the windy western coast where a long beach of white sand is washed by powerful waves. You could come surfing here if you were so inclined. The tide is out and the sand is clean, apart from a few razor shells, white pebbles and shiny strands of seaweed. The beach is empty, but she sees a single set of footprints following the shoreline.

She finds a sheltered spot among rocks and makes herself comfortable while she eats ham sandwiches and fruit. She is finding it hard to get used to this sense of freedom. Nobody will mind if she is late. She can do as she pleases, stay here or move on. Nobody will tug at her hand and tell her to hurry up. The combination of wind and sunlight is dazzling. She leans back against the lichen-crusted rock and closes her eyes. Perhaps she falls asleep for a while because when she opens them again, she feels her cheeks burning. Through the wind, the sunlight is very strong. A small boat is moving slowly across her field of vision and she can hear the remote put-put of its engine. She squints into the distance and can make out that the boat is carrying two or perhaps three people. The hotel advertises fishing trips and she supposes that this is what she is seeing. On board somebody raises an arm in salute and she waves back, watching the little vessel labour round the far headland.

Later on that day, after a nap, a long bath and a good dinner, she sits in the bar again with blistered feet and a sunburnt face, this time nursing a Laphroaig that tastes of peat and smells of smoke and honey. She remembers that her parents used to drink it whenever they were on the island and raises her glass in silent tribute to them. Wish you were here, she thinks.

Mrs Cameron comes and joins her, sitting down and easing pudgy feet out of smart shoes.

'Ah, that's better,' she says. 'My corns can't be doing with tight shoes any more. I've been shopping on the mainland. I think my feet appreciate island life more than I do.'

A small woman with permed grey hair, she is wearing a tight powder-blue summer dress and pearls.

'You've got a touch of the sun!' she says, looking at Alys's scarlet cheeks.

'I know. It was windy and I didn't realise how bright the sun was.'

'It can be very treacherous. You have to take care, you know. Did you not bring sun cream?'

'I forgot.'

Actually Sophie reminded her, but she had thought it superfluous. 'Sun cream? In the West of Scotland?' she had said.

'You'll get some in the shop tomorrow.' Mrs Cameron leans back and gazes at Alys with interest. 'My husband tells me you were admiring our cabinet of curiosities.'

'I think it's wonderful.'

'We've had it valued – with Iain's permission of course. Late sixteen hundreds, they reckon. It's worth a fortune; the contents, too. But Iain won't sell.'

'Maybe he doesn't need the money.'

'Oh, he could do with the money. And if he couldn't, then his son certainly could.'

'But he still won't sell?'

'He says it belongs on the island. And who's to say that he isn't right?'

TWO

Henrietta lay huddled in the stern of the rowing-boat, a thin blanket her only protection from the constant drizzle. She was disorientated, shivering with cold and sick to her stomach. They had blindfolded her with a filthy rag and her hands were bound in front of her. From that first moment, when the two men had seized her, pulling her from her horse, on the road between Linlithgow and Edinburgh, she had been bundled up, carried and sometimes dragged from one place to another, like a piece of baggage rather than a human being: first on horseback, then in some sort of cart or carriage, and again on horseback, for many days, until at last she was lifted aboard a boat that swayed and bucked under her like another horse. She had vomited several times, and one of the men had continually forced brackish water between her lips, talking to her in a language that she couldn't even begin to understand.

She had lost count of the days and nights. Sometimes she had been allowed to sleep on bundles of straw or heather which at least had the virtue of cleanness. Once or twice, in the darkness, she had been tumbled onto a bed, which she knew from the stench of it must have been filthy, but she had been too exhausted to complain and had slept until they lifted her and carried her again. Afterwards a constant itching had been added to her trials: fleas, or lice, she was not sure which. Perhaps both. Only when she needed to attend to her own bodily functions had they let her alone; showing her, with unexpected diffidence, ditches, trees and shrubs she might use in peace. But they had never gone far from her and she had been too uncomfortable and too ashamed to linger, too weak with hunger and shock to try to escape.

Her captors had spoken little during the whole journey: Seamus, whom she remembered as a red-haired young man from her first sight of the pair on the road to Edinburgh, had said almost nothing that was not in his own language, although the older man addressed the occasional remark to her in the Scotch tongue, flinging the words roughly at her as though the very articulation of them made him uncomfortable.

She remembered how her groom had ridden a little way ahead. She had heard the hoofbeats behind her on the road and had called to him to stop, to wait for her, but they were upon her so swiftly and suddenly that the shock of the assault froze her into immobility. They had dragged her from her mount, smothering her head in a woollen blanket. The young groom had ridden back to her assistance, but they had dealt with him, for she had heard his cry as he fell. Then one of her assailants had thrown her over his saddle, and they had ridden off at speed, her terror and the rough motion rendering her bewildered and dizzy.

Now she could hear the slop of the waves and sense the pulling of oars. A cold wind blew about her head; she could smell both sea and land; she knew that they were rowing in darkness, and she was possessed with an overwhelming apprehension about what lay in store for her at her journey's end.

Her captors were speaking to each other, and to somebody else – the ferryman, perhaps – in that strange, liquid language which she now recognised as the Gaelic. 'Uncouth,' her brother Thomas had called it. 'Fit only for animals.'

She felt fingers fumbling at the back of her head and the blind-fold was removed.

'Here, lady.' It was Seamus, the redhead, younger than his

companion and less brusque with her. '*Faodaidh tu sealltainn air na reultan. You may look at the stars.*'

It was dark, although a thin moon showed through the clouds every now and then and glimmered off the oily waves that heaved under the boat.

She said, 'I don't understand you. I don't understand what you are saying to me. Tell me why you are doing this!'

'You are wasting your breath talking to him, lady.' That was the older man speaking from the bows of the boat. He laughed but it was not a kindly sound. 'Seamus has little of the Scotch. You must speak to me or nobody.'

'Where are we going? Where are you taking me?' Her tongue felt thick and heavy in her mouth. She could smell the foulness of her own unwashed clothes and body.

'The ferryman here is taking us to the island. To *Eilean Garbh*.'

She made out that there was a third man in the boat, bent double over a pair of long oars. Then the thought of Gabriel came to her again, as it had during all the hideous waking hours of the journey and she wailed aloud at the pain of it.

'Where is my son? Where is my little boy? In the name of God, what have you done with him?'

'Little boy?' asked Greybeard. He sounded surprised. 'There was no child in the matter. There was just yourself and the groom in it.'

Gabriel had been with Maisie in the carriage. She had ridden alone, glad of fresh air and exercise, leaving him to travel in comfort. So perhaps he was safe after all. But what had become of the poor groom?

'Have you killed the lad that was with me?' she asked tentatively.

Again the highlander seemed surprised by the question. 'Killed him? No. There was to be no killing. Ach, he was no great fighter and it was no great blow. He just went down like a pair of breeks beneath it. He will have had a sore head for a day or two. That is all. It was yourself we were to take just.'

She said, wonderingly, 'But why, when I have done nothing wrong?'

'Whoever said that you had?'

She put a hand to the neck of her riding habit, tugging at the chain that hung there. 'Look,' she said, speaking slowly and clearly, trying to make them understand, 'if you will let me go, I can pay you. I have a gold locket. It is yours. Save that there is a lock of my baby's hair in it, which I would like to keep for myself. And there will be more. Do you understand me? I have money and means of my own. Only take me back to Linlithgow, and I will give you anything you ask.'

Clouds had hidden the thin moon and she could see nothing of their faces in the darkness. The older man spoke again. 'No, no, put it away,' he said. 'There is nothing you can do or pay. It is an insult to us. Put your golden locket away, lady. What we do, we do for our chieftain and the loyalty we bear him. We do it for Manus McNeill of Garbh!'

She began to cry, rocking backwards and forwards and folding her arms round herself.

'I cannot stand her weeping,' said Seamus presently. 'I wish she would give over. It hurts the heart of me.'

'She is crying for her little boy. What do you expect?'

'Her little boy?'

'Aye. That is what she is saying.'

'Dear God!'

'Conscience troubling you, lad?'

'I tell you, I did not know there was a child in the matter and if I had—'

'Quiet,' said his companion. 'We do as we are told. We give her into my Lord Manus's keeping.'

'Aye. And how do you think she will fare in his keeping?'

'He is not a bad man.'

'No, nor a kindly one, either. Ach, Iain, Iain, I am sorry for this day's work. And for the days that have gone before. Truly I am

15

sorry for the wee lass. It was not what I thought it would be . . .'

'But you will be glad enough of the money.'

'I don't deny it. The money will be welcome and besides, I would be afraid to disobey Manus. But the deed weighs heavily on my conscience all the same. And I tell you I cannot bear her crying.'

'You will not have to stand it for much longer. Soon we will be at home upon the island. And then she will be in his keeping, not ours!'

Henrietta dozed in spite of the discomfort, and when she woke it was day and the boat was still. The men did not find it necessary to blindfold her any longer and she blinked in the light. The house rose above the bay where the boat had been drawn up on a stretch of white sand. When she looked upwards, she saw grey stones against a dun landscape. The building seemed fierce and monumental in the cold sunshine of a winter's morning. Seamus set her down on the sand, but her legs collapsed under her. Iain had to carry her up the track from the bay to the house, slung over his shoulder, and when she managed to twist her head so that she could look up again at its grim walls, she could think only of prisons and further misery.

They passed through the oak door of the house and then up a spiral of stone stairs, into the wintry light of a great hall. Henrietta caught a glimpse of a fire that burned at one end, with the ashes of years built up beneath and around it, giving out an intense heat. But the place was deserted at this hour, except for one young woman, who looked up from her cooking pots and came running to meet them. The girl, dark and pretty, with cheeks flushed pink from the fire, was very cross about something. She seemed nervous as well, wringing her hands together and biting her lip. But she was not at all scared of Seamus, who was coming up behind, for over Iain's shoulder Henrietta saw her berating him, and whatever she said to the freckled lad in a high, accusing tone caused him to colour up and slink back down the stairs. Then she spoke to Iain more calmly and presently he followed her, still carrying Henrietta, like a sack of meal, over his shoulder. They went up several flights of spiral stairs and along a dark passage until they emerged at last into a high room, sparsely furnished, stone-cold, and full of the sound of wind and waves and the lamentations of wild birds.

Iain dumped Henrietta on the bed and strode to the door, with the young woman after him, nipping his ear with questions, although he only grunted in reply. He was anxious to be gone. He had played his part and wanted nothing further to do with the whole sorry business.

There was a short spell of silence. Henrietta closed her eyes and breathed deeply, trying to control the faintness that threatened to overwhelm her. The room smelled damp and salty. She could hear the constant sighing of wind and the shrieking of birds. The mattress upon which she lay was fat with feathers, and clean but musty. Disorientated, she sat up on the bed and looked dizzily around her. There was a slight movement from the doorway. The young woman had come back and was regarding the stranger nervously. Henrietta looked at the stone walls of the room, which was empty save for the bed where she lay, one high-backed chair and an oak press.

The girl spoke hesitantly. 'Lady . . . lady, don't you greet so.'

Comforted by the sound of her own language, Henrietta asked, 'Where am I? Why have I been brought here?'

But when the girl spoke next, it was in a mixture of broken English and Gaelic. 'Mistress Dalrymple . . . I have been told to help you. My name is Ishbel. This will be your room. I have brought you some food and wine.'

Henrietta saw that the girl was carrying a wooden board with thin oat cakes, a little pile of white curd cheese, and a cup full of red wine. She was holding them out in front of her, hopefully,

17

offering them to the stranger. All these things looked appetising enough and for the first time in many days, Henrietta realised that she was hungry.

Still, she shook her head. 'I won't eat it. Take it away!'

'You must eat,' aid the girl, distressed. 'Look. There is cheese of my own making—'

'I don't understand what you are saying to me.' Henrietta turned away and began to weep.

'Calm yourself. Oh, do calm yourself, my lady, please.'

But Henrietta was crying too hard to listen. 'I want Gabriel!' She wanted the sweet smell of him, and his little fat arms clutching her neck. She wanted to hear him laugh or to hear him cry: she did not mind which. She would die without him. She would rather die without him. 'I want to go home,' she sobbed. 'I want to go home to my baby.'

The girl came over, set the tray down on the bed and tried to take the strange foreign woman in her arms. She understood enough to know that Henrietta was asking for her child. Her baby. Lord, she thought. Nobody had mentioned a baby. What would Manus have to say about that?

'Now, now,' she murmured. 'Calm yourself.' She looked down at Henrietta's dress in some dismay. 'But you will be needing fresh clothes. These are so dirty! You must be so uncomfortable.'

'I have nothing. Can't you understand me? I have nothing at all!'

Ishbel said, 'There are things in the room below. Gowns and other clothes. I'm sure that my Lord Manus will not mind if you . . .' But again she hesitated, holding Henrietta at arm's length. 'You are in mourning, are you not?' More unpleasant surprises for Manus. 'Your dress is so dirty – you are so dirty. Oh Lord, what am I to do with you? Lady, lady, do not distress yourself so!'

Henrietta pushed her away violently, upsetting the tray,

spilling the wine and scattering oatmeal over the floor. 'Leave me alone! You are all thieves and murderers here!'

She was in a foreign place, surrounded by savages. Highlanders. Terror overcame her again.

'Leave me alone! I want to go home! And I want my baby!'

Ishbel backed away, frightened by the woman's distress. Henrietta wept desperately, uncontrollably, a terrible keening that burst from her and bent her body in two with the force of the emotion behind it.

Ishbel spread her hands. What was to be done?

'I will go and get Manus,' she said at last. 'Maybe he can make you understand.'

It took Ishbel some time to find her cousin, Manus McNeill, and then he was reluctant to come. When he finally accompanied her to the tower room he could hear the wild weeping for himself, even from the stairs below.

'You see, sir?' said Ishbel. 'I can do nothing with her while she is in this state. I am sure she thinks she is going to be killed. But perhaps you can reassure her. Perhaps you can make her understand.'

'Understand what?'

'That we mean her no harm.'

'Do we not? We have snatched her from all that she holds dear.'

Ishbel was silent. Manus listened to the dreadful sounds for a moment and then set off grimly up the stairs.

'She must certainly understand that she cannot go on in this way. You wait here, Ishbel, till I have done.'

Ishbel did as she was told and sat down at the bottom of the stairs. With her forefinger she made patterns in the white sand that always gathered there, blown in on the wind. She wondered what he would do, and felt a pang of pity for the weeping lowlander, but she would never have thought of questioning his orders. He might be her kin, but his word was law in this house as it was on the whole island.

Henrietta was in that state of childlike grief where it is easier to carry on crying than to stop. There seemed no way of stopping and so she just went on wailing, sobbing, choking and retching on her own sobs and then wailing hopelessly again. There was comfort in the repetitiveness of it.

'In the name of God, will you stop your caterwauling, woman!'

A slap on the cheek would not have been more effective. Her sobbing subsided, more from shock at the harshness of his tone than anything else. She was not used to being spoken to like this. Even her captors had been more or less deferential.

'That's better. Now I can hear the thoughts of my own head.'

Manus McNeill. She saw before her a strongly built man, in his thirties perhaps, wearing highland dress, bare legs showing beneath the big blue plaid, which, since he had just come into the house, was still gathered about him. He reminded her of the highlanders she had seen on the streets of Edinburgh where sometimes, dressed in their outlandish clothes, they were perceived as crude figures of fun and sometimes, bristling with weaponry and with the drink taken, as dangerous incomers. She had been taught to avoid looking directly at them in case they took offence, as they were notoriously quick to do. Manus was no figure of fun although she could see that he might be dangerous, a better friend than an enemy, perhaps. He had a thin, sallow face, very weather-beaten and with a certain severity about it, and he was glaring at her in exasperation.

She summoned all her courage and managed to scramble to her feet, the better to confront him, though her head spun with the effort.

'For God's sake, woman,' he said again. 'Will you sit down before you fall down.'

She did as she was told, more out of necessity than obedience. 'Who are you? And why have you brought me here?'

'My name is Manus McNeill and I am lord of this island, such as it is.' Even in her present distressed state, she could see that he was very proud of himself.

'This is my own little kingdom,' he continued. 'You ask me why you have been brought to this place. I can tell you nothing, except that you are here, and here you must stay.'

His gaze was detached. There was concern for her distress in so far as it affected him, but no pity on his face.

'I was visiting my brother and his wife in Edinburgh. I was on my way there, from my home in Linlithgow.'

How long ago had that been? she wondered. She had lost all count of the days. 'I don't understand why this has happened to me!'

Manus lapsed suddenly into his own language, muttering a string of incomprehensible words.

'And I don't understand you!' she interrupted him, beginning to cry again. 'Why do you speak to me in a foreign tongue?'

He stared at her and then, unexpectedly, he began to laugh. 'But it is you who are the foreigner here, lady!'

'I am here most unwillingly!'

He moved closer to her, sniffing the stench of the filth from her journey, and the scent of fear from her body. He was forced to admire her bravery, even now when she was travel- and tear-stained, and quite plainly at her lowest ebb. She turned away, but he seized her by the arm and stared into her face. Emotion had wreaked further havoc there and scars stood out lividly on her pale cheeks. Her hair was a tangled mass of rats' tails.

'Well,' he said, with a sneer in his voice, 'you are a plain wee thing. You have suffered from the smallpox, I see.'

She turned away from him. 'It killed my mother and father . . .'

'No no,' he said, dismissing explanations with a wave of his hand. 'Do not hide your face for me. Why should I care what you look like?'

'Sir, my baby son went in the carriage to Edinburgh with his nurse. They were ahead of me on the road. Do you know what has become of him?'

This was a new and disturbing piece of information. There had been no mention of a child. It startled him for a moment.

'Your son?' His tone was suddenly angry, and she recoiled from him. 'What do you mean?' he asked. 'No one told me that you had a son.'

'He is a bairn. Not yet two years old . . .'

'I know nothing about a bairn. But he will be safe in Edinburgh by now. Our business was with you alone.'

'I pray he will be safe.'

'Lady,' Manus said, slowly and rather loudly, as though speaking to a fool. 'This will be your room. It is spacious enough and you may have a fire and a lamp for the dark nights. Ishbel will wait on you. She will fetch you anything you need, within reason. For you must understand that you are not in one of your fine Edinburgh houses now.'

'But I can barely understand her.'

He shrugged. 'Then she must learn – or you must. You will have plenty of time for study.'

Years, he thought. What had he taken upon himself? Why had he agreed to it? It would surely have been easier for all concerned if she had drowned on the way here, sliding into the deep waters between islands. It might even have been kinder. Iain might have done it for him, even if Seamus would not. Who would have known? And who would have cared? The darkness of his thoughts alarmed him and he came to himself with a little start of horror.

'I have nothing with me. What am I to do for clothes?' said Henrietta suddenly.

He had been on his way out of the room, anxious to be gone from the sight of so much misery, but he stopped and turned towards her again, pulled up short by practicalities he had never considered.

'There are some things which belonged to my wife. I suppose you must make use of them.' He hated the thought of it, but it was the only solution. 'Ishbel will see to it.'

'Wait!' She stretched out her hand to him and he moved backwards a pace, distaste on his face. Was she so repulsive? She saw that she must be abhorrent to him: a filthy, tear-stained, pock-marked creature.

'Yes?' he asked sharply.

'Sir, where must I go? What must I do? Must I stay here – a prisoner – in this room?'

He hesitated. He had given little thought to the consequences of her presence. 'In this room? Why no.' How could he keep her locked up here? It would be unreasonable. One would not keep an animal in that fashion. 'No, Mistress Dalrymple. This is a big house and I barely use the half of it. You are free to roam the house and the island as far as you wish and so long as you do not trouble me. But there is no way to leave the island, save with my permission. So you should have no hopes in that direction – no hopes of escape, I mean.'

'But I may go out?'

'You are free to roam as you please, only I would be glad if you would stay out of my way. I am to keep you here. That is all I can tell you. Whatever you need, Ishbel will show you. If you cannot make her understand you, I am sorry for it. But she must not always be running to me on your account. Is that plain to you?'

'It is.'

He was at the door. 'I will send her to you now. I am sorry for you and that's the truth.'

She saw that it was indeed the truth, but also that he thought of her as a disagreeable encumbrance, like an unwanted horse or a stray dog that had fallen to his unwilling care. He would not murder her in cold blood, but it would suit him well enough if she died and he might even find it in his heart to neglect her until she did. She saw all this as clearly as though she had read his mind.

23

He said, matter of factly, 'I cannot be responsible for the wickedness of others, Mistress Henrietta. You must just make the best of it that you can.'

There was a draught of cold air from the doorway and when she looked up she saw that he had gone.

After a while, Henrietta stood up and made her way over to the window. Outside, seagulls rode the winds in a grey sky. Below her the waves tumbled ceaselessly onto the white beach. How had she come to be here? And where was she? Her knowledge of geography was sketchy at best. She remembered the big globe of the world that always sat on the nursery table in Edinburgh, but she had never paid much attention to it. Henrietta supposed that they had come west, for they had always headed towards the setting sun, but that was as much as she could tell. Why should she be kidnapped by two highlanders at the behest of a third? Who could possibly have ordered it? It was enough to send a person mad. She was at a loss to know what possible benefit her removal could be to anybody. As far as she knew, she had no enemies in the world.

She had once been a much-loved daughter; she still considered herself an obedient and affectionate sister. Indeed, when she was a girl, her brother Thomas had been the sun in her sky. He was her hero, always coming into the nursery or the schoolroom, shamelessly interrupting her lessons with gifts for her: gingerbread men, green ribbons for her auburn hair, or posies of sweet-scented flowers in season. In return she had remained loyal and loving to him, even when she grew older and more aware of his failings. For she could see that Thomas had a streak of recklessness. He liked to drink more wine and spend more money than was prudent, even for a young man of his considerable expectations.

Thomas's wife, Grisel Shaw, had always been her good friend as well as her distant cousin, although when they were children, it was Grisel who had been the poor relation, plain and tall, marooned in that vast, tumbledown house at Linlithgow with her great-uncle, William Shaw. He was a kindly but scholarly man who had assumed the guardianship of his dead brother's child dutifully, but with little enthusiasm. Grisel was the recipient of a good deal of benign neglect and she had often come visiting Henrietta's family in Edinburgh, anxious for company, and also for a glimpse of Thomas, whom she adored.

The two girls had walked in the gardens that ran downhill at the back of the narrow house, just off the Canongate, and had talked about clothes, and courtship and marriage. Poor ingenuous Grisel had made her admiration for Thomas all too obvious, but Henrietta did not think that Thomas returned Grisel's love and she had been truly sorry for it. It would be nice, she thought, if her best friend could also become her sister. And so she had racked her brains for ways to make Thomas like Grisel. None of them had worked. Thomas would bestow brotherly kisses on Henrietta, plant a chaste peck on Grisel's cheek and then proceed to ignore her, as usual.

When Henrietta was fifteen, the horror of smallpox had come to the city. Her parents had caught the disease and died within days of each other. Henrietta had contracted the illness too, but her nurse, Maisie, had coaxed her back to health if not strength. While Henrietta lay sick, something strange and unexpected had happened to Thomas. After their parents' death, and in his anxiety to avoid the disease-ridden city, he had fled to Linlithgow to stay with William Shaw, and there he had fallen under Grisel's spell. Henrietta had never quite understood the change, though it was welcome. Perhaps he had been flattered by her open affection, for Grisel knew little of flirtation. Besides, her face and figure had blossomed so that she might justifiably be called 'handsome'. It had occurred to Henrietta to wonder whether the fact that William had settled a tocher, a good dowry, on his niece, might be part of the attraction. But with both their parents dead, and Thomas the favoured only son, he would have little need of

Grisel's money as well as his own inheritance. So when she recovered from the effects of her illness and from the first devastation of bereavement, Henrietta began to hope that the love between her brother and her friend was genuine.

Thomas and Grisel were soon betrothed and Grisel was to be mistress of the Edinburgh house. 'But you must always think of this place as your home, you know,' Grisel told her, hugging her close. 'You will, won't you, Henrietta?'

Poor Henrietta was terribly scarred. She had looked at her ruined face just once. She had even made Maisie hold the glass steady for her. But she had not looked again.

'Put the glass away for pity's sake,' she told Maisie. 'Put it away!'

What was it Manus had called her? 'A plain wee thing.' Well, even though the scars had faded somewhat over time, it was nothing less than the truth. She had been imprisoned then, in familiar surroundings, imprisoned by the ruin of her looks. Now, after a brief interval of happiness, she was imprisoned again, but this time it was among savages, on a remote island. Was she destined to wither and die among the barren rocks of this place? She lay down on the bed and closed her eyes, willing sleep to come.

A little while later, however, Ishbel came to her bringing a fine linen nightdress as well as a big basin of warm water for washing. When Henrietta did not reject these offerings, she began to smile and showed her where there was a dressing room to one side of the bedroom, and a chilly toilet closet, and then she lit a peat fire in the grate, and helped Henrietta to take off her clothes. They were so verminous that they would have to be burned. Henrietta relinquished them with small regret, keeping only her gold locket, and the two things which had been in her pocket: Gabriel's teething coral and a recipe for 'cosmetic lotion' which she had hoped to make for herself in Edinburgh, and which would, so Maisie assured her, encourage the scars to fade. Then the girl helped her to wash, combed out her wet hair, spread ointment on her sores, slid the nightdress over her head and finally wrapped a clean woollen shawl round her shivering body.

'Poor lady,' she said under her breath. 'Poor lady!'

Ishbel went away again and presently came back carrying another tray of food. This time Henrietta did not reject the meal, and when she had eaten the oatcakes and cheese and drunk the wine, which was rough and heady, she lay down beneath linen sheets and woollen blankets and slept the sleep of exhaustion. The bed was soft, being well stuffed with down. Ishbel had even warmed it with a stone bottle full of hot water, but Henrietta would have slept on solid rock and barely moved all that day.

In the evening, she was aroused by Ishbel bringing in a small iron oil-lamp which smoked constantly and smelled of fish. She took a bowl of broth and more oat bread, and slept again. In the night she opened her eyes and was frightened by the extreme darkness of the place and the low moaning of wind around the tower, but then she caught sight of the faint embers of the fire that Ishbel had banked up before she left, and she was comforted by them, and soon drifted into sleep again.

The following morning she woke to the grey light of a winter's day, and the ill-tempered squealing of seagulls around the old building. Ishbel came in, bringing more peat for the fire as well as warm milk for her and hot porridge in a wooden bowl, with a horn spoon, and with a basin of cool cream to dip it in. At least, thought Henrietta, they didn't intend to starve her to death, whatever else might become of her. Then, with a mixture of encouraging words and signs and smiles, the girl coaxed her out of the room, and took her down the spiral stairs to the floor below, where, in a cupboard recessed into one of the walls, she saw a great many dresses, shawls and petticoats hanging in sad rows. They were damp and musty, although sweet herbs had been strewn among them to deter the moths and to keep the garments as fresh as the building and the climate would allow.

'They are for you,' said Ishbel, urging her forward. It was as though her command of Henrietta's language had been very rusty from want of use, but now that she was forced into it, it was becoming easier. Henrietta ruffled through the silk and brocade, the linen and Indian cotton.

'Who did they belong to? Is Manus some kind of Bluebeard? Some ogre?' she said, half to herself, remembering stories of fairy folk, demons and goblins, told by Maisie in the Edinburgh firelight.

'They are for you to use.' Ishbel held one of the dresses up against Henrietta, frowning. It was dark red brocade with a full skirt, already worn and mended in places, with a heavily boned bodice and pretty French lace on the sleeves. 'She was a bigger lady than you, to be sure, but it is better that way for I can alter them for you and make them smaller.'

'But whose clothes are they?'

'They once belonged to Manus's wife. She died in childbirth.' Ishbel sighed in frustration, searching for the right words. 'She is dead now. With a baby. You understand?'

'So Manus's wife died in childbirth. When?' Henrietta held up her fingers. 'One year? Two years?'

Ishbel held up ten fingers. 'Many years ago now.'

'Ten years?' said Henrietta.'Aye. It was all of ten years ago.'

Henrietta saw the girl's face fall with the remembered sadness of it. But Ishbel could be no more than twenty herself, and must have been a child at the time.

'So Manus's wife died ten years ago. And the baby?'

'The baby died too.'

'And I am to have these things?'

'Yes,' said Ishbel eagerly. 'Yes, you are to make use of all these.'

There was a shelf in the closet with things neatly piled onto it, a pathetic collection of everyday possessions. Henrietta took them up, one by one. There was a pincushion, a pretty little pocket with ribbons for fastening it inside the skirt and a lace handkerchief inside, even a pair of shoes embroidered with lilies and roses: most unsuitable for island wear. Still, this was ghostly gear and, like the clothes, they were sad things with the scent of another woman on them.

Ishbel was picking them up, pressing them upon her. 'Use them. You take them and use them. All the clothes, too. Manus, he never comes here. Never.' She shook her head, echoing Henrietta's own thoughts. 'Too sad.'

Gowns and shawls and lace. A dead woman's shoes. How could she bring herself to wear them? And yet she must. What was she to do for clothes otherwise?

'Let us take some of these back to your room,' said Ishbel. 'They will need to be changed. To be stitched.' She mimed the actions.

'What?'

'They are too big for you. My lady wore them when she was with child. But we can make them smaller. We can make them fit. Help me to carry them.'

Henrietta said, 'You will help me to sew them, to alter them?'

'Yes. Yes, we will do all that. But come back to your room now. I will make up the fire for you, nice and warm, and then we will sew them.'

THREE

On the morning of her second full day on Garve, following a gargantuan breakfast of bacon, egg, sausage, tomatoes and mushrooms (the previous day's quota of fresh air and exercise seems to have given her a country appetite), Alys straps up her blisters, puts on her new tough sandals and strolls in sunshine, down towards the bay and the narrow jetty. She thinks about the island boy baiting their creel, but she still can't remember his name. He was small and wiry and very dark and his father was a fisherman, going out in a wooden boat for crabs and lobsters every day. The boy had lived on the island all his life and knew every inch of the place, though she remembers that the last time they met him, when she was ten and Robert was thirteen, he was about to go away to secondary school on the mainland, staying in a hostel through the week. She remembers it because she had thought how awful it would be to have to go away from home all week long. Robert told her afterwards that the boy wouldn't talk about it. He said he wanted to forget about it until it happened, so perhaps he had felt the same.

Yesterday evening, Ben had phoned from a hotel in Sorrento. 'There are lemons growing outside,' he said excitedly. 'I can see them from my window. Big huge lemons. And there are oranges in the hotel garden. And we're going to walk round the top of a volcano.'

'Well, just be careful. Just take care,' she told him, trying to sound matter-of-fact, cheerful.

She thinks about the trek up Vesuvius and the precipitous path round the crater. In her mind's eye it becomes fraught with danger. Vesuvius is classified as 'deadly and dangerous'. She knows this because she and Ben looked it up on a vulcanology website a few weeks ago. Now she is sorry they did. What if . . . ? She bites her lip and throws stones into the water below the catwalk. She wishes Ben were here, beside her. Little fishes dart away from her stones, through clear water. The sea looks shallower than it actually is, and warmer.

A pink jellyfish swims elegantly along, trailing long reddish tendrils. They are known as 'scalder' and they are dangerous. From some long untapped part of her memory she dredges up the information. The big creatures like swimming lampshades are harmless, but these smaller jellyfish will sting you. Touch them and rub your eyes or other parts of your body and all hell will break loose.

'See, if you get that on your fingers from the creels and then have a pee, by God you'll know all about it!' That was what the island boy told Robert.

When she was ten, she had developed a crush on him. He seemed so capable, so self-possessed, so grown-up. She wore her hair in a ponytail in those days and sometimes, particularly during that last summer, he would chase her and try to pull it and she would run off, giggling, full of a transient but intense delight. Even now, when she thinks about it the memory gives her a little glow of satisfaction. With hindsight, she realises that this was probably the first time in her life that she flirted with somebody.

The tide is out, showing broad expanses of sand, like caster sugar. She decides to walk across the bay — across several bays, really — towards the cottage she can just see huddled beneath a low hill.

31

She takes off her sandals and strides out, paddling through pools, elated by the day and her surroundings. The sand is wet and the prints of her bare feet fade behind her. Below the tidemark are the sandy casts of a thousand lugworms. She remembers digging for them, with Robert and her father, in search of bait for fishing, remembers the excitement of the frantic scrabbling in pursuit of the worm beneath, her fascinated revulsion at the sight of the jam-jar full of purplish creatures, squirming together.

The broad expanse of Scoull Bay narrows to a series of inlets with small reefs fringing them. The cottage, which is much further away than it looks, is very old, with white walls and a grey roof and a thin wisp of smoke spiralling up from the chimney. She comes to it from the sea and notices that a green lane winds among foxgloves and campion and dog roses towards the house. A veronica bush, six feet tall and full of startling blue blooms, guards the gate, and there is a hedge, heavy with fuchsia flowers. There is a vegetable garden too, with neat rows of leeks and carrots and potatoes. Somewhere she can hear hens complaining, faintly but persistently, in the manner of their kind.

Alys sits down on the turf beside a pile of creels, and looks out at the sea. She drinks bottled water and eats an apple. A couple of small craft are moored against a crumbling wall: a white fibreglass affair and an older, clinker-built wooden boat that looks sturdier and smells of tar and has a powerful outboard engine tilted up on the stern. She wonders if this is the same boat that she watched yesterday. The sun is very warm now, and she leans back and closes her eyes, letting the heat beat against her body, smelling that magical amalgam of salt and honey.

The man clears his throat, hesitantly, not wanting to alarm her. But he needs to get to his boat and to do that he has to walk past her.

She opens her eyes, startled, and sees him hovering uncertainly in front of her.

'Excuse me,' he says. He is a man of about her own age or just a little older, and he is holding a pair of long wooden oars and a bulky plastic bag, his lunch maybe.

'I'm sorry.' She starts to scramble to her feet. 'Is this private property?'

'No, no.' He seems embarrassed by the question. 'Not at all. No. Sit yourself down. Don't trouble yourself. I was going to my boat. I didn't want to disturb you, that was all. Have you walked across?'

'From the bay below the hotel. Yes.'

'Ah,' He nods. 'You'll be on holiday, then.'

'For a couple of weeks.'

'Just yourself?'

'Just myself. Do you live ... ?' She gestures towards the cottage.

'Ardachy,' he says. 'Aye. That's where I live. With my father.'

There is something familiar about the name of the place, but at the moment, her mind fuzzy with sleep, she can't remember what.

'You have a lovely vegetable garden,' she tells him.

'Well, I do a lot of it. Though my father ... He does what he can.'

He seems disposed to be friendly but pathologically shy. Just at first, she wonders if he is a few sandwiches short of a picnic. At least, that's how she puts it to herself. The phrase pops easily into her mind and scandalises her. God, she thinks, what am I like? The stranger offers her his smile as a charm against misunderstanding but she misinterprets it anyway as simplicity. He is stocky and dark, with untidy black hair already streaked with a little grey, and his skin is tanned by wind as much as by the sun. He looks directly at her with a frown and says, 'Do I know you from somewhere?'

'I don't think so. Alys. My name's Alys.'

He props the oars against a big rock and shakes her gravely by the hand. 'Donal,' he says. 'Donal McNeill.'

She remembers suddenly that Donal and Iain McNeill of Ardachy

33

are the owners of the embroidered cabinet. How extraordinary, she thinks, and then wonders why she should find it so strange. Why shouldn't this man with his sweet smile, so at odds with the severity of his features, own something so beautiful and not want to let it go? And in that same moment, she remembers something else. The island boy, all those years ago. Wasn't he called . . . ?

'Donal McNeill,' she says.

'That's my name.'

'I know. I mean, you're right. You do know me.'

'Do I?'

'I used to come here on holiday when I was a kid. The last time we came I was ten years old. You and my brother used to hang a creel from the . . .'

'From the old wooden jetty, for crabs,' he finishes. 'Robert. Your brother's name was Robert.'

'That's right. I'm amazed you remember. There must be so many holidaymakers.'

He sits down on a rock, takes a squashed packet of cigarettes out of the pocket of his jeans and offers it to her.'

'No, thanks.'

'Ah, you don't.'

She shakes her head. He puts the packet away.

'But you go ahead. Please.'

'No, it's all right. I'm trying to stop. The old man goes on at me all the time. He used to smoke a pipe but now that he has angina he's got very fierce about it. Anyway, it'll do me good to abstain. Robert and Alys Miller. That was it, wasn't it? You must be Alys Miller.'

'That's right.'

She had never changed her name, even after marriage. Now she's glad. One less complication of divorce. But she doesn't want to talk about any of that to him. Not here. Not now.

'How is your brother?' he asks.

'He's in America. In Seattle.'

34

'Oh yes. That would be . . . ?'

'He's in aero-engineering. He works for Boeing. We speak on the phone and by email.' Sometimes, she thinks. Sometimes, but not often enough, if the truth be told.

'He'll be earning good money, then?'

'He does.'

'And your parents?'

'Both dead.'

'I'm sorry to hear that.'

'Dad had a heart condition. Mum got cancer. They died within a couple of years of each other.'

'I remember they made me very welcome. You seemed like a very happy family.'

'We were happy. I miss them.'

'I miss my mum, too. So does the old man. She died a few years ago. We've still not quite got used to it.'

Deprived of his cigarettes, he takes out a packet of Polo mints and carefully folds down the wrapping before offering them to her. She takes one and they suck in friendly silence for a moment or two.

'That last summer, you had another girl with you. Honey. That was her name.'

'It was. How did you remember that?'

'My uncle in Ardfern had a dog of that name.'

'That's what my father always said. Good name for a yellow lab.'

'She wouldn't go on the boat and you got very cross with her, and you were angry with your brother, too. I remember it.'

'You used to chase me and pull my ponytail.'

'I did.' He ducks his head as though embarrassed by the memory.

'I wanted to go creel fishing with you. They wouldn't let me go because I had to stay and be nice to Honey. You only get to know someone properly when you go on holiday with them.'

'Is that why you're all alone this time, then?'

'Something like that.' Afterwards, she wonders if the remark was as innocent as it sounded. Did it perhaps have an ironic edge to it?

There is a pause. He puts his mints away, jiggles his knee up and down. She suspects he wants to be off. He has work to do.

To her surprise he says, 'I'll take you this time if you like.' He says it as though no time at all has elapsed instead of twenty-five years.

'Will you? Well, that's very kind of you, but I think my time for creel fishing is past.' She thinks of the smelly bait, the struggling crabs and lobsters. She's not averse to eating them, but cowardly about killing them.

'Well, I could just take you out on the boat if you like,' he offers. 'For a little trip.'

'That would be very nice.'

'Look, I have my creels to haul just now and then I'll be working in the gardens at the hotel this afternoon. But I could take you tomorrow. We could go to the wee island over there, where the old graves are.'

'Graves?'

'It was an old burial place once, for the chieftains and their families. The visitors like to go and see it. Sometimes they pay me to take them there, or for a bit of fishing. Not that they catch very much now. The fish have more or less gone from the sound.'

'Have they?'

'They have.'

'Why's that? The sea looks fine and clean.'

'It's clean enough here, but the fish are still few.'

'I'll . . .' She hesitates, not quite knowing how to put it. For the first time in years, her urban self-confidence deserts her. 'I'll pay the going rate, of course.'

'Indeed you won't,' he says, frowning and standing up. She sees that she has hurt his pride and that he can pick up the oars easily in one big hand. 'I owe you the trip after all this time.'

'Well, thank you. Do you think the weather . . . ?'

He glances at the sky. 'Oh, the weather will be just fine.'

'Can you really tell that by looking at the sky?' she asks, deeply impressed.

His lips are twitching slightly. 'No,' he says. 'But I listened to the shipping forecast this morning.'

'Oh.' She feels herself blushing. Daft cow, she thinks. 'What time?' she asks, to cover her confusion.

'I'll come and pick you up at the jetty by the hotel about nine if that suits you. At Port Manus.'

'Port Manus?'

'That's the name of it.'

'OK. That's very kind of you. ' She stands up, too. 'And I'll maybe see you at the hotel, later on.'

'Aye, well. I'll likely be at the back of a lawnmower if you do.'

'Can I . . . Is there a road . . . ?' She looks towards the house.

The island has only one main road that runs from north to south. There are plenty of smaller tracks running east to west, serving farms, houses, cottages. You drive from end to end, turn round, and drive all the way back. Just to vary things a bit, the young men of the island sometimes roar down to the ferry terminal, do handbrake turns and scream up again. There isn't much more to be done in the way of joy riding.

'If you follow the lane there, it will take you back up to the road. It's a good walk.'

'That's fine. I need to work off breakfast. Will I bring a picnic tomorrow?'

'No. I'll fetch us something to eat and drink. Don't you worry about that. You just bring yourself.'

He strides off towards the wooden boat. She sees a barrel, presumably of bait, waiting for him on the edge of the tiny harbour. He hauls it aboard, ships the oars, stows his carrier bag under the seat, casts off the painter and starts the engine with a single pull. The boat potters smoothly out of the harbour and into the bay. She can see the distant orange floats that mark his creels, and watches him negotiate the rocks to reach them. Then she sets off past the cottage.

In spite of the big breakfast, she is beginning to feel hungry again. She has visions of prawn sandwiches and pots of coffee. As she passes the cottage, she sees an old man standing in the kitchen window. He looks as though he may be washing up. He has a handsome, lined face, framed by white hair and a white beard. He doesn't smile, but raises one soapy hand solemnly in salute. He seems quite unsurprised to see her there.

FOUR

One short November day soon blended into another, but for some weeks Henrietta did not dare to leave the shelter of the house. Ishbel stitched away at two or three of the old gowns until Henrietta could wear them: serviceable, heavy brocades and velvets in green and blue. There was a cloak, too, a warm, hooded garment in black velvet with a scarlet lining, and it needed hardly any alteration at all, though it had been torn and neatly mended and there was a little encrusted mud at the hem. Henrietta pictured Manus's wife wrapped in it as she walked the island paths. But then she had presumably been here willingly. Had she, Henrietta wondered, been contented with her lot?

'Look,' said Ishbel, 'I have taken up the hem for you. You could put this on and go outside. A breath of air would do you good!'

'Later,' said Henrietta shyly. 'Maybe later.'

She was nervous of venturing outside. The wide, wild landscapes that she saw from her high window made her head spin. In these first few weeks, she preferred to crouch beside the fire in her room and think about Gabriel. His absence was an ache, deep inside her For a while, she even managed to cling to the hope of rescue. Surely her brother would be hunting for her. If the groom was not dead, he must have made his way to Edinburgh and told his tale. They would be mad with worry about her. She imagined them sending out messages and letters of enquiry. All she had to do was wait for them to find her.

But as time passed, and no word came, she began to see that Manus had been right. This place was too small, too remote, too foreign. However hard they might search for her, they would not find her. Gradually it was borne in upon her that nobody could save her. And whatever they had done with Gabriel, he was lost to her and all of her old life with him.

The new life was a lonely one and she was glad of Ishbel's company, even eager for it, for no one but Manus seemed to have a word of Scots and he never spoke two words together to her in any language. Ishbel was friendly enough, but she was expected to help with the cooking for the whole household, which took up much of her time, particularly now, when deep winter was upon them and supplies must be well managed if they were not all to go hungry at the bitter end of the season.

After a while, though, Henrietta's natural curiosity got the better of her and she made a hesitant exploration of the house. She was always afraid of meeting Manus, so she would wait for him to leave, watching from her high window as he rode away, relieved at the knowledge that she might have the freedom of the house for a few hours. Like a savage, he used no saddle, but only a woven blanket, and he and the horse seemed one. The winter weather affected him little and he was as likely to be riding through driving hail or rain as not. She had asked Ishbel where he went, and Ishbel had said vaguely that he would be with the horses, or working on the land, or collecting rents or settling disputes, for his word was law here.

Sometimes she saw him coming home in the late afternoon, dark hair plastered to his head, his face grimy, his clothes heavy and sodden, bare legs and knees black with mud and she thought he resembled a fey creature; more like a hobgoblin than the civilised men she had known in that other life in Edinburgh, a life that had begun to seem more remote, more unreal with every day that passed.

She soon discovered that the rest of the house was much like her own room: large and shabby and sparsely furnished. Manus had not deprived her of anything; her chamber merely reflected the general desolation. There was dust everywhere, covering surfaces, or airborne in the pale wintry light. She did not know whether it was lack of money, or indifference that made the house so cheerless. There was little warmth in any part of it except the great hall, and less comfort in stone and wooden benches, and the few tapestries, poorly executed hunting scenes mostly, leprous with the damp. It was as though some previous laird, or perhaps his lady, had made a half-hearted stab at civilisation, only to be defeated by the building and the climate.

From every window, she saw a dreary landscape, or grey seas and white-tipped waves with the birds riding them or the winds above them, like dust motes in sunlight. She scurried about the corridors, a bewildered mouse, afraid of footfalls and shadows, trying to efface herself in case Manus should become irritated by her presence, and be tempted to put an end to it once and for all.

Once, however, her curiosity got the better of her and she pushed open the heavy door of a room that lay just above the great hall. A blast of warm air met her and she found herself peering into a big untidy space, with a large oak bed, carved with leaves and birds and men of the forest, in the middle of it. This must be Manus's bedchamber. There was a heap of bedclothes, sheets, a woven coverlet and a feather pillow with the imprint of his head and a few dark hairs stuck to it. Fascinated, she looked around the room, holding the heavy door open, trying to read the man from his possessions. Just beyond the dusty green hangings, the banked-up embers of a fire glowed in the grate, with a litter of clothes, books and papers strewn about in front of it.

Summoning all her courage, she ventured inside, letting the door close behind her. The room smelled of peat, fish-oil and sweat. There was a shabby carpet on the floor, a press set against one wall, with numerous carvings of strange winged creatures like hermaphrodites with big breasts and strong faces, a table with heaps of letters, quills, and pots of ink by the window. Manus was not a tidy man. Then her eye was caught by an unexpected splash of colour amid the gloom. Beside the bed was another table and on it sat a casket. Intrigued, she went over to look more closely. The cabinet – set like a jewel in this grimly masculine room – was richly embroidered with . . . were they biblical scenes? Perhaps. A woman, long red hair flowing, stood amid the yellow corn. But there were other pictures, too: hesitantly, she reached out and traced the designs with her forefinger: the lapwing and the swan, the curlew and the lark. And here were honeysuckle, foxglove and bramble. The birds and flowers of this island, perhaps? Here was a tall house and here the sea.

From outside she heard the hammering of horses' hooves. He was coming back. She hurried into the passageway, closed the door quietly behind her and ran away, back to her own room, her heart pounding with fear. What if he had caught her there?

Ishbel told her repeatedly that Manus was not a bad man, but she was afraid of him. The thought of arousing his wrath terrified her, although he had done nothing worse than shout at her, and that only once. She missed Thomas and Grisel with their warmth and their wit, she missed her husband's patience and his kindliness. She missed Maisie's chatter. Most of all, she missed Gabriel with a suffering that often threatened to overwhelm her. What use was a life without purpose or affection? And then grief for her son would possess her again, and she would spend days huddled beside the fire in her room, unable to rouse herself from the black misery that filled all her waking thoughts and most of her dreams.

By the time December came, Henrietta had lost all track of time. Her acute distress had subsided as she became convinced that she was not to be ill-treated, unless her isolation might be called cruelty. But the yearning for her son never left her. There was a rhythm to it and sometimes it was more acute, sometimes less, but there was no respite from it. How could it be otherwise when there was nothing to displace it, nothing else to occupy her mind? She had found a few mouldering books which must have belonged to Manus's wife: sermons, old poems, a volume of plays and one of political tracts. She read listlessly, and found one rhyme repeating itself over and over in her head.

'Westron wind when wilt thou blow?

The smalle rain downe can rain.

Christ, if my love were in my arms,

And I in my bed again!'

Henrietta recognised her own suffering in that ancient exclamation of anguish; a longing to be elsewhere, and to be comforted. The lines echoed her feelings but they did not console her and every day she slid further into despair.

She ate little, whatever Ishbel served to tempt her appetite, and the gowns that had once belonged to Manus's wife and that had been altered to fit, now hung about her in loose folds. She spoke only to Ishbel. The other servants seemed embarrassed by her presence. Sometimes she would hear Manus giving peremptory orders in the courtyard below. Once, when there were visitors, she heard him laugh, uproariously: a strange and unfamiliar sound. Henrietta was doubly careful to keep out of Manus's way when there was company in the house. Instinctively she knew that she could look for no help at all from that quarter. Manus's guests would be sure to keep his secrets as closely as they guarded their own.

At last, unable to bear the damp and dusty house any longer, she wrapped herself in the velvet cloak and ventured out of doors. But her long confinement had taken its toll, and instead of her usual exhilaration at fresh air and exercise, she felt only panic. Wherever she looked, up towards the hills or down towards the sea, she found her heart racing, her head reeling at the sight of so much space. One of the old women who helped about the house was coming in from the dairy with the day's milk, and Henrietta tried to smile at her, but she only muttered something in Gaelic and Henrietta hurried on.

She picked her way cautiously down the muddy track to the bay where the boat had landed, and sat down on a rock to watch the sea, a succession of long, powerful waves breaking constantly on the sand. The light was steely, a silvery dazzle on the water that chilled her just to look at it. And this was the sheltered side of the island. To the north and west, so Ishbel had told her, the seas were much fiercer.

The sand was white and clean, apart from a few shells and small pieces of glistening seaweed, deposited like question marks, at haphazard intervals. Henrietta got to her feet and walked along the tideline. When she looked back she saw the thin meander of her own footprints and the sight of them made her more desolate than ever. She cried a little, but after a while even that seemed pointless, because what was the use of weeping when there was nobody to comfort you? So she turned and walked back, retracing her footsteps, letting the salty wind dry the salty tears.

All the same, when she got back to the house, the great hall seemed warmer, and Ishbel told her that the walk had done her good. 'You have roses in your cheeks!' she said.

After that, Henrietta went out for a walk most days, and felt better for it, though she still thought the island of Garbh a bleak and cheerless place and found it hard to understand Ishbel's obvious affection for it.

One afternoon, when the two young women were sitting together in the great hall, in the full heat of the fire, Ishbel broached the subject that had so engaged the women of the household. It was a matter of endless speculation, but they had to be very careful not to mention it when Manus was about. Manus did not seem to want to be reminded of Henrietta's existence at all.

'Tell me about your son.' She paused in her stitching. 'If you can bear to talk about him.'

'I should like to talk about him. If I don't, I'm afraid I'll forget what he looks like.' Henrietta faltered. 'I try to recapture his face all the time. But I can't. Only sometimes I see him in dreams.'

'Tell me about him.'

'He is not yet two years old. I don't know what has happened to him. Sometimes I believe he must be safe in Edinburgh with my brother and his wife. But sometimes . . . oh, Ishbel, the thoughts that are in my head!'

'Who would want to harm a child? Nobody would do such a thing. I'm sure he's safe enough!'

'I hope so.'

'Whatever became of your husband?' asked Ishbel tentatively.

'Oh he died. He was quite old, you know.'

'How old?' Ishbel was always interested in marriage matters.

'He was sixty-two when we married.'

'And you were . . . ?'

'I was sixteen.'

Ishbel screwed up her nose in disgust. 'Holy Mother of God, how could you bear it?'

'It wasn't so bad as all that. He was kind to me.'

'Just as well, I'm thinking! How did you come to be married to such an old man?'

She smiled at Ishbel's indignation. 'It is not uncommon!'

'All the same, you'll allow there were a great many years between you.'

And yet in view of all that had gone before, the arrangement had come as a welcome solution to all her problems. After she had recovered from the smallpox, and as she grew physically stronger, a sense of dread had overwhelmed her. Her future, which had once seemed so bright with the promise of marriage, children, an establishment of her own, now seemed to have narrowed to the four walls of her old room in the Canongate house, the room still occupied by the playthings of her child-hood, her wooden dolls, her baby chair, her hobby horse and her building blocks.

Who would want to marry her now? What could she do with the rest of her life except grow shrivelled and resentful in the shadow of Thomas and Grisel's marriage, a disfigured maiden aunt, confined within the house where once she had been the indulged daughter? Grisel offered her nothing but kindness, and yet there was pity in every word she spoke, in every gentle embrace. What was there for Henrietta now, but long years of dependence upon the benevolence of others?

I wish I had died with my parents, she had thought, but she would not have voiced this, for fear of upsetting Maisie, for fear of hurting Thomas and Grisel.

'My sister-in-law, Grisel, had a guardian, her uncle William,' she said to Ishbel. 'She and Thomas thought it would be a good thing if we could be married. And you know — although I objected, just at first — it *was* a good thing. William was no longer young, it's true, but he was very kind to me. He had a big house at Linlithgow and he made it into a beautiful home for me.'

Henrietta smiled, remembering the sunlit rooms, the elegant furniture, the gardens with their orchards of apple and pear trees. She had sat in their shade, with her husband, while they waited for the birth of their first child. Ishbel saw the change that came over her face at the memory, and pitied her even more for her new circumstances.

'He said he wanted to make it into a palace for me. He was a good man. And look at me. Who else would have wanted . . . this?' She touched her cheek. 'No young man, surely?'

Ishbel frowned. 'You have a few scars to be sure, but with fresh air and sunlight they will soon be no more than freckles! Besides, not all men see only the face.'

'But most do. The face and the tocher. Or the tocher and the face. I had neither. Thomas inherited almost everything when my parents died. I had a small dowry from my mother, but that was all.'

'And your brother would settle nothing else on you?'

'Oh, he would. He would have been glad to, if it were needed. But there was no need. I married William Shaw and he had more than enough money for both of us. He said he wanted nothing from me or Thomas. We were happy.'

It was the plain truth. They had been very happy for a while, ensconced in the house at Linlithgow: she, William and Maisie, who had insisted on coming too, to look after them. And when William had finally come to her bed, gently and very diffidently, she had not objected. She had been largely unmoved by his love-making, but not greatly disturbed by it either, for he had been so careful of her comfort, so very kind and polite. She had loved him dearly. A year after that, Gabriel was born and William had adored his little son too.

'What a gift to come to me so late in life,' he kept saying. But the gift had come too late. When Gabriel was still less than two years old, William died very suddenly, complaining of great pain, falling to the ground, clutching at his chest. Henrietta's grief over the loss of her husband and companion had been genuine. It was true that there had been no passion between them, but she had been very fond of William. He had been a good husband and a loving father.

Once the first sorrow at her loss was over, Henrietta found that she had a considerable fortune at her disposal, more even than had fallen to her brother on their parents' death. She could look forward to a comfortable life in Linlithgow, bringing up her son with Maisie's help, and there had been a good deal of reassurance in the prospect. She had much to thank Thomas and Grisel for, and although she was in mourning she made sure that she saw them as often as she could. Sometimes they would visit her; very occasionally they would persuade her to spend a few days in Edinburgh, 'so that we can look after you, dear Henrietta,'

Grisel said. 'And it can be like the old days, when we were girls together.'

'But you'll marry again, you know,' Grisel told her, one fine autumn day. She had been visiting her sister-in-law, and was pulling on a pair of richly embroidered gloves before returning home. Grisel, thought Henrietta, looking at her anew, had become a very fashionable young woman since her marriage to Thomas. She did not begrudge the change, only it surprised her a little.

'Oh, I don't think so.'

'But you will. You're a woman of means now and you are sure to be snapped up, my dear! Or you would be if you could meet anybody suitable.' She glanced at Henrietta shrewdly. 'So why don't you come to us?'

'You will see more of me in the spring.'

'Oh, if you wait till the spring, you will miss all the balls and the parties of winter. No, Henrietta, I mean why don't you come to live with us?'

'To live with you?'

'It would do you good to be back in the city again. You need to meet people, to see more of society. You're a young woman still and you can't hide away here for the rest of your life. We would make you very welcome, you know. There is plenty of room in the house and Gabriel would be a playmate for his cousin. You know they are very fond of one another.'

Thomas and Grisel had a daughter of their own, Janet, who was a year older than Gabriel.

'That may be so, but I like it here.'

'How can you bear to live alone in this horrible old house?' continued Grisel, glancing around with a shudder. 'I always hated the place! I couldn't wait to leave it, although I'll allow it is much improved since I paced its floors!'

'It's my home. Our home: mine and Gabriel's.'

48

'But if you came to live with us, you would at least have some company,' she persisted. 'After all, we are your only family now and we love you dearly!'

Henrietta had declined Grisel's offer, though she didn't doubt that it was kindly meant. She had her son and the means to take care of him herself. She would make her own way in the world.

A few weeks later, Thomas rode out alone to Linlithgow and he too suggested a visit.

'You needn't stay for longer than you like,' he reassured her, 'but you had much better pay us a visit before winter sets in. Come for a week or two, at least.'

It seemed churlish to refuse and she knew Maisie would welcome the trip to the city.

'You could send Gabriel with Maisie in the carriage,' he continued, 'and you could have the pleasure of riding some of the way to Edinburgh. I will send a docile mount for you and a groom to keep you company and for your protection on the road.'

'All right,' she told him, laughing at his enthusiasm. 'All right, Thomas, I agree. I'll come.'

He had embraced her then, laying his cheek against hers. 'Oh my dear,' he said. 'What a splendid little sister you are, to be sure! How blessed I am in you!'

'So you see, I was kidnapped on way from Linlithgow to Edinburgh. But I have no notion of who planned it, or why. Has nobody said anything here? Not Iain or Seamus? Has nobody said anything at all, Ishbel?'

'Iain would not tell me, even if he did know, but I am sure that Seamus knows nothing, save what he was told to do: take you on the road and bring you to the island.'

'I sometimes wonder if it may have been a jealous relative of my husband. Somebody I know nothing about, somebody who thinks he has a claim to my husband's money.'

'That may be so,' agreed Ishbel, frowning.

'But what is worse is that I have no idea what became of my son. He was in the carriage with his nurse. I hope and pray that he is safe in Edinburgh.'

'Surely that's where he must be,' agreed Ishbel. 'Safe with your brother and his wife.'

'Oh, but it is the not knowing. It eats into me, Ishbel. I don't know why I am here!'

'Nobody knows but Manus, and he will say nothing.'

'The island is so bleak and cold. How can I bear it? How can you bear it?'

'But it is not always like this. It is winter now, the very dead of winter. *An geamhradh.*'

'*An geamhradh,*' repeated Henrietta. 'Winter.'

Ishbel smiled at her. 'You should learn to speak a few words of our language, you know. It is not so very hard and it would help to pass your time.'

'I have more time than I need or want. Hours, days, weeks to be filled. Ishbel, can you tell me? When I walk out each day, why do people watch me?'

'They are only curious about you. They see very few strangers. They know you are lowland, but you have the red hair of a highland lass. The fisherfolk think it unlucky.'

'Unlucky?'

'They do not even like to have my friend Seamus on their wee cobles, although needs must when there is a journey to be made and Manus issues his orders.'

'Once, an old woman turned her back on me and crossed herself as though I was casting the evil eye upon her. Who do they think I am, Ishbel? Why do they think I am here? What can he have said? Has he told them I am some criminal or a witch, perhaps?'

'No! No!' Ishbel shook her head vigorously. 'He would not do such a thing!'

'Would he not?'

'Manus McNeill is a good man. He is my cousin you know, on my mother's side. We are of the same blood, he and I, and he is a good man, whatever you may think.'

'Is he?' she asked, doubtfully. 'Well, I find it hard to believe you.' She stood up. 'It's time I was back in my room. The ogre will soon be in his castle once more.'

Manus did not seem at all like a good man to her. She was afraid to move far from the house, afraid that if she walked for any distance she would lose her way among the hills and then people would be sent to fetch her back, much to her humiliation. Even worse was the thought that nobody would be sent to fetch her back and then she would lie out upon some wintry hillside until she died. And perhaps that was what Manus wanted: to be rid of the unwelcome burden of his prisoner.

Henrietta moved to the doorway. 'Oh Ishbel, yours is the only kind face I see. I am nineteen years old and if I am to spend the rest of my life here on this ... this prison ... this savage prison of rock and heath ... Oh, I cannot, cannot bear it. Who has done this to me? And how can I bear to spend the rest of my life here? Alone without my baby. Alone without my son!'

'I pity you,' said Ishbel, half to Henrietta, half to herself. 'Poor lady, I cannot help you more than I do, but I pity you.'

FIVE

In the afternoon Alys lies on her bed, reading. This is an unheard-of indulgence and a pleasure. She can't remember the last time she got peace to read in the afternoon. She can hear the lawn-mower coming and going outside and smell cut grass but when she looks out of the window she doesn't see Donal. The hotel has big gardens: lawns, fountains of pale pink Himalayan roses cascading through trees, a walled garden with bee-ridden clumps of perennials. There seem to be a great many trees on this part of the island: oak, ash, birch and willow creating shelter for more exotic specimens that she can't name. Elsewhere on the island the woods degenerate into wind-tormented rowans or tiny stunted oaks, natural bonsai, but some previous laird must have established a garden here long ago. There are even remarkably healthy palm trees growing on the lawns in front of the house.

Inevitably she falls asleep, and when she does she dreams about Donal. He is offering her the embroidered cabinet. 'I think you ought to have this,' he tells her, smiling at her. 'You might be able to use it. I don't mind if you make use of it.' The dream is a very pleasant one, and when she wakes up to a room full of evening sunlight she finds that it has coloured her mood and she feels extraordinarily calm and happy.

In the evening, showered, changed and well fed, she goes to the bar and is chatted up – there is no other way of putting it – by one of the visiting yachtsman. He is English, his name is Jeremy, and he has come off a large and flashy white fibreglass boat which lies at anchor in the bay. He wears matching white oilskins and a tee-shirt with the yacht's name, Trailblazer, across the front. Blond and blue eyed, he is younger than Alys, though probably not by as many years as he pretends. Looking rather as though he has been moulded from the same sleek material as his boat, he is holding court in a corner of the bar, surrounded by three friends: two more young men and a girl called Lizzie, who seems to be with one of them, but who looks hungrily at Jeremy from time to time. He claims to be a banker from Basingstoke, though Alys finds this faintly unbelievable. Do bankers live in Basingstoke? The yacht belongs to Daddy (a retired solicitor), he says, and Jeremy has borrowed it for an extended voyage around the islands.

He has been here before, several times. It seems to be a regular stopping-off place for him. He keeps talking about 'these people' and 'these places' in affectionate but slightly superior tones. Alys feels her hackles rise defensively. She looks towards the row of fishermen slouched over the bar and senses a general hunching of shoulders. She blushes for Jeremy, glad that she can't see their faces.

Jeremy from Basingstoke invites her to join his party for a drink and she can hardly refuse. When he finds out what she does and where she lives, he obviously thinks it a romantic and endearingly impractical occupation.

'Do you make any money at it?' he asks.

'Well, yes. I wouldn't do it if I didn't.'

'Nice to be able to turn a hobby into a job.'

'Actually, it always has been a job for me.'

She rents a cramped flat in one of the restored buildings off the Canongate on Edinburgh's Royal Mile. It is tiny, picturesque but noisy in summer. Tourists picnic on her doorstep, eating take-aways and drinking from cans, unaware that people are living and working above them. She makes her jewellery in a little back room looking down over the roofs of the city towards the Forth. Ben sleeps in a bedroom which is about the size of a cupboard. She sleeps on a divan in the sitting room and throws a paisley shawl over it during the day.

This is not conducive to forming any new relationship but she isn't looking for one, anyway. She has been divorced for two years and she is wary of introducing a new man into Ben's already disrupted life. The flat is not ideal but it is all she can afford because, in spite of what she has just told Jeremy, she doesn't make any fortunes out of the jewellery. She also rents space in a craft market, just off the Grassmarket, for an exorbitant sum, but it is worth it because the market is awash with tourists for most of the year, and some of them like her work enough to buy it.

Sometimes she pays a friend to mind the shop for her while she goes to salerooms or prowls around antique and charity shops in search of materials: Italian glass beads, old cameos, polished agates and the like. While she is on Garve, her friend Sophie has offered the services of her seventeen-year-old daughter Jasmine. Sophie has never been married. She had Jasmine just after graduating with her first degree and went on to do a doctorate as a single parent, which fills Alys with admiration. Now she teaches Scottish History at the university. Not conventionally pretty but intelligent, fit and sexy, Sophie still manages to attract men, who buzz around her like wasps around candy. She will give them a whirl but only until they start to get serious. 'I say I won't commit myself to them, and I mean it,' she tells Alys, who is smaller and plumper. 'But they never seem to believe me.'

Alys's ex-husband, John, works in IT and has somehow managed to afford a very nice Victorian terraced house up in desirable Bruntsfield (and holidays in Sorrento) with his new partner Millie. He complains that the Canongate flat is no place for a little boy: no garden, no room for friends to stay over. This irritates Alys enormously but she struggles to keep the peace for her son's sake. Since meeting Millie, John seems to have become very grand. He throws dinner parties rather than the casual suppers they used to have. He and Millie collect rare pearlware pottery figures and antique silver. Alys sometimes wonders if they have struck oil in the back garden but realises that their combined salaries amount to quite a lot of money.

Ben has a big room of his own in the Bruntsfield house where he keeps toys and books and another set of clothes. He spends every second weekend there, some Friday nights and lots of time during the holidays. He enjoys himself and gets on with Millie, but he likes the flat in the Royal Mile as well, and seems to accept the change with equanimity. But who can really tell? Have they damaged him in some way? Will he become a difficult adolescent? A delinquent teenager? Sophie tries to reassure her, but it does nothing to assuage her guilt.

Yachtsman Jeremy manages to elicit at least some of this information from Alys by means of a constant stream of questions. It is obviously his way of endearing himself to women. He thinks he is being a good listener. He goes to the bar and buys another round of drinks for them all. He says something to the fishermen and laughs uproariously at his own joke.

I have to get out of this, thinks Alys.

Five minutes later, the door opens and Donal McNeill comes in with his father. They join the fishermen at the bar, who are obviously pleased to see them. They huddle together and talk in low voices, casting covert glances at Jeremy and his party. Then Donal turns round and looks straight at Alys, smiling, raising his dark eyebrows slightly. She waits till she thinks nobody is looking and pulls a face. He grins, and turns back to his drink. After a while, he stands up, pulls a packet of cigarettes from his jeans pocket and takes one out, preparatory to going into the garden for a smoke. Before he can head for the door, his father reaches over and snatches it, deftly crumpling it onto the bar, scooping up the remains and throwing it into the litter bin in the corner.

'Fuckin' hell, Iain,' says one of the young fisherman.

'I told him I would!' says the old man.

'Bloody waste of money,' says the fisherman.

'Ach well, it would just go up in smoke anyway, Ronnie.'

Donal says nothing. Unprotesting, he leans on the bar, finishes his drink and orders another for himself and his father. He looks at Alys again and mimes holding a glass but she shakes her head and smiles at him. 'No, thanks.'

'Know him, do you?' asks Jeremy in a low voice.

'Kind of. He's an old friend.'

'Salt of the earth,' says Jeremy with unctuous wisdom. 'That's what they are, you know. Salt of the earth.'

Alys is just beginning to think that she will have to get up, excuse herself on the grounds of fatigue and go to bed, when the Trailblazers grow restive and come to a communal decision to sweep Jeremy along with them.

'Cheese toasties!' says Lizzie, by way of enticement. 'Come on, Jeremy. Let's get going.'

'Coming back to the old girl for a nightcap?' he asks Alys. 'Nice calm night. I'll bring you back to the jetty later. She's a beautiful boat. You'd be very welcome.'

'Thanks, but no. I think I'll just go up to bed.'

'Had a busy day, eh?'

'Not really. Just a lot of fresh air.'

He nods sagely and dons his slick white oilskin jacket. She finds her bag and heads slowly in the other direction. She would like to stop and have a drink and a chat with Donal and his father, maybe ask Iain about the cabinet, but Jeremy, at the door of the bar, is still waving at her. If she lingers, he will probably take it as encouragement and come back in. God forbid.

'Good night, sleep tight,' he calls. 'Mind the bugs don't bite.'

The fishermen splutter into their beer. 'Fuckin' hell,' says Ronnie again, but under his breath.

She finds herself alone in Reception, looking at old photographs of the island and its people, moments in time: men in caps and navy sweaters, women in long dark skirts and aprons, people working in the fields or on boats, people sitting outside stone cottages, watching the photographer with calm curiosity. The bar door swings open. It is Donal on his way to the lavatory. He is wearing a navy pullover, like the men in the pictures, and faded jeans. But no flat cap. He has been running his fingers through his hair and it is standing on end. She thinks he looks very nice. Just that. Nice.

'Off to bed?' he says gruffly.

'I think so.'

'Well, he's enough to tire anyone out, that one.'

'I know. I got persuaded into joining them. Then I kind of wished I hadn't.'

'He comes here every year or so. Stays for a night and pretends he knows all about the place.'

She shrugs. She supposes it is what she does as well. Except that she has been away for twenty-five years.

'Incomers eh?' she says, drily. 'Aren't we terrible?'

'I didn't mean you!' She can see that he would die rather than be openly impolite to a stranger. He will be gently ironic or he will say nothing at all. But he will never be rude to the person's face, no matter how great the provocation.

'I wanted to ask you about the embroidered box .'

'Oh yes. You've seen it, then.'

'I have.'

'My father can tell you something about that. It sat up in our loft at Ardachy for years.'

'It's very beautiful.'

'It's a treasure, right enough.'

She finds herself yawning. She really is tired now.

'You'd best go to bed,' he tells her. 'You have to be up early in the morning.'

'I do, don't I?' She pauses at the foot of the stairs. 'Nine o'clock at the jetty.' She is looking forward to it.

'That's right.'

'We don't have to go anywhere near Trailblazer do we?'

'Ach, he'll be gone in the morning. It's what he always does. You're lucky you didn't get him started on the finer points of seamanship. You'd have still been there at midnight.'

'Goodnight, Donal.'

As he walks away, he says, 'Bigger bum than ten arses, that one!'

She splutters with laughter all the way up the stairs.

'Sleep sound, Alys. See you in the morning,' he calls after her.

SIX

Manus saw her from some distance away, a tiny figure, standing on the very edge of the cliff, facing out to sea. He narrowed his eyes against the wind that slashed at his face. She looked as though she had become rooted to the land with the damp weight of her dress, which was just as well, because it seemed to him that she was poised there, ready to tumble over into the oblivion of rock and boiling sea below. He didn't know whether to call out to her. He didn't think it would do any good. She hadn't even heard the approach of his horse; the quarrel of wind and water was too loud in her ears.

In the mid-afternoon Ishbel had come looking for him in a great panic. Henrietta had left the house that morning, saying that she was going for her walk, but she had not returned. She had eaten no breakfast and drunk nothing save a mouthful or two of buttermilk. Ishbel had been too busy with the cauldron-broth, simmering the remains of the winter vegetables, onions and kale with a piece of mutton in the big stock pot, too busy and impatient to persuade her to take more. It was too much to expect of her, she had thought. Too big a burden. Why should she have the well-being of the poor woman on her conscience when it was none of her doing? Then there had been the dairying to see to, and the spinning and she had not missed Henrietta until much later on, when she and the other women realised that the girl had not been seen all day. The afternoon was wearing away, Henrietta had taken no food or drink with her and Ishbel was suddenly afraid for her. They all were.

'She has been so sad!' Ishbel's tone was severe. She was usually much too deferential to criticise her cousin, but her concern for Henrietta had overridden all that.

Manus felt an unfamiliar pang of guilt. He had paid no attention whatsoever to his unwelcome guest, preferring to forget about her existence as far as possible. Ishbel had made it easy for him and he had resolutely shut Henrietta's suffering out of his mind. He was not the cause of it, so why should it worry him?

He frowned. 'Why did you not tell me sooner?'

'Because you did not want me running to you with her troubles. You told me as much, sir. Do you not mind what you said to me, that first day, when she was so distressed about her baby? About her situation here? Do you think she is any better now? Did you not wish that she would somehow take herself out of it and leave you in peace? Dear God, Manus, she even hurries out of the great hall in case you find her there.'

'Nevertheless, it is not for you to . . .' He stopped abruptly. It was true enough. He had often wished Henrietta dead. Gone from his house and his island. But not in this fashion.

'We are wasting time,' he said sharply, angered as much by his own guilt as anything else. 'I'll take the mare and look for her. She cannot have gone very far.'

'No, for she is not strong. Not strong at all.'

Even on horseback, he was a long way from the house before he saw her, far to the north. How had she walked so far and how had she known about this place where land so abruptly gave way to sea? Had she come here often, standing on the very edge of oblivion, steeling herself to make the leap? Had she waited until the sorrow inside her threatened to come bursting out of her heart, until the pain became so intense that it could no longer be borne? He knew that pain well. It had not left him, either, since the deaths of his wife and his son. In ten years, he had simply learned to live with it locked away inside. And then it came to him that Henrietta did not even have the cold comfort of the finality of bereavement. The fate of her son must be a constant torment to her. He reined in his horse and watched her for a moment, undecided. Then he saw her move, fractionally, in the direction of the edge, and called out in alarm, 'Mistress Dalrymple! What are you doing?'

She ignored him but stood still and he urged his mare on, with hands and knees, until he was closer to her. Then he dismounted and left the horse to its own devices. But he did not dare to go too near. He had a sudden insight into how much he frightened her. He had shown her no kindness in a place where custom dictated a measure of generosity towards the stranger at all times.

'What are you doing here?' he repeated, shouting above the lash and thunder of waves below. He could see the place where the tides met, a line of dizzying whirlpools around the base of the cliff. Even from here he could see it. Nobody could survive in that sea.

'What?' She still did not turn, her gaze intent on the horizon. 'What did you say?'

'What are you doing here?'

'I am watching the seabirds.'

'The cliff is dangerous.'

She was not quite so close to the edge as he had thought, but too close all the same. One little rush and she would be over. He felt sick at the thought. Until now he had been able to blame others for her predicament. But if she died, it would be his fault. He had not cared enough – still did not care very much, if the truth be told. But for the first time the perception of his own indifference worried him.

'Is it?' she said listlessly, and turned to face him. The misery he saw etched into her features made him flinch. He saw hopelessness in every line of her.

'Will you move back, Mistress Dalrymple? Please will you move back? Here. Take my arm.'

'No!' She recoiled from him and he braced himself to seize her if she should make the leap. Even at the risk of his own life, he knew he could not let her go unhindered. There would be no honour in allowing it to happen, and what was a man's life worth if he had no honour?

'I'll not hurt you,' he said, stretching out his hand, as gently as he knew how. It was the way he treated the wild horses, presenting himself to them but sliding his gaze away from theirs, unthreatening.

There was a pause, and she turned back to face the sea.

'Last night,' she said, 'I looked at the new moon. And I thought that he might be looking at the same new moon. My little boy. What am I to do without him? How can I bear it?'

Again she turned a thin, sorrowful face to him. Her cheeks were wet with rain and her eyes were desperate. She was not even wearing the cloak, and her dress hung sodden about her. The gorse had torn it as she walked and there were deep scratches on her forearms where the spikes had torn her skin, too. Her feet were bare and black with mud, red with blood where the stones had cut them. He felt a rush of genuine pity for her and anger at himself. How could he have ignored such misery? It struck him that he would not have treated an animal so. The very horses in their stable were better cared for than this young woman.

Why had nobody told him? But the answer was plain to him already. Because you did not want to know, he thought. And who among your people would dare to tell you? Certainly not Ishbel, or old Mhairi, or even Iain or Seamus or any of the other men and women of the island. Have I become such a despot? he asked himself. A profound sadness came to him and he felt tears prickling behind his eyes. He blinked them away, ashamed of them and glad of the obscuring rain.

'Come back from the edge at least, Henrietta.'

Unwillingly, she responded to the concern in his tone and his unfamiliar use of her name, and moved a pace or two backwards, turning towards him.

'If you like. But I was only watching the sea.' She felt that an explanation was necessary. She saw him frowning at her; he would be angry with her. 'I was only watching the sea and the birds drifting like ashes in the air. Do you see them? How they ride the wind! They are not bound by the island. It is their home, not their prison. They can go where they please!'

'You are so close to the edge, Henrietta.'

'I was thinking that if I were one of those birds, I might fly. I might soar up into the air and fly away home.'

'Are you mad?'

'Mad?' She shook her head. 'No. I am just . . .' She hesitated. How could she explain? They had so few words in common – few thoughts in common, perhaps. He was foreign to her. 'Sad,' she said at last. He must know what sadness was. 'I am much too sad.'

He stood still, with his hand stretched out to her, and at last she made a decisive movement away from the edge of the cliff, towards him, and towards the horse that was gently cropping at the short turf of the edge, but she swayed with fatigue as she walked.

'I'll take you home now,' he said. 'Let me help you, Henrietta.'

He lifted her onto the horse She was ice cold and so thin – a little rickle of bones beneath his fingers. No weight at all. The dress was heavier than she was. 'A bhoireannaich! Woman!' he exclaimed, his stock of patience all exhausted, but his own sorrow running in his mind, like a lamentation for something lost. 'You are wet through with the rain. I must take you home.'

He vaulted up behind her, unpinned his plaid off one shoulder and wrapped it round her so that the dry side of it, still warm with the warmth of his body, was against her sodden frame. He felt her relax against him.

Her strength, physical and spiritual, was all worn out, and he was warm and strong. She was like a small moon drawn into the orbit of a larger and more powerful planet. With her cheek against his chest she smelt the musky sweat of his body, and closed her eyes. The steady beating of his heart soothed and calmed her. She felt safe. The words of the little rhyme came into her head again.

'Westron wind when wilt thou blow?

The smalle rain downe can rain.'

He turned towards the house and they rode in silence for a while but at last she asked him drowsily, 'How long have I been here now? I have lost all count of the days. One is so like another.'

'You have been here for almost three months.'

He walked the horse onwards as fast as he dared, afraid of her fragility. Every step would jar her bones. She fell silent again.

'Spring is coming,' he observed in an effort to lift her gloom. 'Do you not see the signs all around us?'

She raised her head for a moment and forced her eyes open. She had almost been asleep, wrapped tight as a baby. It was so long since she had been close to anyone. She did not want to speak, only to rest against him for a while, absorbing his strength.

'I hardly know what to look for. This landscape is so foreign to me.' Her tongue felt thick and strange in her mouth.

'But you have seen the golden blossoms on the whins. And smelled their scent on a sunny day.'

'The whins bloom all year long.'

'Aye,' he said. 'When the gorse is in bloom, kissing's in season. That's what folk say.'

'Well, they are full of cruel spikes, at any rate.'

'I know, I know. But look!' He glanced upwards. 'The swans are flying in. That is a sure sign that winter is almost gone.'

She followed his gaze and her spirits were lifted in spite of herself by the sight of the graceful creatures overhead. 'What a din they make!'

'It is the music of the beating of their wings, not their voices. They have no voices, but they sing anyway.'

She fell silent again, closing her eyes.

He urged the mare on. The house was in sight now, but there was still some way to go.

'I cannot believe how far you have walked. No wonder you are soaking wet. Henrietta, you must not do this again. You will make yourself ill.'

'What would that matter? You would be rid of me. It is what you want. I have seen it in your face. I am a trouble to you.'

He had no answer for her but her words roused his conscience all over again. He thought of his father and his grandfather before him, telling him about the ancient duty of hospitality to strangers, the law of the Gael that must never be broken. How could his wilful neglect of her be counted hospitality?

At last she said, 'I can't forget my son, you see. No matter what I do, the pain never stops.'

'I had a son once.' He could barely get the words out. In ten years he had spoken of this to no one. 'He survived his mother by two days. He was just a wee seven-month wean but she died giving birth to him. And then he followed her, two days later. There was no strength in him, though I willed him to live anyway and prayed for him; and when prayer failed I cursed God. I would have gone with them as well if I could. But I was the strong one and had to stay behind.'

'I'm sorry.'

'Why?' His gaze was fixed beyond the woman and on the broad back and strong neck of the mare. 'You cannot wish me well in any way.'

'No. But I know what it is to lose a child.'

They walked on in silence until they came into the courtyard of the house. Night was falling. He dismounted and lifted her down.

Deprived of his warmth, she instantly began to shiver, her teeth chattering with the cold. And she could not stand unaided. She would have crumpled and fallen had he not caught hold of her again.

'You smell of her,' he said, half to himself. He had been thinking it all along and it had been a torment to him. 'You are wearing her clothes. Dear God, you have the scent of my wife.'

'What else must I do but wear your wife's clothes? I have nothing of my own.' It was not a complaint, but a simple observation.

He lifted her again and carried her inside, not as Iain had carried her on that first day, like a sack of meal, but tenderly, holding her against him like a tired child.

'No, no,' he muttered, 'I don't mind at all.'

Up in the great hall, he set her down on an oak settle, pulling it right up to the fire. Ishbel came rushing forward with a blanket to wrap her in. He seized the stone bottle of whisky that always sat on the table and forced her to drink. She coughed and spluttered at the unfamiliarity of the peaty spirit, but he still held the bottle to her lips . 'More,' he said. 'It will warm you.'

She drank again and he was relieved to see the colour returning to her cheeks.

'Where was she?' asked Ishbel. 'You have been so long and I was so afraid for her.'

'She was standing by the cliff.'

'At the north end? As far as that?'

'Aye. And I fear she is unwell. You must look after her. Do not leave her alone, Ishbel. Do you understand me?'

'I understand you very well.'

'Some of the other women must take turns to watch over her. Put her to bed and make her eat if you can.'

'I will do my best sir, but she is so . . .' Ishbel hesitated.

'I know what is wrong with her, and there is little I can do to remedy it. But she is in my care and I would not have her . . . In all honour, I would not . . .' He could not finish the sentence.

66

Instead, he went and bent over Henrietta where she sat staring into the fire. Her cheeks were flushed, but when he spoke she looked up and seemed to hear him.

'Mistress Dalrymple, I am going to the mainland in a day or two. I shall be gone for a few weeks just. Is there anything you need that you do not have here? Is there anything at all that I can bring you?'

'I need my son,' she said, so quietly that he could hardly hear. 'Indeed, I do wish that you could bring me my son.'

SEVEN

Donal is waiting for Alys down by the jetty, working with a sharp knife, cleverly splicing two ends of rope together. She hangs back and watches him for a moment, admiring his absorption in the job. It reminds her of the way she herself works. She recognises and identifies with that expression of concentrated involvement. Then he looks up and smiles at her and his smile changes his whole rather grim face.

'Good morning,' he says.

'What's the weather going to do?' she asks. She woke up to the rattle of rain against the windows, but now it has stopped.

He glances over to the west, where the cloud is already breaking up.

'I told you, it'll be just fine. Showers clearing from the west.'

He takes her bag from her and then helps her down into the boat.

'Put your foot right in the middle,' he says.

He has to hold her hand, to guide her to a seat. His fingers are strong and rough as sandpaper, the nails cracked and broken: a working man's hands, she thinks, with John's soft pink hands coming into her mind. Then he casts off the painter and gives it to her to coil up, pushing the boat away from the jetty.

'Sit well back, now. You don't want my elbow in your face.'

He starts the outboard with a single pull. The boat smells of tar and diesel, and faintly of fish, though he has left the barrel of bait behind. There is a battered rucksack under the seat, which she assumes contains the picnic. She wonders what he has brought. The whole expedition seems bizarre, and she reflects that at home in Edinburgh she would never consider setting off for a day's outing, alone like this, with a stranger. But then she supposes he isn't a stranger at all.

'You'll be fine with Donal McNeill,' said Mr Cameron this morning as she left the hotel. 'He knows these waters like the back of his hand. I'd trust him to take me anywhere on the island or over the waters around it.'

The boat motors steadily out into the bay. The water deepens and darkens but she can still see the bottom where sand has given place to rock.

'Port Manus,' she says.

'That's its name.'

'So who was Manus?'

'He was a chieftain of the island a long time ago. Another McNeill, for sure.'

'How come?'

'Well, we McNeills once ruled the whole place.' He grins at her. 'How we are come down in the world. That's what my father is always saying. But we have survived. We're still here.'

Donal manoeuvres the boat slowly and competently between rocks. She can see that he knows exactly what he is doing. Mr Cameron was right. She feels safe with him.

After a little while he switches off the engine altogether and takes up the oars. Alys sees that the water has become shallow again as they approach the little islet which is their destination. They are rowing through a corridor between rocks. She peers down and finds a looking-glass garden spread out beneath the boat, clumps of weed, sinuous fronds, great heaps of some fantastic growth that foams over the rocks like sponge.

'Can't you use the engine here?'

'I can, but I thought you might like to see the seals.' He nods at the rocks and she is enchanted to see them basking there, almost blending in with their surroundings. One of them raises a lazy head and eyes the boat suspiciously, barks at them but can't bring itself to move out of the sun.

'They don't much like engines, though they'll follow me for the last of the bait when I've finished with the creels. Bloody nuisance when I'm fishing. But they are picturesque, I'll give you that.' He says the word ironically, with a little chuckle.

She watches him pulling strongly and smoothly on the oars and realises that the sight of him is giving her immense pleasure. He is wearing a faded blue tee-shirt and she is brought up short by his arms, sinewy and powerful and downed with dark hair. She realises that her breathing has quickened and she swallows hard. She acknowledges that the sheer physical strength of the man is attractive, but also that he is totally unaware of it. She wonders what kind of image he has of himself and then suspects that he doesn't care. He just gets on with living. Maybe two years of celibacy have made her susceptible to this kind of unselfconscious masculinity.

'Do you know where all the rocks are?' she asks him, to distract herself. 'The rocks in the sound, I mean.'

'No,' he says. He glances up at her from beneath sooty eyelashes, the only feminine thing about him. 'But I know where they're not, and that's good enough for me.'

Donal rows into a tiny bay where a thin strip of white sand divides undergrowth from sea. Alys helps him to haul the boat up the beach and make her safe, tying her to a rusty iron ring let into one of the rocks. Behind the beach, a tangle of flowering bramble gives place to green turf patched with swathes of bracken. There is the ruin of a cottage, just a gable-end and two sad walls fringed by nettles. Further up the hill, the stones of an ancient chapel are visible. Like the seals, the islet basks quietly in the sun. Donal takes the rucksack out of the boat, and shrugs it onto his back.

'There's a path,' he says. 'But it gets very overgrown. Just follow me.'

'So tell me about this place.'

He talks over his shoulder at her as she comes up behind him. 'The story goes that it belonged to one of St Columba's monks. He built himself a cell and lived here all alone, praying and fasting. Anyway, he must have impressed the islanders for they converted to Christianity soon after. Later on they started to bury their chieftains in the graveyard. It's just up the hill. Come on.'

He strides off through shoulder-high bracken. Alys wrinkles her nose at the sour smell of it. It seems to be a breeding ground for flies.

'The bracken is a menace,' Donal comments, reading her thoughts. 'The sheep used to keep it down, but there are not enough of them now. It used to be up to every farmer to control the bracken on his land, but now they don't bother. Besides, for some years there were not enough working farms on the island and so it covers everything.'

'Not very nice.'

'No. It's poisonous, the flies love it and it stinks. Still, one of the bigger farms is up for rent now, so things may get better. If you come here again in spring, before it grows, I can show you more.'

'Maybe I will.' She thinks it would be good to bring Ben to this place. He would love it. But she will have to bring him while he is still young enough to be enchanted by boats and beaches; by digging for worms and trapping crabs and other simple pleasures.

The islet is roughly pudding-shaped and soon they are through the bracken and out among silvery green heather-tips and flowering thyme. Donal pauses for her to catch up.

'I need to get fitter,' she says, panting.

'It's living in cities that's the killer.' He moves on again immediately.

'Hold on a minute, Donal. Just let me get my breath back.'

'Sorry.' He shrugs off the rucksack and gives her a bottle of water to drink.

'Have you ever?' she asks him.

'What?'

'Lived in a city?'

'I was in Glasgow for a few years, after I left school.'

'Were you?'

'I thought since I had made the break I ought to give it a try. That's what happens to our kids, you see. Once they go to the mainland they seldom come back.'

She can't imagine him in the city. 'What did you do in Glasgow?'

'I worked in the Botanical Gardens. It was nice there, but it wasn't like home. They sent me to London to do a course, and I stuck it out but I didn't like it much. I found it . . .' He pauses, narrowing his eyes against the sunlight. 'I found it suffocated me. I couldn't breathe there. The place just closes in on you, somehow. Anyway, that was where I met my wife.'

'Your wife?' This surprises her very much. Somehow she hadn't thought that he would be married.

'I was married for a couple of years, but I'm divorced now.'

'Oh. Snap,' she says.

'She moved up to Glasgow with me. She was from Glasgow originally but she had been living in London. Then she said she wanted to come and live here. She took it into her head that she wanted us both to move to Garve. God knows why. She was a city girl, a real city girl. But she had some romantic notion about living on a small island. You know? The way people do.'

She wonders if he is having a little dig at her, but perhaps he is simply trying to tell her the truth about his wife. They stand still, halfway up the hill. She can see Port Manus, and Scoull Bay and the hotel behind it. The yachts have all left their moorings, even Trailblazer.

'Didn't you want to come back?' she asks him curiously.

'Oh, I wanted to come, all right. That was how she persuaded me. There was nothing I wanted more. But I knew what I was coming to, and I didn't think it would suit her.'

'Why not?'

'As I said, she was a city girl.'

'And did she like it here?'

There is a long pause.

'I'm sorry. It's none of my business, Donal.'

'It isn't important – not now. She liked it at first but then she got bored, I think. She lasted for a couple of years just. Then she packed her bags and went home. I got the divorce papers through soon afterwards.'

'I'm sorry.'

'It was inevitable, I suppose. She couldn't cope. She couldn't cope with the silence and the darkness. She wanted street lights outside her window and shops and cinemas.'

'Surely she must have known what it would be like?'

'She said she only realised how much she missed all those things when she didn't have them; which is reasonable enough.' He pulls at a piece of bracken. 'There was no quietness inside her. She couldn't adapt to the pace of the place, and it sure as hell wasn't going to adapt to her. And I was too young to know what to do about it.'

'Would you know now?'

He shrugs. 'Maybe we should have moved back to Glasgow. She might have been happier there.'

'But you wouldn't.'

'No. No, I wouldn't. Not then. I thought she had made her bed and had better lie on it. "What do people do?" she kept saying. It was as if I had transplanted her into sandy soil and she couldn't survive. Maybe she had a fantasy about this kind of place. People do, you know.'

'What kind of fantasy?'

He is staring into the distance, remembering. 'People imagine

73

that an island like Garve will be a bolt hole for them. A place where they can hide away, let the rest of the world go by.'

'And?'

'And they forget, or maybe they don't care, that other people are involved: people who live and work here, people like me and my father who depend upon the place for their survival. Folk think that they will escape to an island, but they always bring themselves along for the ride.'

His articulacy surprises her and then she is ashamed of her surprise, ashamed of the arrogant assumptions she has made about him so far. He lapses into silence while they negotiate the last stretch of hillside.

'Do you have any children?' she asks, scrambling up behind him.

'No.' He reaches down and casually hauls her over a ridge of rock. 'Just as well. What about you, Alys?'

'I have a wee boy. Ben. He's away on holiday with his father.'

'How old is he?'

'Eight.'

'A nice age.'

They have reached a low wall of loose stones, which protects an acre of turf overspread with a few grey slabs lying flat or protruding at odd angles from the ground.

'This is it.' Donal leads the way through a gap in the wall. 'The old burial ground where the lairds were laid to rest. The new cemetery is back over on Garve, close to the village.'

Alys walks among the stones, stooping to examine them. The breeze that has accompanied them all the way from Garve drops suddenly. A skylark tumbles through the sky. A rabbit, startled by their approach, leaps from between the stones and rushes away, its white scut bobbing between heather stalks. The stones are cracked and broken by the weather, covered in yellow lichen, with ancient designs – patterns, spirals, zigzags – only just visible upon their pitted surfaces.

'Some of these must be very old.'

'Aye, very. The old minister knew a great deal about them. He used to get me or my father to row him across here sometimes. He thought that some of these were as early as the fifteenth century. But they cover three or four hundred years.'

'When the MacDonalds were Lords of the Isles,' she says, remembering her history all of a sudden.

'Aye. They are the graves of men of consequence, no doubt. Although you see that there are no names attached to them.'

'But they could be McNeills?'

'They could. Almost certainly they are.'

They sit on a flat tombstone and he pours cups of good coffee, strong and black with a little brown sugar in it. There are sandwiches, too, soft bread, cheese and tomato, tuna mayonnaise and cucumber. She wonders if he made them, or perhaps his father. Opposite them, Garve lies long and hilly like a strange, hump-backed animal. Behind are the pale silhouettes of other islands. Bumblebees busy themselves in the thyme. Alys has one of those intimations of pure happiness that come and go quite suddenly.

'So Manus might be buried here?' she asks him.

'I wouldn't know. That doesn't come into the stories.'

'What do the stories say?'

'They only say that he had a great treasure, which he lost. And also that he had a bride from the sea, who went back to it eventually. Maybe those are memorable things.'

They pack away the remains of the picnic and he helps her to her feet. His old-fashioned courtesy touches her. He is so kind, so polite, so anxious not to give offence.

'This is probably the most interesting of all. Come and see.'

She follows him across the turf to a corner of the graveyard where a large stone sits at an odd angle, like a broken tooth. She bends to look at the symbols carved into the surface.

'It's not so badly weathered as some.'

'No. The minister thought that this one was later than the others. You can still get a good idea of what it must once have been like. There's the figure of a man – do you see? He may be wearing a plaid.'

It is a rudimentary figure, like a child's clay model of a man, arms akimbo, sword to one side. But there are other images carved onto the stone, too. Donal traces the outlines with his finger. 'Do you see a creature which may or may not be a swan? There. Close by the man. And here above the two of them is the crescent moon, which is a very old symbol. And this – it may be a boat with oars. Who knows?'

They sit down on a mound of turf and stare at the stone. There is something simple and poignant about the arrangement of the carvings, a picture puzzle that you could decipher, if only you had the key.

'The mute swans still fly to the island,' he tells her. ' They always go to the same place as well, one of the lochans. *Ealachan*, that's what my father calls them. That's their name.'

'Do you speak Gaelic?'

'Only the odd word. But my father spoke nothing else until he was eight. He can still think in the Gaelic when he wishes and he tells me it's quite different from thinking in English.'

'I didn't know you could switch it on and off like that.'

'No, neither did I. But you don't argue with the old man. He tells me it's the language of heaven, and who am I to argue with him? He spins a good yarn, I'll say that for him.'

'I must meet him. Properly, I mean. All I've done is wave to him in passing.'

'This is one of his favourite places. He still rows over here sometimes on his own. He likes to sit here and think.'

'I'm not surprised. It's very peaceful.'

'He tells me that this is a very thin place.'

'What does he mean?'

'He means that the border between life and death, between the natural and the supernatural, is very thin here.' But Donal says it with a wry twist of his lips.

'And is it?'

'Maybe it is. You know, I sometimes think they ought to tidy the place up a bit, and preserve the stones from the elements. But then I reckon that it would spoil it, make it too tidy, and too touristy, and that wouldn't do at all.'

Donal smiles at Alys in the sunshine and she realises that his eyes are grey. Grey eyes fringed by long black lashes. Physical desire hits her again, as it did on the boat, like a blow to the pit of her stomach. This won't do at all, she thinks. She hasn't wanted anybody like this for years, literally. But there is nothing remotely suitable about Donal. The border between his world and hers is anything but thin. His gaze slides away from hers, diffidently. All she would have to do would be to stretch her hand out, and slip it into his. But she doesn't do it. And Donal, she thinks, would be much too shy. There won't be enough time for Donal to do it. She will be back in Edinburgh in less than a fortnight.

They walk down the hill together. On the beach, she prepares to help him to slide the boat into the water.

'Wait a moment,' he says.

'What's the problem?'

'Not against the sun.'

'What do you mean?'

'You don't turn a boat against the sun. It has to go sunwise. Sorry.' He is half embarrassed, half defiant.

Intrigued, she helps him to turn the boat with the sun, and then scrambles aboard again.

He starts the engine and takes her, not back to Garve, as she had expected, but further out, motoring smoothly over the glassy surface of the sound, shifting direction occasionally to avoid submerged rocks. Going where they aren't. He is absolutely at home here, calm, and very capable. She once went out on a boat with John when Ben was little. They were on holiday in the Lake

District and she was on pins the whole time because, although they were wearing lifejackets, she didn't trust John's bluff 'I love messing about in boats' confidence. But she would trust Donal to take herself or her son out any day. She gets the feeling that whatever happened he would probably know what to do.

'You have to respect the sea,' he says, confirming this belief. 'You don't take anything for granted, least of all your own abilities.'

She watches the deserted coastline change shape slowly.

'There's a Viking buried in that bay somewhere.' He points out a broad stretch of sand, backed by green, between steep arms of rock. 'They dig up things occasionally but nobody is quite sure where the actual grave is. And there . . . the old stone house perched above the bay. That's the oldest house on the island. Auchenblae.'

'Is it derelict?'

'Not quite, but nobody is living there. Not now. It was known as the Old Laird's House once upon a time. Then some wealthy incoming owner built the place where you are staying now.'

'You can see why, I suppose. It's much more sheltered.'

'And do you see that wee hill there looking out to sea? That's another burial mound. They say a great king was buried there, and people used to come on pilgrimage to it from Ireland maybe two thousand years ago. And up there, over the hill, is the Well of the Winds, although the place is so overgrown that hardly anybody knows where it is. Once upon a time, if you had a voyage ahead of you, you could go there and take some of the water and ask for a favourable wind, but the story goes that if the well wasn't capped with a big stone the water would spill over and the flood the whole world.'

'How do you know all this, Donal?'

'I had it from my father, mostly. The visitors like to hear these tales. I am giving you my tourist spiel!'

'Well, it's very entertaining.'

He shades his eyes and peers across the water. 'Hold on,' he says, and takes them further out still. The air is suddenly full of seabirds, diving crazily, hungrily, on a shoal of small eels which she can see wriggling in the waters below them. She watches, enthralled by the strangeness of it all.

He switches off the engine, and lets the boat slop about for a bit while he takes a cigarette out of his pocket.

'I thought you were supposed to be stopping.'

'I am.' He sticks it in his mouth, looks at her sheepishly, takes it out again and shreds it into the water. 'I have. I've stopped.'

He dips his fingers in the water and then says 'Fuck!' and then 'Sorry.'

'What's wrong?'

'Scalder.' His fingers are red where they have just touched the long, fine tendrils. 'You'd think I'd know by now, wouldn't you?' he says, shaking his head. 'Bloody painful.' He gestures at the rucksack. 'There's vinegar in there. It helps.'

She rummages in the bag, brings out the bottle of vinegar and a tissue, holds his hand and dabs expertly at his fingers.

'You can tell you've got a wee boy,' he says, with a grin.

'Of course. I'm really good at ministering to minor injuries. There now, is that better?'

Ben would expect a kiss, too, she thinks.

'Yes, thanks. Much.' She could swear he gives a little sigh. 'I suppose I should get you home again.'

Instead of taking the boat into Port Manus below the hotel, however, they go into the bay at Ardachy and Donal invites her up to the cottage.

The house is four-square, facing the sea, with two dormer windows above. It is full of the accumulated clutter of a lifetime. Or several lifetimes. A fire of bleached driftwood splutters in the big room that serves as kitchen and living room combined.

Alys sits down on the sagging couch and looks around, while Donal makes tea. 'Unless you want something stronger?' he asks.

'No, thanks. Tea will be fine.'

'Don't worry,' says Iain. 'He'll take you back to the hotel. You won't have to walk today.'

'It's further than you think.'

'Aye, it is. The road winds about a lot.' He makes it sound as though the road moves of its own accord.

She loves other people's houses, loves to try to read them. This one, she reckons, has once been very neat, very spick and span. There is an underlay of china ornaments: vacuous dogs and pretty painted ladies, each standing on its own hand-crocheted doily. But it is as though the years have gradually overlain these elements of femininity with something altogether more careless and robust, for every surface is littered with newspapers, mugs, fish-hooks, coils of nylon rope and other masculine debris. The cottage smells of an odd but pleasant mixture of tar and smoke, whisky and soap powder.

Donal comes over to the fireside, carrying a wooden tray, on which he has set out mugs, milk and sugar, a big red teapot and a square china plate of shortbread fingers. The tea is strong, made with real tea leaves.

'I can't be doing with teabags,' says Iain scornfully, 'and neither could my wife.' He gestures at a photograph sitting on top of the television. It is a black-and-white studio portrait of a young woman with a round, placid face and cherry lips. She would look like a doll, if it were not for a certain keen intelligence in her eyes. Donal, Alys thinks, looks much more like his father than his mother. Iain is what Donal will come to, in time.

Iain questions her politely about herself and her family.

When conversation flags she looks around and says, 'I do like your cottage.'

Iain looks around, too, as though seeing it through her eyes. 'Ach, it's full of clutter. A lot of it was my wife's and I haven't the heart to clear it out. I still feel that she might come walking into the room any moment.'

'I was admiring your little cabinet up at the hotel.'

'Ah, the casket.' He looks at her shrewdly. 'It was in our loft for many years. There was an old blanket box with clothes in it, and when we were first married my wife decided to have a bit of a clear-out. There it was, in among the old dresses and shawls and things, which were all falling to pieces. We kept it safe for a long time, but then we thought other people should have the pleasure of seeing it. The clothes are still up there in the kist. She said she didn't have the heart to throw them out, so she wrapped them in tissue and put some lavender in among them. I never look at them, but I like to see the wee casket.'

Alys gazes at Iain. Grey eyes, she thinks. Just like his son's. Sun and wind have etched deep lines into his face. The same thing will happen to Donal.

'I think it's very beautiful. I wish it were mine.' Whenever she is in the hotel, she keeps going back to look at the cabinet, fascinated by it. 'I don't know why, but there's a kind of sadness about it. I feel it here.' She taps her chest briefly, surprised at her urge to confide in him. 'Like a real pain. Does that sound daft?'

'Not at all. My grandmother always used to tell me that it came from the Old Laird's House many years ago. , You'll have seen the place from the sea, likely?'

'Yes. Donal pointed it out to me.'

'I fancy the building has changed somewhat. A grand stone-built house it was once, like a tower. But it has shrunk and turned in on itself with the passage of time.'

'Do you think that maybe the casket was Manus's treasure?'

Iain grins at her. 'What nonsense has my son been telling you? Manus's long-lost treasure? The things are precious to us right enough, but maybe three hundred years ago they would have been quite ordinary.' He glances over at his son. 'I suppose he took you to the little island.'

'He did.'

'It's a nice peaceful place.'

'Tell her about the seal woman,' says Donal suddenly. 'Tell her the story about the selkie.'

Iain pours out more tea, the dregs of the pot, strong and leafy. He looks at Alys. 'Are you not bored by this stuff?'

'Not at all.'

'But you'll have heard this kind of story before, no doubt. It is better in the Gaelic, you know.'

'Tell me anyway.' She glances at Donal but he is staring out of the window.

Iain makes himself comfortable. 'Well, now,' he begins. 'A fisherman of the island was out alone in his boat. A sudden squall blew up, his coracle overturned and he was tipped into the water. Like most fishermen in those days, he could not swim. Not a stroke. He would have drowned for sure, but he was saved by a seal woman, a selkie. She was young and strong and beautiful, with long dark hair and grey eyes like the sea on a wild day, but she had a tail like a seal. She brought him to the bay where he had his home, and she shed her sealskin so that she could pull him up the sand and make sure that he was safe. For she had the power to assume human form when she wanted. And since he was a good-looking young man she gave him a kiss or two for luck. He may have been half drowned but he wasn't daft. He asked for her name and the poor foolish selkie gave it to him.'

'Why foolish?'

'It meant she had given him power over her, of course. That was the way of it. Words are powerful things. He took her into his house, and she couldn't deny him. Then he hid her sealskin so that she could never go back to the sea, and he married her. But they were wrong for one another. She had a hundred words for water and he had very few. He knew the names only of what he could catch and eat, and she despised him for that. The children she bore him pinned her to the land like fish-hooks in her flesh.

She stayed with him, but she was never happy and he knew it.'

'What happened?'

'Well, I suppose she just made the best of it, but whenever he was at the fishing, she hunted high and low. First she tried the cottage, then the boathouse, and at long last she tried the caves at the back of the bay. And one day, of course, she found her sealskin where he had hidden it, wrapped up in a tarpaulin and stored in an old wooden box among nets and ropes.'

'What did she do?'

'She waited till they were all fast asleep, the fishermen and her children. She kissed them goodbye, one by one, and the tears fell from her eyes because her love for them was strong. But the call of the sea and of her own people was stronger by far. Once she had put on her sealskin, she forgot all about the land. She slid into the waves and was never seen again. And there he was, poor man, left alone to bring up a family of children with long, dark hair from which the white sand fell constantly, and they had webbed feet and the sea in their eyes besides.'

Alys glances over at Donal. He is still sitting looking out of the window. She sees that his big fists are clenched. He gets up. 'I'll make more tea,' he says.

A little later, Donal offers to take Alys back to the hotel. He gives her the choice of going in the van or the boat, and she chooses the boat. Apart from anything else, the van looks as though it might fall to bits at any moment.

They tie up at the jetty in Scoull Bay and he hands her ashore.

'I've kept you from your work,' she says. She thinks, fleetingly, about offering him money again, but senses that his pride will be hurt by it. He divides his time between the hotel gardens and the creel fishing. He has told her that he also does maintenance work on the bikes which the hotel hires out to visitors, as well as odd gardening and household jobs for elderly islanders. He can turn his hand to plumbing and knows a bit about car mechanics. It all adds up to a busy but not very lucrative working week.

'That's all right,' he says. 'I've enjoyed it.'

'Me too.'

'We could . . .' He hesitates.

'Yes?'

He obviously needs encouragement.

'We could go for a walk. Over the other side of the island. There are lost villages there. And the views are very beautiful.'

'I'd like that.'

'Later in the week, then. I'll see you at the hotel.'

'I'll look forward to it.'

She walks up the jetty and turns to see him pulling across the bay. He hasn't bothered to start the engine, but is rowing for the pleasure of it. The boat is brown and sweet as a nut in the water. His dark head is bent over the oars. She watches him until he pulls the boat towards the harbour at Ardachy.

She shakes herself. Don't be daft, Alys, she thinks. Don't lose your head.

But afterwards, when she is almost at the hotel, she thinks that it isn't her head that worries her so much as her heart.

EIGHT

For the second time in her life, Henrietta was so ill that those caring for her thought she might die. The soaking that day by the cliff, after months of self-starvation, compounded by the shock of her kidnapping and the separation from her son, all culminated in the onset of a chill which quickly developed into a raging fever. It worried Ishbel that Henrietta had no strength and perhaps no desire to combat her sickness.

Manus had left for the mainland and could not be contacted. Besides, what could he have done? Day after day, Ishbel sat beside the bed where the young woman lay, twisting and turning, crying out and moaning and clutching at the covers. It seemed as if Henrietta was wasting away before her eyes; burning up and then dwindling like a spent candle. She would cry out for her mother or for Maisie, but most of all, she would whisper the name of her son: 'Gabriel. I want Gabriel.'

Ishbel would not leave Henrietta. She persuaded others to take over her household duties and made up a bed of heather, covered with a woollen blanket, so that she could sleep beside her patient and be there whenever she was needed. Sometimes old Mhairi, who was alone in the world and whose legs and hips were crippled, would come to relieve her, bathing the sick girl's head and hands and feet in an effort to cool the fever that raged through her emaciated body.

'Tis a crying shame, so it is,' the old woman said at last. 'What crime has the lass committed that she should be reduced to this? Do you know the truth of it all, Ishbel? Has the Laird taken you into his confidence, for I know he sometimes does?'

Ishbel sat up on her bed, yawned widely and drank the buttermilk that Mhairi had brought her.

'I know very little. He only told me that I was to take care of all her needs. But she has committed no crime, I know that much. How is she?'

'Still burning up. I wonder if she'll live to see Manus return?'

'Well, he'll be home soon. He sent Seamus ahead of him with the news last night.'

'She may die yet, Ishbel.'

'If the fever only passes and she can eat and drink, we may manage to build up her strength.'

'The lass needs more than that. She needs a reason to live.'

'Aye,' Ishbel agreed. 'But she has none that I can see. It would be enough to drive a body mad, to be so torn from hearth and home and bairn.'

'If she dies it will be on all our consciences.'

'It will be on Manus McNeill's conscience most of all.'

'Ach.' Mhairi shrugged. 'I expect he will bear it. He has been a good friend to me all these years, but he has broad shoulders and his conscience is a moveable feast at the best of times.'

'I know it.'

'But the poor lass. The poor wee lass!'

That afternoon the ferry carried Manus McNeill back to the island. Ishbel met him at the door and was surprised and touched that his first enquiry was for Henrietta.

'She is gravely ill, sir. There have been times when we thought that she would not live to see your return.'

'I feared as much when I left. We must treat her more kindly in future.'

86

'I have always treated her with kindness, sir.' There was reproach in her tone – or as close as she would ever come to it – and he acknowledged the justice of it.

'I know you have. The fault is all mine. Is she awake?'

'I'm not sure. Sometimes she wakes, but then the fever takes her again.'

'I must speak to her. I have news for her and it cannot wait. It had much better not wait.'

'Is it about her son?'

He nodded. 'But let me tell her first, Ishbel. She must have the news before anyone else.'

Ishbel led him into the sickroom. Henrietta's face, in the middle of the piled pillows, looked flushed and vulnerable. If she had been slender before, she was skeletal now.

Ishbel stroked her forehead. 'Henrietta, wake up. My Lord Manus is here. There is news for you.'

Her eyes flickered open, and she moved, groaning a little at the pain in her limbs.

Manus gestured to the door. 'Leave us for a few moments, Ishbel. You should not be party to this. The less you know the better.'

'Very well, sir.'

She left, puzzled by his words. Something very wrong had taken place, she knew, and now he was sorry for it. He could be a hard man when the times and the circumstances demanded it, but brutality was not in his nature. He had once been a compassionate man, but that was when his wife was alive.

Henrietta made an effort to focus on him. Then she tried to sit up and burst into a fit of coughing.

'No,' he said, in some alarm. He put a cool hand on her forehead. 'Lie down, Henrietta. I have something to tell you. Will you just listen to me for a moment?'

'Has spring come, then?' she asked him eagerly. 'Has it come at last?'

'Aye, the spring has come. And I have news for you.'

'The last time I was so ill as this,' she said, 'my parents had died. I woke up to the news that my parents had died. Who is dead this time?'

'Nobody is dead, thank God. Although I think you yourself have been very near it. But I have seen your wee boy.'

She struggled to sit up again and would have seized his hand but he laid her gently back on the pillows.

'Gabriel? Is he here?' she asked.

'No. No, he is not.'

'Ah! I thought perhaps you had . . .'

'Don't turn your head away. I have good news for you. If I could have brought him with me, I would. I have been to Edinburgh on business of my own. I have not spoken with your brother or your sister-in-law. I could not do that. But I certainly spent some time observing their house.'

He had been very careful but still it had been a risk. If they had seen him loitering there, who knows what they might have accused him of?

'I think I have seen your son. But is there another wee one in the house? A lass?'

'Yes. That would be Janet, Thomas's daughter. She is just a little older than my Gabriel.'

'And your lad? Tell me, is he two or maybe three years old, with hair much like your own, and bright eyes, and a high colour to his cheeks?'

'Aye, he is, he is.'

It was him, to the life and Manus's next words confirmed it.

'Then I have seen him. He and his cousin were in the charge of a handsome, motherly woman with iron-grey hair.'

'Maisie!'

Relief flooded through her. It did not negate the sorrow or the regret, but it served to calm something of the terrible apprehension that had eaten into her all these months. If Maisie was taking care of Gabriel, all would be well with him.

'My dear Maisie. How Gabriel loved her!'

'And still does, I think. They were playing at the ball in the back court of the house. And I'll tell you this, he is by no means as ill fed or as sad as yourself at this moment. He was toddling about on wee fat legs and laughing fit to burst.'

'He was laughing?'

'Aye, he was. Indeed he seemed very fond of his cousin, too, for she put her arms around him and kissed him heartily on both cheeks and he did not object. But I saw him run after her, crying, kiss, Janet! Kiss!'

'Then he has forgotten me,' she whispered.

He tried to say 'Surely not', knowing it to be a lie. But she confounded him by seizing his hand.

'Oh, thank God,' she said. 'I would rather he forget me and be happy with Maisie than remember me and be sad. And thank you for this news. You bring him before my eyes. God bless you for your kindness!'

He stood up and withdrew his hand gently, tucking hers under the coverlet. 'Don't thank me, Henrietta. You have little enough to thank me for. Only get well soon. Do this for me, and then I will show you the island wearing a different garb.'

For the first time in many weeks Henrietta slept peacefully. She woke only to drink a little wine and water, then slept again, and when she woke for a second time Ishbel took Manus the news that the crisis was past and she was hopeful of seeing her patient regain her health and strength once more.

By the time Henrietta was able to leave her bed, spring had truly come to the island. She was still weak, but growing stronger by the day. Manus had brought sugar plums and gingerbread back from Edinburgh. He said, 'They are for you, Mistress Henrietta, to tempt your appetite. You must eat.'

Better than sweetmeats however, was the traditional

'springtime soup' which Ishbel cooked and brought to Henrietta in the middle of the day. It was an appetising meat broth enriched with chopped sorrel, wild garlic, watercress and the tender shoots of young seaweed. There were, besides, soft-boiled eggs served in the morning with buttered bannocks, and white cheese, and what Ishbel called 'old man's milk': a concoction of eggs and cream, beaten together in a blue delft bowl, sweetened with honey and strengthened with a good dash of whisky.

'It is to put flesh on your bones and you are to drink it every night,' said Ishbel. 'Those are my Lord's orders and you are to do as he says.'

Henrietta smiled at her. 'It is so delicious that I could hardly refuse!'

'Well, I'm glad of it. I am to build you up and make you strong.'

'For what?'

'Why, so that you can make the most of the fine weather and see the island as you should. You might even find yourself loving it as we do.'

Henrietta could not imagine herself loving the island, but the sunlight and the sweet scents that came drifting in at her window encouraged her.

One day she said to Ishbel, 'Does this place have a name?'

'You mean the house?. This house is called Achadh nam Blàth. It means 'field of flowers' in your tongue.'

'I saw no flowers.'

'They are blooming now. All along the shoreline and beyond.'

'And the island itself. Does it have a name?'

Ishbel looked at her in disbelief. 'Of course it has a name, lady.'

'I fancy the men spoke a name when they brought me here but I have forgotten it. Nobody has mentioned it since.'

'Not even Manus?'

'What occasion would he have to tell me the name of the place where he keeps me a prisoner?'

'Why, it is called Eilean Garbh,' said Ishbel. 'I think it means "rough island" in your tongue.'

'A fitting name.'

'It is rough no longer. You have hardly set foot out of doors for many weeks, but when you do, you will find the island full of flowers!'

Ishbel sang about her work now, partly from relief at her patient's returning health, but mostly from joy at the coming of spring to the island and Henrietta listened to the strange melodies, humming them over to herself. There was a sadness about them, even when the lilt in Ishbel's voice told her that the song was about love. Sometimes she would try to say the words in Gaelic, laughing self-consciously at her own attempts, until at last Ishbel said, 'Now you have it!'

It helped to pass the time. Her curiosity and her intelligence were both aroused and engaged and she did not find the language as savage as she had once thought it. There was a liquid beauty in words and music, and the more comprehensible they became, the more melodic they seemed.

Manus still avoided her, though when he met her in courtyard or corridor he did at least acknowledge her with a smile and a bow of his head. She suspected that it was not aversion that dictated his behaviour now, but lack of practice in the social graces.

Then came the day when she was seated on the stone bench outside the house door, hemming petticoats for want of anything better to do. She drank in the sunlight and the sharp scents of green and growing things that mingled with the more robust farmyard smells drifting from the back of the house. She sang under her breath as she worked, words which Ishbel had taught her, and which she still barely understood.

> *'Is tu sgàil anns an teas,*
> *Is tu fasgadh anns an fhuachd,*
> *Is tu sùilean don dall,*
> *Is tu bata don eilthireach,*
> *Is tu eilean aig muir.*
> *Is tu ceum an fhèidh air a' bheinn,*
> *Is tu steud-each air còmhnard ...'*

> 'You are shade in the heat,
> A shelter in the cold,
> Eyes to the blind,
> A staff to the pilgrim,
> An island at sea.
> You are the step of the deer on the hill,
> The step of the steed on the plain ...'

Manus had been standing in the shadow of the doorway, brought up short by her singing, and the unexpectedness of the language. Now he found himself joining in.

> *'Is tu eireachdas an t-eala a' snàmh,*
> *Is tu àilleachd gach miann àlluinn ...'*

> 'You are the grace of the swan swimming,
> You are the loveliness of all lovely desires ...'

She turned round at the sound of his voice.

'How do you know this?' he asked.

'Ishbel taught me. But I don't really understand its meaning – or only a little of it. I sing the words because the sound of them is sweet, that is all. I have learned them by heart.'

'But you sing as though your heart is in them. It is a wedding hymn and was addressed to a maid who was to be married.' He came out into the sunlight. 'Mistress Henrietta, I am happy to see you well again.'

'I am glad to be well again. I have not been so ill since the smallpox deprived me of my looks. Such as they once were.'

He remembered the day of her arrival and what he had said to her then. He had not even honoured her with common politeness. His late wife, Frances, who had been a good-natured and kindly woman, would have been horrified. Well, it was too late to make amends now.

Nevertheless, he observed, 'The scars are very small. Who would notice them? The fresh air has done you good.'

'Your words are very kindly meant but I hardly think that they can be true, Mr McNeill.'

He said, brusquely, 'For God's sake, my name is Manus.' And then, more gently, 'Call me Manus, just.' I must have grown utterly unfit for polite society, he thought, looking at her startled face, when every word I speak alarms her.

'If you wish,' she said mildly, and he saw that she was not alarmed at all but only surprised by his vehemence.

'I do wish.'

'You know, until you brought me news of my baby, I think I had lost all desire to live.' She found herself anxious to be on friendly terms with him. 'And even now I cannot help but be jealous of Maisie. But I do feel better, and it is your doing. I cannot thank you enough.'

'It was the least I could do.' He hesitated. 'Henrietta, do you enjoy sewing?'

'Well, it keeps my hands busy.'

'Do you think that you could make use of this?'

She saw that he was holding out a wooden knotting shuttle, inlaid with a floral motif in gold leaf and with a pretty piece of edging still attached.

'It was my wife's.' He seldom mentioned her and the word did not come easily. 'She used to make edging for her petticoats with it. She brought it with her from the mainland and she said it sat well in the hand.' He smiled at the memory. 'Can you use it?'

She took it from him, touched by the gift. 'Yes. I could make good use of this. But are you sure?'

'It would please me to see it in use. My wife would not have approved of her possessions lying idle for so many years. Of all things she loved to be busy.'

'And so do I.'

'I know. I have watched you.'

'Have you?'

'My wife came here from the mainland. She was of a lowland family but one loyal to the Stuart cause. We were very happy for the year or two we were together.'

He had been a different man then: younger, less embittered, less disillusioned. Life had held many prospects for happiness: all taken from him at a stroke. It had made him furiously angry. But with what? With whom? He had railed against God for a time, but God had not deigned to answer. Then the anger had turned in on himself.

'So short a time!'

'Aye. We did not have long together. Frances was her name.'

'That is my name too, my middle name,' she said, impulsively

'Is it? They did not tell me.'

Who did not tell you? she thought. But she did not ask. There were things she would rather not know, not yet awhile.

'And you are giving me this?'

'If it will be useful for you. You have little enough. Take it. Frances would not have wished to see another lass so . . .' He paused, seeking for the right word. 'So desolate here,' he said, and then, as though ashamed of his own emotions, he went quickly back into the house.

She had not thanked him properly. But then maybe he did not want her thanks.

Later, she showed the knotting shuttle to Ishbel, who seemed surprised to see it. Her brown eyes opened wide, 'I wondered what had become of it. He must have kept it close beside him. And Manus gave you this?'

'But perhaps I should not have accepted it.'

'Oh yes, you should. It would have hurt his pride terribly if you had refused the gift.'

'Then I did the right thing?'

'Of course. It was well meant. He is not a man to make such gestures lightly. Make good use of it. It will give him pleasure to see you using it.'

Ishbel, reflected Henrietta, was ingenuous in her loyalty to her cousin. Giving Manus pleasure was not an idea that would have entered her head until now. But still, if it eased her life on the island with him, there was surely a great deal to be said for it.

NINE

At the first opportunity, Alys asks Mrs Cameron about Donal's wife, but for somebody who usually likes to indulge in a little gossip she is surprisingly cagey.

'Anne Marie?' she says, pursing her lips. 'Hm. Not a marriage made in heaven that one – not so far as I know, anyway. Who told you about her?'

'Donal. When he took me out in the boat.' Alys doesn't want to seem too inquisitive. 'I didn't know he had been married, that's all.'

'It didn't last. And she didn't get on too well with Iain, I believe.'

'Well, it can't be easy, living with your father-in-law.'

'Maybe not, but what else were they to do? Thank God we're going to get a few new houses on the island at last. We need a bit of decent housing, if all our young people are not to go away for good. But it wasn't an option at that time. Not for Donal and Anne Marie.'

They are sitting in the residents' lounge, over a tray of coffee.

'Tell me, are you getting on well with him?' Mrs Cameron stirs brown sugar into the milky liquid and selects a chocolate biscuit.

'Oh yes,' says Alys, enthusiastically. Too enthusiastically, perhaps. 'I mean, he's such a nice man,' she qualifies. 'So polite. He's a gem.'

'Yes, he is.' Absentmindedly Mrs Cameron dips her biscuit in her coffee and sucks the glistening chocolate.

This is one of Alys's pet hates and something she scolds Ben about, though that never stops him doing it. She almost taps Mrs Cameron on the hand and says, 'Don't do that!' but catches herself just in time.

'Poor Donal,' says Mrs Cameron.

'I knew him years ago. When I used to come here on holiday.'

'So I hear.' She eyes Alys thoughtfully. 'He needs a good woman. We're all agreed on that.'

'Well, I'm sure it wouldn't be too hard for him to find one, if that's what he wants,' she says, defensively. 'He's a very attractive man.'

For God's sake, she thinks, why can't you zip your lip, Alys? But it's true. She finds him extraordinarily attractive.

'You'd be surprised, my dear,' says Mrs Cameron. 'Not everyone wants what Donal has to offer. This is a very small place and Donal isn't a rich man. Besides, I think it's a case of once bitten, twice shy with him.'

'I know how he feels.'

Mrs Cameron looks a bit taken aback.

'I'm divorced, too,' explains Alys. 'I'm on reasonably good terms with my ex, but it does make you cautious about new relationships, especially when there's a child to consider.'

'You have a child?'

'A little boy. He lives with me but he's on holiday with his dad just now.'

'Ah well, that's the civilised way of going about things, right enough.'

'We try.'

'There were no children, not for Anne Marie and Donal. I'm surprised he mentioned the divorce. He doesn't often talk about her. She was Scottish herself but I think she was living in London when he took up with her. A flighty wee girl.'

Alys finds the old fashioned expression funny, but it is characteristic of Mrs Cameron.

'He told me she just got tired of the island.'

'Yes. Well, that was true. She didn't exactly take to the way of life here – though some folk might say she took to parts of it all too well.'

'What parts?'

Mrs Cameron restrains herself with an obvious effort. 'Oh, there's no point in going over old ground, Alys. Let's just say she let him down and on an island the size of this one, that's a little unwise. People all knew what was going on. We had only been here at the hotel for a few years ourselves when it happened, so I remember it well. He should have been very angry and no doubt he was, but he kept that side of it to himself. He just retreated into his shell and stayed there.'

It is Alys's turn to say, 'Poor Donal.'

'We're all very fond of him here, you know.'

'I'm sure you are,' agrees Alys, puzzled.

Mrs Cameron looks uncomfortable again. She hesitates. 'You see, Alys, you're just visiting, aren't you? You'll be gone in another week's time, back home to Edinburgh.'

'You mean I shouldn't upset him all over again?'

'Well . . .'

'Oh, Mrs Cameron, he's just being friendly and so am I. That's all there is to it.'

'Well, that's good.' She pours more coffee. 'I expect you're thinking I'm a nosy old cow,' she says, much to Alys's embarrassment, 'and you'd be right in a way. It's absolutely none of my business. It's just that I've got a very soft spot for Donal and I wouldn't like to see him get hurt a second time. Nobody here would.'

Ben phones the hotel. They have been to the Isle of Capri ('All right') and to Pompeii ('Magic'). 'Mum,' he says excitedly, 'there were bodies. Well, they poured concrete into the holes and when it set, it came out in the shape of bodies. There were people, and there was a dog. It was the . . .' He pauses, getting the words right. 'It was the pyroclastic flows that did it.'

'Let me speak to Dad,' she says, eventually.

'Hi,' says John. 'How's your desert island?'

'Beautiful. Even better than I remembered. How's Sorrento?'

'Equally lovely, thank you. And sunny.'

'So's Garve. You'll be back next Friday afternoon, right?'

'We will.'

'I'll be home on Saturday. There's a ferry around ten thirty.' She has left the car in the ferry car park on the mainland. 'I'll be home by mid-afternoon, maybe a bit later.'

'It's all right, Alys. We won't throw him out into the street if you're not back in time.'

'I miss him,' she says.

'So do I. You see more of him than I do.'

This could easily develop into one of those interminable 'Your deal is better than my deal' arguments, so she says, 'I know. Listen, put him back on, would you?'

'Why?' he asks suspiciously. She can hear Millie whispering in the background.

'Because I want to say night-night, that's why.'

She and Ben blow noisy kisses into the phone. Eventually they turn into raspberries. She waits for him to hang up first. 'Night, Mum, night, Mum, night, Mum,' she can hear him saying as he retreats, giggling.

'Oh God,' she thinks as she replaces the receiver. 'I do so miss my son.'

The second week of her holiday passes very quickly. She sees Donal once or twice in the hotel bar, usually with his father or his friends. He buys her a glass of wine and she buys him a beer, and they talk casually about the weather and the fishing, and how she has spent her days. He doesn't mention the walk on the other side of the island, and she is too inhibited to ask him in case he has already decided that he doesn't want to take their relationship any further. He seems to have stopped smoking altogether.

She hires a bike for the day and cycles up and down the road. She lingers on the pier at the south end of the island for a long time, watching a pair of grey mullet foraging about on the sandy bottom. Once or twice, she realises that she is gazing at the Old Laird's House, blending so perfectly with its surroundings that it looks more like a rocky outcrop of the land itself than a dwelling. She finds the meandering track to the windy beach she visited on her first day. She gathers razor-fish shells and white quartz pebbles. She reads a couple of novels. But she spends most of her time sitting on a succession of rocks and staring at the sea and is amazed by how quickly the time can pass in this effortless meditation.

She is not remotely bored. Most of the time she misses Ben with a constant low-key hunger but the island has brought back all kinds of memories: small remembrances of her mother and father, her brother, and Donal, too. She thinks about her father 'making camp'. Wherever they went, he would plant his walking stick in the ground and say, 'Now let's make camp,' even if it were only for a lunchtime picnic. She has a sudden image of her mother frying steaks for all of them, including Donal, on a primus stove in the rain, swearing under her breath but not really minding. She remembers Donal saying, 'I like your mum and dad. They're good fun.' She misses her parents all over again, and not for the first time is aware of the profound division that exists between those who have lost their parents and those who haven't.

Then she recalls Donal, chasing her along the beach hell-for-leather, running madly for the sheer joy of it. She remembers them all climbing the highest hill on the island and sliding down a long, gentle slope of heather on the other side, like a toboggan run, shrieking with laughter, bruising their backsides on hidden rocks, and ending up in a breathless heap at the bottom.

She sends her brother a succession of picture postcards of Garve, sliding them into the red box outside the post office. 'Do you remember this?' she asks him. 'And this? And this?' She writes him a long letter, telling him how little the place has changed, telling him all about Donal and what has happened to him since they trapped crabs together. She takes pleasure in writing about Donal, even in spelling out his name. When she tries to make sense of her feelings, she decides that maybe she has a crush on the place and the man. She finds him physically attractive but there is also a pathos about him that makes her sorry for him . As the day of her departure comes closer, she is smitten with a feeling of urgency. It seems that she will have to make the first move. He can only refuse.

On the Thursday before she is due to go home, she seeks him out in the hotel garden. He is weeding a rose bed and cursing the thorns that catch on his shirt and sometimes in his hands.

'Worse than bloody fish-hooks,' he says. 'Savage. I never planned to be a gardener, you know.'

'Didn't you?'

'I just fell into it somehow. I always thought I would be a fisherman like my father.'

'Isn't that what you do now?'

'In a way. But I could do with a bigger boat, an electric winch, things like that.'

'Would that be expensive?'

'Aye, it would. With the licence it would. It would run to thousands.'

'I thought you said there were no fish.'

'There are crabs, lobsters, crayfish sometimes. The Spaniards will buy all the shellfish we can send them.'

'You could sell your cabinet of curiosities. Get a new boat with the proceeds.'

He looks at her, frowning. 'That belongs to my father. And he won't ever sell it, never in a million years, so I'll just have to stick with the gardening. Besides, the wee box belongs here. It can't leave.'

But I can, she thinks.

'Do you know I'm going home on Saturday?' she says, in desperation. He has haunted her dreams all week. She is still not really sure what she wants from him; or what he might be prepared to give.

He looks shocked at the news. 'Jesus, I didn't realise. Time flies, doesn't it? I thought you had another week.'

'No. Ben will be back at the weekend. My son. And I'll be off to Edinburgh.'

He brushes his hands on the knees of his grubby canvas trousers.

She should go and leave him in peace to get on with his work but she hesitates. Then she looks down, and sees a small metallic creature squirming over her foot. She gives a shriek and leaps out of the way. 'A snake!'

He starts to laugh, picks it up, moves it gently into the shade of a shrub. 'Don't be daft. Don't you know a slow-worm when you see one?'

She shakes her head. 'Of course I don't. I've never seen one in my life before.'

'Well, that's what it is. A legless lizard.'

'You learn something new every day.'

He clears his throat. 'I said I would take you for a walk, didn't I, over the other side of the island?'

'Yes, but if you don't have time . . .'

'Would you really like to go?'

'I would.'

She realises that what she has taken for reluctance has been simple shyness. He has been waiting for her to mention it. You fool, she thinks, meaning herself.

'We could go tomorrow,' he says. 'I suppose it would have to be tomorrow if you're going on Saturday – if you have to go on Saturday.'

'I do have to go. But that would be lovely.'

Beneath his tan, his face has turned scarlet. 'I'll call for you after breakfast. You'd better wear strong shoes,' he says abruptly and turns his attention back to his weeding.

TEN

Henrietta was well again. She had blossomed in the long days of the island summer and Ishbel declared herself satisfied with her patient's progress. Her face and her figure had filled out and now that she had had encouraging news of Gabriel, she felt less desperate, more prepared to engage with her new surroundings and the people who inhabited them.

As her physical strength returned she had begun to explore the island, in company with Ishbel. Gradually she was becoming familiar with this enclosed world where a couple of big villages and a host of smaller clachans were linked by a maze of narrow pathways as well as two broad tracks that ran to east and west of Eilean Garbh. They had walked to the windy north but had avoided the steep cliffs there. They had walked to the green south and watched fishermen hauling their long lines aboard small and precarious boats, which they handled as skilfully as Manus handled the horses he loved.

She would pause to listen to people singing at their work, spinning, weaving, waulking the cloth, and they would not fall silent as they had once done. Now when Henrietta passed islanders engaged in peat cutting or haymaking – for there was good grassland on the island – they would raise a hand in salute or call out a greeting to her. She was beginning to feel much more at ease with her surroundings, and even to appreciate them.

Ishbel told her that Manus enquired after her every day but

he still kept himself aloof and she saw little of him. Henrietta, however, began to question Ishbel about her cousin.

'He is almost fifteen years older than I am.'

They were sitting in the sunshine, watching the play of cloud shadows on the water. 'He is the only surviving son of the old laird and a cousin of my family on my mother's side. He had a brother and a sister, but they both died young.'

'How old was he when he married?'

'He was twenty-four and his wife, Frances, was lowland like yourself. My mother came to wait upon her, and they became great friends. My mother always said that she loved to laugh, and she made Manus laugh as well. I was a girl at the time, but even I could see the change in him.'

'You know him better than most, Ishbel.'

'I suppose I do. But Manus is close to nobody now. And I am glad that I have my father's house nearby, for that is my real home.'

'And of course your father lives next to Seamus of the red hair, doesn't he?' asked Henrietta, slyly.

'I have known him since we were children together and we would scramble barefoot among the rocks for shellfish.'

'Do you think you will marry him?'

'Well, nobody else would have him!'

'Oh, Ishbel!'

'And one day he certainly will pluck up the courage to ask my father for my hand and then I expect we will be married. But I would like to see Manus content as well. There is no reason why he should not remarry.'

'It is a long time since his wife died.'

'It is, and he should have put his loss behind him by now. I don't mean he should have forgotten about her, but he should be remembering her with love, and travelling onwards. That is what my own father has done, although to be sure he has not married again either.'

'Manus must have loved Frances very much.'

'She was taken too soon. And of course he lost his child, too.'

'I know what that means.'

'He frightened us all. He drank too much and he neglected the island and its people. He went away to the mainland and they say he spent a small fortune on gambling and the Lord knows what else. When he returned at last, the fires that raged in him had died, for he was much calmer. But it was as though something else in him had been extinguished as well. His pleasure in life had all gone.'

'I see that in him,' said Henrietta. 'But I had thought it was only with me.'

'No, he is the same with everyone. We bear it but we do not like it. Everyone has felt the lash of his tongue at some time. Only the animals escape it; he is always gentle with them.'

'I know. I've seen him.'

Ishbel sighed. 'It is as though he has concluded that nothing human matters very much, whereas in Frances's time everyone down to the smallest stable boy mattered to Manus. He was a good man and we regret the change in him. We want our old Manus back. We have sometimes wondered if he was embittered by his time in Edinburgh.'

'Oh, it isn't so bad.'

'But we have heard such dreadful stories.'

'What stories?'

'Why, that the city is a terrible heathen place, where people live crowded together like rabbits, and that lowlanders are little better than thieves and robbers.'

'They say much the same thing in Edinburgh, only they say it about the Highlands and Highlanders.'

'And what do you think now?'

'I think that we were both wrong. I think that there is much to be said for both places and peoples.'

Soon after that conversation, on a very fine day in July, Henrietta emerged from the house, blinking in the sunlight. A tracery of clouds came rolling across from the west, lace over blue silk and the air was heavy with the scent of summer flowers. It was a day to lift the spirits and Henrietta had decided that she must be out of doors. She had breakfasted early and then lingered in the great hall, hoping that Ishbel could be persuaded to come with her, but the girl was too busy.

The women of the house would not allow Henrietta to work, except at the spinning and weaving, which was thought to be a suitable occupation for a lady. They had a rhythm and a meaning to their lives but there was nothing for her to do. She hated to be so useless. She had a sudden desire for friendly conversation on this fine morning, but if she could not have that, at least she could have sunshine and exercise as a substitute.

She fastened on the pair of serviceable leather brogues Ishbel had given her.

'My father made them,' Ishbel had told her. 'He is shoemaker for the whole island.' She laughed. 'Not that that amounts to much, since the great majority of people here go barefoot most of the time!'

Henrietta kilted up her skirts and clambered up the hillside behind the house, following a meandering track that was surely made by animals rather than men. She walked until she had left the house far behind. The heather was springing into new green leaf, but the dry tips of last year's flowers cut into her ankles and she was glad of the brogues. Her feet were not yet as tough as island-born feet. The whitish-pink blossom of the bramble was everywhere – there would be a good harvest of fruit in the autumn – and the flag irises were just dying away from the marshy places.

Henrietta climbed higher and higher, until she felt the springy turf of the uplands with its embroidery of purple thyme beneath her feet. Behind her and then ahead of her, too, as she breasted the spine of the island, she could see blue sky and a turquoise sea and a pattern of islands, near and far.

Delighting in her own health and strength, she walked on and on, until at last she felt the need to rest and sat down on a stony hillside below which the land sloped into a basin containing a *lochan* like a grey eye, fringed with bright green marsh or pasture – she could not tell which, at this distance – far below. There was a gathering of stone buildings beside the water and tiny white dots upon it which she thought must be swans. She was thirsty and wished she had brought something to drink.

She heard his horse's hooves drumming on the turf before she saw him. Manus had ridden to the north end of the island with the first light of dawn, and now was on his way home. She had not thought he would return so soon, although she knew that he rode like a madman. He caught sight of her and reined in his horse.

She raised an arm in greeting. '*Latha math dhuibh*! Good day to you!'

To her surprise, for she had expected him to acknowledge her and ride on, he cantered over to where she sat, and dismounted, taking a leather water bottle from the saddle and then freeing the mare to crop the short turf.

'And good day to you, Henrietta! Ishbel is proving to be a good teacher, I think.'

'She tries hard and so do I. But her Scotch is far better than my *Gaidhlig*.'

'Have you walked so far by yourself? Or have you one of the wee ponies hidden away?'

'Oh, I have walked.' She smiled up at him, remembering another day when she had walked a long way. 'I could not bear to be indoors on such a fine day.'

'You must be thirsty.' He offered her the bottle.

'I was wanting a drink and you have come in answer to my wish. I thought there would be a spring up here.'

'No. Not on this hillside. There is only one and it is down there, a long way down, where the houses are. But here, drink your fill and welcome.'

He watched her drink, and then took the bottle back and satisfied his own thirst.

'Who would not want to be outside on such a day?' he said. 'May I sit with you a while?'

'Of course.'

He sat down beside her, clasping his knees with his hands. His arms were brown in the sunlight, his bare legs likewise. She stole a covert glance at them. She had seen few men dressed in this fashion before she came to the island, save the odd highlander in the streets of the capital, where they were thought to be savages or figures of fun, depending upon whether they were young and finely made, or old and ugly. She and Grisel Shaw had once giggled together over them. The thought gave her a pang of homesickness, but she put it quickly to the back of her mind; the day was too fine for misery. Besides, Manus's proximity was faintly disturbing. They sat in silence for a moment, their faces turned towards the sun, until a peewit, disturbed by the foraging mare, shot up into the air in alarm.

'What is that bird?' he asked. 'I mean in your tongue?'

'It is a whaup.'

'A whaup,' he repeated in the Scotch. 'And the wee bird up there?' He pointed high in the sky where the bird sang and tumbled almost beyond sight and sound. '*Uiseag*?'

'A skylark.'

'A skylark. You see, I am quick at the learning.'

'You are. But it seems to me as if you know these words already.'

'I have dredged them up from my memory. My wife taught me. And some of their names I have asked Ishbel over the years. My wife told me the name of the swallows – the *gobhlain-ghaoithe* that cry about my old house down there. But what are the black-and-white birds with bright yellow beaks that patrol the shore?'

'They are oystercatchers. My father took me down to the sea at Cramond when I was a wee girl, and showed them to me, otherwise I should not have known, either.'

'One should know the names of things,' he said gravely. 'Words are powerful things.'

'My father was learned in the lore of birds and beasts and liked to read about them. There were books at home, with pictures . . . I loved them.' She paused, shading her eyes. 'Are there swans on the loch?'

'Aye. *Ealachan*. And they are magical creatures. They bring healing in their wake.'

'Do they?'

She wondered why he was disposed to be friendly. Perhaps he, too, had wished for company on such a fine day.

'They do.' He grinned. 'Ach, you are very ignorant, it seems to me, Mistress Henrietta.'

'I am ignorant of all kinds of things about this place. Only Ishbel has taken the trouble to inform me.'

'That's because only Ishbel can understand you. And I myself—' He broke off, then smiled again. She wished he would smile more often.

He said, 'But Ishbel will not have told you about the water bull that lives in the *lochan* down there.'

'A water bull? I have never heard of such a creature.'

'Have you not? Well, it is a strange creature to be sure and it is sometimes seen swimming about the water. It has a long neck and a wee head and a great humpy, warty back.'

She shook her head. 'Now you are making fun of me! And I do not believe you!' She began to laugh. 'I do not believe a word of it.'

'Do you not?' he asked, all innocence. 'There is a *clachan* – a small village – down there as well. Do you see it?'

She squinted into the sunlight, following the direction of his hand. 'I think I see smoke from the chimneys – if chimneys they are.'

'They are chimneys after a fashion, only in that the smoke must go somewhere and finds its way out through the roof as best it

110

can. Well now, one of the men there swears that he has seen it; but then Hector is very fond of his dram.'

'I'm sure he is.'

'Ah, but there are better men than Hector have seen it, too. My own grandfather, for one. He used to swear that he had had sight of it in his youth.'

'And have you ever seen it yourself?'

'I cannot in all truth say that I have. No. But there is always a first time, is there not, Mistress Henrietta?'

'I will look out for it and I will be sure to tell you when I do see it.'

'Indeed you must.'

He was pulling at the turf, nipping at the small flowers that grew there. 'What do you call these?' he asked. He held the flowers out to her.

She bent over his outstretched palm. 'That is self-heal I think. And this yellow one is trefoil. Maisie used to tell me the names of the flowers.'

He repeated the words, 'Self-heal and trefoil,' and then paused, shredding the little flowers with his peat-stained fingers.

'And tell me, what is the butter-coloured plant that scrambles among the hedgerows and smells like the scent of heaven..'

'I think you must mean honeysuckle.' She would not have said that he was a man to notice flowers or the scent of them.

'Honeysuckle. Yes. I knew that word but I had forgotten it. My wife told me.' He glanced at her. 'You bring it into the house, do you not?'

She put it in her room, and sometimes she left a jug of it on the big table in the hall, amid the dishes and pots. Ishbel had tut-tutted, saying it would attract insects, but had left it where it was.

She hesitated. 'I do. But if you do not like it . . .'

'No no. I like it fine. I like it just fine. It has been much too long since there have been flowers in my house.' He brushed his hands together, and she saw with some regret that he was preparing to

111

get up. 'Mistress Henrietta, I must be going. There is work to be done and here I am lingering in the hills with you like a gypsy.' He paused. 'But the day is beautiful just.'

'Manus?'

'Henrietta?'

'I have a question for you.'

'Ask away.'

'You say there is work to be done. Is there nothing I can do?'

He looked incredulous. 'What could you do?' he asked, doubtfully. 'You with your soft fingers and little strength in you!'

'But I am not as weak as you suppose – indeed I am not weak at all now. And your house is – forgive me – your house is very neglected.'

She saw that she had injured his pride. He got to his feet and whistled to his horse, two fingers in his mouth. The chestnut mare raised her head at the sound and came cantering over to nuzzle at his hand.

He said stiffly, 'I am not in the habit of spending much time there.'

'But I am,' she persisted. 'And now that the summer is here, the sunshine shows all the cobwebs and a distressing quantity of dust. And the drapes are disgraceful.' To her alarm, she heard her mother's voice, practical and precise, issuing from her own mouth. Still, she had better go on, now that she had begun. 'I know that there are kists upstairs full of good woollen and linen cloth. I have seen them.'

'Have you now?'

'There is a great deal that Ishbel and I could do if you would give us permission. There is so much that we could do to make your house more . . .' She hesitated. Oh well, she thought, it must be said. 'To make it more . . .'

'*Siobhalt*,' he finished for her, with a kind of distant irony, keeping his temper. 'Civilised. Is that what you are meaning to say?' He stood up. 'Are you saying that I am an uncivilised highlander, Mistress Henrietta Dalrymple?'

She stood up, too. As well be hanged for a sheep as a lamb. But she saw his mouth twitch and thought that he was laughing at her after all, that the day had wrought its magic on him and he was still in indulgent mood. Well, she would tell him the truth.

'It is nothing to do with you being Highland or Lowland. It has much to do with you being a man . . .' Again she hesitated. 'A man alone.'

He gave a little sigh of agreement. 'Aye, well, you are right there. And my wife would have said as much herself.'

'I think any woman would.'

The mare butted at him impatiently and he rubbed her soft nose.

'Henrietta, are you coming home with me? You may ride if you please and I will walk beside you.'

'Very well, if you don't mind.'

'No. I don't mind.'

He lifted her onto the mare and then stood a moment, regarding her steadily, running his fingers up and down the animal's silky mane.

'Henrietta, you may do exactly as you please upon my island, except that you must not go walking beside the cliffs for I tell you now that my heart will not stand it. And you may do as you please with my house. I have neglected it these many years past and you are right in all you say. And besides, I have beasts to see to and rents to collect and quarrels to settle. So you can do it with my blessing. Tell my wee friend Ishbel that you and she can make of the house what you will.'

He turned away from her, taking up the reins. 'Let us go home,' he said.

'Yes,' she said. 'Oh yes, Manus, let us go home!'

ELEVEN

Alys and Donal have walked for most of the morning. She can hardly believe that such a small island can encompass such a complex landscape. She and her family rambled the island footpaths years ago, but today Donal has taken her to places she has never seen before, where well-defined paths are few and far between. Most of the time they have simply scrambled across country, with Donal stopping now and then to get his bearings. There are marshy places below and patches of scree above; oceans of bracken and tumbled heaps of impassable boulders. You could get lost for days here, she thinks. Or for ever.

Now, though, for a mile or so, they have been following a track along the western side of the island. It is narrow but reasonably well defined. Sometimes a stone bridge, often just one big flagstone, carries it across a trickle of water. 'This used to link the old villages of Garve,' says Donal. 'But they are long gone and the people with them.'

'How do you know where they were?'

He shrugs. 'We just know. I've always known. Sometimes you'll see a patch of marshy ground where the yellow irises grow. Look, over there.'

'I see it.'

'Well, that was maybe a spring, and do you see beside it, just a patch of grey?'

'Maybe. It's hard to tell.'

'Aye, well, it's hardly there. The ghost of a patch, then. But that will have been a cottage or more than one. A *clachan*, my father would call it. A small village.'

'It's so sad.'

'Aye, it is. This was once a populous place with maybe five or six hundred people.'

'Why did people move? Was it the clearances?'

He shakes his head. 'Nothing so definite. No landowner came along and threw people off to make room for sheep. Not here, anyway. But people were very poor and often harshly treated by landowners and factors alike. The prospects elsewhere were better, so folk just trickled away. And then, of course, the twentieth century hit us. And the twenty first.'

'You need more people to come and live here.'

'We need work to bring them and more houses.'

'Do you think it will happen?'

'Maybe. Things are looking better than they have done for a while.'

New developments are afoot: craft workshops, small-scale projects that might make all the difference. In the twenty-five years since Alys last visited the place the population has fallen drastically, so the changes have come not a day too soon. But talking about all this seems to make Donal angry, and he strides out so that she has to run to keep up with him.

'Slow down!' she says.

'I'm sorry.' He halts and waits for her to catch up. 'We have to turn off here anyway.'

Further on, the track becomes impassable where rocks have fallen into the sea, so they cut across a steep ridge, towards the middle of the island. There they rest on a springy slope looking across a green basin of land, and drink mineral water and eat chocolate.

'Up there,' says Donal, pointing to his left, 'is an old Celtic fortress. You can just make out the shape of it. And very strange it is, too.'

'The rocks are like teeth.'

'They say Diarmid brought Grania there.'

'You mean the one who was married to Finn McCool?'

Alys listens to BBC Radio Four as she works and absorbs all kinds of bits of knowledge, subconsciously.

'I can't remember the details of it,' he says 'But Diarmid stole Grania from Finn, who was a great hero. He brought her to the Dun up there, but she had her wicked way with the local lad as well, and then Diarmid killed him.'

'The hussy.'

He grins at her. 'There's always a woman at the bottom of these things, Alys.'

'I don't know about that.'

'I do.'

They lean against each other, watching the clouds roll over from the west. He is very solid and strong and warm. She wonders if he might kiss her but he is still shy. She wonders if she should just kiss him, but is fearful of rejection. He is so hard for her to read, so foreign to her.

'Say something in Gaelic'

'What am I to say?'

'I don't know. Something about me,' she says, casually.

'*Oh, m'eudail, a ghràidh!*' he says. '*A bheil thu fhathast airson m'fnàgail?* Oh, my dear, my darling. Do you still want to leave me?'

'What did you say?'

'You'll just have to guess.'

'Is it rude?'

'Not at all.'

'Tell me.'

'No, I can't!'

He shakes his head and then thinks for a bit and says, chanting the words slightly, making them sound formal:

> '*Is tu ceum an fhèidh air a' bheinn*
> *Is tu steud-each air còmhnard,*
> *Is tu eireachdas an t-eala a' snàmh*
> *Is tu àilleachd gach miann àllainn . . .*'

'Gosh,' she says. 'I'm deeply impressed. I thought you couldn't speak the language.'

'I can't. But it's a kind of song. My dad used to say it to my mother.'

'And I don't suppose you can tell me the words to that one, either?'

'Yes, I can.'

'Go on, then.'

He thinks about it for a moment and then in a low voice says:

> 'You are the step of the deer on the hill,
> You are the step of the steed on the plain,
> You are the grace of the swan swimming,
> You are the loveliness of all lovely desires.'

The words trail off. A whaup shoots across the sky like a falling star, the notes trailing behind, drilling into the silence.

'What a magical place this is,' she says.

He moves, impatiently.

'What's wrong?' she asks, aware of his change of mood.

'I don't know, Alys.' He sighs. 'It *is* magical. And the old man is quite right when he says it's a thin place. But it does us no good at all to say so. We've had too much bloody Celtic twilight over the years, if you ask me.'

'I suppose so,' she agrees, reluctantly.

'Too many people try to make this island into something that it's not.'

'What do you mean?' She's defensive in the face of what she

takes to be criticism of herself as a visitor, an incomer.

'Look,' he says, half apologetically. 'It's a very beautiful place, right enough, and that's important. We owe it a duty of care, if you like. But folk are just the same here as anywhere else.' He has turned to face her and now he takes her hands in his own. 'They fall in love and they quarrel, they're kind and they're spiteful. They laugh, and they cry and they complain. Oh, how the buggers complain! People need to eat and to earn money here just the same as anywhere else. So why shouldn't they have the right to live here and do that, rather than in Glasgow or Edinburgh? I love the place in my bones but that's the only magic I know here. The human kind.'

'Oh God, Donal,' she says suddenly. 'I don't want to go home.'

'Do you not?'

'I really don't want to leave.'

She looks into his eyes, with their long sooty lashes. Grey eyes with the sea in them. And she is lost.

He leans across and kisses her, very gently, on the lips. 'Hush now,' he says. He puts his arms round her and pulls her close. She can feel his heart beating strongly through his shirt. He kisses her again. Through the sensation of his lips on hers, dry and warm, she is aware of the scent of the island, the sound of the skylark, the green of the turf and the blue of sea and sky. All these things are bound up together. She closes her eyes and sees Donal as a young boy, rushing along the beach with sandy legs, sees him as a grown man, pulling strongly on his oars, narrowing his eyes against the dazzle, staring out to sea. She feels as though her whole life has been aimed at this moment like an arrow shot from a bow.

They are brought up short by a little squall blowing in suddenly from the west, showering them with rain.

He pulls her to her feet. 'Shall we go back to the hotel?'

She nods. 'My knees are wobbly.'

'Are they? I don't often have that effect on women!'

'How would you know?'

She sways against him and he steadies her.

'Is there a short cut?' she asks.

'Not really. But it won't take long.'

When they get back, she smuggles him up to her hotel room. There is something very funny and very stimulating about this.

'I feel as though I'm sixteen again,' she says. 'But I get the idea that Mrs Cameron wouldn't approve.'

'Why? Do you think the gardener shouldn't be found in a guest's bedroom? Do you worry that I'll lose my job?'

'Maybe.'

'I don't think so, Alys. There's nobody else to do it, for one thing.'

'Anyway, I didn't mean that. I just don't think she would approve of me.'

'Ah, you mean she'll think you've seduced me, wicked lowlander that you are!'

'She's very protective of you.'

'Is she?' He grins but offers no other comment.

He hangs the 'Do not disturb' sign on the doorknob and locks the door. She draws the curtains. They take off their muddy boots and then, suddenly shy of each other, they start to take off their clothes.

Much to her amusement, he fumbles in his jacket pocket and brings out a couple of condoms in their little packets.

'Good God,' she says. 'Did you plan this?'

It occurs to her, fleetingly, that contrary to all her assumptions he might do this all the time: opportunistically seducing the hotel guests.

Perhaps he should be hurt by the question, but he takes it in his stride.

'I don't make a habit of it,' he says mildly. 'But with you, I just caught myself hoping. You know?'

She lies on the bed looking up at him, enjoying the sight of him. 'Do they sell them in the post office?' she can't resist asking.

'My ex-wife left a job lot of them behind,' he says drily. 'Hope to God they're not past their sell-by date.'

They start to laugh and their mutual embarrassment dissolves.

His body is pale and hard, but his arms are very brown. They roll and sway together among the white sheets with a passion that alarms them both. She sees his dark face above her, and then he is kissing her, long, deep kisses that make her moan with pleasure, his tongue inside her mouth, and at last he is deep inside her and they are moving together. She closes her eyes and sees seals, moving in deep water. She sees a boat breasting the waves. She sees him rowing, pulling strongly on the oars, carrying them both to shore.

They come quickly, violently and at the same moment, trying to be quiet for the sake of Mrs Cameron's feelings. They sleep briefly in each other's arms, and then they wake to make love again, more slowly. He is shy and considerate at first, as though embarrassed by his earlier loss of control, but all at once he is abandoned and passionate again, and that arouses her even more. Their bodies go well together. It is as simple as that.

She drags her feet to slow time down. She counts the minutes. She looks at the clock. Time, she keeps thinking. We have no time. Only a handful of hours. I have to go away and we have no time.

The sun dips down the sky. 'My father will be wondering where I am,' says Donal apologetically. 'He will think I'm in the bar, drinking. Or lurking outside with the other addicts and smoking.'

'And I'd better put in an appearance at dinner.'

'Do you really have to go?'

'Don't. I can't bear it. I can't bear it.'

'Why?'

'Because I never meant to do this.'

'Are you sorry?'

'No, of course not. But I have to go home, don't I? To Edinburgh, to my son. I have to go home to my son.'

'There are telephones, Alys, and the postman comes. Even on Garve.'

Guiltily they creep downstairs, but there is no sign of Mr and Mrs Cameron. The barman grins at them as they go through the empty bar, but says nothing. None of his business, he thinks. But good man, Donal. Go for it.

Alys sees all this on his face and blushes. The flesh between her legs is swollen and a little bruised from the unaccustomed lovemaking. Her breasts, too. She can hardly bear for Donal to leave her.

They kiss in the garden, underneath the overhanging roses.

'Go, then,' she says pushing him away. 'You'd better go.' The space between them is a mile wide and cold as death. She is dizzy with the pain of it.

Why? she wonders. They are both adults, both unattached. Why can't he simply stay and have dinner with her and spend the night?

But then people would know and she would still have to get on the ferry in the morning.

From the gate she watches him climb into his rusty old van and drive away towards Ardachy. Turning back, she thinks she sees Mrs Cameron, watching her from one of the upstairs windows. She goes up to her room and begin to pack, methodically folding garments and shaking the fine white sand out of her shoes.

TWELVE

Summer was already passing and September had brought a different flush of colour to Eileen Garbh. The weather was still mild, and the sun shone on heather that flamed orange over the hills as it withered. But the days were shortening and after sunset there came a little chill of frost in anticipation of winter. Ishbel had taken to lighting a fire in Henrietta's room again, although that room, together with many others in the house, was certainly more 'siobhalt', more civilised than it had been a few months previously. Walls and windows were hung with curtains that were, if not new, then cleaner.

There were few carpets, but such as there were had been washed. Henrietta had taken old Mhairi's advice and had them soaked in lye, then rinsed and trampled with soft soap and warm water for half an hour until all the dirt was out of them. She would have pinned up her skirts to take part in the barefoot trampling herself, had not Mhairi forbidden it.

'A lady such as yourself cannot do it — it would be a shame to the household! My Lord would think shame to see it.'

'He would not see it. I would make sure of that.'

'Nevertheless, you must not do it, Mistress Dalrymple!'

And so she had to keep herself apart and watch the other lassies enjoying themselves, cavorting amid the soapsuds with their skirts kilted up to their knees.

All summer long, however, she and Ishbel had worked together, sewing drapes and curtains and cushions, cleaning and polishing the old furniture with beeswax and oil of lavender, and airing and beating the mildewed tapestries, disturbing the lairs of a thousand spiders, until all the cobwebs were banished along with as many woodlice and earwigs. The whole house smelled of polish and of the sweet herbs that they had strewn about: chiefly dried meadowsweet, which grew in the boggy places down by the shore.

While they worked Ishbel had taught Henrietta more of the Gaelic and had sung songs for her. 'I have never thought about it before, but so many of our songs are sad,' she said. 'But perhaps when we are truly happy we have no time for poetry.'

Henrietta had been diligent in learning the words, for she agreed with Manus that there was power in knowing the names of things. She had taught Ishbel many Scotch songs in return: the ancient and mysterious ballads that Maisie had once sung to her, tales of love and loss and betrayal such as 'The Demon Lover' and 'The Three Corbies' and 'Edward, Edward'. She still thought about Gabriel constantly, but with less of the desperate misery that had once beset her. The idea of him had become a counterpoint of regret to all her days, but she found solace in the work and in her companionship with Ishbel and with the other women of the household.

Manus came and went in the middle of all this activity, affecting not to notice what was going on, but he certainly smiled more often and his manner to Henrietta was altered in other, more subtle ways. For one thing, he was much less prickly with her. She suspected that there were times when he was actually glad to see her, when the occasional conversation or passing courtesy gave him pleasure.

For Henrietta herself there had come a moment of revelation. It had been at the very height of summer, not long after their meeting above the *lochan* of the water bull, when she had glanced from her window in the tower and seen Manus riding along the shore towards the house, at his usual mad gallop, spurring the mare on with heels and knees. The plaid flowed out behind him, blue against the white sand. Watching him, she thought that he looked beautiful as a hero out of the old ballads. Afterwards she realised that it had been very unwise of her to conjure such a strange and enticing image, but there it was, and she could not easily dismiss it once it had come to her. After all, he had a pleasing appearance, and she was still very young and very lonely.

That day, she had watched him until he rode out of her sight and into the courtyard of the house. She had heard him shouting for the boy to come and take his horse, and then the slam of the big oak door. She could picture him throwing himself onto a bench while Ishbel brought him his dram, and the thought of him gave her pleasure. The sensible part of her acknowledged the folly of this enthralment. The fine white sand of the island filled her brogues, and blew about the floor of her room, and even trickled softly out of the sheets of her bed in the morning. It had infiltrated her life in much the same way as this fascination with Manus had trickled inexorably into her head.

She could not decide whether it was her growing absorption in Manus or her gradual adjustment to life on the island that had wrought the change in her, but as the summer wore on she had begun to think that if she must be imprisoned – and it seemed that she must – then there were worse places in this world to have to live out her days. Like her marriage to William, it was turning out to be better than she had feared, and the people of the island were very far from being the brutes she might have expected.

They were poor, certainly, and led lives heavily circumscribed by the landscape. They sang their songs – often as an aid to a daily labour that was bitterly hard or downright dangerous – and they worked within the constraints of the land and its seasons, understanding it more fully than city folk ever would. The island was remote and the outside world impinged on them very little.

They were polite to her and wished her no ill, and for her part she was growing to value them as friends. Although the reasons for her kidnapping and her loss of Gabriel still tormented her, Henrietta's natural disposition was to make the best of things. It had always stood her in good stead until now.

But this physical awareness of Manus was disturbing. She had not known that her body could betray her in this way. At first the feelings were so strange that she could not even name them. She had never known this longing that was as palpable as hunger, even for William, who had come to her very gently and carefully as though ashamed of himself for loving her, and had left her body unhurt but largely unmoved. She could only hazard guesses now at the nature of her own sensations, remembering the whispered conversations she had sometimes overheard between young servants in Edinburgh and later at Linlithgow.

She kept her desire a secret even from Ishbel and began to avoid Manus as far as possible, not as she had once avoided him, out of fear, but out of confusion and to try to preserve her peace of mind. But sometimes she found herself watching him: the way his brow creased in a frown when he was concentrating, the way he laughed out loud at something one of the men said to him. She watched the way he stood, the way he rode, the way he sprawled in a chair, wondering at her absorption in something so ordinary.

For the past nine months her body had been starved of human contact as never before. All her life she had been petted and made much of: by her mother and her father, by Maisie and by Thomas, during her childhood. Later William had been a loving companion and then Gabriel had clung to her and suckled at her breast, for she had insisted on feeding him herself, much to Grisel's disapproval: 'You should find yourself a good, respectable wet-nurse.' But Henrietta would not be deterred. Now she found that she missed the warmth of human contact, the simple touch of hand upon hand, with an acute longing.

It would be enough, she found herself thinking, if he would

take my hand sometimes. Then it came to her that it might not be enough at all. And so she flung herself into the work of the house with more energy than ever. But at nights she lay awake long after the household was asleep, and thought about Manus.

In early September, he went to the mainland again. He told her briefly that he was going to Edinburgh, and that he would try to catch a glimpse of her son if he possibly could, but the enterprise was fraught with danger. He had even forsaken his plaid in favour of breeches and an old blue travelling coat with engraved silver buttons that had once belonged to his father. 'It would never do to draw attention to myself,' he said. 'And so I must pretend to be as lowland as you are, Henrietta.'

'Oh, you will never be that.'

He frowned at her sharpness. 'I will do what I can to bring you news of your boy, but you are not to expect too much.'

'I know that I can expect very little from you, sir,' she said stiffly.

'Then you won't be disappointed.'

He could never bear what he called her 'city manners', her moments of formality. It always made him defensive and cross with her.

'I had thought to bring you something from Edinburgh.' He was ready to go, gazing at her from the doorway of the great hall, where he stood with his arms folded, leaning on a stone pillar. 'But how would I know what to bring you? Uncivilised highlander that I am.'

She mustn't let him go away like this. What if misfortune befell him? What if he never came back?

'You could bring me something, Manus. If you would be so kind.'

'What?' He came marching into the room, and then hesitated. 'Do not say your son again. You know I cannot do it.'

'I would not say my son again. I would not dare.' She felt a lump in her throat and tears forming wretchedly behind her eyes. She clenched her fists so that her fingernails dug into her palms.

He came over to her and took her hand, his face softening all of a sudden.

'I am sorry, Henrietta. I am ill tempered at the nature of my errand, but I should not vent my anger on you of all people, my little friend. What do you want me to bring you? Name it – whatever you like within reason – and I will do my best to find it for you.'

She thought, I should like a pair of white silk stockings, and some scarlet taffeta for a new gown, and a set of scarlet and white ribbons for my hair. But I cannot tell him as much. It would shame me to tell him. And he would not fetch them, anyway.

She said slowly, 'I think I should like some plants. Bulbs and perhaps seeds.'

She could not have surprised him more had she actually demanded the silk stockings and scarlet taffeta.

'Plants?' he asked. 'What plants?'

'I should like to establish a garden here.'

'But there is a kitchen garden already.'

'Aye.' She pulled a face. 'But it grows only kale stalks and sour gooseberries. I should like a flower garden and perhaps a herb garden.'

'Henrietta, the whole island is a flower garden.'

'But I should like to have one of my own. Not a wilderness but a garden, however small, where I can plant things and weed them and . . . and tend to them. We had such a garden in Edinburgh. It fell away down the hill in terraces and you could see Fife beyond the water. And in Linlithgow there was an old walled garden where there was an avenue with walks. There were columbines, hollyhocks, poppies and marigolds. Oh and such roses! The scent of them on a summer's evening . . .'

'You cannot grow hothouse blooms here, woman! They would not survive.'

'No. But all that I have named will grow out of doors in Scotland. In fact, I think the winter was colder at Linlithgow than here. I should like some bulbs to plant so that they will flower in the spring. And I should like tulips best of all.'

'Henrietta, they will cost a king's ransom and they will never grow here. The sea winds would blight them.'

'I am sure they would grow. I am sure I could make them, if I could find a sheltered spot. It is windy here, but there are few frosts. And the willows provide some protection from the winds. Ah but you are right,' she conceded with regret. 'They are too expensive. So if I cannot have tulips it must be something else. Anemones, perhaps, and Lenten lilies. Bulbs from Holland. I care not what. Lavender roots and some marigold seeds. And roses. I should very much like to have roses, Manus.'

'Well, well . . . I cannot promise to bring you a garden, but I will see what I can find.'

She never ceased to surprise him. He turned and left her, and as he strode down to the shore he was already wondering how he might manage to bring her what she had asked for. Tulips were rare and exotic. He had seen them on few occasions himself and then they had seemed very foreign to him, almost sinister with their dark hearts, their whorls of colour and fringed petals. Why did he feel the need to please her? As the boat which would take him to the mainland rolled and heaved under him, he found himself wishing that he had kissed her goodbye, even if it had only been a decorous kiss of friendship on the cheek.

Henrietta found that she missed Manus very much. She missed the sight of him going to and from the house. She missed his infrequent smiles and his teasing words. She worried about him, too, fretting that in her desire for news of her son she might have sent him into danger. But then she thought that he would never be so foolish as to risk overmuch for her sake. She had sent him nowhere; he had gone away on business of his own. The enquiry after Gabriel was only incidental. Nevertheless, she also worried about what business he might have in the capital. Highlanders of his persuasion were not welcome in Edinburgh and might be arrested upon any pretext.

At last – and much to her relief – the night came when his step was heard on the stairs and he came striding into the great hall, where Henrietta was seated before the fire. She couldn't hide her joy at the sight of him and ran to greet him. He embraced her warmly in return and then flung himself into a high-backed chair on the opposite side of the fire. Ishbel had brought ale in a tankard and he drank deeply.

'How I hate your city, Henrietta,' he observed, wiping his mouth, where three or four days' growth of beard shadowed the skin, 'And how very glad I am to be back here upon my own island. Not even a storm would have kept me from the sound tonight.'

'I'm glad to see you safe.'

'Are you?' He was silent and suddenly subdued, casting her a strange, shrewd glance. He shook his head. 'Oh, Henrietta!'

'What is wrong?'

'Nothing. There is not a thing wrong – now. Now that I am back here. And you are safe and well. And I have to tell you that your son is safe, too. Maisie still has the care of him.'

'Have you seen him?'

'I have not. But I sent one of my friends, a young man of great charm and wit, even though he is also highland like myself,' he added. 'And he had a long conversation – nay, several long conversations – with your sister-in-law's maidservant, I believe, a lass called Anna. He was not to mention you at all, but only to ask for the little lad. And when I could get him to leave off telling me about Anna and all her charms – I think I have encouraged a most unsuitable match there — he was able to tell me that the child is well and thriving. They are all kind to him for they say he is much less thrawn than his cousin Janet who is, by all accounts, very free with her slaps and pinches. But she does not slap or pinch Gabriel, for she loves him more than any other in the house, and will not allow him to be punished under any circumstances. And even Grisel does all her bidding.'

She could not help but laugh at this. 'Thank God for your news. You do not know how it gladdens my heart.'

'I think I do know. But I have even more to cheer your heart, Mistress Henrietta.'

'Oh?'

He raised his voice and called, 'Iain! Where are you with the box, man?'

'I am coming, sir. I am coming,' said a resentful voice from the stairs. Iain struggled into the room with a sizeable but rather battered wooden kist and set it down in front of Manus.

'No, no,' said Manus, irritably. He was very tired from his journey and inclined to be cross. 'No, Iain. They are for the lady, not for me. I shall have nothing whatsoever to do with them. Although I expect you will have plenty, for she will expect you to dig for her and plant for her and do all the other things that are demanded of a gardener.'

'A gardener?' said Iain, casting Henrietta a wild-eyed sideways glance, like a wary horse.

'Aye. Somebody must help her and I am certainly no gardener. Nor do I intend to become one just to please Mistress Henrietta here.'

During this exchange Henrietta had been opening the wooden kist and unpacking various interesting objects from the straw that cushioned them: a collection of bulbs and corms and plants with the earth still clinging to their roots. There was a paper inside with a list of contents written out in a thin hand: anemones and narcissi, lavender roots and roses both red and white, tiny packets of seeds and – 'Manus! Oh, Manus, you have brought me tulips!'

A little leather bag contained some half dozen of the nut-brown bulbs.

'Aye.' He took another draught of his ale. 'I found a nurseryman in Edinburgh who supplied me with all these other things, the lilies and the lavender and the like. But I had to go elsewhere for your tulips. They were more difficult. And you had best take good care of them, Henrietta, for they cost more than all else put together. And the man owed me a few favours at that.'

'You should not have been so extravagant!'

'Why not?' He shrugged. 'It is my own money and I will do as I please with it. And besides, you do not mean that. You are very glad indeed that I have been extravagant on your behalf so you may as well own to it and thank me properly for my trouble.'

'Well, perhaps I am,' she conceded, 'And I do thank you most heartily for your kindness.'

She went over to him and planted a kiss on his prickly cheek. He didn't flinch from the contact, though the surly Iain coughed disapprovingly in the background – she thought he would probably go home and call her a forward hussy, or whatever its Gaelic equivalent was.

She began to lay the plants and the bulbs out, gloating over them.

Iain hovered in the doorway, looking miserable. 'I'd best be going to my home, then,' he said.

'You had.' Manus grinned. 'But you can come back tomorrow and make a start on digging Mistress Henrietta's garden.'

'Where am I to dig?'

'Wherever she tells you. I know nothing about such things.' He waved his hand airily towards the window. 'She must go around the house and choose the best spot, which only she will know, and then you can dig, and carry seaweed up from the shore in a basket, for the soil is very poor, and the ground will need a great deal of preparation. That is what I was told in Edinburgh. You will have a very hard job of it.'

Iain was allowed to go, with the promise that he would come early the following morning and make a start on the garden. The room fell very quiet. Henrietta was still kneeling by the kist, engrossed in her plants. Manus sat with his legs stretched out in front of him, and an empty ale mug in his hand. Casting a little glance at him, she saw that his eyes were closing. But suddenly he sat up.

'Mother Mary, I almost forgot,' he said. 'I have something else for you.'

'Something else?'

'Yes. Now where did I put them?' He felt in the pockets of his blue coat. 'Ah, here they are.' With the air of a magician, he drew out a skein of silken ribbons, scarlet and white. 'They were selling them at the booths near your old home, and I saw them and thought . . . well, I thought they would do very nicely for you, Henrietta.'

'Ribbons.' She took them from him, and coloured up, almost as bright scarlet. 'You are very good!' She ducked her head, not knowing what else to say to him. 'You are a good friend to me.'

'I hope I am. God bless your wearing of them.'

'Amen to that. And thank you.'

She knelt by the kist for some time, fingering the ribbons in her lap, and when next she stole a glance in his direction she saw that he had fallen fast asleep.

THIRTEEN

It was a warm September night and Henrietta was seated by the window while Ishbel brushed her hair before bed. Big white moths blundered in every now and then and singed themselves against the lamp. Maisie had brushed Henrietta's hair every night; it was only occasionally that Ishbel offered to do it, and Henrietta was shy of asking her, but tonight she had volunteered .

'Ishbel,' she said, 'tell me what is happening on the island. Everyone seems so busy.'

There was a sense of preparation, a feeling of excitement in the air.

'I always forget that you know so little. In a while, it will be the feast of Micheil.' Ishbel was plainly excited too. 'St Michael, you would say. It is a time of great celebration for the whole island. But do you not have this feast in Edinburgh?'

'No. Not at all.' Henrietta could not imagine that the Kirk would approve of such things. 'What happens?'

'Well . . .' Ishbel paused in her brushing. 'On the eve of the feast we make the *struan Mhicheil*.'

'And what is that?'

'Oh, it is a great cake, baked from oats and barley and rye. We have harvested all these things and ground them into meal.'

'And where is it cooked?'

'Down in the great hall. The lads bring a big flagstone in from

133

the moors, specially for the purpose. And a prepared lambskin is placed on it, and that is to spread the batter on. The fire is special, too. For there are certain kinds of wood which must not be used.'

'Why not?'

'They are not holy, not good for this purpose: the aspen and the blackthorn chiefly. You can come and help if you like!'

'Yes, I should like that. How is the cake made?'

'The meal is mixed with milk, and then there is a batter of cream and eggs and butter which is put upon it in layers and cooked.'

'Oh, it sounds very good, Ishbel.'

'It is very good – you will see. And besides that the lassies make wee *struans* to give to their special friends, to their sweethearts, you know? They put cranberries or brambles into them, but my Lord Manus likes the blaeberries best of all.'

'Does he? And do you make him a *struan*?'

'Oh no!' The girl looked horrified. 'Well, I generally make one and he eats it, right enough, but I would not give it to him, you understand. Whatever would he think? But I may make one with brambles for Seamus. For he is very fond of the taste of them.'

'So does no one make a *struan* for Manus?' Henrietta persisted.

Ishbel began brushing vigorously. 'No one in the house would dare. Well, old Mhairi might, for she loves him dearly, but then she is an old woman and she has known him since before he could walk.' Ishbel laughed. 'She once told me that the heather used to hurt his little toes and he would come crying to her and she would feed him bannocks and cream and honey to take the pain away.'

'Good God, I cannot imagine such a thing.'

'No. It is hard to think that he was once a wee lad himself, isn't it? But that is how Mhairi remembers him.'

One afternoon, soon after this discussion, Henrietta went up into the hills with Ishbel to pick blaeberries. 'Though it is late in the season' she observed, 'and we will not find as many as earlier. The birds will have eaten their fill.'

Henrietta had to be shown which were the blaeberry bushes and how to look beneath them and close to the stem to find the hidden berries: somewhat sparse, now that autumn was coming, but fat and juicy and aromatic nevertheless. Ishbel also showed her how to avoid the glossy but poisonous ling berries which grew among the blaeberry scrub. It was an absorbing occupation, and soon Henrietta – always pursuing a bigger bush, with better fruit – strayed some distance from her companion. At last, seeing the distant smudge of Henrietta's dress, as she clambered among the rocks, Ishbel called, 'I must go home now! Will you come too?'

Henrietta straightened her back, which was aching from the constant stooping. Flies buzzed about her head and she brushed them away. She looked at the half-empty basket by her side.

'Not yet awhile.'

'Very well. But don't be too long. The days are shortening.'

Ishbel went back down the path towards the house, while Henrietta carried on picking, occasionally popping one or two of the berries into her mouth to refresh herself. She clambered over a ridge and seeing a hollow ahead of her, soft with heath and fern, and planning to rest there for a spell, scrambled down into it and almost tripped over Manus McNeill, who was lying full length on a bed of heather, staring at the sky, his arms pillowing his head.

She almost dropped the basket of berries.

'Manus! What a fright you gave me!'

'And you me,' he said. He had raised himself on one elbow, but remained cushioned among the heather.

'I'm sorry if I disturbed you.'

'This is a favourite place of mine. No one can find me here. Unless someone trips over me as you have just done.'

'I'm sorry,' she repeated.

'I don't mind, Henrietta. I don't mind at all, since it is only yourself. You are always careful not to disturb me.'

'Ishbel must not be coming to me with your problems. That is what you told me.'

'So I did. Well, well,' he said, making room for her, 'we can always change our minds. And often we do. Why don't you sit down, now that you are here?'

She sat down beside him in the heather. He was right. It was a comfortable and sheltered spot.

'What are you doing up here?' he asked

'Picking blaeberries. For the *struans* for the feast of Micheil.'

'What do you know of the feast of Micheil?' he asked, squinting at her in the late-afternoon sunlight.

'Nothing at all but what Ishbel has told me. She says that cakes are made, and that blaeberries and brambles must be gathered to flavour them and so I offered to help.'

He peered into her basket. 'I love blaeberries!' He began to take them out and eat them, weighing them in the palm of his hand. 'I think they have the best taste in the world.'

'So Ishbel told me.'

'Did she? Then why will nobody ever make blaeberry *struan* just for me?'

'Because you are their chieftain!'

He looked rather dispirited. 'All the same, I think I should like it.'

'Then I must make you one.'

'So you are not afraid of me any more?'

'Only when you frown at me.'

He seemed genuinely amazed by this. 'Do I frown at you?'

'Oh yes. Quite often. It makes you look very stern.'

'Then I must try not to do it. God knows I have little enough cause where you are concerned.' Absentmindedly he began to pick at the berries again.

She snatched the basket away from him. 'I have been hours picking these and you have half of them eaten already. Leave them alone, will you, or I will be frowning at *you*, Manus McNeill.'

'Surely you can spare me one or two?'

'One or two? You have taken a good handful already.'

'Then I will just have to help you pick more.'

'Aye, you will.'

There was a silence for a moment, then he said, 'Henrietta, I have been thinking about your husband.'

'About William? What about him?' She was surprised that the thought of her dead husband should even enter his head.

'I was wondering, were you happy, you two?'

'Very happy. He was a good man.'

'But much older than you?'

'Who has been telling you these things?'

'Ishbel. But don't blame her, for I asked her.'

'Why?'

'I was curious about you. About your life before you came here. Forgive me, Henrietta.'

'No, I don't mind. I would have told you myself if you had asked me. It might have been a disastrous match but my brother and his wife thought that we would do very well together, and strangely enough they were right.'

'I'm sure they were happy about that.'

'Well, they were.'

She remembered the day when she had finally capitulated. Thomas had already broached the subject with her but she had rejected the idea out of hand.

'I cannot marry William Shaw. He is old enough to be my grandfather.'

'But, Etta!' It was what her father had called her and her brother used the name in a conscious effort to influence her. 'Etta, can you not see that it is as good an offer as you are ever likely to get? He is rich, he is kind, he has a comfortable house.'

All of it was true. She had her own small dowry, her tocher, and William had promised to settle a very large sum of money, a jointure, on her. Her future would be completely secure.

'Why can I not stay here in Edinburgh?' she asked, plaintively.

'Has anybody told you that you cannot?'

'But you want to be alone with Grisel.'

'Oh, Henrietta, you can surely forgive us for wanting to spend a little time alone together. That is not the point. The point is that we have your best interests at heart.'

'You make me feel as though I will be a burden to both of you.'

'I would not have put it that way,' said Thomas, quietly.

'But it is the plain truth.'

'Then, my dearest Henrietta, why will you not listen to me?' He spoke affectionately, his arm around her shoulders. 'We both love you very much, Grisel and I. Grisel in particular wants to be sure that you do not feel forced into a marriage of convenience. But William Shaw will give you an establishment of your own. He will be kind to you. He will protect you.'

'I should have no need of his protection.'

But she knew that she was already defeated and the words were half-heartedly spoken.

Thomas pressed home his advantage. 'You do not need it. You will always have Grisel and myself. But it would be good for you, all the same. You should agree to this marriage, Henrietta. Believe me, you will never have another offer like this one.'

And so, in the late autumn of the year in which her parents had died, not long after her sixteenth birthday, Henrietta Frances Dalrymple had been married to William Ignatius Shaw in a simple ceremony with few witnesses save her old friend and servant Maisie, her brother Thomas, and his betrothed, Grisel Shaw. Thereafter Henrietta removed herself and her possessions to William's house in Linlithgow and took Maisie with her.

In the middle of the ceremony Grisel rushed out of the kirk and was found later, leaning on a tombstone, her face pale and with beads of sweat on her brow. She had been violently sick. She and Thomas were married some three weeks later; Grisel came to the altar with a loose dress disguising her already swollen belly and when the baby was born, barely seven months after the wedding, it was a plump and bonny girl, nothing like the sickly infant that might have been anticipated. There was a good deal of talk among friends and servants, but Thomas was genuinely delighted with his daughter and they named her Janet Thomasina.

'So it was a good match?' asked Manus, looking at her gravely. 'And you were content?'

'He had been a bachelor for so many years that it must have seemed very strange to him to be married. But he was gentle and attentive and altogether very kind to me. I had no cause for complaint.'

'He was lucky that you accepted him. Your brother should have found a younger and more suitable husband for you,' said Manus indignantly.

She was touched by his anger on her behalf. 'You forget, my looks were against me.'

His gaze met hers for a moment. 'Yes, Henrietta, I do forget. I forget all the time.'

He took a few more blaeberries from the basket, eating some and holding the rest out towards her. 'They are very good, you know. Taste for yourself.'

'I know.'

'Taste!' he insisted.

She opened her mouth and he put the berries on her tongue, squashing them gently so that the juice flowed onto her lips, staining them purple. She felt a great lurch of desire for him. He was still watching her, steadily, with a half-smile on his face.

'Open your mouth again.'

He fed her with more berries from her basket, pushing them gently between her lips. 'Your tongue is purple.'

'So is yours.'

'And your lips . . . Your lips are stained with juice.'

His hands were on her shoulders. And then he was kissing her, and she was kissing him fiercely in return, clinging to him, falling over backwards with him on top of her, and the weight of his body was pinning her down upon the bed of heather. He was kissing her as though he could not help himself, twisting his hands in her hair, whispering to her in his own language. She was dizzy with new sensations. The blue sky reeled above her and she could smell the blaeberries, and the musk of his body as she clung to him. Then all at once there was a cold space above her, and he was standing up.

'Henrietta, I'm sorry. Oh dear God, I am so sorry.'

She tried to get up and he reached down and hauled her to her feet none too gently.

'It doesn't matter,' she said.

'But it does matter, it does. Henrietta, I cannot . . . I cannot . . .'

'Why can you not?'

He shook his head. 'How can I? Oh, God help me, Henrietta, it cannot be right that you are . . .'

'What? I am what?'

He groaned. 'That you are bought and sold in this way! God help me, I cannot do it!'

She didn't know how to reply. She didn't understand his words.

His face was grave. 'I will take you back to the house. Give me your basket. There are plenty of berries left.'

He went ahead of her down the hill, carrying the basket and occasionally holding out his hand to her, to help her down the steep places.

She laid her hand willingly in his, and could not help but be aware of the tingle of his skin against her own. She wondered if he felt it, too, and could only suppose that he did. But he was intent on restraining himself, and he could not stop frowning, a deep sad furrow on his brow, which was still there when they reached the hall door.

'Goodnight, Henrietta.' He bent down and planted a kiss on her forehead. Then he left her.

She did not see him again for a few days. When she did at last meet him on the stairs, he was polite, but intensely formal. He stood back to let her pass. She smiled at him and pretended that it did not matter, all the while searching his face for signs of desire. But she could make out nothing except a kind of puzzled despondency.

FOURTEEN

After Garve, Edinburgh seems like a suburb of hell: the traffic is too loud, the smells are too pungent, the noise is appalling. On this Saturday afternoon in July, the city which Alys usually finds so beautiful, so vibrant, just seems filthy, crammed with too many people and cars, all its pavements leopard-spotted with squashed chewing gum. She wants to be anywhere but here. She wants to be sitting on the turf at Ardachy, watching the sea. She wants to be with Donal. Her body aches for him. She drives in via busy Morningside Road, where all the traffic lights are against her, and picks Ben up in Bruntsfield. The house is a cool, quiet oasis. Ben is playing in the walled back garden with Millie's dog, a King Charles spaniel, but he comes running up the path to greet her with the liver-and-white dog at his heels. Not given to public hugs, he stands very close beside her nevertheless. He has begun to miss her. Two weeks, she thinks, was much too long. One week would have been enough.

'Two weeks was a bit long for him,' says John, much to her surprise. 'He was all right but then he started to miss you pretty badly.'

'I missed him, too.'

'You look well,' he says.

Millie has taken herself off to the kitchen to make tea. Relations are still a bit strained, though Millie wasn't the cause of the divorce. He met Millie later. At least that's what he tells Alys, and she believes him, now that he has no reason to lie to her. There was someone else, she knows. In fact there had probably been several 'someone elses' while they were married, but not Millie. Millie works in 'Human Resources'. She is charming and pretty and hugely efficient, but Alys always feels that she is being analysed for personality traits and occupational suitability whenever she is in her company. Analysed and, on the whole, found wanting. Millie thinks that Alys has a chaotic lifestyle. At least, that's what Alys suspects, but in her more rational moments she realises that she might just be paranoid about the whole thing.

Millie brings through a tray of tea and a glass of freshly squeezed orange juice for Ben and a plate of home-made biscuits ('You mean the woman actually makes biscuits?' Sophie will say incredulously when she hears about it later. Alys has been known to make the odd cake or tray bake; Sophie barely knows where her own kitchen is. She doesn't do gardening, either: not even a window box.)

Alys asks about Sorrento. 'John never took me to Sorrento,' she says cheerfully, with an effort at humour, but it misfires.

'Oh dear,' says Millie who is wilfully literal. 'I am sorry. Maybe you'll go there some day anyway.'

'I was only joking,' she says. 'But I'd love to go to Sorrento and I'm sure I will some day.' Next year, maybe, she thinks, if they can afford it. But would Ben want to go again?

'I want to see Garve,' he says, suddenly. Small Scottish islands, the Bay of Naples: it's all equally exciting to Ben.

The exhibition is called 'Children in Seventeenth century Scottish Art'. It's a summer show, and part of the official festival programme. Going was Sophie's idea. Alys has a kind of aversion to the festival. There's just too much going on. Like a child in a toy shop, she grows bewildered and cross and finishes up enjoying nothing at all. Besides, she has a horror of being part of an audience that is smaller than the cast of the play, and she is sick of fending off half-naked young actors promoting this or that production as she tries to negotiate the Royal Mile just to get to her own front door. But exhibitions are different. This is Sophie's period. It's what she teaches, among other things: Women in Scottish History after the Reformation.

'Come on,' she says to Alys on the phone. 'You'll like it, honestly. Come with me.'

'Only if we can get carrot cake in the café.'

'I promise there'll be carrot cake.'

Ben is spending the day at his granny's house in Linlithgow. John's widowed mother, Katy, with whom Alys enjoys a warm and lasting friendship, will be bringing him into Edinburgh on the train later on. Alys has arranged to meet them at five o'clock, so there will be plenty of time for the exhibition.

She and Sophie move inside the gallery and the racket of Princes Street traffic is replaced by the buzz of conversation and the echo of footsteps on wooden floors. The place smells of polish: beeswax and lavender. She always forgets how much she loves this gallery until she visits it again. It was a place of refuge for her, even when she was a student. The canvases evoke another time and place. A confident little boy stands behind his sister, who, seated at a spinet, is all unaware of him wielding a pair of scissors with malicious intent against the ribbons of her dress. A moon-faced girl in a lace cap clutches a wooden doll. Plump and pretty sisters dance together in a summer garden. There are whole families captured in rural settings with trees and flowers – and whippets.

'Why always whippets, I wonder?' asks Alys.

'They were fashionable canines,' says Sophie. 'Do you know King Charles spaniels were bred as foot-warmers for ladies? A sort of fur-covered hot water bottle.'

Alys has a sudden vision of Millie in a sedan chair, dog at her feet. It seems highly appropriate.

She stops in front of a large canvas depicting a miniature lady wearing a long yellow silk dress with a low, square-cut neck and nipped-in waist, dark curls caught up in tiny ringlets at either side of her head. It is a pale, clever, elfin face, half smiling, and one hand is stretched out to touch a rose.

'How old do you think she is?'

Sophie shrugs. 'She doesn't look very childish to me. She looks like a grown woman with a baby face. But that's par for the course.'

'Pretty, though.'

'Yes. She's very pretty. But they all look like little old women, don't they. Poor wee sods!'

'Who is she in all her finery, then? And how old is she? You've got the catalogue.'

Sophie consults the glossy booklet. 'Young Girl in a Garden, 1683,' she reads, and fans herself theatrically with the book. 'She could be twelve or twenty-two. Who would know?'

'It's just the way she's dressed.' Alys leans closer to examine the picture.

'Be careful,' says Sophie. 'The alarms will go off.'

'Look. Her hands are still quite podgy. And look at the curve of the cheek. That's childish enough.'

'Mm.' Sophie glances dubiously from her friend to the picture and back again. 'Well, she's a very elegant little lady, anyway,' she says. 'God, just look at it. Girlhood as a prelude to matrimony. And we think our kids are precocious! Come on, Alys, I'm desperate for a coffee.'

'1683,' says Alys. 'I'll bet . . .'

'What?'

'It must be the same age as the embroidered cabinet I was telling you about. The one on Garve.'

'That's right. Seventeenth-century. So?'

'I don't know. It just brings it to life somehow. The idea of somebody all those years ago making it, keeping it, putting all her things in it.'

'God, Alys, don't be so . . .'

145

'What?'

'I don't know. Sentimental.'

Alys only sighs.

Sophie looks at her in exasperation. 'What's the matter now?'

'I don't know.'

'You haven't been right in the head since you got back from that bloody island.'

'I know.'

'If I didn't know you better, I'd swear there was a man involved.'

'Well, maybe there was.'

'Is there something you're not telling me?'

'I've already told you about him. Donal McNeill. The man I used to know years ago, when we were kids.'

'So? You weren't very forthcoming about him. You just mentioned him in passing.'

'I know.'

'I need a coffee.'

'Me too.'

'Let's go find the café.'

Over coffee and carrot cake Sophie questions her friend, but Alys is already regretting her indiscretion. She hadn't meant to tell Sophie much about Donal at all.

'It was nothing,' she says. 'Just a bit of a fling.'

'Jesus!' says Sophie. 'I know you better than that. You don't go in for casual flings, Alys. That's my department.'

Alys shrugs. 'Well, this time I did, OK? I was footloose and fancy-free for once. I don't usually go anywhere without Ben, do I? But I think it was a mistake.'

'What's he like?'

'He's an islandman born and bred.'

'Oh yeah. Whatever that means!'

Not likely to want to leave the place, thinks Alys. Not ever. To change the subject she says, 'Can you look something up for me?'

'What?' asks Sophie. Now that she has topped up her caffeine levels she is happy again. 'What do you want to know?'

'Something to do with the history of Garve. I thought you might have access to . . . I don't know . . . records and things up at the university.'

'For Garve? Not likely.'

'Well, for Clan McNeill, then.'

'There you go with that name again. McNeill.' Alys kicks her under the table and she relents. 'Well, I could probably find some stuff, even if it's only on the net. But you could do that for yourself. Mind you, there are some specialist academic sites that only I can get access to. What do you want to know?'

'There was a McNeill who was laird of Garve. A long time ago.'

'I'll need a bit more than that, Alys. Do you know how many references you get when you type "McNeill" into a search engine?'

'I think the McNeills were given the island by the MacDonalds.'

'They would be. Most of those places were in the gift of the Lords of the Isles at one time or another. So what do you want to know?'

'I'm not sure, really. But his name was Manus: Manus McNeill.'

'Well, thank God it wasn't Iain or Allan.'

'Why?'

'Because it's reasonably uncommon, Manus.'

'Oh, I see.'

'Some remote forebear of your Donal, I suppose . . . ?'

'Maybe. I haven't the faintest idea. And he isn't my Donal.'

'Wait a minute. I need more coffee. This stuff's half froth.'

Sophie loves researching things. She gets the bit between her teeth and never gives up. She fetches two more cups of coffee and takes a notebook out of her bag.

'Now,' she says, suddenly businesslike. 'Manus McNeill. Possible dates?'

'I'm not sure about that, either.'

'Doh! Big help, Alys. How the hell do you expect me to do anything useful?'

'Well, say late sixteen hundreds and after? Early seventeen hundreds as well.'

'Same date as your embroidered cabinet, in fact.'

'Maybe.'

'Where are you getting your information from?'

'I'm not. It's just a long shot.'

'OK. And he was a chieftain of Garve?'

'That's what they say on the island.'

'So what do you want to know?'

'Oh, anything at all. Was he married? Did he have children?'

'Who told you about him? No, wait, let me guess. Donal McNeill, maybe?'

'Not just Donal. There are place names. And there are stories about Manus on the island.'

'What stories?'

Alys puts sugar in her cup and stirs her coffee, round and round, licking the froth off the spoon. She heaves a sigh. 'They say he had some great treasure, but he lost it. And they say . . .' She hesitates.

'What?'

'They say he had a bride who came from the sea.'

'Good God, Alys,' says Sophie, exasperated. 'It isn't much to go on! Folk tales.'

'I know. But I just wondered . . .'

'What?' Sophie is really curious now. 'What's so interesting about him?'

'I don't know. I've got a bee in my bonnet for some reason.'

'I can see that.'

'And I get the feeling that there's a connection with the embroidered cabinet.'

'Maybe so. Sounds like typical seventeenth-century raised work to me.' Sophie can't resist showing off her knowledge. 'They used to call it stumpwork but that's inaccurate and we're not supposed to use it any more – not rigorous enough, you see.' This is one of Sophie's obsessions: fashions in terminology, academic jargon.

Alys ignores the diversion. 'I think it belonged to Donal's family. But the things, the things in it . . .'

'Go on.'

'They're all very obviously women's things. Oh God, Sophie, I'm being stupid I know. There's probably no connection at all between the cabinet and Manus McNeill, whoever he was. But then again . . .'

Sophie snaps her notebook shut. 'What you mean is that you sense a pattern of some kind but you can't see it properly, and it's driving you nuts.'

'Sort of.'

'That's what drives me all the time. You'd make a good academic, Alys.'

'I don't think so.' Alys did an MA in Fine Art, years ago. Sometimes she has thought about going back to studying, but not recently.

Well, I'll see what I can do.' Sophie drains her coffee cup. 'You might be surprised by how often folk tales contain a germ of truth. You just have to tease out the fact from the fiction. Does this have anything to do with the way you feel about your own Mr McNeill?'

Alys blushes. Sophie pretends not to notice.

'I don't know. I don't think so. And he isn't my Mr McNeill – far from it.'

'Will he come and see you, do you think?'

'We speak on the phone. Sometimes. On the landline. The mobile signal's rubbish there. He phones me and then there's a gap when he doesn't phone at all and I can't stand it any more, so I phone him.'

'Bad move, Alys. Keep them guessing, that's my motto.'

'But he always seems pleased to hear from me.'

'I expect he's flattered by your interest.'

'You sound like an agony aunt.'

'If I ever decide to give up the academic life I'll bear it in mind. Probably more lucrative. Anyway, about your Mr McNeill . . .'

'I just don't know. I don't think it's going anywhere. How can it go anywhere? I'm here, he's there.'

'Well, since you've been phoning him, why don't you ask him to visit?'

'Do you think I should?'

'I don't see why not. He sounds a bit shy to me. He might be glad of the invitation. He could do the whole tourist bit, you know?' She grins, puts her notebook away, stands up. 'I should go, Alys, and so should you.'

'Yes, I have to be at the station for Ben.'

'I'll see what I can find about this Manus McNeill. But don't hold your breath. You haven't given me very much to go on.'

'I'd just like to know.'

'There'll be records on the island somewhere.'

'Too long ago.'

'There'll be stories.'

'I've told you all the stories.'

'No. I mean other stories. The tales they don't tell outsiders, interlopers like you and me.'

'Do you think so?'

'Maybe. Sure to be, in fact. As I said, you'd be surprised how many facts about the history of places and people are embedded in tales. Passed on, passed down. It's like when they find shells in rock strata, miles from the sea. You think it's all nonsense, fairytales, fantasy. Only somewhere inside the fantasy there'll be this nugget of truth. If only you can dig it out.'

A week later, Sophie telephones Alys, who has just bought a box full of antique Venetian glass beads at an auction sale and is gloating over them, covering a sketch pad with tiny designs, her head full of new ideas.

'Manus McNeill,' says Sophie abruptly.

'You've found something?'

'Not a lot. But I went over one lunchtime and dug about in the School of Scottish Studies library and found some old stuff about Garve.'

'And?'

'Well, it seems he was married as a very young man.'

'Right.'

'He married one Frances Hamilton, who was a lowlander. Quite a rich family. God knows how they met but they did, and she went to the island. Only she died within a year or two, presumably in childbirth. Lots of women did in those days. It was common for a man to go through two or even three wives. Though I suppose it could have been some illness or other that carried her away. And another thing. There's no record of him having remarried, so maybe he was really heartbroken.'

'So that's that. Poor Manus. But was she his Bride from the Sea then? And why on earth would they have called her that?'

'I'm not sure. So far as I can see, her family had nothing to do with the sea at all. There's another interesting thing, though.'

'What?'

'Well, he was widowed in his mid-twenties. And then there are almost no more references to him. He kept his head down, politically speaking. He hardly set foot off the island, or if he did nobody knew about it. We don't even know when he died. And if he had some treasure or other, he didn't go in for conspicuous consumption either . . .'

'But? I sense a "but" coming, Sophie.'

'Well, there's just one more thing.'

'What's that?'

'How come,' says Sophie, thoughtfully, 'if he was widowed as a young man, how come he finished up as the father of four sons and a daughter?'

FIFTEEN

Although she generally passed her evenings in her own room, Henrietta came downstairs on the eve of the feast of St Michael. Ishbel had been sent to tell her that she must join in the celebrations: it was what Manus wanted. She noticed the absence of men. They had been gone from the house for some time and she wondered where they were – they must be about other business in connection with the festival, she supposed.

At one end of the room an excited flock of women, young and old, were gathered around the big fireplace where the *struans* large and small were being cooked. It had always surprised Henrietta that there was no separate kitchen. At both her homes, in Edinburgh and Linlithgow, the kitchens and other offices had been kept well removed from the rooms where the family lived and conducted their business. But here on Eilean Garbh, no such distinctions were maintained. People lived and worked together. Not, she thought, that the differences of station were ignored: Manus's word was law here and the island was troubled with few visitors from the outside world. Those who did come were near neighbours or family, clan and kin, and their arrival was generally cause for celebration. She had gradually come to realise that the way in which the whole of life was organised here was different from anything she had known, and that difference was dictated largely by the landscape in which people lived and worked. Each man and woman worked both for themselves and for the benefit of the community, though not without a certain amount of grumbling and sometimes downright bad temper. It was a desperately hard life, and an uncomfortable one, particularly in winter, but it had its compensations. They were a big and often quarrelsome family, with Manus at its head. This was all very well when the head of the household was a fair man like Manus, with the best interests of his people at heart. But she could imagine that it might be quite otherwise with a despot in charge.

The other women fell silent as she walked among them until Ishbel came forward and led her towards the fire. 'Mistress Henrietta. Welcome.'

She said to the other girls, ' Why don't you carry on with the cooking. And don't be staring at the lady in that fashion. You will make her embarrassed, to be sure.'

Henrietta went over to the fireplace, putting aside the chair that one of the girls had brought forward for her. 'No, no. I shall just stand. I cannot sit and see you all active like a . . . like a chaperone at a ball.'

She watched for a while as the big *struan* was cooked, each young woman taking a turn at brushing the batter onto the cake. The scents that rose from the cooking were a tantalising mixture of butter, eggs, and flour. After a while, she plucked up enough courage to ask, 'May I try, Ishbel?'

'Of course. After all, you are almost the lady of the house now.'

Henrietta was glad that this part of the great hall was dark and smoky from the cooking. 'Hardly that,' she whispered to Ishbel. 'You should not say such things.'

'But I am sure that is how *he* thinks of you.'

'Hush,' she said. 'You know that I am very far from being the lady of this house. You must never let Manus hear you say so. He would be very angry. Now, what must I do?'

Ishbel pursed her lips but did not argue. Instead she handed

Henrietta her own bunch of twigs. 'Well, now, you just paint the batter on with this. But carefully . . .'

Henrietta had been well warned. To break the struan would bring ill luck for the forthcoming year. She dipped the twig in the batter and painted another layer delicately into position on the big cake, watching as it set and changed colour in the heat. And again the sweet scent rose from it.

Ishbel nodded in approval. 'And when this one is finished we can make some smaller ones. Perhaps you will make a blaeberry struan . . .'

'Why would I want to make a blaeberry struan?'

'You could give it to Manus. For as I told you, he always goes without!'

'You told me you would not dare to give him a struan. What makes you think that I would do it?'

'Because you are very fond of him. And he of you, I think.'

'Nonsense!'

'Well, now, I cannot remember him ever feeling the need to buy tulips before. Or making Iain dig a garden for them, which I think the poor man did most ungraciously. All that carting of seaweed up from the shore. Iain's wife told me he was fair demented with it!'

'It serves him right!' said Henrietta with feeling. 'He treated me like a parcel when I was first brought here.'

'Well, well, he is paying for it now.'

Henrietta was glad that Ishbel did not know about the ribbons. She had hidden them in the pocket of her dress, too shy to show them, too shy to wear them.

'I think your garden will be very beautiful when it grows and flowers,' remarked Ishbel.

To give him his due, once he had overcome his early reluctance Iain had worked hard, bringing many baskets of seaweed up from the shore, digging it into the poor soil and planting willows round about to shelter Henrietta's chosen plot from the prevailing winds. It would never be like a city garden, but it might be a little enclosure of civilisation in the heart of the island. Next spring they would all see and admire it.

'When do we eat these wonderful cakes?' asked Henrietta, with a sudden lifting of her heart.

'First we take them to the church to be blessed, and then we eat them for breakfast, together with the fat lamb which we are cooking now.'

'And which smells so good.'

'I am hungry already,' agreed Ishbel. 'And we shall all eat together and pray that good Michael will protect our flocks and our harvest and ourselves throughout the coming winter.'

'The church?' It seemed an unlikely ceremony for a minister to perform. Henrietta had seen the small stone kirk on her walks, but only from a distance. It was set on a hillock, close by the huddle of low houses that Ishbel was pleased to call a village. Once or twice it had occurred to her that she might flee there and throw herself upon the minister's protection, but her natural caution had always exerted itself. She could not imagine that even a minister of the Kirk would defy Manus upon his own island.

'We are all of the old faith here,' said Ishbel simply. 'The new ways have not yet come to Garbh, though I know that on many of the islands singing and dancing are forbidden along with all of the old celebrations. Which is a pity. And upon some of the islands I am told that the people still pursue the old beliefs, even in defiance of their ministers, who are always telling them it is heathen nonsense. But Manus will have none such here. We follow the old ways like our fathers and grandfathers, and their fathers and grandfathers before them. And I tell you it would be a brave minister who prevented a fisherman from turning his boat with the turning sun!'

Henrietta rubbed the smoke from her eyes and watched the batter pucker and settle in the heat. So she was come to a pagan place, truly, but she had met nothing but kindness.

'Where are all the men?' she asked after a while. 'I see none of them about the house.'

'No. They will be out in the stables, standing guard over the horses. I always forget that you know so little. Tonight it is permissible to take a horse away from wherever you can.'

'To steal it, do you mean?'

Ishbel frowned and shook her head. 'You misunderstand me. It is a borrowing just, for the sake of the feast. The poor beasts will be returned afterwards, though in much worse condition, I'll allow. But nobody will get the better of Manus, for he will be in the stables, too, in among the horses the whole night long with the other men of the house. And let me tell you there are few can outwit him.'

'I'm sure you're right,' agreed Henrietta.

She could not imagine that anybody would dare to steal one of Manus's horses, but it seemed that anything was possible, any mischief, on this night of the year.

'You do not have this custom in Edinburgh, either?' Ishbel asked.

'No. And it is very strange to me, I confess. You must tell me more. What are the horses to be used for? Why are so many needed?'

Ishbel regarded her companion with a certain pitying wonder, as though only now was she comprehending the true depths of the girl's ignorance.

She drew Henrietta to one side, while the rest of the women got on with the business of *struan* making. 'Well now, in the morning, after we have breakfasted, the whole household together, everyone will ride to the church again, to process round and about the churchyard, in honour of St Michael. For everyone loves the great archangel.'

'Why St Michael in particular?'

'Because he was a bonnie fighter, of course! The greatest fighter of them all, for he fought with Lucifer himself, and cast him down to hell. And you had better have Michael on your side if nobody else in the heavenly throng.'

'And you go round the churchyard? Is that right?'

'We begin from the east and follow the course of the sun himself.'

'The sun?'

'Aye, the sun in the sky. I have already told you, you cannot go against the sun. Even the fishermen do not turn their boats against the sun, have you not noticed? That would be terrible bad luck. You must always go with him and not against him. And then all will be well with you and yours.'

Luck seemed very arbitrary, thought Henrietta. There were rules which you might unwittingly break, as you might break the *struan*, bringing down the wrath of heaven. Was that what had happened to her? She had done nothing knowingly to bring such misery upon herself, so perhaps she had broken some unwritten rule, though it seemed as unreasonable to suppose that as to suppose the opposite: that damnation or salvation was all mapped out for you beforehand. Yet that was what the minister had told them in Edinburgh when she had gone to the kirk each Sunday with Maisie and with her parents.

'The procession is always the same,' added Ishbel. 'The priest leads the way, with my Lord Manus behind, and then the rest of us follow after, even the old and young on horseback, as well as they may.'

'And who will you ride with?' asked Henrietta with interest.

'I have always ridden up behind my elder brother, but this year Seamus has asked me to ride with him.'

'Has he now? And will you?'

'Oh, I think I will. In fact I have already told him I will be glad to. And my wee sister will sit up in front of my father as she always has done since our mother died.'

'Has she been long dead, your mother?' asked Henrietta. When Ishbel was not up at the big house she spent her time in one of the smoky cottages with her widowed father, her younger sister and her unmarried brothers.

'She died a few years after Manus's wife. Both of them in childbirth. My young sister survived, although Manus's baby son did not. My mother had waited upon my lady Frances, and was very fond of her. They were good friends. It was from her that my mother learned the Scotch tongue, and then she taught me while I was a child. But I have learned much more from yourself this past year.'

'You have,' said Henrietta. 'But I have also learned so much from you.'

'And from Manus himself, I think,' said Ishbel, with a smile.

'Just a little.'

'But to be sure,' said Ishbel, reverting to her preoccupation with the procession. 'I do not know who you will ride with. Perhaps one of my brothers would take you.'

'I do not think I will ride at all,' said Henrietta. The thought of participating in the festival had never occurred to her.

'But you must! You cannot miss it. It is such a day. After the procession there are always games. There will be racing and riding and storytelling. And in the evening there will be dancing, which is held in the great hall here at Scoull. And everyone pays a little for the pipers and the fiddlers. You must ride, you must!'

'Well,' said Henrietta. 'We shall see. But it may not be allowed.'

'Who will not allow it?'

'Manus may not allow it. You forget that I am still a captive here, no matter how much freedom I am allowed in this house and on the island. You forget my position here, Ishbel.'

'I never forget it for a moment. And it saddens me to think of it. Oh, but you should ride with us. Manus will not mind. In fact, I am sure he will welcome you to the celebrations. It is a good day and I think it would make you happy to take part in it.'

The following morning Henrietta was urged downstairs by Ishbel. The *struans* had already been taken to the church and blessed, and now all the people of the household were seated round the big oak table, eating fresh cake and slices of lamb that had been roasted with herbs the night before, as well as butter, soft-boiled eggs, cheese and honey and cream. It was a feast such as Henrietta had never seen set out here before. Manus smiled at her from the head of the table. Ishbel brought her a chair, and once she was seated beside him, Manus served her with his own hands, encouraging her to try this or that delicacy.

'And here is a blaeberry *struan*,' he said. 'Which Ishbel tells me has been made specially for me.' He tasted the cake and pronounced it very good.

She buried her face in her cup.

'I wonder who can have picked these blaeberries?' he persisted.

'I wonder.'

'But I am also wondering if they might not taste better out upon the open hillside. What do you think, Henrietta?'

'I think they might taste very fine. Out upon the open hillside.'

After that Manus fell silent, although he still seemed in genial mood, smiling at his household. But he occasionally lapsed into deep thought, and once or twice she caught him staring at her with a puzzled, speculative gaze as though he were wrestling with some great conundrum.

Later, when the breakfast had been cleared from the table, Manus disappeared to make himself and his horse ready, and the rest of the company prepared to ride off in procession. There was much laughter and joking among the young people, in such quick, liquid Gaelic that Henrietta could understand little of it, but she knew its import. She retreated into one of the window alcoves, watching them all with a kind of hungry interest, spiced with regret. She had never known the kind of loving, tantalising teasing that went on among them, or not for many a long year, and none of it would have been so free and easy within her sheltered circle at home in Edinburgh. Even with her parents, even with Thomas and with her friend Grisel, as they moved away from childhood, there had grown that edge of formality.

There was formality here to be sure, but it was of a different order. People were less concerned with outward show and more with the observation of a set of ancient customs, most of which, she now saw, had been formulated simply to assist people to survive in an unforgiving place. Family was more important than society here, but Manus's 'family' extended to the whole island and beyond. Life in Edinburgh had been quite different, but she was no longer so sure that it was better. And with that realisation came a sudden longing to give in, to be part of this place, a foreigner no more. She was not yet fully at ease here, but the possibility of calling it home lodged in her heart. 'I wish I was highland,' she thought, surprising herself with the strength of her desire. 'I wish I belonged.'

The morning was fine and chilly, and the horses were stamping and shuffling on the stones of the yard, when Manus rode up, leading a lively silver-grey pony on a long rein behind him.

He dismounted and strode over to the door. 'Well, Mistress Henrietta,' he said. 'Are you ready?'

'For what?'

'For the procession, of course.'

'I shall bide here and take care of the house and tend to the fires for you. Somebody must stay.'

'But there is old Mhairi. She is happy to bide here and mind the fires and the house and dream of her youth. Is that not the truth?' he asked Ishbel, who had appeared in the doorway, carrying Henrietta's brogues and a soft woollen shawl of red and blue dye.

'Aye, it is true enough,' agreed Ishbel. 'It is all beyond Mhairi now, the procession and the games. She prefers to remember what once was.'

'So you see there is no need for you to stay here, Henrietta, and you must come. I am depending on you.'

'You certainly cannot miss it,' agreed Ishbel. 'I said that she might ride with my brother.'

'Mistress Dalrymple will have her own pony. I have it here. Indeed, I have been guarding it all night long for her. And she will ride alongside me. I'll have no argument, Henrietta. Put on your brogues and your shawl and make yourself ready. There is little time to spare and I am waiting for you, so you had better make haste.'

She saw that he had chosen her mount – a good-natured beast – with care, and that he wished only to please her. It would be ungracious to refuse. So she fastened on her shoes, wrapped the soft woollen shawl around her shoulders, and allowed herself to be helped up onto the pony. Then they set off in procession towards the village.

It was still misty but sunlight was already beginning to filter through. She rode behind him towards the church that stood close to the village of Scoull, a tumble of dark thatched houses. Behind them wound a long procession of islanders: men, women and children, old and young alike, and brindled dogs, running among the horses' hooves to their own great peril. The people were singing and chanting variously in Gaelic, but Henrietta could make out nothing of their words. She urged her pony on, so that she was riding beside Manus and asked, 'Are you not afraid to take me to the church?'

He cast an amused glance at her. 'Why should I be afraid of such a thing?'

'Well, are you not fearful that I might denounce you to your priest? For holding me here, against my will.' She had fleetingly pictured herself rising up in the saddle and calling out accusations.

Manus laughed. 'Do you think that he does not know?'

'He knows?' She looked at him in astonishment laced with a certain amount of relief that she would not, after all, have to speak out.

'Aye, he knows. And disapproves. In fact, he tells me that I am bound for hell fire because of you. But he holds his peace for the sake of his flock, who would suffer greatly if ought befell me.'

She had not thought about it like that. She cast a backward glance at the straggling procession behind. To see almost the whole population of the island, several hundred people, gathered together like this was salutary. She had not known that Garbh gave shelter and sustenance to so many. And they all relied on him, on Manus McNeill. They paid rents and gave him labour and a share in the fruits of it. But in return the old and the sick called upon him for help, and he would not turn them away. Some, like Mhairi and a number of other elderly men and women, he installed in his own household; all of them he cared for in some way or another. It was true enough. They would suffer greatly if any ill befell him. He held the fate of the island and its population in the palm of his hand.

She thought, They are not only the priest's flock. They are Manus McNeill's flock, too. And they love him as much if not more than they love the priest. But she only said, 'I see,' very quietly, and rode on for a while.

At last, to break the silence between them, she said, 'What are the people singing?'

'Old songs to the blessed Micheil the archangel, whose sword is keen to smite and his arm strong to save; a bonnie fighter indeed. He is our warrior of the sea, the protector of boats and boatmen everywhere, as well as of all horses and horsemen. But come, Henrietta. We must hurry. The real procession is beginning and we must follow the sun.'

Later he settled her in a sheltered spot, spreading a woollen blanket on the ground for her to rest upon, the grey pony cropping the turf beside her.

'I will leave you here now to watch the games, if I may. Are you sure you are warm enough?'

'I am,' she said. 'I am fine and warm.'

He mounted his horse and prepared to ride off.

'Will you be gone long?' she asked anxiously. It was all so

strange to her and Ishbel was nowhere in sight – she had affairs of her own to see to, thought Henrietta with a pang of envy. Affairs of the heart, perhaps. She had seen Ishbel riding proudly with red-haired Seamus, leaning back against him, his bare, freckled arms clasped lovingly round her. She felt very much alone today when all the islanders seemed to be paired off: husbands and wives, mothers and sons, fathers and daughters, brothers and sisters.

'Not very long.' Manus smiled down at her. 'And besides you will be quite safe here. Nobody will trouble you and you can watch the games and the riding. There are many people here from the remoter parts of the island. It is a great gathering and it will save me time if I can speak to some of them today.'

'I didn't know . . . I wasn't aware that you were . . .' She hesitated, not sure how to finish.

'What? What were you not aware of, Henrietta?'

'Only that these people seem to rely on you very much. And they seem to be very fond of you.'

Fond was too weak a word. They respected him. Above all, they expected a very great deal of him, and not without justification. He was responsible for them. He was their protector just as much as the blessed Michael.

'I am very fond of them, too,' he said. 'In fact, I am more than fond. I love them and this place very dearly. I'll allow I went mad for a spell after my wife and my bairn died, but these folk did not desert me. They supported me through thick and thin. They are a fine people. And, chiefly this past year, I have begun to feel more like myself. Even grief has its seasons, Henrietta.'

'Aye, you are right. Even grief has its seasons.'

SIXTEEN

September in Edinburgh is wet and windy. The Venetian beads have all been made into necklaces, earrings and brooches and some of them have been sold. Alys has mixed them with turquoise and amber, liking the contrasts of colour and texture. She's at her happiest when she's absorbed in her work, and when she's spending time with Ben. But sometimes dissatisfaction with the rest of her life threatens to overwhelm her. She has never felt this so strongly before, even when she was divorcing John. She wonders if it is Garve that has done this to her, or Donal. Every night, in the period between waking and sleeping, she thinks about him. She finds herself going to bed early so that she can indulge in memories of him, in fantasies about him, his face gazing down at her, the roughness of his hands and the softness of his thighs, the touch of skin on skin, the warmth of him moving inside her.

There is so much – too much – that she doesn't know about him, but on Garve she had felt comfortable with him as she had with no one else in her life so far, not even John. Her relationship with John had been a giddy switchback of highs and lows. She suspects that with Donal things would be different. She can imagine herself being contented with him but she is not quite convinced that he would be contented with her. She knows, too, that any deepening of their relationship would involve huge changes for herself and her son, and the thought frightens her. It's well out of her comfort zone, as Sophie would say. Sometimes she thinks that it is all immaterial anyway, because she will probably never see Donal again. Mostly, she feels vaguely depressed rather than really sad.

The endless bickering with John over Ben's arrangements doesn't help. Maybe if they didn't live in the same city she might get on better with John and Millie, but perhaps that would be unfair to Ben. At the end of August, he had two birthday parties, two cakes, two sets of presents. If they were really civilised they might manage to co-operate enough to have one big party, one cake, but Ben isn't complaining.

'I suppose this is the upside of divorce,' she tells Sophie, 'for the kids at least. Two of everything. They talk about it at school, you know. How to play one parent off against the other, how to get the best deal. It's shocking.'

'No, it's not. Kids are nothing if not opportunists. And it's us who give them that opportunity, so they might as well make the best of it.'

Sophie has found out nothing more about Manus McNeill. 'How's the other man in your life?' she asks.

'What man? There isn't one.'

'The other Mr McNeill.'

'Donal? Oh, I don't know. I haven't heard from him for a while.'

'Holiday romance, eh? All over and forgotten?'

'Probably.'

But he is not even beginning to fade from her mind. And neither is the island. She cannot shift the island from her consciousness. She thinks about it every day. It worries her that she can't forget the place, can't set it to one side and get on with her life. It is becoming an obsession with her, like a love affair. It occurs to her that she thinks about the island almost as much as she thinks about Donal. She badly wants to go back. In all her daydreams she walks its paths and beaches. It is as vivid now as it was immediately following her return.

Then, one evening when she is sorting out her clothes cupboard for winter (the size of the flat means that a measure of tidiness is essential; otherwise she won't be able to get in the door), she picks up a pair of shoes and shakes them. A slew of fine white sand drifts onto the floor. Two passions collide in her head. The call of the island and the man together are irresistible. An hour later, fortified by a couple of glasses of wine, she telephones Ardachy.

She is embarrassed when Iain answers the phone, but he seems pleased to hear her.

'Alys. Nice to speak to you, lass. How are you?'

'Oh, fine. Fine. Really.'

'Work going well?'

'More or less.'

'And your son? Ben, that's his name, isn't it?'

'He's asleep at the moment, but he's fine, too. I must bring him to Garve.'

'Bring him in the spring, before the bracken grows. Then you can go walking and show him the sights.'

'Maybe we will.'

'You'll be wanting Donal, I suppose.'

'If he's around,' she says, blushing at the thought of wanting Donal. Does she want him? Of course she does.

'Just give me a moment. He's fetching in some wood.'

She hears the distant creak of a door, the murmur of voices. A muted altercation. Or is that just her imagination? Then Donal.

'Hello, Alys.' His voice shakes slightly.

As soon as she hears him, she realises just how much she has been missing him.

'It's good to hear your voice,' she says.

'And yours.'

'Do you fancy a trip to Edinburgh?' she asks. Sophie would be proud of her.

He seems taken aback. There is a moment's hesitation and she prepares to make some excuse, hang up. Don't do this to me, she thinks.

'Well. That would be nice,' he says at last, cautiously.

'I was just wondering . . . Ben has a week's holiday in October, mid-term. We could show you the sights.'

'Do you have room for me?'

She has already warned him that she lives in a listed shoebox.

'I could make room. I'll borrow a camp bed. We'll squeeze you in somehow. If your dad and the island can spare you for a few days.'

'Oh, I expect they can,' he says. 'How would I get there, I wonder?'

'I thought you might drive.'

'Not in my van.'

'Why not?'

'Jesus, I can't take it off the island.'

'Oh, I see.'

'No I mean it's fucked. It——' She can hear Iain remonstrating with him in the background. 'The old man's telling me not to swear at you,' he says. 'But I'm not swearing at you, I'm just telling you the truth about the van.'

'And the van's fucked,' she repeats, beginning to laugh. No MOT, she thinks. Probably no insurance, either. Definitely not much of an exhaust.

'But I could get a bus. If you're sure you want to see me.'

'Yes. Of course I want to see you, Donal.' I'm desperate to see you, she thinks. But she doesn't say it.

'I'll get back to you as soon as I've worked out the details, then.'

As the next couple of weeks pass by, Alys finds that she is more and more apprehensive about seeing Donal again. Why should that be? Will he be so different, out of his environment? Maybe. She thinks about the seaweed in Scoull Bay: sinuous and sexy in the water; a sad, glutinous mass at low tide.

'Oh, God,' she says to Sophie. 'What if I can't stand the sight of him?'

'That's hardly likely. He isn't going to have changed that much, Alys!'

'No, but it's possible. What will I do?'

'It's only for a few days. You've been telling me what a nice man he is ever since you came back from your holidays.'

'Distance lends enchantment to the view.'

'Bollocks.'

'Don't be so crude, Sophie.'

'There's nothing quite like being up close and personal, Alys, particularly after a few months' absence. You'll be absolutely fine.'

'I sometimes wonder if it isn't . . .'

'What?'

'The island.'

'What about the island?'

'I sometimes wonder if it isn't the island that I've fallen in love with and not Donal. I think about the island all the time, you know.'

'In that case, you've got a bit of a problem, darling, haven't you?'

She tells him to get a taxi when he gets off the bus; it will be easier than trying to meet him with the car. In the event, though, he hikes up the Mound with his battered rucksack on his back and arrives on her doorstep in the late afternoon. When the doorbell rings, her heart gives a great lurch. Sociable Ben goes scurrying down the stairs to let him in and then gets all tongue-tied with shyness. Alys feels tongue-tied as well, and what with Donal being quiet anyway, she thinks they are probably in for a silent week.

She opens a bottle of red wine, and watches him as he sits,

resting his elbows on her pine dining table. He pushes up his sleeves and drinks.

'Pasta OK?' she asks. She has no idea what he likes to eat.

'Oh, fine. Yes. Thank you. I'll eat anything.'

He is wearing a soft sky-blue fleece and jeans. He isn't anything like seaweed out of water. He's not exceptionally handsome. But he looks dark and stocky and tousled and somehow exotic in this setting, especially with the sea-grey eyes and the sooty lashes. All through the week he will continue to look as though he belongs elsewhere. Even when they hear him speak, people in the shops will sometimes mistake him for a foreigner, ask him where he comes from. Maybe it's the accent or maybe it's something to do with men who work out of doors, or on the sea, she thinks. Maybe it's working on the water that gives them that quality of detachment. He's calm and careful in everything he does. She remembers something else that she has liked about him, right from the start: she feels safe with him. He's a practical man in the way that John never was.

Still, there's something else about him that she can't quite come to terms with: a sense of . . . if she had to put it in one word, she would call it hopelessness. Intermittently, there is a profound and disturbing air of hopelessness about him. She sensed it on Garve, but she feels it even more here in the city: his vulnerability. It is as though he cannot allow himself to feel too strongly about anything. It makes her heart turn over with pity for him, and pity is so close to love. But no substitute for it. She cannot afford to make any more mistakes. After all, she has Ben to think of, and Ben will always be more important to her than herself.

To add to the complexity of the situation, Ben takes to Donal instantly. She had half wanted her son to be suspicious of this interloper but Ben is quite unthreatened by him. And Ben senses no hopelessness whatsoever, but perhaps that is because whenever he is with Ben, Donal seems like a different person, much more relaxed, less inhibited. They sit there like two adults, talking

169

casually about this and that. She has never seen her son behave so maturely so quickly, and she is slightly resentful of it.

On the night of his arrival, she shows him to the camp bed she has borrowed from Sophie, managing to find space for it in the room where she works. 'I hope you'll be all right on this.'

'Yes, this'll be fine. But I don't want to keep you from your work.'

'I wouldn't be doing much with Ben off school, anyway. I can always make up for it later.'

She wonders if he can guess how much the sleeping arrangements have exercised her and Sophie over the past two weeks. If she puts the camp bed in the living room, where she herself sleeps, will Ben be upset? Will Ben tell his father? Will John and Millie be angry and do they have any right to be angry? ('Tell them to get stuffed if they say anything,' says Sophie.) If she puts the camp bed in the workroom will Donal be upset? Will he draw the obvious conclusion that she wants to put a little distance between them, that she doesn't want to rush into anything? And would that be such a bad thing? Isn't it the truth, anyway? So eventually, and much against Sophie's robust advice, the bed goes in the workroom, and Donal doesn't seem to mind. If anything, he seems relieved by the measure of privacy it affords him. On that first night, he unpacks his rucksack and brings out a parcel.

He has brought her a gift: a book about the island, a leather-bound history of Garve by the Reverend Bartholomew Scobie, published in Edinburgh in 1900. Bartholomew Scobie was, it seems, one of those eccentric clergymen and part time antiquarians who used to cycle about the Scottish countryside gathering songs and stories, and scouring the landscape for prehistoric remains. Urn burials, hill forts, standing stones: they were all grist to the Reverend Scobie's mill. He had had a particular liking for Garve, and seemed to spend large chunks of his summer neglecting his own parish, wherever that was, and making notes on the antiquities of the island.

'Donal, this is wonderful! Just the kind of thing I like.' She flicks through it. 'Is there anything about Manus in it?'

'Only what you know already: the treasure and the bride from the sea. But there's lots of other stuff about the lost villages and so on. I found it on my dad's bookshelf and thought of you. He said you were welcome to it.'

Self-consciously, she kisses him on the cheek, when Ben isn't looking. 'Thank you,' she says. He catches hold of her hand, squeezes it and then lets go.

He has brought something else with him from the island, something for Ben. He digs a shoebox out of the bottom of the rucksack and opens it. In it is a plastic carrier bag. He takes it out and shakes its contents gently onto the table. There is a flurry of feathers and a rattle of bones.

'Wow!' says Ben in astonishment.

The bag is full of wings. They are the wings of the birds of Garve. Most of them are skeletons, though many still have feathers attached. There are the white wings of seabirds, and the tiny, delicate bones of the wren. There is the lark and the peewit. There are swans' feathers. There are a couple of small avian skulls thrown in for good measure. Alys doesn't know whether to be horrified or fascinated. She is attracted by their intricate beauty and revolted by them at the same time.

'Aren't they dirty?' she asks. 'Won't they smell?'

'They smell of the sea,' says Ben, sniffing them, fingering them delightedly.

'No, these are long past having any flesh on them. They are dry bones. But you can see the way they are made. You can see what lies under.'

'So I see.' As an artist she should be fascinated and she is. But still . . .

'I didn't kill any of them,' Donal hastens to reassure Ben. 'They die for one reason or another. Perhaps old age. And they are washed up on the beach from time to time. I used to draw them when I was a boy. Maybe you could take them to school.'

'Are they all for me?' asks Ben.

'If you like.'

'Cool,' says Ben. 'I'll start a collection. Mum, when can we go to Garve and get some more?'

That night, she lies awake in bed, conscious that Donal is also lying awake across the tiny hallway. Desire is driving her crazy but neither of them dares to move for fear of waking Ben, whose cubbyhole is between them. And Ben is having some trouble sleeping. Over-excited, he calls for glasses of water and then pads off to the loo.

What in God's name am I doing? she thinks, but there is an inevitability about it. It doesn't seem to matter that they are lying in separate beds. Donal is somewhere in her head. There is no getting rid of him. Like the fine white sand of the island, she will never quite shake him off now.

When she does at last fall asleep, she dreams about swans flying in across the bay and thinks that she hears the music of the beating of their wings.

They see the sights of Edinburgh together. They do the Castle and Holyrood House and, more prosaically, the Scotch Whisky Centre, which he enjoys very much. He tells her, sheepishly, that he used to overdo the drink a bit but he is more careful now. They drink countless cups of frothy coffee in small cafés, where Ben and Donal also eat large amounts of chocolate cake, and then they climb Arthur's seat. Donal strides ahead, Ben scrambles after him, and she brings up the rear, panting. She sees that this is the way they will always be. She is touched and alarmed by how much they already feel like a family.

At the top, he spreads his jacket, an old and shabby army parka which smells faintly of fish, on the damp ground and they sit on it, huddled together to admire the view, while Ben climbs and jumps and whirls round and round, with his arms spread wide.

Donal says, 'This reminds me of your mum and dad – those picnics.'

She has been thinking much the same thing. 'They were good at picnics, my mum and dad.'

He slips his arm round her waist and squeezes her tight against him.

He is so warm, his grip on her so firm, his sheer physical presence so overwhelming that she can't help herself. She turns and kisses him on the lips. 'I love you,' she tells him. 'I love you so much.'

Ben has not noticed the kiss. He is still whirling round, making loud brumming noises, absorbed in the moment of being something.

Alys puts her arms round Donal and hugs him close, sniffing the oily wool of his sweater and the clean shampoo scent of his hair. Over his shoulder she can see all the picturesque verticals of the city. 'I don't want to let you go,' she tells him. 'I hate the space between us. We're so right together.'

'I know.'

They kiss again, and the urge to topple over, to press their bodies close, breast to breast, thigh to thigh, is almost overwhelming.

But Ben has come to a halt. He has made himself dizzy with whirling and queasy with chocolate cake and now he wants to sit down on the parka. 'Any room?' he asks, plaintively.

Donal moves first. 'Course there's room, Ben,' he says, making a space. 'Always room for one more in here.'

John and Millie issue a dinner invitation, but a drink with them is all Alys is brave enough to endure. She can't bear to think of them scrutinising Donal and finding him wanting, lacking in the urban sophistication they seem to prize so much. But when they do meet, she realises that her fears have all been unfounded and once again she has underestimated Donal. He slips into another mode altogether, highland and witty and ironic. Almost deliberately so, she thinks, slightly disapproving of the ease with which he becomes a chameleon, taking on the colours of his surroundings.

He asks all the right questions, wraps them both round his little finger. They talk about art and music and theatre.

'You deliberately set out to charm them,' she says, accusingly, when they are on their way back to her flat.

Donal shrugs. 'What's the harm? I only told them what they wanted to hear. Didn't agree with half of what they were saying. But there was no sense in antagonising them, now, was there? We all have to get on together, don't we?'

'What a nice person,' Millie says afterwards. She is in bed with John and they are lying like two spoons, breast to back, tummy to bum. 'What a nice, funny, sensible man. Do you know, I think he'll be really good for her.'

'Ah,' says John wisely. 'Salt of the earth. They don't make them like that any more.'

Donal is planning to stay for five nights. All too soon, his last evening comes round and though they have managed the odd kiss and cuddle they have not yet made love. The result of this is that they are now wild with desire for each other. Tonight's the night, she thinks, even if she has to give Ben a spoonful of Calpol to send him off to sleep. But on his last evening, the telephone goes while they are eating pizza from the Italian takeaway down the road. It is for Donal. She watches him while he takes the call, sees his cheeks go suddenly ashy. He puts the receiver carefully down on the table and covers his face with his hands.

'What's the matter?' asks Ben.

'Hush,' she says, frowning at him. 'Just go on with your pizza.' She lifts the receiver and talks to the person on the other end. It is Mrs Cameron, phoning to tell Donal that his father is dead.

Mrs Cameron is distressed and so she talks quickly, and at length. Alys can barely get her to shut up.

'He would insist on going to the creels, though I know Donal told him not to. But he said he wanted to make himself useful. The engine broke down halfway across the bay and Iain started to row, but it must have been his heart. Robbie McLean, his neighbour, saw the boat drifting and found him there. There was nothing to be done. He was gone already. Poor Iain. Poor Donal. What will he do now, do you know?'

'I'll get back to you in a while,' says Alys, and hangs up.

'I must go home,' says Donal. He stands up, looks about him as though the wish were the deed. 'I'm sorry but I must go home now.'

'You can get the first ferry in the morning.'

'Jesus Christ, how can I?' He runs his hands through his hair. 'How can I get to the ferry? Is there a train or a bus I can get? What will I do, Alys? What will I do?' He starts to pat his pockets helplessly. 'You don't have a cigarette, do you?'

'I don't smoke.'

'God, I need a cigarette.'

Ben gets up and fetches the bottle of Laphroaig and a couple of glasses. 'Would you like a drink, Donal?' he says, like a little old man. 'I think you need a drink as well, Mum.'

Very carefully he pours out two measures of the golden spirit.

Donal looks at him and blows his nose. Takes the glass. 'Thanks, Ben.' He pats the child's hand. 'You're a good lad, do you know that?'

Alys phones Mrs Cameron again. 'He'll be home as soon as he possibly can. I'll drive him to the ferry myself.'

'Well, there's really no hurry now, my dear, is there?'

'No.' She is almost in tears herself. She looks at Donal's face and can't bear the sorrow she sees there. 'But he needs to be on the island.'

'Of course he does.'

'And I think I'd be better to drive him, don't you?'

There is a pause.

Mrs Cameron says, 'Take care of him.'

'We will. We'll be on the first ferry in the morning.'

She makes a pot of strong coffee, puts Ben to bed, and feeds Donal more whisky, but has none herself after the first mouthful. He agrees with everything she says. 'Yes,' he says and 'Thank you,' and 'That's fine.' He will do anything she tells him. His mind seems to be quite elsewhere. She knows what he is feeling: periods of numbness interspersed with the intense pain of the realisation that he will never see the old man again, never hear him laugh, or cough, or walk into a room.

'I'm coming with you,' she says.

'What about Ben?' His teeth are chattering.

She puts her arms round him and kisses his forehead. 'Don't worry. I'll sort it all out. Just you get your things together and I'll make a few phone calls. You leave everything to me.'

SEVENTEEN

Henrietta watched the riding and the races in honour of the feast of St Michael, with a great deal of pleasure and amusement. In the early afternoon, Ishbel came back to her briefly, bringing water in a stone bottle and food tied up in a cloth.

'You needn't stay with me,' Henrietta told her. 'You spend enough time with me as it is. Go to your Seamus. He's waiting for you.'

She had seen the red-haired lad hovering anxiously in the background. He could not take his eyes off Ishbel, and it was plain that he was in love.

'Well, if you don't mind . . . I'm sure Manus will be back soon.'

'I don't mind at all. And Manus has work to do. So go – go and enjoy yourself.'

In the warm afternoon sunshine, she fell asleep for a while and dreamed of Michael the Archangel standing guard over her with a fiery sword. She was awoken by Manus shaking her gently by the shoulder.

'Have you been sleeping long?' He helped her to her feet.

She looked up at the sun. 'Only a little while. It was pleasant.'

'There's nothing quite like a nap out of doors on a fine day.' He touched her cheek, briefly. 'You've caught the sun!'

He clicked to her pony and it trotted over to him obediently

'Have you enjoyed the games, Henrietta?'

'Very much.'

'They are good horsemen and -women, to be sure. It is a great tradition upon Garbh. But we must go back now and make ready for the dancing.'

'Do you always hold the dancing up at Scoull?'

'Always, although for these many years past my heart has not been in it.'

Her silver-grey pony nuzzled his hand, obviously a favourite with him.

'Henrietta,' he said, 'I fear my own horse is lame. I have stabled her here in the village, but if you would like to mount your pony I will lead you back to the house.'

She got to her feet and wrapped her shawl about her shoulders. 'I shall walk with you, if I may, and we'll lead the pony.'

'Just as you wish.'

They set off together along the track that wound from the village back to the big house, and soon they had left the sounds of galloping hooves far behind them. The heavy grey-brown clouds of night were already rolling in from the west.

'Wrap your shawl tight about you, Henrietta. The evenings grow cold.'

'And darker. Soon I will have been here for a whole year.'

'I know it.'

They walked on in silence for a few moments.

'Manus?' she asked presently. There might not be another time when they were alone together like this, when she felt so at ease with him, and could broach this subject. The uncertainty of her situation still ate into her and she must have answers to her questions.

'Yes?' He was not going to help her out, that was plain.

'What happened?' she said, at last. 'I have to know.'

'What are you asking me?'

'You understand me well enough. For all of this long year nobody has offered me a proper explanation, save that I am here and here I must stay. Yet I was kidnapped. Snatched away from everything I held dear.'

He strode ahead so that she had to scurry along to keep up with him.

'And I fancy it is only thanks to you that I have not been brutally treated here,' she persisted. 'What harm had I ever done you?'

She pulled his arm and he stopped at last, shaking his head. 'You had done me no harm,' he said slowly, 'no harm at all. And well you know it.'

'Then who ordered you to do such a thing. And why? In the name of God, tell me why?'

'I was not ordered.' He turned to face her and she saw that he was both angry and embarrassed. 'Nobody ordered me!'

'Then I don't understand why you did it.'

'Oh, Henrietta, I needed the money!' The words came bursting out of him and she heard the raw shame in his voice. 'I had gaming debts that I wished to clear. It is no good excuse. In fact, it is no excuse at all. But it is a reason of sorts and I give it to you because you have asked me and I cannot lie to you – to you of all people. I wanted to make a fresh start.'

'So you were bribed.'

He sighed. 'I was bribed. But it has to be said in my defence that they had information about my political allegiances which could have gone ill with me and my people – which could still go very ill with me. My clan chief is content to swither this way and that. We McNeills are cautious by nature but I am less so than most. So yes, to my eternal discredit, I say to you that I was persuaded. And I was paid.'

'Who paid you? Who had information? Who? Manus?'

They had come to a halt on a stretch of flat turf overlooking the sea. A little evening wind, cold with the threat of winter, angled over the rocks to chill them both.

'My dear Henrietta,' said Manus, 'you are no fool. You must surely have guessed long ago. Who had most to gain from your "disappearance"? Ask yourself who.'

'I don't know! A relative of my husband's, perhaps. Somebody who thinks they have more right to his money than I have.'

'You have said it yourself.'

'But I do not know this person.'

'You do, Henrietta. You know this person – these people – very well indeed.'

There was another silence. A sudden sharp gust blew in from the sea, and buffeted Henrietta so that she took a step backwards. Instinctively he put out his hand to steady her, but she shook him off. The wind was nothing. It was her whole world that had rocked on its foundations.

'Good God,' she whispered. 'You are talking about my brother. And Grisel, too?'

'Grisel most of all.'

'How can I believe you?'

'You must believe me. Would I tell you this if it were not the truth? *A ghràidh*, you don't know how much I have tried to shield you from this.'

'But they are my kin!'

'They betrayed you, Henrietta. They betrayed you most cruelly.'

The words burst out of him, more loudly and coarsely than he intended. They hurt her heart: a twisting pain in her breast.

'Why would they do it?'

'Are you daft, woman?' he asked. 'Or can you still not bear to face the truth? Now they can have the managing of your wealth and your son's inheritance as well as their own. You stood between them and a considerable amount of money.'

'It cannot be true!'

'Oh, think about it, Henrietta,' he said in exasperation. 'There has been a longstanding conspiracy against you. William was possessed of a great fortune but Grisel was never his principal heir. If he had died unmarried, it would certainly have gone elsewhere.'

'I believe he had left a small legacy for Grisel, but yes, there was a nephew, somewhere in the south, who was to inherit everything else. I had heard Grisel speak of it with resentment. In fact, this past year I have sometimes suspected . . .'

'You suspected him, a complete stranger, of having you brought here. Well, William's nephew, wherever he is, is as blameless as yourself. Your husband thought that he had provided well enough for Grisel and Thomas. He was no fool and I expect he saw how things lay with their greed and their profligacy, even when you didn't.'

'But they were always so kind to me.'

'Of course they treated you well, lass. You were their milch cow. First they conceived the plan of making a match between you and William.'

'It was their suggestion, certainly, but William agreed most readily.'

'He was very fond of you. I think your husband was a good man. But he was also an old man who refused to accept his own mortality. Oh, I have thought long and hard about all this. The way I understand it is that your brother and his wife hoped – nay, they planned – that after William's death, they would have the managing of your fortune as well as their own. You would be a helpless widow, albeit a wealthy one. What else could you do but return to your loving brother's house? And who can say how long you would have survived there?'

'But how could they know that William would die so soon?'

'They didn't know. But the prize was well worth waiting for. Besides, I think Grisel already suspected that he was ill, even before the wedding. They were hoping for a swift marriage and a swift despatch for William, and that is what they got.'

'No!'

'Oh, I think so. But, for all that, things began to go awry for them. They had not imagined that you might have William's child. And that, after his death, you might be set on independence. A

181

young widow with a healthy son, a fine house and a good fortune at her disposal! My God, scars or no, you would have been a very marriageable proposition.' Manus almost spat the words out, in his disgust. 'Ach, it is all money. They would do anything for silver. They would even betray their own close kin. So you see they had to change their plans very quickly. And Grisel is not a woman to tolerate any opposition. Not from what I have seen and heard of her.'

'You think it was all her idea?'

'I would say that she had the bigger hand in it. Although your brother must have been a coward, at least, to go along with her in disposing of his only sister in this fashion.'

'I thought she was my friend,' said Henrietta. 'I thought she was my oldest and my dearest friend.'

'Aye and maybe so she was, once. But you are an innocent if you cannot imagine what the desire for such a large sum of money will do to a fair-weather friendship like Grisel's. I have seen it destroy even close families where you would have thought that the demands of love and honour would overcome greed. What hope was there for you, *a ghràidh*?'

'So they paid you to kidnap me,' she said, slowly, as she realised the full implication of what he was telling her. 'And I suppose they are still paying you to keep me here.'

A profusion of terrible thoughts rushed in on her. Over the past year she had grown to love the island and its people. Eilean Garbh had become a refuge rather than a prison to her, but it was Manus himself who had been instrumental in her acceptance of life here. Gradually, she had begun to see him as her friend and protector. But now all her carefully constructed faith in him threatened to come tumbling down. She remembered that day on the cliffs when she had wanted to fly away with the wild birds and she saw herself teetering on the edge of oblivion again.

There had been a conspiracy against her, but what hurt her most was that Manus seemed as culpable as Thomas and Grisel.

Suddenly she found herself calling all his other motives into question. Had his offer of friendship been genuine, or had he merely been entertaining himself with his captive? And exactly what was she worth to him? Was this what he had meant when he spoke of her being 'bought and sold'? When did the money change hands, and how often? She saw clearly that Grisel and Thomas had bought his complicity. They had stopped just short of murder, and he was fulfilling his part of the bargain, keeping her here, keeping her alive. She swayed, sick and dizzy at the thought.

'I am sorry, Henrietta. I am so sorry, but I thought you must know, or would have guessed.'

Those who should have been most concerned with her care and protection after William's death had betrayed her cruelly. And Manus, even Manus, was motivated by greed. The words he had used came into her head: 'milch cow'. Is that what I am to him, she thought, his milch cow, a source of income? Hot tears of anger and disappointment coursed down her face.

'Don't cry, Henrietta,' he said. 'It hurts the heart of me. Don't weep for them, for God's sake. They are not worth your tears.'

She turned on him. 'No, they are not worth my tears and I am not crying for them. Or for you. Why should I expect anything from you but the occasional crumb of kindness? Dearly bought, I have no doubt!'

She was too distraught to see how he flinched at the words.

'But they have my son. I tell you, Manus McNeill, there is not a day, not an hour, goes by but I am thinking of him! And weeping for the loss of him.'

'Oh, my dear, don't cry, please. I cannot bear it. I cannot bear your sorrow!'

The pony had wandered on and come to a halt some distance ahead of them. Now it whinnied quietly, impatient to be at home in its warm stable. She rubbed her face, trying to dry the tears with her fingers.

'And you?' she asked. 'What of you, my Lord Manus? I suppose that they are still paying you to keep me here? They are still making it worth your while? No wonder you are glad to have me here since I am a source of much-needed money for you and your island!'

There was a long pause.

'Well,' he said at last. 'That is not quite the truth of it.'

'What do you mean?'

He cleared his throat. 'You have every right in the world to be angry, to hate me. But will you listen, Henrietta, before you judge me?'

'Go on, then.'

'There is a man called Ravenscroft. Your sister-in-law uses him as her intermediary.'

'I know the name. I used to see him when I was a child. He came to our house sometimes. He is an old friend of Thomas's. But I thought Grisel did not like him. She told me he led Thomas astray.'

'Led Thomas astray? Aye, well, I fancy that would not be a hard thing to do. But I also think that Grisel has been leading Ravenscroft astray. Anyway, I saw him not long ago.'

'When? And where?'

'The last time I was on the mainland. In Edinburgh, when I bought you your flower garden.'

He had brought her tulips and roses. She did not suppose that Grisel would have seen fit to pay for tulips and roses. And what of the silk ribbons? And the knotting shuttle? Why had he given her such things if he had no affection for her?

'Your brother had been attacked and robbed while walking in the Grassmarket at night and lay injured for some time.'

'Poor Thomas!' The exclamation came involuntarily, but perhaps it was not the present-day Thomas who was in her mind, but the charming elder brother she remembered, bringing her sweetmeats and sugar plums from the booths, taking her hands and dancing with her. 'Why did you tell me nothing of this?'

'Ach, don't be pitying him,' said Manus, in some disgust. 'He deserved all he got and more, there is no doubt of it. I told you what you needed to know at the time. That your wee boy is well. That your old friend Maisie still has the care of him and his cousin.'

'Aye. Thank God for that at least.'

'However, there is more. There was more that I did not tell you, for I did not have the words. I found that, when it came to it, I just did not have the words. Neither in your tongue, nor in my own.'

'So tell me now. My brother is ill. And this has affected your financial arrangements, I suppose.'

He seized her arms and would not let her shake him off. 'It has, it has. But not in the way you think. Listen to me, Henrietta. I have done wrong, it is true, but I am not the villain you suppose me. While Thomas lay so ill, Grisel took matters into her own hands. There was to be no more money for me.'

'No more money?'

'Well, there was one last payment but it was in the nature of a valediction. And then I was to do with you as I pleased.' The words tumbled out, low and grim and savage. 'Keep you or kill you, it was all one to her.'

'Keep me or . . .' she repeated, but could not bring herself to say the appalling word aloud. 'Does Thomas know of this?'

'I fancy he does not,' Manus conceded. 'I think he would not go so far. But the fact remains that I was to do as I pleased with you. Those were the words that were conveyed to me by Mr Ravenscroft.'

He remembered Ravenscroft's face, pale in the smoky light of the tavern. He remembered the man's fear of him, the way he had sweated and sighed, as though fearful that the highlander might produce a dirk from the folds of his coat and stab him. But Manus had responded with nothing more than a quick frown.

'Well, well, if that is to be the way of it . . .' he had said, rising easily from his seat, even shaking Ravenscroft by the hand. He had seen the relief on the other's face.

'Am I to convey any message to Mistress Grisel?'

Manus shook his head. 'Only that she had better take good care of herself in this life.'

'And why is that?'

'Because it seems to me that she is little likely to enjoy the next.' Manus laughed, and the sound made Ravenscroft shiver.

'But what will you do?' he asked.

'Oh, Mr Ravenscroft, you surely do not want to know that!'

'No, I suppose I do not.'

'Keep the lady or kill her. If that is what I am to do, then that is what I must be doing. The decision is mine, and mine alone. But the less you and Mistress Grisel know about what I choose to do, the better for all concerned, surely?'

Ravenscroft nodded but said nothing.

'I think you should go now,' said Manus. Suddenly he wiped the hand that had touched Ravenscroft's own, up and down his coat, a quick involuntary movement, like a man who has inadvertently touched a slug or a spider. He could not help himself. 'I find the sight of you offensive and I hope never to see you again. But you may tell the lady one more thing from me.'

'What is that?'

'She had better take good care of the wee lad. I find that my highland pride will balk somewhat at cruelty to bairns. I have friends in this city she knows nothing of. Tell her she may be watched. Tell her she should not harm the boy.'

'There is no fear of that, Mr McNeill. She loves him like her own son.'

'A mixed blessing, perhaps. But it is just as well,' he said, grimly. 'We savages can bear grudges for many a long year. We are like the animals you think us in that at least, Mr Ravenscroft, and we do not easily forget an injury. Go now. Go and leave the fate of my prisoner to me.'

And now he was gazing at Henrietta, with his fingers digging into her arms. She stood still and looked into his eyes. It seemed to her as though he were struggling with a great dilemma. There would be no more money for Manus. What was she but a liability to him? One more mouth to feed when he had a whole community to care for. And yet she had no fear for her safety. She knew him well enough for that. It would be against all his ideas of honour, his deep sense of what was right. He might have imprisoned her but he had also begun to treat her as his guest and at last he had extended his friendship and perhaps even his love to her. But she was afraid, all the same, and her fear was broader, and more ill defined than any physical terror. Would he simply set her free? Would he send her away, back to Edinburgh? Would she become a wanderer with nowhere to call home? She realised that what she feared most was losing her dearly won place in this small world of Eilean Garbh. And with that realisation came the perception of just how much she had grown to love the island.

'What will you do?' she asked, her voice little more than a whisper.

He misunderstood her at first, perhaps deliberately. 'What *can* I do?' He released her, turned and walked on, striding after the pony.

She hurried in his footsteps, pulling his arm.

'No! Wait!' she said. 'I mean what will you do with me? Now that you are not being paid to keep me here?'

'What do you think I will do?' He stopped and peered at her again in the growing gloom.

'Well, I don't know. I don't know where I belong any more.'

He was his old tetchy self again. 'I may have my faults, Henrietta, but brutality to women is not one of them. I will leave all that to your fine city gentlemen. But we must walk on. The dancers will be close behind us and we will not be ready for them. Ach, enough of all this nonsense. I see now that it is all nonsense! I don't know why I have let it worry me so much. It is all completely immaterial.'

'What is?' she asked him, amazed at his change of mood. He seemed suddenly light-hearted.

'The money. It does not matter at all – except in one particular only.'

'And what is that?'

'I used the last payment to buy you your flower garden. And your ribbons. Which you have never yet worn, so you can do me the favour of wearing them for the dancing tonight. Now, let me put you on the pony. We will go quicker that way.'

'But you haven't answered me. What are you going to do? Will you send me away? Will you send me back to Edinburgh?'

'Send you away? For God's sake, woman, why would I want to do that?'

'I don't know. I'm not sure about anything any more.'

'No. No, I can understand that,' he said gently, as he lifted her onto the pony. He clicked to it and it followed him of its own accord. He looked back at her and though the twilight obscured his face, the words came warm and clear.

'I suppose I will just have to keep you,' he said.

EIGHTEEN

In the early hours of the morning Donal, with his rucksack on his back, carries a sleepy Ben downstairs in his pirate pyjamas and his yeti slippers, while Alys carries her own bag and an assortment of bedding. They find the car, parked too far away for convenience, in the little residents' car park behind the houses, and make Ben as comfortable as possible with rugs and pillows tucked around the child seat in the back. Snug and warm, he closes his eyes almost immediately. Then Donal gets in beside Alys, and she drives across Scotland, west towards Garve. There is very little traffic at this dead time of night, even on the motorway. Later, they pass through eerie towns and villages where shift workers cycle homewards along silent streets. Ben hardly stirs. She tells Donal to try to get some sleep too, but he stays awake, gazing straight ahead.

Well before dawn, they pull into a deserted carpark beside a picnic place on the shores of a sea loch. They drink coffee from a flask and eat chocolate. When she winds down the window, briefly, the air outside is chilly and smells of autumn. A bird flies overhead with a plaintive double call. The public toilets are closed and shuttered, so they take turns to pee on the grass verge in the shelter of a clump of willows, easier for Donal than for Alys. She finds herself suppressing the urge to giggle as she crouches beneath the slender trees. Ben wakes briefly, scrambles out of the car to relieve himself, shivering with the excitement and oddity of the situation. For him, it's an adventure. She takes him back to the car, gives him a drink of juice and a biscuit, settles him down again. Donal begins to fidget the closer they get to his island, like a dog sensing home. With the light growing, they drive onto the first ferry of the day. The ferryman shakes Donal by the hand and then suddenly hugs him, patting him hard on the back.

They leave Ben to eat breakfast with Mrs Cameron at the hotel and head home to Ardachy, where Iain lies on his bed in his bedroom for the last time. Ever since her parents' death Alys has lost her squeamishness about the dead. She remembers a time when she would have found it unthinkable, but now she sees nothing gruesome in Iain's presence. He is a quiet companion. Where else should he be but in his own home for these last few hours?

Donal goes in alone to see him, but spends only a little while there.

'He's gone,' he says, when he comes back into the kitchen. He stands at the window staring out at the sea, drumming his fingers on the sill. 'He just isn't there. I don't think I realised before how completely . . . I never saw my mother after she . . . She died while I was away in London and I came back for the funeral but I never saw her.'

Alys understands him. 'It's very definite, isn't it?' she says quietly. 'The difference between life and death.'

'It's certainly that.'

'My father was so ill before he died,' she tells him. 'He clung on and on and we waited. When he did die it struck me as being like the answer to a question. I didn't know where he'd gone, but he certainly wasn't there any more. I used to be frightened of death, but after that the fear went away.'

Donal comes over to her and she puts her arms round him. His cheeks are wet with tears. 'Thank-you for bringing me back.'

'Oh, my darling,' she says, and the intensity of her feelings sweeps over her. Suddenly, there is no denying it. It isn't just pity for him. It's the real thing, fierce, undeniable, overwhelming. 'I do love you so much!'

He pulls her close, kisses her fiercely, then buries his face in her hair. 'What will I do without him?' he whispers, and after a pause, 'And what in the name of God would I do without you?'

Alys stays on Garve for the funeral. The service is in the new church at Scoull; the church is full to overflowing, which is astonishing to Alys, considering the size of the island. But lots of people knew and loved Iain, and many friends have come over from the mainland specially for the wake. There is even a distant cousin who has flown in from Canada. The minister talks about Iain for a long time. Alys is surprised to learn that, though he was born at Ardachy and was the last of a family of seven, he spent some time in Canada before coming back to Garve. Donal's mother came from the mainland, from Oban, but her own father was a fisherman and the families had been friends.

Iain is buried in the cemetery on the hillside overlooking the village, with the rain coming down like stair rods and the new grave smothered beneath a mass of flowers. There are cakes and sandwiches accompanied by whisky and strong tea at the hotel afterwards. Donal looks pale and awkward in a dark suit and black tie, going round to speak to people, shaking hands. People keep clapping him on the back as though the constant touching will comfort him. And perhaps it does. Alys lurks in the background, anxious not to intrude. Besides, she knows hardly anyone except a handful of islanders. So she hangs back and talks to Mr and Mrs Cameron and Donal's neighbour, Isa MacLean, and to Agnes Galbreath from the post office.

After the funeral, she offers to stay on and help Donal sort out his father's things, but he refuses.

'No, Alys, I think that's something I must do for myself, don't you?'

Alys and Ben have been staying at the hotel. She wanted to stay at Ardachy with Donal, but she is acutely aware that this is a small community and people will talk. Besides, there are assorted relatives staying in the cottage and who knows when they will leave? She can go away back to Edinburgh but Donal would have to stay behind and cope with the gossip. 'And the old man hardly cold in his grave,' they would say. So she has booked a twin room in the hotel and goes back there every night.

Ben has spent most of his time with the Camerons. He has also made friends with a little girl called Kirsty, whose mother, Shona, is the one and only teacher at the island's school.

'Kirsty says there are only nine pupils in the whole school!' he says, wide eyed. 'Oh, Mum, I'd really like that!'

In Edinburgh, there are twenty-five pupils in Ben's primary-school class, and more than ninety in his year. Although the classrooms are quiet enough, the playground is a riot of running, shrieking children. Ben has never liked school much. He howled constantly for the first week and, although things have improved, he would still rather be at home than at school.

'I love being ill,' he once told Alys, 'just a little bit ill. Then I can sit at home and watch TV, with you working in the other room. It's really nice and peaceful doing that.'

'I wish I went to a school like the one here,' he says. 'It would be great just to have one teacher and to know everybody.'

'Yes, but what about secondary school?'

'What about it?'

'You'd have to go to the mainland to school. That's what the children do here.'

'Maybe Donal would take me in his boat. And bring me back.'

'I don't think so, Ben.'

'Donal can do anything.'

Alys looks helplessly at Mrs Cameron, who has been dispensing apple juice to Ben and Kirsty. They have been playing with an old set of French boules on the soggy hotel lawn.

'No, no, Donal wouldn't have to take you in his boat.' Elspeth Cameron hands him a biscuit. 'Would he, Kirsty?'

'No,' says Kirsty. 'The big ones can come home at nights now. That's what my brother does.'

There is an early ferry, specially laid on for school days, and a bus to take the children into town. 'Before that they had to stay in hostels. It wasn't very suitable,' Mrs Cameron says, pursing her lips. 'They were supposed to be supervised but I believe they got up to all kinds of things in the evenings.'

'See, Mum?' says Ben. 'We could stay here. We could stay at Ardachy, couldn't we?'

Alys is touched and slightly alarmed by his growing attachment to Donal. She has always worried that she might meet someone she likes, only to find that Ben objected. Ben's approval has always been crucial in her eyes. But it has never occurred to her that Ben might pre-empt her by deciding to love someone as much as she does. She should be glad of it but she finds that it puts her under even more pressure to make some kind of commitment to Donal. But then, she thinks, Donal has made no real commitment to her, and now he is shellshocked by bereavement.

She does what she can. She goes down to the post office and general stores to fetch groceries for him: milk, bread and butter, tins of corned beef and packets of cream crackers. The post office smells exactly as it used to when Alys visited it as a child: a glorious compound of home baking, disinfectant, earthy potatoes and a little spice of firelighter for good measure. The shop sells everything from newspapers to cheese, from wellington boots to notepads. When she was young, Alys remembers, this was where they bought their fishing nets to go guddling in the pools down the seashore. The same long-handled fishing nets are still stacked at crazy angles in front of the shop, along with a net full of beach balls, and yellow plastic buckets and spades hanging in rows.

Agnes Galbreath, who runs the place with her husband Ewan, is friendly but slightly reserved with Alys, as though she doesn't quite know what to make of her. Alys feels the need to underline the fact that she is staying in the hotel and not with Donal. She senses that this community is protective of Donal, and not just because of his bereavement. It is, no doubt, something to do with his first marriage, with Anne Marie. But he hasn't told her much about that, and it doesn't look as if he ever will now. With Iain's death as well, they have all closed ranks. Sometimes she thinks, What am I doing here? I don't belong here. These people don't even like me much. And she knows with miserable certainty that, although she loves him, it is never going to work and that she will return to Edinburgh and resume her normal life and try to forget about him.

In any case, it's high time she was home in Edinburgh. The October holiday is over, the funeral is past, and John has been telephoning her irritably, wondering why Ben isn't back at school, why she is spending so much of her time in 'the back of beyond', as he calls it. Also, Sophie's daughter can't mind the shop any longer and her business will be going to pot.

'I must go,' she tells Donal. 'I don't want to leave you but I have to go home. So if you're sure there's nothing else I can do to help?'

Ever since his father's death Donal has been quiet and remote, his face shuttered. They have kissed sometimes and held hands whenever they are able to snatch a moment of privacy. But the cottage is still full of relatives indulging in an extended wake, and such moments are few and far between. They have not yet managed to make love, although the awareness of mortality engendered by the funeral has given her a fierce physical desire for him all over again.

'You should go, then,' he says. 'I'll be fine.'

'But what about when everyone goes away?' The cottage is littered with the bags and baggage of several visitors.

'I kind of wish they would!' he says ruefully. 'I could do with a bit of peace and quiet. Besides, I'll be fine. This is my own place, Alys. People look after each other here.'

People have been coming to Ardachy with eggs and tins of

home baking or pans of soup. His near neighbour, Isa MacLean, pops in every day, 'Just to see that you're all right.' Someone else, Robbie perhaps, has been lifting his creels for him. Mr Cameron has cut the hotel grass for the last time that year, thoroughly enjoying himself on the back of the motor mower, then oiling it and putting it away in the garage till spring.

Alys feels a little coldness around her heart. Donal is telling her that he can do well without her. He doesn't need her. She must go and leave him to get on with his grieving in peace.

She packs up their things that night, not forgetting the yeti slippers, and prepares to drive down for the early ferry. As she is stuffing bags into the boot of her car, Donal drives into the hotel car park in his old van and draws to a clattering halt beside her. She sees that the exhaust is now tied on with baler twine. Soon the van must dissolve into its component parts.

'I came to say goodbye.' He holds out his hand to her, shyly.

She takes it and then leans over and kisses him chastely on the cheek.

'Thank you,' he says. 'Thanks for all your help.'

Ben comes running out of the hotel clutching his bamboo-handled fishing net in one hand and a bulky plastic carrier bag in the other. He has been waiting for a parcel of clam shells which the chef has promised him from the kitchen. The shells will go into his collection, along with the wings donated by Donal. She thinks of the wings of all the birds of Garve, bleached by the sun. Grounded. She is taken aback to see Donal open his arms wide. Ben rushes into them and he gives the boy a huge bear-hug.

'Oh, Donal,' Ben says, his cheek against the man's chest, 'I really, really don't want to go home!'

She looks at the dark man, over the blond top of her son's head, and bites her lip. 'Neither do I,' she mouths at him. With one arm round Ben, he leans over and touches her gently on the cheek. It is a gesture at once so intimate and so loving that it takes her breath away.

'Come back, then,' he says. 'Come and spend some time with us, and see how we get on.'

'Do you think I should?'

'I would like it very much. We could ... you know ... we could sort things out. There's so much unfinished business between us.'

'Then I will.'

She prises Ben away and manages to get him into the car, though his lip is trembling and his cheeks are scarlet. She winds down the window. Again they touch fingers.

'Write to me,' he says. 'Or phone me. Keep in touch, Alys.'

'I will. I promise I will.'

She drives away, and onto the ferry. The sky is pale gray with a fine mist that is almost drizzle. The CalMac safety announcements are being played over the tannoy. The waves are an oily mass heaving beneath them. On board the boat, she and Ben clink-clunk up the slippery stairs onto the upper deck, so that they can watch the island fading into the distance, assuming its familiar long and hilly silhouette. The smell of the wet metal rail stays on her fingers all day. It has always been painful to leave this place. Today, it is almost unbearable.

NINETEEN

As soon as Henrietta and Manus arrived back at Scoull, Henrietta went upstairs. The first of the guests were already arriving and Manus was soon distracted by the demands of hospitality.

'But you will come down again?' he said anxiously, and he looked so concerned that she could only agree.

She said, 'I need to change my dress for something more suitable,' but the truth was that she needed an interval of peace and quiet. She felt exhausted, as though she had come through storm and shipwreck, to be washed up high and dry on a foreign shore. She was much too weary for dancing, but she knew that if she tried to excuse herself, Manus would probably come and fetch her. So she washed and then with Ishbel's help made herself presentable in a pale silk gown and threaded the red and white ribbons through her hair.

'These are pretty' said Ishbel. 'Where did you get them?'

'They were given to me.' Henrietta couldn't go on.

Ishbel frowned but didn't pursue the matter. 'Are you well?' she asked.

'I'm just tired.'

'But there is a long evening ahead of you. Manus should not have kept you out so late.'

'I slept this afternoon for a little while. Besides, there were things we had to talk about.'

'Oh?' Ishbel raised her eyebrows. 'And is all well between you now?'

'I think so. I'll be better when I've had something to eat and drink.'

'We don't want you fainting in the middle of the dancing, do we?'

'No. We don't want that.'

'I'll bring you some *struan* and a glass of wine. You sit before the fire for a spell. I'm sure my cousin will manage without you for a wee while longer.'

By the time Henrietta came down into the hall, the guests had all arrived and the music had begun. The noise was deafening. There were fiddlers and pipers. There were people eating *struans* and cold meat and cheese, or devouring great bowls full of brambles and jugs of cream, and drinking ale, wine or whisky. There were people laughing and talking and dancing. They were the men and women, young and old, that she had seen in her solitary walks about the island. Now they were dressed in their best, which was often ragged enough, but still they had taken trouble as a tribute to the day, and the saint, and as a tribute to their chief, too.

Feeling more than ever like an incomer, Henrietta took a seat by the wall with the older women, hoping to efface herself as far as possible, and watch quietly. But they were all dressed in black and her pale silk gown, Frances's gown, made her stand out among them like a dove among rooks. Besides, she had the scarlet and white ribbons threaded through her hair.

Manus caught sight of her immediately and came over to where she sat, holding out his hand to her. 'There you are! I was wondering what had become of you. Will you dance with me, Mistress Henrietta?'

'Oh, I don't think so. The dances are not what I am used to.'

They seemed wild and energetic. The young men flung their partners recklessly about the floor.

Manus stood his ground. 'You have danced country dances

before, surely? I thought that all young Edinburgh ladies were taught to play and draw and dance.'

'I have learned to dance.' She smiled up at him, remembering the few gatherings she had been allowed to attend at the homes of family friends. 'I have, but they were stately affairs.'

'And not scenes of wild abandon such as this?'

'Well, no.'

'But the steps are the same, only we are more lively than you town-bred folk. And that is because there is more love of life in us.' He took her hand. 'You will not be sitting by the wall all night long. I'll not allow it. So you had better do as you are told.'

She allowed herself to be pulled to her feet. 'Very well then, if you insist.'

'I do.'

As they joined the set, she felt her fatigue leave her, to be replaced by something like excitement.

'But I don't know the dance,' she said in sudden panic, and Manus shouted, above the clamour of the fiddle music and the laughter that accompanied it, 'No matter! We will push you the way you ought to go!'

They did indeed push her, so vigorously that there was nothing for it but to keep on dancing. She was birled about until she grew dizzy. She was passed from hand to hand and arm to arm, smiling at a dozen faces, until she found herself with Manus again. Each time he would spin her around and cast her to somebody else like a top, and they would be off again. The wildness of the music, the speed and the rhythm of it, carried her along. Her feet barely touched the floor. The room was a blur around her. But at last the music halted and she stopped, fanning herself with her hand and gasping like a netted fish.

'You see?' he said. 'You can dance!'

'Why are you not even breathless?'

'Because I was born to it. Did you enjoy it?'

'I did. But I think I need something to drink.'

He led her to a seat, and served her food and wine with his own hands. She ate and drank with an appetite, and realised that she felt extraordinarily happy. It was as though some exotic flower had begun to blossom inside her, as though whenever her thoughts turned inwards she found it there, and marvelled at it.

From time to time, Manus left her to attend to his duties as host, but always he came back, and danced with her more than once. The celebrations went on until at last the stragglers stumbled down the path towards the village, or rode, bent low over their ponies' necks, each man leaving his mount to find its own way home. There would be many 'darkenings' that night, men who had drunk not wisely but too well. A few guests even slept down in the great hall, slumped over the tables amid the debris of the party. Henrietta was ensconced on a settle before the fire, half asleep and yawning, when Manus finally came back to her and offered her his arm. He looked tired, but sober.

'Would you like a breath of air, Henrietta?'

'I think I would.'

'This has been a long and difficult day for you. Come with me. We will go outside for a while.'

She took his arm and allowed herself to be led away from the house, to where an old lichen-covered rampart looked out over the sea. With nightfall, the wind had dropped, and the sea was calm now; the waves a gentle accompaniment, rather than the thunderous clamour that they would all too soon become with the onset of winter. Owls were calling around the house as they did every spring and autumn. She glanced back and saw its walls looming above her, but there were lamps in the windows and it seemed by no means so forbidding as she had once thought it. She turned towards the sea. A full moon sailed towards them, now large as a galleon, now veiled in thin clouds.

'The night is sweet,' she said.

'But you can already smell the approach of winter. The birds of summer know it, too. They are flying or have already flown.'

'And I must stay.' She spoke without bitterness, as a matter of fact only. She leaned on the wall and looked down at the sea, catching glimpses of the movement of waves in the fluctuating moonlight. Manus stood companionably beside her. He had pushed up the sleeves of his linen shirt in the heat of the dance and she could feel his bare arms against her own, and the warmth of his body against hers.

'It was what you wanted in the spring,' he said. 'To fly with the birds. Do you mind that day?' He remembered her desperation. He remembered the damp scent of her as he had lifted her onto his mare, and the sudden rush of sympathy that had come to him. 'Do you still want to fly from here?'

'I still want my son.'

I will always want him, she thought. The loss of him will be there, a hollow wound inside me. And time will heal it over, but the wound itself will be there, just below the surface. And I will have to live with it, all the days that remain to me. But perhaps I can learn to live with it and not die of it.

'He will have forgotten me,' she said. 'He was so young when we were parted, and he has Maisie. At least he has not lost her.'

'Do you still want to go from here?' The question came again, tentatively, from the darkness.

How could I go? How could I ever leave Manus when I love him so much? she thought, and the truth of it struck her like a blow to the heart. It was not just friendship she felt for him. It was love; a raw, unmanageable passion that she had never known before.

' 'Do you still want to leave me?' he repeated. 'Henrietta? I must know what your wishes are.'

'Why do you ask me when it isn't possible?'

'But if it were possible?' he persisted.

She paused for a moment. 'Listen,' she began. 'You cannot imagine how frightened I was when I first came here.'

'I remember it all too well.'

'I had been taught to believe that highland folk were little better than savages.' It was easier to say such things to him in the darkness.

'I remember your saying as much: thieves and murderers. It was the day when you threw your food at Ishbel and deafened me with your wailing.'

'I was beside myself.'

'And I was not kind to you. Not kind at all.'

'No. You called me a plain wee thing.'

He shifted his arm on the wall, and took hold of her hand. 'I did. And I'm sorry for it now.'

'But you see, I have changed my mind as well.'

'Have you?'

'I have received a great deal of kindness upon all sides. And I find that you are all more *siobhalt* – more civilised – than any of my Edinburgh acquaintance.'

'That is because you have made yourself a part of this place.'

'I grow more used to it with each day that passes. I begin to understand the speech and the way of life. And now that I have the names of things, the words themselves give me strength. I love the music and the singing. Oh, Manus, I think I love your island.'

It was true. There was that in her which responded to all the sounds and scents of the place.

'And your house is warmer than it was,' she observed.

'Which is your doing. But you have made your mark on more than the house, Henrietta. I think it is my heart that is warmer than it once was.'

'Grisel thinks me dead.'

He stirred impatiently at the mention of the name. 'She *hopes* you are dead. I would wager that she will make no further enquiries. If she hears nothing, she will make up some tale for Thomas and do her best to forget all about you.'

'You are probably right. Such malice. I can barely believe it even now.'

'What wrong had you ever done her?' he asked. 'Were you aware of having offended her in some way?'

'I think, when we were both young, I may have been unkind to her. Or not even unkind so much as careless of her feelings, maybe.'

She, too, had been wondering what lay at the root of Grisel's spite. And as she had slipped into the pale silk dress, before the dance, a memory had come to her of an afternoon in Edinburgh when they were little more than children. She remembered herself, prancing about in a new gown, while Grisel had watched with greedy admiration, spiced with jealousy.

'You do not have such a gown, do you, Grisel?' Henrietta had said, more out of pride in herself and by way of offering friendly advice than from any real desire to humiliate Grisel. 'You should ask your uncle if he will buy you one. Thomas says he has plenty of money but you wear such old-fashioned clothes. Why do you not ask him to buy you some new dresses and petticoats?'

Had that been what lay at the root of it all? she wondered. Could one thoughtless, childish remark be responsible for so much misery? She doubted it.

'I was woefully spoilt, it's true,' she said. 'But I cannot believe that her malice was only to do with envy of me. I suppose she may have wished herself in my place from time to time. William was a kind man but I'm sure he was of no help to a growing girl. He changed when he married me. It was as though something awoke in him, late, but true all the same. As though he woke up to life. But when Grisel was young, he gave her little affection. She envied me but she adored Thomas and for a time he would not even give her a second glance. Then, after I had the smallpox, our positions were reversed. So she got her wish after all.'

'She should have pitied you for that.'

'She should. And maybe she did for a while. But I know that the money would have weighed heavily with her. Grisel always counted the cost of everything. She loved things for their price, not for their value. Thomas was of the same mind. It strikes me that if they had each married different people, things might have turned out quite otherwise. So I can only believe that you are right. It was simply her craving for money, a very great deal of money, that prompted her to do what she did. And that made Thomas agree to it.'

'Listen,' he said. 'If I were to tell you that I would let you go – take you to Edinburgh and leave you outside your brother's town house on the Canongate – what would you say?'

The moon was veiled again. She could not see his face properly but she knew from his tone of voice that he meant it. He would take her to Edinburgh and leave her there, but only if that was what she wanted.

She hesitated. 'Grisel and Thomas would be greatly embarrassed by my unexpected return.'

'They would.'

'But more than that,' she said slowly, 'I think they would be threatened. And so they would find a way of implicating you – nay, of blaming you for the whole enterprise.'

He would be a hostage to their accusations and insinuations. He was a known Jacobite. A highlander. While Thomas was a lowlander of good family with considerable wealth at his disposal. And she, Henrietta, was a helpless woman, not long widowed. Nobody would listen to her, no matter what she chose to say. She had few friends in the capital and none of them had Thomas's influence or authority.

'They would have you arrested,' she told him. 'And then I would be at their mercy all over again. You would not be able to help me. I would be a prisoner and my son would not even know me.'

'It is what I most fear.'

'I cannot allow you to risk it,' she said. 'And besides. I would never again smell the *machair*. Or hear the owls crying around the old house.'

She turned to him. The moon sailed out from her cloak of clouds.

'And I would never see your face.' She reached out and touched his cheek, gently tracing the lines of it. 'Oh, Manus, don't ask me to decide.'

'You would not wish to go?'

'I would not wish to leave this place.' In spite of everything that he had confessed to her, perhaps because of everything, she still had her own confession to make. 'I would not wish to leave you, Manus.' The relief of saying the words aloud, acknowledging the truth of them, flooded through her. 'I think it would break my heart to leave you.'

She moved into his arms. His lips on hers were cool, and though his manner was grave she sensed some excitement in him, some passion that he was doing his best to control.

'Will you come indoors with me now, Henrietta?' he asked her. 'I have a gift for you. Something I want you to have.'

She knew that on this day there had been a great exchanging of gifts between the young men and women. *Struans* had been swapped for ribbons and in some cases even jewellery made of stones or pretty shells. She had seen Ishbel proudly wearing a necklace of serpentine pebbles from the shore, that Seamus had polished up for her.

'It is only fair. Why should you not have a gift like the other lassies? Come with me and I'll show you.'

TWENTY

At home in Edinburgh Alys tries hard to resume normal life, but with only limited success. November seems to go on indefinitely. The winds that blow up from the Forth are bitterly cold and laden with tiny particles of ice that make her face ache. It is much too cold for snow. John is so tetchy and cross with her that she begins to fear that he may be going to ask for custody of Ben. The thought throws her into a complete panic.

'Ask him what's wrong, for God's sake,' says an exasperated Sophie. 'I can't imagine that he would want to rock the boat like that. Millie's very fond of Ben but I don't think she wants him on a full time basis, do you?'

Sophie has a new man in her life, and Alys has not been seeing quite so much of her. Sophie has a new man roughly every nine months, but that is as long as they last, like pregnancy. After that she gets bored with them and looks around for somebody else, though they usually persist in calling her for a long time afterwards. She hates what she calls 'the overlap'. This time seems different, however. This new man is easy-going and even-tempered but independent. He doesn't sit making cow's eyes at Sophie. He is pleasant and undemanding and Sophie is uncharacteristically meek when she talks about him.

'God,' says her daughter, Jasmine, who has come to help in the craft market on a particularly busy Saturday in late November when people are beginning their Christmas shopping. 'I hope this is finally the one!'

'Do you like him?'

'He's OK,' says Jasmine casually. 'His name's Clive and he's a philosophy lecturer. Mum likes him and that's all that matters. He's the best of the lot so far. What she really needs is somebody who'll take care of her without trying to bully her.'

'Don't we all?'

'Well, Mum thinks she doesn't. But I'll be off to uni soon. I've got my own life to lead and I don't want to be worrying about her all the time.'

Alys is touched by Jasmine's concern. 'Would you?' she asks. 'Be worrying about her, I mean?'

'Well, maybe not all the time,' concedes Jasmine.

'I always think your mother's so self-sufficient. She seems perfectly happy to me.'

Jasmine pulls a face.

'Heavens,' says Alys. 'If Sophie isn't contented with her lot, what hope is there for the rest of us?

'Well, she is happy most of the time. But everyone needs company. I'm like . . . I don't want her to rush off and marry the guy. Just give him a chance, that's all.'

Jasmine wears long black Victorian skirts and black boots with pointed heels and toes, or big chunky black lace-ups. She is fond of chantilly lace shawls with their intricate sooty florals, dark lipstick and nail varnish. She has a delicate tattoo on her back, and a necklace of silver skulls round her throat. She is a very pretty girl, tall and elegant, and the look suits her. She is wrapping up a pair of earrings for a customer, with long-purple-nailed precision.

'Will you be asking Mum to your house for Christmas?'

'I expect so,' says Alys absentmindedly. They have had Christmas dinner together ever since the divorce.

'Because I've got plans,' says Jasmine.

'What plans?'

'I've been invited to spend Christmas in Florida. My uncle and aunt have a place there, and my cousins want me to go, but I can't if Mum's going to be on her own.'

'What about the new man?'

'Oh, I think he might be around. But I don't know what their plans are for Christmas. And I don't want to say I'm going away or even ask mum about it until I know for sure.'

'Don't worry about it. Me and Ben will take care of her. And Clive can come too, if he wants.'

'Thanks,' says Jasmine. 'I was hoping you'd say that. I only hope he's still around by Christmas.'

The next time John brings Ben home, Alys manages to entice him in for coffee and takes him into her workshop, leaving Ben engrossed in his Playstation in the living room.

'What's wrong, John?' she asks. 'You seem edgy these days.'

John gulps down his coffee. 'You still know me well, don't you?'

'I used to think I did.'

'I've been meaning to tell you, but I didn't know how to put it.'

'Put what?'

'Millie's pregnant.'

This news takes her breath away. She has somehow never thought about Millie wanting children. She is a couple of years older than John, thirty-eight or -nine to his thirty-six. Alys has always imagined that Millie's profound attachment to small dogs and her work signalled a decision not to have children. Which is daft, when you come to think about it. Broodiness can strike at any age.

'Good God!' She goes to the fridge and takes out a bottle of wine. 'Do you want a drink?' she asks.

'I'm driving.' But he accepts a small glass anyway.

She pours herself a much larger one and takes a big gulp. 'Was this planned?'

'She'd got the mother-hen thing in a big way, I know that.'

'And how do you feel about it?'

'Now that I've got used to the idea? I'm happy. I just wondered how you . . . ?'

'Ben will be delighted,' she says quickly.

'Will he?'

'Of course. He's always going on about wanting a baby brother or sister.'

'And you? How do you feel, Alys?'

'What does it have to do with me?'

'I don't know, really. I just feel that it does. I wondered if you might mind.'

Does he think I'm still carrying a torch for him? she wonders. 'No. I don't mind in the slightest,' she reassures him. 'Why on earth should I? I'm quite fond of you as Ben's dad. And I still kind of like you. But I don't love you any more.'

'That's me told, then,' he says ruefully, switching on the boyish charm that has long since ceased to move her. 'Besides, there's something else.'

Alys shifts uneasily. Here it comes, she thinks.

'I've had the offer of another job.'

'Oh?' This is unexpected.

'I've been headhunted, I suppose. It's almost too good an offer to turn down.'

'I sense a "but" coming.'

'There is a fairly big "but",' he says evenly. 'It's in London – London, Ontario. We'd have to move there for three years at least.'

'Oh God. That's a long way.'

She suddenly realises how much she still relies on him for help with Ben, for doing the things dads do, attending meetings, picking Ben up and dropping him off, taking him to the doctor and the dentist sometimes, just being there. If he goes, she really will be alone. A single mum.

'What do you think?' he asks.

'I don't know. We'll miss you. Ben will miss you.'

'I haven't said yes yet.'

'What about Millie?'

'She says it's up to me to make the decision and I have to ask you as well, but I think she'd like to go.'

'I'll bet she would.'

Of course Millie will want to go. Much as she likes Ben, with her own child on the way she will be glad of a fresh start.

'What about you?' she asks.

'I've thought of nothing else for the past month. I have to decide within the next week or so. And we'd move in the New Year.'

'So?'

'I need to know how you feel about it, how Ben feels about it. I'd be flying to and fro pretty often, you know. And he could still come for holidays. The world's quite a small place.'

'And he's growing up fast.'

'But I'll still worry about you.'

'I know.'

She has a sudden vision of Donal, his arms round Ben, dark head bending down to blond. Why is life so bloody complicated? she thinks.

'I think you should go. To Canada, I mean.'

What is at the back of her mind? Would his absence somehow give her permission to leave Edinburgh as well, taking Ben with her? Would she then be able to go wherever she wanted? To Garve, for instance?

But all these thoughts are only half formed. Besides, she doesn't know if Donal would want her. More to the point, she doesn't really know if she wants to go. Would she miss the city too much? Would she, like Anne Marie, miss the shops and the cinemas and the restaurants and the . . . Would she miss the buzz? What about the winters? says the cautious voice in her head. What about the wind and the rain and that small circumscribed world of the island where everybody, absolutely everybody, knows your business? What about the next year and the one after that?

'Alys,' says John, 'what are you thinking about?'

'Nothing. Just that you can't plan your life too meticulously. I think if you've been given the opportunity you ought to go. We'll work round it. We'll manage. Ben can come to visit you. I may even come to visit, you never know.'

'That would be good.'

She is astonished by how civilised and sensible she is being. Only a year ago, she could not imagine herself ever behaving like this. Suddenly all her perspectives seem to have shifted. It is quite a revolution.

John stands up. 'I'd better get home.' He stops on the way out. 'Thanks, Alys. Thanks for being so understanding. You've given me a lot to think about.'

Same here, she thinks, but she says nothing, watches him kiss Ben, pecks him on the cheek, waves him away from the door.

'You have to go back to Garve, of course,' says Sophie, after Christmas dinner. 'You can't possibly decide until you've been. It's been too rushed if you ask me, and yet too half-hearted at the same time. You've had no time at all to get to know each other. You need to have a good long talk with the man, find out what he's really like, find out where you stand.'

'I don't think I stand anywhere at all right now.'

'Then you have to ask him. Tell him you can't go on like this. You have to know one way or another. Does he want you or not? Do you want him? Can you bear to up sticks and move there? It's simple.'

'For you, maybe.'

Clive, who has a passion for orienteering and genealogy, has come for Christmas dinner as well. When Alys issued the invitation to Sophie, it turned out that Clive had nowhere else to go, either.

'Are you sure you don't want a nice private party?' asked Alys. 'Just the two of you together.'

'Christ, no,' said Sophie. 'I adore Christmas. But it has to be sociable. We see plenty of each other anyway.'

'Do you?'

'Well, you know . . .' said Sophie, evasively.

Like birthdays, Ben manages to have two Christmases, two sets of presents, two Christmas trees; this one and another celebration with John and Millie on Boxing Day. He has treated the news of his father's impending move to Canada with equanimity, and Alys realises that he still has little idea of distances. If he can visit his father and Millie and the new baby – and John has assured him that he can – then that's all right by Ben. Bruntsfield, London, Ontario, what does it matter? His only worry has been for the dog, but John has assured him that it will be going to Canada as well.

'Just so long as I know,' he says.

Clive is down on the rug, wrestling with the assembly of a new and complicated Lego space vehicle. Ben is helping him.

'I do want to go back to Garve,' says Alys thoughtfully.

'Why don't you go at Easter? It's so lovely on the islands then, and you won't have John belly-aching about time off school for Ben.'

'I don't think you should take kids out of school for holidays,' says Clive, mildly, from the rug.

'I was never in school for more than a fortnight together,' says Sophie, who was an asthmatic child, 'and it never did me any harm.'

'Yes, but you were a prodigy.'

'Oh, whoof,' she says, making a dismissive little noise with her lips, and kicking at him with her bare foot. Sophie likes academic flattery, Alys has noticed, though comments about her appearance leave her unmoved.

'It's me that's had too much time off already this year, never mind Ben.'

'Nonsense. Anyway, John will be giving you more cash soon, won't he?'

'He will.'

Her ex-husband has surprised her by proposing that he increase his monthly maintenance payments. Perhaps it is his way of saying thank you for not rocking the boat where his new job is concerned.

'I have been invited, you know. To Garve, I mean.'

'By Donal?'

'Yes. He sent me a Christmas card.'

'Wow!'

Alys doesn't offer to show it to Sophie. It is a flimsy affair with an unfeasibly large robin sitting in the snow, and she has propped it on her work table. She can imagine Donal buying it in the post office, but knows that Sophie would greet it with a hoot of laughter.

'Why do we let men get away with being so feeble?' asks Sophie of no one in particular.

'How do you mean?'

'Well, if it was a woman friend – me, for instance – you would have expected a Christmas card and been hurt if I didn't send you one. Just because it's a man, you're deeply impressed that he bothered. I can tell you are.'

Alys shrugs.

'It's because you think yourselves so superior,' puts in Clive from the rug. 'You let us get away with it, and we do.'

Sophie kicks him again. 'Away back to your Lego,' she says. 'So what does Donal say?'

'He says he's feeling better and he's done a bit to the house and do we want to go and stay with him when the weather improves?'

213

He has also sent his love and a row of kisses, but she doesn't tell Sophie that.

'What are you waiting for, then?'

'I don't know.'

'Listen, if you're waiting for him to throw himself at your feet and declare undying passion, you'll wait for ever.'

'Do you think so?'

'He doesn't seem the type, but then what do I know?'

Sophie looks fondly at Clive, who is frowning over a miniature set of wheels on a bright blue plastic strip.

'Do people ever do stuff like that?' asks Clive, wonderingly. 'Declare undying passion, I mean?'

'There,' says Ben. 'Look, it goes in there.'

'Oh, so it does,' says Clive, all thumbs.

Ben takes it from him kindly and slots it into place.

'Gosh,' says Clive. 'Is that where it goes?'

'What type is he, then? Donal, I mean?' asks Alys in a low voice, leaving the men to their engineering.

'You mean you don't know by now?'

'I mean I want to know what you think.'

'I hardly know the man,' says Sophie. 'I only met him a couple of times in October.'

'So what were your first impressions?'

Sophie pauses and takes a large gulp of port for inspiration. 'Mm. That he's attractive, in a rural sort of way.'

'Oh God, Sophie.'

'Well, you asked! He's got that weather-beaten look. You'd get like that, too, if you went to live on the island. I can see you in a year or so: hair like straw and a face like a turnip.'

Alys pours herself another glass of wine. 'Hell's teeth, Sophie!'

'Well, if I'm being serious, I think he seems kind, capable, practical, sexy.'

'Really?'

'In a weather-beaten sort of way.'

Alys nudges her and she chokes on her port, chuckling.

'What else?'

'Nice eyes. Really nice eyes. A bit sad. Hidden depths there, I should say.'

'What kind of hidden depths?'

'Oh God, Alys, I don't know. I just got the impression that he constantly hides his real feelings for some reason. Partly it's that self-contained, understated islander bit. But there's something else. He's afraid of . . . I don't know. Being hurt? Losing something? If you don't make a commitment you can't get hurt, can you? If you don't trust anybody, then how can you be betrayed?'

Alys thinks that Sophie should know this better than most, but doesn't say so.

Sophie says it for her in a low voice: 'I recognise it in other people because it's my problem, too. But honestly, I don't really know what kind of man he is, and that's the truth.'

'The trouble is that I don't know what kind of man he is, either. So I'll just have to try to find out.'

TWENTY-ONE

Manus offered Henrietta his arm, and led her back to the house. To her surprise, they went in by a side door that she had never used before, thinking that it gave access to some cellar or food store. Instead a narrow flight of spiral stairs, dimly lit by an oil lamp, wound upwards. He went ahead of her to show her the way. 'Be careful,' he told her. 'The stones are very uneven. I know them so well that I hardly notice it.'

'I didn't know that this stair existed, Manus.'

'Nobody uses it except myself.'

At the top, he opened another heavy door, pulled aside a musty tapestry and led her into the big warm space that she instantly recognised as his bedchamber, though it was much tidier than when she had first caught sight of it, all those months ago.

'Oh!' she said, in some confusion. 'Here we are.'

'Have you been in here before then?' he asked, puzzled.

She nodded.

'When?'

'It was only briefly. Last winter. I was exploring the house all by myself. You had gone out. I looked in here.'

'Good God, did you? No wonder you thought me an uncivilised highlander.'

'I saw only your bed, and the big carved press there. Then I heard your horse's hooves in the yard, and ran away back to my own room.' She didn't mention that she had seen the embroidered cabinet.

'My poor Henrietta. Did I frighten you so much?'

'You did.'

He took her hand and led her to his high feather bed, very neat today, and covered with a heavy woven blanket. Without asking her leave, he lifted her up so that she was perched on the edge of it.

'I have a gift for you, *a ghràidh*.'

'You don't have to give me presents. I like you well enough without them, you know.'

'Do you like me, Henrietta?' He looked as though he needed her reassurance. 'This evening, on the way home, I thought I might have forfeited your friendship. I thought I might have lost your trust for ever.'

'And I feared you might send me away.'

'But you didn't want to go?'

'No! The thought of leaving you and this island filled me with such dread. And then I saw how it really was. Oh, Manus, it is more than liking, more than friendship, but it is all of that as well. I love you most truly.'

'And I you. Which is why I want you to have this.' He took up the embroidered casket from beside the bed, and put it in her lap. 'It belonged to my wife. The work is all her own. But that is not the reason for the gift. I don't want you always to be looking over your shoulder and wondering what Frances would have done or said. I want you to have it because it is precious to me, and so are you.'

She looked down at the cabinet where it lay, heavy with the promise of happiness. 'Manus, it is beautiful.'

'She did some of the work before our marriage and brought it with her to hold all her small possessions. Then she finished it here because she grew to love the island dearly.' He bent down to show her. 'You see, it is the story of Ruth,' he explained. 'But the flowers are the flowers of this island. And so are the birds. Here is my house and here is the sea. You can keep your own work in it if you choose. And I know that you like to take shells and pebbles from the shoreline sometimes.'

It was true. She collected pearly shells and stones like glistening chunks of ice, whenever she went walking along the flat white sand of the bay. He must have been watching her.

'See.' He leaned over and opened the doors, to reveal more embroidery, sliding out one of the drawers inside. It smelled of lavender and lemon balm. A fine feather floated up. She caught it. Swansdown. So Frances, too, had gathered small remembrances of land and sea.

'And you are giving me this?' She pulled open another drawer. The knotting shuttle would fit inside perfectly. The generosity of the gift took her breath away.

'Do you like it?'

'I love it. I'll take care of it. Always.'

Henrietta slid open yet another drawer of the cabinet and found a hand mirror, set with stones in the shape of flowers.

'And that is for you, too. It was my mother's and it is very old. It was given to her by a visitor from France.'

'I try not to use mirrors.'

'I have noticed it. You cannot bear the sight of your own face. But if you look into it, Henrietta, you will see only the dear face of the woman I love.'

He shifted the cabinet carefully to one side, and – on a sudden impulse – buried his face in her lap. She put her hand on his head, stroking the thick dark hair, shot through with grey. He looked up at her.' Henrietta, I find myself sorely in want of a wife!'

'I would agree with you there.'

'You would?'

'Oh, I would. After all, I have already set your house in order.'

'And now I suppose you want to organise me in the same way.'

'I think I do.'

'Then will you consent to become my wife?'

She hesitated. One last doubt remained, but it was a large one. 'You are not asking me out of pity for my situation?'

'Oh, Henrietta!' He sounded not so much angry as exasperated. He rose to his feet, lifted her and laid her gently down on the bed. His face hovered above hers, grave, loving.

'Ah, God!' He leaned down and kissed her and she felt her body's intense arousal to him. 'Do you think me so foolish that I would seek a life's partner out of pity?'

'No, I don't think you are at all foolish. But my face . . .'

'Henrietta, listen to me. The scars have faded with each month that has passed here. And even if they had not, they do not matter to me. If I do not notice them, why should you? You have a sweet face and a happy disposition.' She could feel him trembling and the passion in his voice was unmistakable.

He moved away from her, controlling himself with an effort. They lay together on top of the bed, hand in hand, and she had the fleeting and faintly disturbing thought that they were like figures on a tomb: a knight and his lady. She looked up at the carving on the pillars of the bed, strangely alive in the firelight. She thought how good it would be to stay like this, close beside him in the warmth of this place, and never to have to go back to the drafty tower room again.

'*Oh m'eudail, a ghràidh!*' he said, 'Oh my love, I should have spoken to you months ago. But how could I, when I feared that you might think yourself bought and sold?'

'I should not have thought that.'

'You say that now, but it might have been so. It would have been so. Henrietta, you do not know how it gladdened my heart to hear that . . . that villain Ravenscroft repeat those words: "You may kill her or keep her."'

'They were terrible words.'

'Aye, they were. And they were the measure of their wickedness. But they released me from my foolish bargain – and yet it was not so foolish, for it brought you to me, and God knows what other evil they might have attempted if I had not agreed. All that was left to me, after that, was to offer you your freedom.'

'I had grown to love my prison and my captor most dearly.'

'Aye, but I meant it, you know, Henrietta. I would sooner see you go back to Edinburgh than keep you here against your will.'

'My only regret is for my son.'

'I know.' He sighed. 'It even came to my mind that I could have him taken as we took you, and bring him here. But by then it would have been a cruelty to the little lad.'

'It would.'

'I tell you, Henrietta, it was a judgement of Solomon.'

'Besides, even if you had brought him here, we would not have been left in peace together, he and I. And the consequences for you, and for this place and your people, would have been terrible indeed. As long as Gabriel is well cared for, I can be happy, too.'

He turned and slid his arms round her again, holding her close.

'You should go back to your chamber, to your own bed. For the sake of propriety,' he said, with his arms still wrapped tight round her.

'I should.' She made no attempt to leave him. In fact, it was quite beyond her to get up and go, and it was plain that he felt the same. She started to laugh. 'But how on earth am I to do it?'

'I don't know at all,' he said, still not moving. 'Perhaps we should follow the custom of some of our people, and put the bolster between us, so that we can lie together without temptation.'

'And how do they fare?' she asked. She had heard of the tradition among country people, where houses were small and opportunities for courtship were few.

'Well, sometimes I am told that the bolster is but a poor barrier to love, with the results clearly demonstrable in nine months' time.'

He slid his knee between her legs. The silk of her dress was creased and crumpled beneath the weight of him.

'Ah, God,' he said. 'What will we do?'

'You are lord of this island,' she said at last. 'That is what you told me on my first day here. Your word is law here, is it not? And everything on the island belongs to you?'

'Aye. That is true. But what of it?'

'Then why do you not tell me that I must stay here with you?'

'And will you do as you are told?'

'Of course. In this at least I will be glad to. For the truth is that I can't bear to leave you.'

'Then stay. Tonight, and every night to come. For the long and the short of it is, Henrietta Dalrymple, that I am as much in love with you as any man could be and I want you for my wife. And believe me, my treasure of treasures, it is not out of any misplaced pity that I ask you, but because I cannot any longer bear to be under the same roof as you, and not take you to my bed and my heart.'

TWENTY-TWO

It is Easter on Garve and Alys and Ben are staying with Donal at Ardachy. This time they haven't booked into the hotel. Donal has had what he calls 'a bit of a clear-out'. He himself has moved into his father's room with its big mahogany double bed. This leaves Donal's old room, with two neat single divans, for Ben and Alys.

'I got them delivered from the mainland,' he says.

Some of the clutter has been, if not removed, then at least dusted and rearranged. Things have been tidied away. Everything smells faintly of bleach, disinfectant or lavender furniture polish. Alys suspects that he has had help in preparing for their visit: Mrs Cameron from the hotel? Perhaps she would disapprove. His neighbour Mrs Maclean, then? Agnes Galbreath from the post office? Elderly Mary Fleming, who lives alone in the village with a large dog of indiscriminate parentage for company and is said to 'have a soft spot for Donal'? It could be any, or indeed all of these ladies together.

When Ben is asleep in bed, they sit up late at the kitchen table and talk. It is a well-scrubbed deal table, and Alys imagines Donal's mother rolling out her pastry on it, or kneading bread dough. Not an ambitious cook, she nevertheless finds herself thinking that it would be nice to potter about on this table, making meals for herself and Donal and Ben.

Tonight, they are drinking whisky, a smoky island malt. The bottle sits between them, its gold reflecting the lamplight, and the occasional moving flame from the fire. Alys likes the idea of having a kitchen like this with a real fire. She looks around at the old cupboards and the shabby couch and wonders why anyone would want a fitted kitchen.

'Would you ever think about moving here?' Donal asks her.

She hesitates, surprised by the way in which he has come right out with it. 'Well, maybe. But it would be a big step to take. There's Ben to consider. I would have to be absolutely sure it was the right thing to do. For both of us.'

'Ben loves this place.'

'That's true. He does.'

Alys thinks Ben loves Donal as well, but she doesn't say as much. Treading carefully, she says, 'Where would we live? Surely there aren't many vacant cottages on the island?'

His eyes slide away from hers. He cradles his glass in his hands. He does not say, 'Come and live with me.' Instead he asks, 'What about your ex- husband? How would he react?'

'He'd get used to the idea.'

'I don't want to tread on any toes,' he says, which irritates Alys intensely.

'Why would you be doing that? John and Millie are in Canada. What does it matter to them where we live now?'

Ben had wished them both a tearful farewell, but John Skypes or phones him every week and emails him most nights and sends him photos of what he and Millie call 'the bump'. The baby is due soon, and that's something else for Ben to be excited about. They are planning to come back to Scotland later this year to show off the contents of 'the bump'. Millie has become a confirmed advocate of natural childbirth. She is making plans for John to video the birth. Alys just knows that she will keep the placenta in her freezer, cook it like liver with a few chopped onions and eat some of it to prevent post-natal depression. She has placed a small bet with Sophie that this will happen, but Sophie cannot believe that anyone could actually bring themselves to do it and is confident of winning ten pounds. Alys thinks she knows better.

'All right, all right,' says Donal mildly, aware that he has upset her. 'So what's the problem?'

The truth is that there is no reason in the world why Alys can't work on the island, and sell her jewellery from here, online as well as to the tourists. And, that being the case, why not move here? Her mind goes leaping into the future. She knows from conversations with Mrs Cameron that there are new developments planned: a host of initiatives aimed at increasing the population, providing work and accommodation suitable for the island and its unique and fragile landscape. She knows there has been talk of a small arts and crafts gallery at the hotel, for one thing.

'We'll need somebody to run it,' said Mrs Cameron in the bar one lunchtime. They were sitting, eating baskets of chips and egg sandwiches, waiting for Donal, who was doing some spring-time planting in the garden. 'You could consider it. That is, if you're absolutely set on coming to live here.'

'Do you think I should, Mrs Cameron?'

'For heaven's sake, will you call me Elspeth?'

'Elspeth,' she says, 'do you think I should move here?'

'Oh now, I wouldn't presume to give you advice, my dear. It's a good place to bring up a child, sure enough. But could you adjust to the pace of the island?'

'I don't know.'

'Before I came here, my husband told me that this was a place where there was no word with quite the urgency of *mañana*. I didn't believe him, but there was some truth in it. Mind you, that was a while ago now. Things have changed. Young people here want more. There's a lot more get-up-and-go about them. But still . . . You'll just have to make your own decisions, I'm afraid.'

Now Alys and Donal are sitting in the kitchen at Ardachy and discussing the possibility of Alys and her son moving to the island.

She becomes aware that he is talking about the possibility of them moving to Ardachy as well. He beats about the bush for so long, with so many ifs and buts and maybes, that eventually she interrupts him. 'Donal? Hold on a minute. Are you asking us to move in with you?'

A flush overspreads his dark skin. 'I suppose that's what I'm saying. Yes.'

'Are you sure?'

'Oh I'm sure. But, you see, I don't know how you feel about it. I find it so hard to read you, Alys. Sometimes I think we don't understand each other at all.'

He lays out his ideas before her, like offerings. He stumbles over his words in his haste to tell her everything. It seems he has plans for redecorating the whole place to suit her.

'We could get some new furniture if that's what you want.'

'Not in here,' she says in some alarm. 'I like this kitchen just as it is.'

'Do you?'

'Yes, I do. Don't you start rushing about and changing everything for my sake.'

He is, however, hoping to have central heating installed and she agrees that this might be a good thing.

'They deliver oil from the mainland now. I could make it nice for you.'

'It's nice the way it is, Donal.'

'But I want to do things for you. And I'll make you a flower garden.'

'The garden's beautiful, too – the fuchsia hedges and the veronica by the gate. Don't be digging those up, for heaven's sake!'

'No, but there's more that I could do. Not just vegetables but roses if you like. Stuff like that.'

She realises, to her amazement and her love, that he must have spent a whole winter dreaming about this. There is an outhouse to one side of the cottage, which he says he could turn into a studio workshop for her. He thinks she and Ben would be happy on the island. He will do all he can to make them happy.

He takes her hand, across the table. His fingers are rough; the dirt of fishing and gardening remains deeply engrained there, no matter how often he scrubs them. But his hands are one of the things she loves most about him.

'I miss you when you're not here. You can't know how much I miss you both when you're not here.'

That 'both' clinches it. After all, she and Ben come as a package now.

He is waiting for an answer and suddenly she knows what it will be, knows that there is an inevitability about it. This is where she is meant to live. The island and the man have been waiting for her to come back to them. Upstairs, Ben calls out in his sleep. The unfamiliarity of the room, with its silence, has impinged on his dreams.

'I'll have to go and see to him.'

'All right.' He doesn't try to stop her. 'Maybe we can talk about this tomorrow,' he says. 'We have plenty of time.'

'Yes. Yes, we have.'

In the bedroom she crouches beside Ben's bed and strokes his head, until he settles down again. Then she undresses and listens to her son's quiet breathing. He lies curled up, clutching his favourite soft toy, a threadbare dog called Cecil. Or Thethil, as Ben used to call him when he could only just talk. Cecil used to squeak but has been dumb for many years.

Now she stands in her long white Victorian nightie, with a baggy grey cardigan that used to belong to Iain over the top, and looks out of the dormer window and down towards the sea. There is a faint luminescence coming from the water. Out there is the dark Christmas-pudding shape of the islet they visited last summer. She wonders where the seals go at night. She thinks they should have buried Iain on the islet, but he had to make do with the neat cemetery beside the village. He would have been happier out there, with his McNeill forebears, beneath a long stone carved with enigmatic symbols.

'Oh, Lord,' she says aloud, but quietly, so as not to wake Ben. 'Oh, Lord, what shall I do?'

There is a muted knock at the door. She goes over and opens it. Donal is standing there in a white tee-shirt and navy shorts.

He says, 'Oh, my love, I could not go to sleep without a sight of your face.'

The words hang in the air between them, oddly familiar, like the words of a song.

She slips out of the room and closes the door behind her. Ben sleeps on. Donal takes her into the other bedroom, his own room. Carefully – 'decorously' is the word that comes to her mind – he helps her out of the woollen cardigan, which still smells faintly and comfortingly of Iain: tar, soap, gardening. Then he lifts the long white nightie over her head. He covers her with the sheet, which smells of lavender, and he strips off his shorts and shirt and slides in beside her.

'Alys, Alys,' he says.

He kisses her and gently nudges her legs apart with his knee and slides into her, and since this is what she has been wanting all day, all week, all year, perhaps all her life and beyond, she is open and wet and ready for him. Momentarily she thinks that this is the bed where Iain lay. But that doesn't alarm her. Then her thoughts slide away from Iain, away even from Donal whom she loves. Her thoughts slide back to all those other McNeills, husbands and wives who have been together in this room, and elsewhere on the island. She thinks, too, of the embroidered cabinet up at Scoull. Ruth, standing amid the alien corn. Thy people shall be my people. And then there is nothing but Donal, and her body's fierce, passionate response to him.

Later in the week, they start to talk again about ways and means, although now they are assuming that she and Ben will come to

Ardachy. Ben, too, has begun making assumptions. 'When we come to Garve,' he keeps saying. 'When we're living on Garve.'

Donal has inherited the tenancy of the house at Ardachy, and that, at least, is secure. In a year or two they will be able to buy it if they want to. Donal has also inherited the embroidered cabinet and again Elspeth Cameron has asked him if he wants to sell it. It is becoming difficult to insure it where it sits in the hotel. At the very least they will have to buy a more secure case for it; preferably one with an alarm fitted.

'But maybe you can persuade him to sell it,' she says to Alys. 'It really ought to be in a museum. Just think what you could do with the money.'

'It's nothing to do with me, Elspeth. I'd rather not persuade him, one way or another.'

Elspeth looks at her shrewdly. 'You're a nice lady, Alys.'

'I hope I'm an honest one. But you're right in a way. It's such a massive responsibility. And the money would come in handy. He could get himself a bigger boat, for one thing.'

'And you could do a lot of work on that house. You could make it a lot more civilised for the three of you.'

If Alys is honest with herself, though, she thinks that the cabinet ought to stay on the island, and to hell with the value of it. Some things are more important than money. But she is also forced to admit that the value of it is, in some sense, a burden to them. It is too valuable for comfort. And so, one afternoon, when they have just finished a late lunch, and when Ben is down in the village, playing with Kirsty, she asks Donal, 'Do you think maybe you ought to sell the embroidered cabinet, then?'

There is a long silence.

He is looking at her in shocked surprise and she instantly wishes she had never mentioned it. 'Sell it?' he says. 'How can I sell it?'

'Well, I should imagine plenty of people might want to buy it.'

'But it can't possibly leave the island. It can't go from here.'

'I only thought you might be able to . . . I don't know' – she shrugs, smiles at him – 'do things with the money. Put it towards the house. Buy another boat. Stop gardening, if you want to. It was just a thought. It doesn't matter.'

A defensive expression has crept into his eyes. He is folding his arms and scowling. 'But it does matter,' he says. 'Why would I want to stop gardening?'

'I just feel you're not appreciated. I mean, the money would give you choices. You've got a lot of talent. You could really make something of yourself, Donal.'

The words are out before she has time to think about them. She wishes she could take them back but they hang in the air between them. Terrible. Irrevocable.

He could make something of himself.

Oh Jesus, she thinks. Oh fuck, Alys, why did you say that? What did you want to say that for? Apart from anything else, it is exactly the kind of thing Millie might have said.

'Make something of myself?' he says, slowly. 'So you think . . . you think I am nothing, do you? You think I am an uncivilised islandman with nothing to offer you.'

'Don't be silly. I didn't say that.'

'No, but you think it, all the same. It is what you have been thinking all along. I can see it in your face.'

'Don't be daft!'

'I'm daft, am I? Because I have some feeling for history and tradition? Because I do not care to sell my inheritance?'

'I didn't mean that.'

'Make something of myself!' he repeats. 'I see it now. I'm not good enough for you. Is that the problem? Or maybe I'm good enough for a quick screw now and again – is that it? Is that what you think?'

She tries to touch him, but he flinches away from her. He paces about the kitchen, frightening her with his scarcely contained anger, though he seems in danger of hurting himself more than her.

'You're like all the rest of them!'

'What do you mean "the rest of them"?' she asks. 'How many of us have you had?'

This pulls him up short, but only for a moment.

'Well, like my wife, then,' he mutters. 'She was the same. She told me I was a useless bugger.'

'I never said anything of the sort, Donal.'

'She wanted money, a new house, new furniture. I was always doing my best for her, trying to make things nice for her, but it was never enough. She would throw things at me. You see that?' He points to a small dent in the wall beside the kitchen door. 'That was where she threw a dish at my head. She would drink and throw things and she would hit and punch and kick me. Once she took a bread knife to me. I have the scars still.'

Alys sees that he is serious and she is dismayed. 'But how could she?'

Donal is not a tall man but he is strong and stocky, with the powerful arms of a fisherman.

'She could because there was nothing I could do about it. She was a small woman and I couldn't hit her back. So she got away with it. I couldn't tell anyone, either. How could I? It would have shamed me to tell anyone, and who would have believed me, in any case? She used to say that. She used to say "No one will believe you. I'll tell them you started it. I'll tell them you beat me up and I retaliated!"'

'Oh, Donal." She tries to touch him again, but he moves away abruptly and leans against the wall as though the memory has made him tired.

'I put up with it all,' he says. 'I tried to please her but that didn't suit her, either. She took me for a bloody fool. She said I was a weak man with nothing to offer. "Who would want you?" she said. "Who would ever want a dumb bastard like you?"'

The words come tumbling out of him, hurting Alys as much as they hurt himself. She wants to take him in her arms but he won't let her near him. He shakes her off and that hurts her even more.

'So you know what she did? She went off and found herself another man, and another and another. There was the ferryman and there was one of the barmen at the hotel that year and there was one of the seasonal farmworkers and Christ knows how many more besides. "Real men", she called them.'

'I'm sorry. I didn't know.'

'Did you not? Did nobody tell you?'

'No. Who would tell me? Who would talk to me about you?'

'People used to look at me in the post office and the hotel and shake their heads. And then they would be so fucking kind to me to try to make up for it, but I knew what was going on. I knew that they thought I was a big soft bugger for putting up with it. I should have turfed her out long before she decided to go.'

'But I'm not like that,' she tells him, trying to exorcise the past, trying to bring him back into the present. 'You can't blame me for Anne Marie. I wouldn't do any of those things to you. You must know that!'

'She had her eye on the cabinet as well. "That must be worth a bob or two!" she said. "Why don't you make something of yourself, Donal? You don't want to be a fisherman all your life. You don't want to be a gardener all your life." Well, maybe I do!'

'Please, Donal, calm down!' She tries to take his hand but he will have none of it.

There is too much hurt in him and it all comes tumbling out, filling the kitchen with resentment, with painful memories.

'And now you say the same thing. Do you know, she wanted me to put the old man in a home. She wanted me to sell the cabinet and put my father in a home. It's a good job he's dead now, isn't it? Maybe you'd have wanted the same thing!'

He stops and now it is his turn to be aware of what he has said, suddenly brought up short by the insult he has offered her.

This is Alys, he thinks. Not Anne Marie. But it is too late.

His words hurt her so much that it is like a physical pain, somewhere around her heart.

'God!' she says, and she feels the tears gathering behind her eyes. 'Well, if that's what you think of me . . .'

'Oh, fuck!' he says, his head in his hands.

Alys realises that this is what he has always expected of her. Fundamentally, he has always expected that she will be the same as Anne Marie, that in the end she will leave him too, taking his self-respect with her. It is as though he has planned for it. She tries to touch him again, one last time, but he shakes her off.

'Leave me alone!' he shouts. 'Just fuck off and leave me alone will you?'

But it is Donal who goes. He storms out of the house, slamming the door behind him. She hears the van revving up and then driving at speed up the dirt track to the main road.

TWENTY-THREE

She finds herself in tears but after a while, when he doesn't come back, she dries her eyes and blows her nose. Grow up, Alys, she thinks. You always knew something like this would happen, something to spoil it all. Why else would you have been so cautious?

She waits a while longer, walks about the house, and then goes down and looks across the bay to the islet. It is late in the afternoon and quiet except for the distant clamour of seabirds as they jostle for position on the offshore rocks. She climbs down into Donal's boat and sits there for some time, looking at the sea, smelling tar and fish, thinking about the boat's owner. In the bottom of the boat are a screwed-up cigarette packet, a coil of rope, and a wooden box containing a miscellaneous collection of flotsam: an old green bottle, barnacle-encrusted and rather beautiful, a piece of driftwood shaped like a snake, a chunk of grey flint, a fragment of blue sea-glass, worn smooth by the water. She lifts them up one by one and examines them, wondering why Donal has kept them. Then it occurs to her that he has been collecting them for Ben.

Below her another pair of grey mullet are swimming about the harbour and she remembers the ones she saw at the south end of the island, all those months ago. You can never catch them, Donal has told her. They will come up and sniff at your bait but will seldom take the hook. Too clever by half.

At last the thread of her patience snaps. She goes back to Ardachy and packs their bags, glad that Ben is away playing with Kirsty. She puts everything in the car, always half expecting Donal to come back, put his arms round her, kiss her, beg her to stay. But there is no sign of him. They have missed the last ferry of the day, so she gets into the car and drives up the bumpy track to the hotel, where she books a double room for the night. Then she picks up a protesting Ben, and takes him back to the hotel as well.

'What's happened?' he keeps saying. 'I don't understand. Why are we at the hotel? I thought we were staying with Donal until the end of the holidays.'

'We're going home, Ben. Home to Edinburgh.'

'Why?'

'Because ... because we have to go home, that's all. I've changed my mind.'

He loses his temper then, in much the same way as Donal, and has a massive tantrum of a kind he never had, even when he was much younger, when she and John were divorcing. He throws books and clothes about the bedroom and stamps on Cecil, and she sends him to bed, where he sobs himself to sleep. She hates Donal for doing this to him but she hates herself even more.

Elspeth Cameron takes one look at her pale, tear-stained face, and makes a large pot of tea, bringing it into the residents' lounge, which is empty since almost everyone is at dinner.

'Don't ask,' says Alys. 'Just don't ask. I don't want to talk about it any more.'

'But, my dear, surely ... I mean, might it not just be a little tiff?'

'It's over. He's the most bloody unreasonable bastard I've ever had the misfortune to ... Jesus!' She can't bring herself to go on. 'I'm sorry,' she says. 'I shouldn't be swearing at you.'

'He was hurt very badly,' says Elspeth, mildly.

'Maybe he was, but that's no bloody excuse, is it?'

'Excuse for what?'

'For treating me like . . . for treating me . . .' She stops, afraid of bursting into tears again. There is a lump in her throat and she is trembling.

Elspeth shrugs, helplessly. 'No. But it's an explanation of sorts.'

There is nothing she can do or say to comfort Alys. It's up to Donal to make amends, and nobody seems to know where he is. She makes a few phone calls but nobody has seen him. Then a farmer called Angus Fraser reports that Donal's van is parked up at the north end of the island. There is a period of general panic until half an hour later when Angus reports that Donal is in his van and has told Angus to fuck off and leave him alone. Since he has a blanket and a bottle of whisky and the night is forecast to be warm, Angus thinks it best to do just that. Nobody sees fit to tell Alys any of this. They don't see how it will make matters any better and maybe they are right.

In the morning, when there is still no sign of Donal, Alys rouses Ben and makes him eat a piece of the toast which Mrs Cameron has provided, though it tastes like cardboard in her own mouth. Then she gets both of them into the car and heads for the early ferry. Fury at her lover's wilful stupidity drives her forwards.

'What are we doing, Mum?' Ben keeps saying.

'We're going home to Edinburgh.'

'But we can't! You said we'd stay the whole holiday. I thought we were going to stay for ever.'

'Well, I've changed my mind. We're going home now, today.'

'But what about Donal?'

'He's changed his mind, too. He doesn't want us.'

Even while she is saying it she is aware of the damage she is doing and hates herself for it.

Ben bites his lip, his eyes full of tears.

'I don't believe you,' he says. 'You're just saying that to be mean. He wants me. He's my friend.'

'Well, you can send him a postcard from Edinburgh, can't you?'

'Why do you have to spoil everything, Mum?' he asks her angrily, and she doesn't know how to answer him. In any case, she gives herself no time to think.

This is it, she says to herself. Finished. The whole idea was stupid, anyway. We have nothing in common. How could we possibly have anything in common? I'll go home to Edinburgh and forget all about him and his bloody primitive little island.

Hers is the last car to drive onto the ferry. Ben is snuffling and sobbing and whingeing beside her. Her guilt at putting him through this wars with her anger at Donal for making her put him through this. How the hell is he ever going to get over it? She has just turned off her engine, at a thumbs-up from Ewan the ferryman, when she hears the frantic hooting of a horn and the clank and rattle of Donal's van. The exhaust is now dragging along the ground. He has come driving down the road to the ferry so rapidly that the racket has aroused all the other passengers, islanders going shopping on the mainland, holidaymakers on their way home. He bounces the van down the road and then stands on the brake and squeals to a halt, a car's length away from the ferry ramp. The exhaust instantly clatters onto the road. The passengers have all come out of the cabin to watch and are arrayed on the upper decks with an entertaining grandstand view.

Alys stands beside her car, keys in hand.

Ben jumps out of the front seat, still pink with emotion, his cheeks wet, his eyes swollen. 'It's Donal!' he says, delightedly. 'It's Donal, it's Donal! I knew he'd come!'

Donal opens the door of his van and an empty whisky bottle tumbles out. It rolls down the concrete slip and comes to a halt against the ramp. Donal shambles after it, and stands there, a picture of grim defiance.

'Donal McNeill,' says the ferryman. 'What are you at, you silly bugger? Can't you see she's leaving?'

'She's bloody not leaving!'

'This bloody ferry's leaving whether you like it or not.'

'Fuck the ferry!' shouts Donal. 'Reverse the car! Alys, will you reverse the bloody car or must I come and get you?'

He looks tousled and unshaven and very much the worse for wear, having spent the night in the van with only whisky for company. He also looks remarkably sexy, all things considered.

'What?' She looks at him, wondering if he has gone completely mad. Her body betrays her, the sudden thump in the pit of her stomach catching her off guard. Oh God, she thinks, I can't possibly leave him when I love him so much.

'I said, reverse the bloody car.'

'Why?'

'Because I love you, that's why. I love you and I love your son and I don't want you to go away, ever, that's why.'

Some of the passengers on the upper deck begin applauding. This is too much for Ben, who blushes bright red, says 'Oh, Mum!' and gets back in the car again. Alys doesn't know what else to do, so she gets back into the car as well, starts the engine and, narrowly avoiding Donal and his bottle, reverses up the ramp and onto the road. Donal follows after, looking white and crumpled, his hair practically standing on end.

The ferry, full of waving, cheering passengers, leaves without her and Ben. She gets out of the car and then Ben gets out of the car, and Donal puts his arms round both of them and hugs them as though he will never let them go.

'Bloody hell,' he says in her ear. 'I'll have to do something about that bugger of an exhaust.'

Much later that day, they sit on the springy turf, leaning together, watching two seals swimming lazily in the bay below Ardachy.

They have hugged and kissed and apologised repeatedly to each other until Ben has told them to 'Stop it, the pair of you!' They have eaten bacon rolls in the kitchen; they have slept, curled up on the couch in a heap; and they have drunk lots of mugs of strong tea. Some time that afternoon Donal wandered off to have a bath and change into clean jeans and a sweatshirt. Now he has made a big pan of soup, with all the vegetables he could find, and they are waiting for it to cook, slowly and thoroughly, on the old stove, which might merit the description of Aga if it were not so elderly and decrepit.

Ben is down at the water's edge, skimming flat stones across calm water, counting the bounces.

'We used to do that,' says Alys. 'Do you remember?'

'You could never get enough bounces.'

'No. Half the time mine just plopped straight into the water. I used to get so angry. And you were the champion.'

'I was. It was my father taught me, though.'

'My dad was pretty good as well. I could never get the hang of it. Ben tells me I'm pathetic. Just as well he'll have you now, isn't it?'

'We should get a dog,' says Donal. 'I think we need a dog, don't you?'

'Good idea.'

'Oh, Jesus, Alys, I thought you might go for good.'

'I thought you wanted me to.'

'I was in the van and I was calling myself for everything, for being such a bloody fool and I was so sad that I started drinking and then I had a . . .' He hesitates. 'I had a slight darkening.'

'A slight darkening? Is that what you call it?'

'It's what the old man always called it.'

'And do you do it often? Have these darkenings?'

'Not often, no. Once in a blue moon just.'

'I'm glad to hear it.'

'Look, Mum, Donal!' says Ben, pointing up.

Above them they hear the eerie sound of swans, a pair of them flying in over the bay.

'I heard that noise in my dreams,' she says.

'They always come back. Year after year.'

'I'll have to go back to Edinburgh, you know; sort things out. But it won't take long.'

'It had better not. Or I'll be coming to fetch you.'

'Don't worry. Everything that matters is here. With you.'

'I thought I might lose you. My treasure of treasures.' There is a small pause and then he says, 'Like Manus McNeill.'

'Like Manus?'

'He lost his treasure.'

'Yes. But we still don't know what it was, do we?'

'Well,' he says, carefully, 'some of us do.'

'You mean you know?'

'I do.'

'What was it, then?' she asks, intrigued. 'Was it the little cabinet after all? Is that why you won't let it go?'

'Oh no. No, it was not, though the cabinet is precious to us here for all kinds of reasons. Even Elspeth Cameron doesn't know the whole story.'

'Then what was it? If you know, why won't you tell me?'

'It's a secret,' he says. He takes her hand. 'But maybe I can tell you. Only first tell me this. Are you going to stay here?'

'Yes, I am.'

'And are you going to marry me?'

'Are you asking?'

'I'm asking.'

She follows Ben's progress along the shore. 'We'll have to talk to my son about that one. I can't see him objecting, can you?'

'No, I can't. But you're quite sure you can stand the place?'

'I don't think I can stand to leave the place, which is more to the point.'

'All right.' His catechism is complete. 'Now I'll tell you the whole story.'

'Did your dad know all about Manus?'

239

'Of course he did.'

'I don't understand.'

He slips his arm round her. Ben is foraging happily among the stones at the water's edge.

'You see, the way the story goes is this. Manus was twice married.'

'Well, we wondered, Sophie and I. She did some research for me, you know. But there's only one wife on the records.'

'Exactly. His first wife came to the island but died a year or so later, and took their baby son with her.'

'She died in childbirth?'

'That's right.'

'Poor Manus.'

'Poor Manus indeed. But then later, much later, he married again.'

'Who did he marry?'

'Her name was Henrietta. Henrietta Dalrymple. And she was his captive in a way.'

'His captive?'

'Aye. She was kidnapped to this island at the behest of her relatives. There was some plot, to do with money, inheritance. They wanted to be rid of her, and this place was as good a prison as any. So they arranged for her to be kidnapped by Manus, and held captive here.'

'You mean up at- what was it called? At Auchenblae? At that old house?'

'Or Achadh nam Blàth as it was then. Just so. At the old laird's house. She was widowed but she had a child. The story goes that her relatives wanted to get their hands on her fortune. So they brought up her son in Edinburgh while they had her kept a prisoner here, on the island.'

'Poor Henrietta. She must have felt absolutely desperate.'

Donal looks at her for a moment, frowning. 'It would have been a foreign and uncivilised place to her, that's true. She would not even have been able to speak the language. They say she almost went mad with the pain and the grief of it.'

'So how come . . . ?'

'So something happened. She changed her mind. And Manus changed his mind, too, it seems. It happens.'

'I know.'

'Tradition has it that they married for love, but secretly, because her relatives wished to believe her dead. And the only way she could be safe, really safe, was if they *did* believe her dead. So you see nobody must know about it. That was what Manus and Henrietta decided. Nobody but the islanders. They were married for many, many years but nobody outside Garve ever knew.'

'You mean you knew all this? Even when I was asking?'

'Of course. I have known it for most of my life. My father, too. We are people who can keep a secret for a thousand years if we must.'

'If you must?'

'Well . . .' He grins at her. 'We are also people who like to keep secrets for their own sake. Just for the hell of it!'

'And the things in the little cabinet? They're her things, aren't they?'

'Some of them belonged to Manus's first wife but some of them are Henrietta's, right enough. He gave them to her. And they say that he made her a garden. They say he brought her plants from Edinburgh and made her the first real garden on the island. You see, she was his . . .'

'She was his treasure,' Alys finishes for him. 'She was his treasure of treasures. And his bride from the sea. She came by boat, in secret.'

'She was. And she did.'

'So, if he loved her so much, how come he lost her?'

It is night in the great hall of the Laird's House at Achadh nam Blàth, the field of flowers Manus sits alone, with the embroidered cabinet in front of him, fingering its contents, lifting them out one at a time, looking at them. Ishbel has left the cottage where she lives with Seamus and their children who are now almost grown, and she has come back to her old home for a few days, to do what she can, to help Manus and his family, although there is nothing to be done now except grieve. She comes into the room and stands watching him anxiously.

Then she is aware of a movement in the shadows beside her, and looking down she sees that little Frances stands there, fists clenched. Tears stream steadily down her face and the girl does nothing to wipe them away. She is twelve years old and with each passing day, thinks Ishbel, she grows more like Henrietta, except that her skin is clear and pale and smooth with no scars. She loves her father dearly, this last, late child, and can bear her own grief more readily than his. She moves forward, but Ishbel restrains her for a moment.

'Wait a moment,' she whispers.

He is chanting quietly. It is a song for the dead, a funeral song:

'Thou goest this night to thy home of winter,

To thy home of autumn, of spring and of summer.

Thou goest this night to thy perpetual home,

To thine eternal bed, to thine eternal slumber.

Sleep, thou, beloved, and away with thy sorrow,

Sleep, thou, sleep and away with thy sorrow.'

When he falls silent, Ishbel comes forward and puts her hands on his shoulders, where the thick grey hair falls down onto them. And then Frances is pushing her aside, and flinging her arms round him.

'What shall we do? What shall we do without her?'

'Manus, my dear, can I fetch you anything?' asks Ishbel.

He looks up and then, putting his arm round his child, says. 'No, nothing, thank you Ishbel.' He touches his daughter's cheek tenderly. 'I have all that I want here.'

Ishbel slips quietly away. There is nothing more for her to do.

Manus holds out the locket to the child. 'This was your mother's. But it is yours now, *a ghràidh*. She always wore it, but she had left it behind because the chain was broken.'

'I know. She told me to leave it there in the cabinet. She said you would mend it for her.'

'Aye. It was always my job to mend things for her. I would have mended the world for her — I could have mended the world for her, save for one thing only . . .'

He takes more things from the cabinet, and looks at them as though he might conjure the woman from the objects.

'See, there are stones she gathered, and shells. Here is swansdown. And here is her knotting shuttle. It used to belong to my first wife, to the other Frances. That was her name and your mother's middle name and now it is yours, too. And the wee mirror. She did not want that at first, for she was ashamed to look at her face.'

'You should try to sleep, Father. The lads have long since gone to their beds.'

They had come to her, dumb in their sorrow, Frances's brothers, Henrietta's young men. Their own grief was sharp but they were more worried about their father and could do nothing to help him. So they had come to Frances, as before they would always have come to their mother. And seeing them, Frances had felt the heavy weight of responsibility descend on her shoulders. Lord, she thought, how would she cope with them all? How would she make the best of things? How would she make the best of them without her mother to help her?

'And even her receipt for cosmetic lotion. She kept it all these years. Did she ever make it for herself, Frances?'

'Not that I know of. Though she always meant to. Ishbel tells me that she always meant to.'

'Well, well,' he says. 'She had no need of it. She was just beautiful without it.'

'She was.' Frances embraces her father, hugging him tightly. 'You should at least try to sleep.'

'How can I? The house is so lonely. The light has gone out of the place. I should not have let her go rowing across to the wee island. I blame myself entirely. It was altogether my fault.'

'It was an accident. It could have happened to any of us. She had made that journey a hundred times in safety. And the strait between Ardachy and the islet is so narrow.'

'But she drowned, all the same. I should not have let her go without me. I would rather the sea had taken us both than for me to remain here without her.'

Frances sits beside her father. Nothing will ever be the same, she thinks. But they must just make the best of things. It is what her mother would have done.

'You know that she loved to go to the burial ground and the saint's chapel. She liked to be alone there and watch the seals in the water and the birds flying. She liked the silence and the solitude. You know that she liked to sit quietly . . .'

'Aye, and think of your brother, her little lost Gabriel,' finishes Manus. 'I would have brought him here, if I could, you know. I would have fetched him for her as I fetched the tulips and the roses to please her. But time passed. He would have forgotten her. It would not have been a kindness to him to bring him to *Garbh*. She knew that.'

'She knew that well enough. For she told me so herself.'

Henrietta had told all her children about her firstborn son. They knew that somewhere in that distant, foreign city of Edinburgh, they had a half-brother. Of them all, Frances was most fascinated by the thought of her unknown sibling. Again and again she had begged Henrietta to describe him to her. And she had tried to imagine her mother's longing for that one lost child. But it had been beyond her, and would remain beyond her until a few years later when she married Alistair, a younger son of Clan Galbreath and gave birth to her own first child, whereupon she looked into his face and said, 'Now I understand what my mother must have suffered.'

'Donal,' says Alys suddenly.

'Yes?'

'Did you tell Anne Marie any of this?'

'Of course not. Besides, she never asked about the past, neither mine, nor the island's. She always said it was dead and gone. Boring, that's what she called it. Old stones, old stories. She didn't give a toss about the past. It was the future that mattered.'

'Well . . .'

'I know. Maybe she was right at that. I sometimes think we live too much in the past here.'

'Maybe. But then, as your father said, it's a thin place.'

'It is. And we ignore that at our peril as well. I think we just have to learn to strike a balance.'

She has a sudden vision of the island, like a polished pebble: the layers one on top of the other, past, present, future, all part of some mysterious whole, or like a small planet, spinning through time. Maybe that's the secret, she thinks. Everything matters and nothing is lost. She imagines that she can hear music, from the hotel maybe, but it is so faint and far away that she cannot be sure whether it is a lament or a love song, and maybe it is just the remote call of some seabird on one of the far skerries.

'We should be going in.' Donal stands up and holds out his hand to her, pulling her to her feet. 'Ben!' he calls. 'Time to go home!'

It is already late and night is falling, but they have left the lights on at Ardachy, and she can see the yellow gleam in the windows, signalling a welcome.

'Maybe a cat as well?' she says.

'As well as what?'

'As well as a dog, of course.'

'Why not?'

'Oh, I will make such beautiful things here!'

'I know you will.'

'I have so many ideas! I can't wait to start.'

She steadies herself against him so that she can shake the fine white sand out of her shoes.

'You'll never get rid of it, you know,' says Donal.

'What?'

'The sand. It gets into every crevice. Wherever you go, you'll find a few grains of the white sand of Garve in your luggage.'

'I'm not planning to go anywhere,' she says. 'Well, not for long, anyway. And when I go it will only be to come back again.'

She thinks about all the arrangements that will have to be made, the things to be packed up, the paperwork, the complications involved in shifting their whole lives to Ardachy. She thinks, with some trepidation, of the phone calls to Canada. But she will do it joyfully. And at the end of it all she will come home to Donal for good, bringing her son with her.

'She came from the sea and now she has returned to it,' says Manus quietly to his daughter. 'Now the sea has taken her from me. She was the brown swan and the mute swan and the loveliest of swans on the lake. But my bride from the sea, my treasure of treasures, where will I ever find your like again?'

Alys turns to face Donal. She stands close, breathing in the familiar scent of him, enjoying the warmth of his body. 'I have come back for you,' she says. 'I have come back for the island, but most of all for you.'

'Oh, *m'eudail, a ghràidh.*' He kisses her forehead. 'Oh, my treasure of treasures.'

She can hear Ben running up the hill to join them. 'Mum! Donal!' He is holding something in his hand. It could be a feather. It could be a shell or a quartz pebble. But whatever it is, it will be dusted with the fine white sand of Garve.

'Look what I've found!' he shouts. 'Just look what I've found down on the seashore!'

THE END

ACKNOWLEDGMENTS

Many thanks to Hamish Wilson, finest of radio producers, who some fifteen years ago, nurtured my original BBC radio trilogy from which this version of *The Curiosity Cabinet* eventually emerged. Thanks too to my husband Alan and son Charles for all their loving support, to my friends and family, but especially my sister-in-law Jackie for her patient and perceptive reading, to the remaining Kilmarnock Writers for years of friendship, to Sarah Ballard for editorial help, and to Kevin MacNeil, Ceit Kearney, Marjorie McDonald and Catriona Haston for help with the Gaelic. I'm indebted as ever to Sara Hunt of Saraband for help, support and inspiration. Thanks must also go to the late and much missed Vie Tulloch who showed me the 'wings' of the Hebridean birds and last, but by no means least, to redoubtable islandman and friend, Willie McSporran, who – among so much else – knows where all the rocks aren't.

Catherine Czerkawska

ABOUT THE AUTHOR

Catherine Czerkawska is a Scottish based novelist and playwright. She has written many plays for the stage and for BBC Radio and television, and has published eight novels, historical and contemporary including *The Physic Garden* and *The Jewel*, for Saraband. Her short stories have been published in many magazines and anthologies and as eBook collections. She has also written nonfiction in the form of articles and books and has reviewed professionally for newspapers and magazines. *Wormwood*, her play about the Chernobyl disaster, was produced at Edinburgh's Traverse Theatre to critical acclaim in 1997, while *The Curiosity Cabinet* was shortlisted for the Dundee Book Prize in 2005. Catherine has taught creative writing for the Arvon Foundation and spent four years as Royal Literary Fund Writing Fellow at the University of the West of Scotland. When not writing, she collects and deals in the antique textiles that often find their way into her fiction.